Southern Ireland

CRUISING COMPANION

A yachtsman's pilot and cruising guide to the
ports and harbours from the Shannon Estuary to St George's Channel

Robert Wilcox

Photographs © 2009 Robert Wilcox, Joe Wright, Chris Hutchings and Mike McNeal

Aerial photography ©John Herriott photography and design
Kilbeg, Bandon, County Cork
www.irelandaerialphotography.com

Additional photography:
Page 6 ©Discoverireland.com; Page 43 (Natterjack toad) ©Christian Fischer; Page 61 (bottom) ©Kells Gardens;
Page 106 (bottom) ©John Comloquoy*; Page 128 ©Dr Charles Nelson*; Page 133 ©Bantry House and Garden;
Page 143 (bottom right) ©Kilravock Gardens; Page 171 (top) ©Pierce Hickey;
Page 214 (bottom) ©Sir Charles Colthurst, Blarney Castle & Rock Close Gardens
*can be contacted through www.geograph.org.uk/http://creativecommons.org/licenses/by-sa/2.0/

This product has derived in part from material obtained from the UK Hydrographic Office with the permission
of the UK Hydrographic Office, Her Majesty's Stationery Office.
© British Crown Copyright (2009). All rights reserved.

THIS PRODUCT SHOULD NOT BE USED FOR NAVIGATION
NOTICE: The UK Hydrographic Office (UKHO) and its licensors make no warranties or representations, express or implied, with
respect to this product. The UKHO and its licensors have not verified the information within this product or quality assured it.

For Wiley Nautical
Executive Editor: David Palmer
Project Editor: Lynette James
Assistant Editor: Drew Kennerley
Content Editor: Claire Spinks

For Nautical Data
Cartography: Jamie Russell
Art Direction: Lucinda Roch and Jamie Russell
Cruising Companion series editor: Lucinda Roch

ISBN-13: 978-0-470-71381-5

IMPORTANT NOTICE

This Companion is intended as an aid to navigation only. The information contained within should not solely
be relied on for navigational use, rather it should be used in conjunction with official hydrographic data.
Whilst every care has been taken in compiling the information contained in this Companion, the publishers,
author, editors and their agents accept no responsibility for any errors or omissions, or for any accidents
or mishaps which may arise from its use.

Neither the publisher nor the author can accept responsibility for errors, omissions or alterations in this book.
They will be grateful for any information from readers to assist in the update and accuracy of the publication.

Readers are advised at all times to refer to official charts, publications and notices.
The charts contained in this book are sketch plans and are not to be used for navigation.
Some details are omitted for the sake of clarity and the scales have been chosen
to allow best coverage in relation to page size.

Correctional supplements are available at www.wileynautical.com and on request from the publishers.

Printed by SNP Leefung Printers Ltd, China

Contents

Area chart 4

Introduction 5
Weather 6
Tides 9
Charts 11
Navigation 13
Sea Crossings 14
Deciding an itinerary 14
Communications 17
Emergency Services 17
Useful information for overseas visitors 19
Symbols and Abbreviations 22

Chapter one
Kilrush to the Blaskets 23
Kilrush 26
Carrigaholt 31
Kilbaha Bay 33
Fenit 35
Barrow 39
Magharee Sound and Islands 40
Scraggane Bay 42
Brandon Bay 44
Smerwick Harbour 46
The Blasket Islands 48

Chapter two
Dingle to the Skelligs 51
Dingle 54
Ventry 59
Kells Bay 61
Knight's Town 62
Cahersiveen 66
Portmagee 69
Ballinskelligs 72
The Skelligs 74

Chapter three
Kenmare River 75
Derrynane Harbour 79
Derrynane Bay 83
Rath Strand and White Strand Bays 83
West Cove 84
Illaundrane 84
Sneem 85
Coongar 89
River Blackwater 89
Dunkerron Harbour 89
Kenmare Town and Quay 91
Dinish Island 94
Ormond's Island 95
Lehid Harbour 95
Kilmakilloge Harbour 96
Ardgroom Harbour 99
Cleanderry Harbour 100
Ballycrovane Harbour 100
Eyeries Quay 102
Travara Quay 102
Ballydonegan 103
Garnish Bay 103
Dursey Sound 104

Chapter four
Bantry Bay 107
Black Ball Harbour 110
Pulleen Harbour 110
Lonehort Harbour 111
Bear Haven 112
Dunboy Bay 114

Castletownbere 116
Mill Cove 120
Lawrence Cove 120
Adrigole 123
Trafrask Bay 124
Glengarriff 125
Bantry 129

Chapter five
Dunmanus Bay 135
Dooneen Pier 138
Kilcrohane Pier 138
Kitchen Cove/Ahakista 139
Dunbeacon Harbour 141
Dunbeacon Cove 143
Dunmanus Harbour 144

Chapter six
Long Island and Roaringwater Bays 145
Crookhaven 149
Goleen 152
Croagh Bay, Colla Quay and Long Island Pier 154
Rossbrin Cove 155
Schull 156
Cape Clear Island 160
Roaringwater Bay 165

Chapter seven
Baltimore to Kinsale 169
Baltimore Harbour 172
Sherkin Island 174
Baltimore 175
Barloge Creek for Lough Hyne 178
Castlehaven 180
Glandore/Union Hall 183
Tralong Bay/Mill Cove 186
Dirk Bay 186
South Ring 187
Dunworly Bay 188
Courtmacsherry 189
Kinsale 192

Chapter eight
East Cork Coast 197
Oyster Haven 200
Cork Harbour 201
Crosshaven 203
East Ferry Marina 209
Cobh 211
Cork, Penrose Quay 213
Ballycotton 215
Youghal 217

Chapter nine
County Waterford 221
Ardmore 224
Helvick 227
Dungarvan 229
Dunmore East 233
Waterford Harbour 236
Waterford City 236
Duncannon 244
Passage East and Ballyhack 246
King's Channel 247
New Ross 248
Kilmore Quay 250

**For the following background information
visit www.wileynautical.com**
Government; Population; The Provinces; Religions; Time;
Public Holidays; Flag; Tourism; The History of Ireland;
Sports; Restaurants; Getting to Ireland by air or ferry;
Medical insurance; Mobile phone networks; Glossary

Headlands, Major Towns, Bays and Mountains

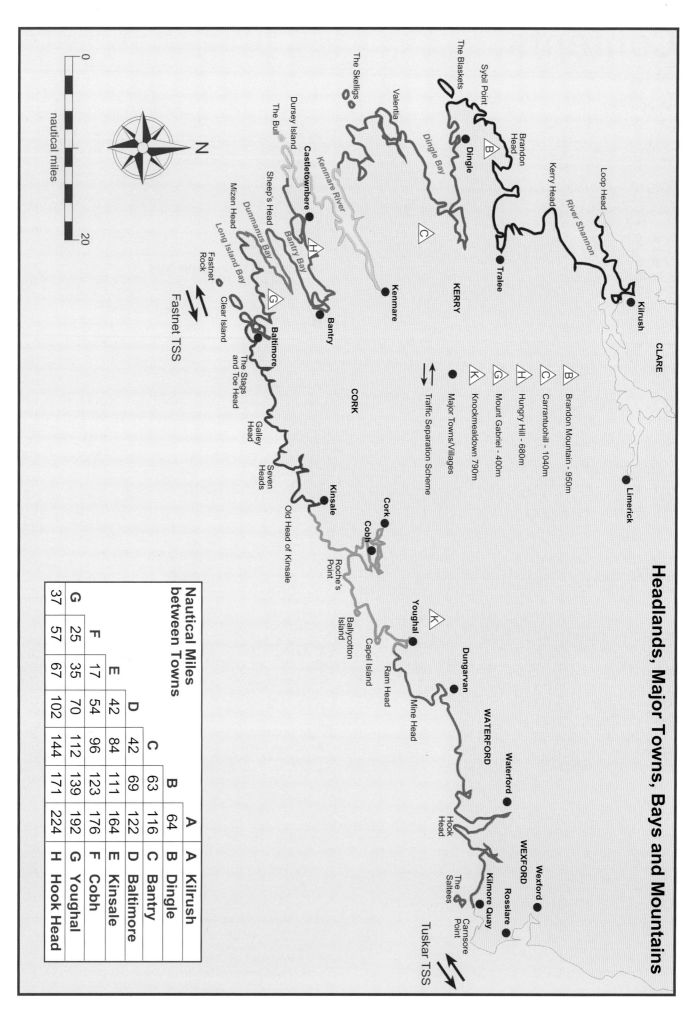

nautical miles

0

20

N

The Blaskets

Sybil Point

The Skelligs

Valentia

Brandon Head

Kerry Head

Loop Head

River Shannon

CLARE

Limerick

Kilrush

B

Dingle

Dingle Bay

Dursey Island

The Bull

Castletownbere

Kenmare River

C

Sheep's Head

Mizen Head

Dunmanus Bay

Bantry Bay

H

KERRY

Tralee

Kenmare

Bantry

Long Island Bay

Fastnet Rock

Fastnet TSS

Clear Island

The Stags and Toe Head

Baltimore

G

Galley Head

Seven Heads

Old Head of Kinsale

CORK

Kinsale

Cork

Cobh

Roche's Point

Ballycotton Island

Capel Island

Ram Head

Mine Head

Youghal

K

Dungarvan

WATERFORD

Waterford

Hook Head

WEXFORD

Wexford

Rosslare

Kilmore Quay

The Saltees

Carnsore Point

Tuskar TSS

B Brandon Mountain - 950m

C Carrantuohill - 1040m

H Hungry Hill - 680m

G Mount Gabriel - 400m

K Knockmealdown 790m

● Major Towns/Villages

Traffic Separation Scheme

Nautical Miles between Towns								
							A	**A Kilrush**
						A	64	**B Dingle**
					B	63	116	**C Bantry**
				C	42	69	122	**D Baltimore**
			D	84	111	164		**E Kinsale**
		E	42	96	123	176		**F Cobh**
	F	17	54	112	139	192		**G Youghal**
G	25	35	70	144	171	224		**H Hook Head**
37	57	67	102					

Mizen Head

Introduction

Wide open seas, plentiful, secluded anchorages, interesting navigational challenges, beautiful scenery and, in the event of poor weather, great hospitality ashore – it is very difficult to think of any negative aspects of sailing the South and South-West Coast of Ireland. This companion describes harbours and anchorages in Counties Kerry, Cork and Waterford between Kilrush, County Clare and Kilmore Quay, County Wexford.

Offshore, ocean winds and wide estuaries encourage vigorous sailing unfettered by shallows, merchant ships rounding busy headlands or narrow channels. A good day's sailing is rewarded with overnight moorings that are often serene yet convenient for excellent hostelries and good humoured company. Fellow yachtsmen are rare enough that socialising and an information-sharing camaraderie are natural.

Navigation depends as much on the eyeball and natural features as navigational aids. Adjacent rocks and distant leading lines substitute for buoyed channels, yet good planning and careful selection of harbours and refuges will yield a safe sail.

The scenery varies from mountainous to pastoral: To the west, the cliffs around the Dingle peninsula are majestic while the Castletownshend

Harbour Seals and Grey Seals are abundant

anchorage, midway along the south coast, is rustic tranquillity defined.

West of Kinsale the coastal communities are individual and somewhat idiosyncratic. When it is fine, there is no better place to be afloat and when the weather is foul there's no friendlier place to be ashore. Going ashore, however, brings its own set of challenges. Walk-ashore berths are few, making anchoring or mooring on a visitor buoy the more usual means of securing for the night.

Ireland's highest mountains cling to the south, west and north coasts while the landlocked counties are predominantly gentle rolling terrain – quite the reverse of most islands, but as will often be repeated later in this book, Ireland is a different place. These mountains and the many headlands will become old friends as we progress along the coast. The graphic on page 4 depicts the highest 'mountains', towns and large villages along the coast and positions the main bays and inlets. Distances by sea can be read from the matrix on page 4.

Cruising along the South-West Coast, west of Baltimore, is also different from sailing many coasts in that it is a linear progression along a series of bays that penetrate deep inland. Inside a bay, a skipper has the option to criss-cross between harbours.

Oscar Wilde's revered teacher, Sir John Mahaffy, aptly summarises the Ireland that will be encountered along this coast:

'In Ireland the inevitable never happens and the unexpected constantly occurs.'

PLACE NAMES

To assist the stranger, place names, with rare exception, are taken from the Admiralty charts. Irish, anglicised interpretations and local names are given where applicable, interesting or useful.

Weather

As the Atlantic Ocean dominates the weather around these coasts, having a reliable weather forecast is significantly more important here than in more protected European waters. Apart from the normal good practice of receiving an up-to-date forecast for sailing, it is prudent to plan for an extended blow of two or three days and ensure it is experienced in comfortable surroundings. The optimal refuge may be around a headland, or two, that should ideally be rounded before the bad weather arrives. The weather can, and does, change several times within a day and a canny skipper will be able to capitalise on these weather windows. There may be occasions when it is essential to find protection against an untamed Atlantic Ocean.

For the majority of cruising yachtsmen, including the locals, the main season off this coast extends from May to, perhaps, mid-September. Although Ireland is famous for its rain, the sunshine hours are higher along the coast compared to just a few miles inland.

The best months to visit are May to July when the winds, on average, are lighter, sunshine hours at a maximum and most facilities are open for business. Summer gales and fog are statistically rare, with fog a little more likely in June. The months with the highest average number of sunshine hours are May and June.

SEA AREA FORECASTS AND CURRENT CONDITIONS

Thankfully, the authorities provide a wide variety of readily available sources of weather information. The Coastguard broadcasts Sea Area forecasts every three hours commencing at 0103 local time. An initial announcement is made on Ch 16, advising which channel carries the broadcast locally. These channels are also listed chapter by chapter. Gale Warning and Small Craft Warning broadcasts are preceded by an announcement on Ch 16. They are broadcast on receipt and are repeated at the following times: 0033, 0633, 1233 and 1833 local time.

Radio Telefis Éireann (RTE) Radio1 broadcasts four times a day on FM (in the west the main transmitter is on 90.0MHz and in the east 89.6MHz – auxiliaries transmit between 88.2 and 89.7MHz) and LW (252kHz) at 0602, 1253, 1655 and 2355 local time, although it would be wise to be ready for the broadcast a few minutes previous to these times.

The Met Éireann website is well thought out and provides simple navigation to useful data. The yachtsman can extract relevant information quickly using Wi-Fi, an internet café terminal or even restricted bandwidth on a smart phone.

The Sea Area forecast is at www.met.ie/forecasts/sea-area.asp and includes gale warnings and small craft warnings. Additionally, a simplified website is available for smartphones – www.mobile.met.ie/mobile/.

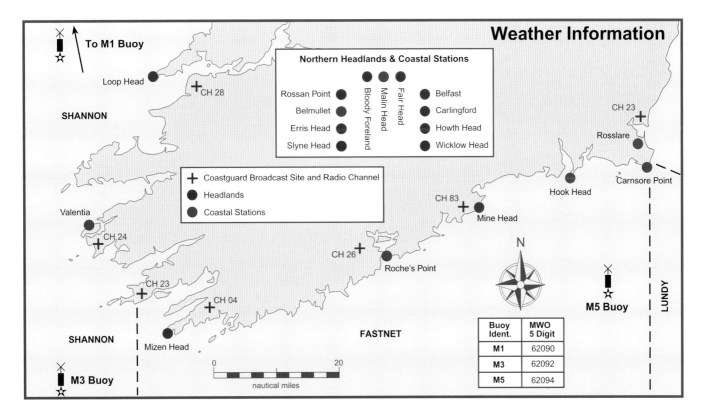

The forecast and coastal reports are both repeated on one RTE website for even greater convenience – www. rte.ie/weather/marine.html.

Each Met Éireann Sea Area forecast refers specifically to an area between selected headlands. The selection of headlands is customised to match the expected conditions and will vary constantly. Geographic ambiguity is usually eliminated by defining three headlands (in a clockwise direction). A minor downside to this otherwise excellent method is that the headlands used for reference change forecast by forecast and a stranger arriving from overseas could be forgiven for not having the location of these headlands at immediate recall. The chart above lists all the headlands that may be used, in geographical sequence. (Download multiple copies of the proforma on page 8 from www. wileynautical.com to assist in recording the broadcast). Each forecast concludes with the current conditions at selected sites ashore and 'met' buoys offshore.

The current conditions data from the local 'met' buoys and from those further afield can be useful for planning sea crossings. There is an easy way to access this data. Dial-A-Buoy is a free service provided by the USA. A phone call to 001 888 701 8991 will cause a computer generated voice to read out the latest conditions at buoys worldwide (in imperial units, for example, wave height in feet). Follow the instructions and key in the buoy's five-digit code when requested. A call to retrieve data on one buoy should last less than one minute. In addition to the buoys listed on the diagram, the following buoys may be useful to skippers trying to decide if the weather is suitable for a longer crossing:

Five Digit Code	Location	Approx Lat/Lon
62107	Sevenstones	50°06'N 06°05'W
62303	Pembroke Buoy	51°36'N 05°05'W
62052	Ushant TSS	48°30'N 05°35'W
62081	K2	51°00'N 13°18'W
62301	Aberporth	52°17'N 04°30'W
62093	M4 Donegal Bay	54°40'N 09°04'W
62105	K4	54°33'N 12°22'W

BBC and NAVTEX Sea Areas

From Kilrush in County Clare to Bantry Bay, the Sea Area is 'Shannon'.

From Bantry Bay to Kilmore Quay, the Sea Area is 'Fastnet'.

Knowledge of conditions in Sea Area 'Sole', which lies to the south and west, will frequently hint at weather arriving in the near future.

The BBC broadcasts on LW (198kHz) four times a day (0048, 0520, 1201 and 1754 Local Time).

NAVTEX weather is broadcast locally from Valentia (Station W on 518kHz) at 0740, 1140, 1940 and 2340 UT.

Other Met Éireann websites

A today/tomorrow depiction of isobar, cloud, rain and temperature can be found at www.met.ie/forecasts/ atlantic-charts.asp.

A simple but very useful one-page summary of current coastal/buoy reports and sea conditions can be found at www.met.ie/latest/coastal.asp. This is predominantly a text web page and is therefore mobile phone friendly.

Valid until:

Gale Warnings

Small Craft Warnings

General situation @   Hrs

Forecast for coasts – 1

From: To: To:

Wind:

Weather: Visibility:

Forecast for coasts – 2

From: To: To:

Weather: Visibility:

Forecast for coasts – 3

From: To: To:

Weather: Visibility:

Outlook for a further 24 hours: Wind:

Weather:

Reports from Coastal Stations at _____ Hours

Malin Head:

Buoy M5:

Tuskar Light:

Roche's Point:

Valentia:

Belmullet:

Dublin Airport:

A bright and breezy April day near the 'Waterford' buoy

Tides

There is no comprehensive tidal stream atlas for this area and charts are unusually free of tidal information. Most of the data was gathered in the 19th century.

OFFSHORE TIDAL STREAMS

Firstly, it is important to understand that the flood tidal stream around the western shores of Britain and Ireland is interrupted by Ireland's south-west landmass, which causes the stream to divide near the Skelligs.

The stream caused to head north past Dingle Bay and the Shannon is uncomplicated and slow, rarely exceeding 1kn (inshore in Blasket Sound it can reach 2-3kn – see below).

The other component of the stream initially heads in a south-easterly direction past Mizen Head and Fastnet Rock and then north-easterly past the East Cork coast

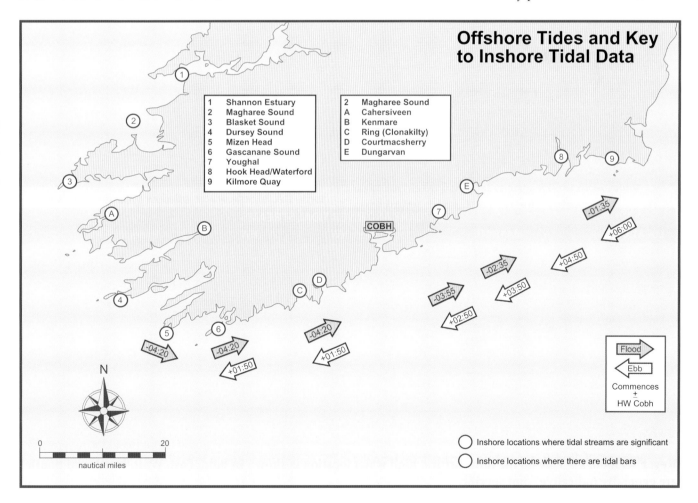

Offshore Tides and Key to Inshore Tidal Data

1	Shannon Estuary
2	Magharee Sound
3	Blasket Sound
4	Dursey Sound
5	Mizen Head
6	Gascanane Sound
7	Youghal
8	Hook Head/Waterford
9	Kilmore Quay

2	Magharee Sound
A	Cahersiveen
B	Kenmare
C	Ring (Clonakilty)
D	Courtmacsherry
E	Dungarvan

COBH

Flood
Ebb
Commences
+
HW Cobh

0   20
nautical miles

◯ Inshore locations where tidal streams are significant

◯ Inshore locations where there are tidal bars

5 or 10m at LAT, while the pale blue shading signifies greater depths. Soundings are represented in metres and tenths of metres, showing the depth of water above chart datum with the underlined soundings referring to drying heights above chart datum.

Sea Crossings

Each of the sea crossings to Ireland has its own challenges, which can be summarised as follows:

FROM SCOTLAND (AND SCANDINAVIA) WEST-ABOUT IRELAND

An option for yachts arriving from Scotland and the Nordic countries is to travel the West Coast of Ireland where exposure to the full effect of the Atlantic is along 350M of coast that has few harbours or refuges. This is a voyage for a well-founded boat (and crew). Kilrush, Fenit or Dingle would be appropriate arrival harbours.

FROM SCOTLAND AND WALES EAST-ABOUT IRELAND

Crossings are short, protection is closer to hand and the challenges are run-of-the-mill. They include some tricky sandbanks along the east coast of Ireland, the strong tides of St Georges Channel and busy shipping lanes. Kilmore Quay is the favourite arrival harbour.

FROM ENGLAND AND FRANCE – CELTIC SEA

This is a much longer crossing than many yachtsmen will have previously undertaken and crosses not only busy shipping routes where yachts are rarely seen (or expected) but also seas that are thrown up as the untamed Atlantic Ocean meets the continental shelf. There are no refuges. Recommended arrival harbours are Kinsale and Crosshaven because replenishment and crew changes, using Cork airport, are so easy. If the wind and sea are favourable, it is also worth considering continuing directly to Dingle, which has a range of alongside facilities, reasonable sailing distances to the more remote destinations in Kerry and Clare and good air links (at Kerry and Shannon airports).

The prevailing wind is from the south-west. This book therefore addresses the coast in an anticlockwise movement in the expectation that the cruising experience will be improved by having the benefit of a favourable breeze.

General observations: Man has had little impact offshore here but be aware of two potential dangers along the coast:

Gas fields

The Celtic Sea has seen the development of several offshore production platforms. Collectively they are known as the Marathon or Kinsale Head Gas Field. The two platforms are 24 and 26M south-east of the

Old Head of Kinsale at 51° 22'.00N and therefore, primarily, of concern to yachts on passage to and from England/France destined for Kinsale or Cork. The westerly platform is at 08°01'.00W and the other is at 07°56'.70W. Obviously, give them both a very wide berth and do not navigate between them!

Merchant shipping

There is very little inshore merchant shipping except a) large tankers bound for Bantry Bay or b) ferries, cruise ships and a wide variety of other shipping entering Cork and Waterford harbours on the south coast or the River Shannon estuary on the west coast.

Cobh is a popular destination for cruise ships

Deciding an itinerary

Presented with 250 miles of previously unexplored coast, it can be difficult to decide how to get the best out of the time available. One question going through many skippers' heads on a first cruise will be 'What will I regret not visiting ….. ?'. Faced with tourist guides that replicate phrases such as 'Kinsale – the gourmet capital of Ireland', it can be difficult to make choices.

From the hundred or so harbours described in later chapters, here is a personal 'top twenty' with a few notes to justify their inclusion – these may help in culling the 'long-list' to a 'short-list' to match any time constraints.

1. **KILRUSH**: It is always good to start and end a cruise in a degree of comfort, clean and defect free. Kilrush supports all that along with easy access to Shannon Airport – one of the most connected airports in Europe (see table on www.wileynautical.com).

2. **BRANDON/FENIT**: Brandon is a hamlet with Brandon Mountain as its back drop and a broad, sweeping bay viewed from a pub garden bench – a majestic lunch stop followed by a restful night on an alongside berth at friendly Fenit, where the history of St Brendan is depicted along the walk to his nearby statue.

3. **THE BLASKET ISLANDS**: Great Blasket supported habitation by Irish speakers into the second half of the 20th century. Glimpse how a community, living on the very edge of Europe, kept the Irish language going and allowed it to be recorded for posterity. The scenery is magnificent and raw.

4. **DINGLE**: Dingle Town, almost Disney, is fun with good food, drink, a friendly dolphin and excellent protection from an Atlantic blow. Yes, it is tourist driven and nothing like 'Old Ireland', but it retains character and is a safe harbour with full facilities and plenty to do if weather-bound.

5. **SKELLIG MICHAEL**: Marvel at the ability of humans to live 200m up this isolated rock over 15 centuries ago. Trust in the Portmagee trip boatmen for a landing and have a more satisfyingly direct encounter. This is definitely one occasion to put self reliance aside.

6. **DERRYNANE HARBOUR**: The harbour nestled under the high hills of the 'Ring of Kerry' gives a skipper a true sense of what it means to navigate in South-West Ireland. The reward is a magnificent harbour, fine beaches and good hospitality.

7. **LAWRENCE COVE MARINA**: A quiet oasis under the dominating Hungry Hill providing protection and also rarely available alongside berths, fresh water and fuel.

8. **GLENGARRIFF**: The harbour is a beautifully tranquil spot surrounded by verdant shores nurtured by the benign microclimate. A visit to the famous Mediterranean style gardens is a bonus.

9. **AHAKISTA/KITCHEN COVE**: A beautiful haven and away from it all anchorage for those with a little time.

10. **CROOKHAVEN**: Good company, food, drink and fun.

11. **FASTNET ROCK**: Few will resist a trip around one of sailing's icons.

12. **SHERKIN or CAPE CLEAR ISLAND**: Both offer sheer 'other-worldliness' of a land time forgot and plenty of character.

Dunmanus Bay. Dawn breaking on a fine day in early June

Kilmore Quay, County Wexford

13. **CASTLETOWNSHEND**: A picture postcard anchorage leading to Mary Ann's renowned seafood restaurant. A visit here would be in the top three destinations.

14. **GLANDORE**: A popular sailing haven and an attractive harbour. It is a delightful overnight stop.

15. **COURTMACSHERRY**: The village is a convivial, unhurried place because it is off the beaten track for road users. With a character peculiarly its own, it has alongside berths and enough facilities and features to make it a welcome destination.

16. **KINSALE**: Kinsale's reputation is well justified. It is a splendid, interesting town both ashore and afloat. This is a 'do not miss' destination. Another advantage is it is very convenient for Cork city and airport.

17. **CORK HARBOUR**: Crosshaven is the epicentre of Irish sailing and venue for 'Cork Week'.

18. **YOUGHAL/ARDMORE**: The weather will dictate whether either of these two historical centres can be visited. Between them they have well preserved buildings from many eras of Irish history and are unmatched elsewhere on the coast.

19. **NEW ROSS**: This could be described as idiosyncrasy as a place – 18M from the open sea via a swinging railway bridge, New Ross retains more of 'Old Ireland' than most other places. A perfect location for sitting out ugly weather offshore.

20. **KILMORE QUAY**: A visit here is valid for the same reasons as given for Kilrush, positioned as it is at the other end of the coastline. Kilmore Quay also has several excellent seafood restaurants.

Unlike many other cruising decisions, the programme for a visit to this coast needs to be considered very carefully. In deciding where to experience these wonderful sailing grounds, it is important to know how to satisfy the crew's expectations:

Circumnavigation style: The Fastnet Rock, Mizen Head, Dursey Sound, The Skelligs and The Blaskets may all be added to the passage plan without diverting too far from the shortest route. For the time being, Kinsale and Dingle are the most useful harbours offering proximity to the route, a full range of services and protection.

Short cruise style (less than two weeks on the cruising grounds): A one-way cruise makes tremendous sense. To put this in perspective, with reasonably favourable weather, Dingle to Kinsale will take one week and will allow a visit to the 'must-dos' en route. Two weeks would permit a trip further east to Cork and Waterford or time for more destinations.

Long cruise: However, if a longer experience is planned, it is important to recognise that 30-90 days will be needed for anything other than a 'dash' that will generate regrets about harbours omitted.

One alternative, often adopted by overseas visitors, is to separate the long passages and the coastal cruise, taking advantage of the frequent and reasonably-priced flights to convenient airports to make crew changes. Public transport to most harbours along the coast is available, in season, for the final leg of the journey.

Communications

MOBILE TELEPHONY AND MOBILE BROADBAND
Fortunately, mobile telephony coverage is very reliable at most locations along the coast as phoning ahead during working hours to make berthing arrangements or calling for a taxi to a remote anchorage is more the norm in Ireland than elsewhere. There are four mobile networks. Overseas visitors to Ireland should check with their home network before departure to establish economically priced roaming rights.

Alternatively, Irish SIM based pay-as-you-go services are available from at least five operators. This avoids the possible shock of a large bill for international calls upon return home. Top-ups are available at many locations, including small grocery stores. In either case, there is no need to prefix local telephone numbers with the international prefix when dialling within the country. Mobile broadband is increasingly useful to establish Internet access to obtain weather forecasts.

BROADBAND BY WI-FI
There is a rapidly increasing availability of Wi-Fi in marinas and even remote moorings along the coast, making the carrying of a suitable computer or smartphone a useful proposition. There are three styles of provision. Some locations see the provision of free Wi-Fi as a basic facility equivalent to a water tap. Others make access free once the user has checked in to the marina or paid a mooring fee. Finally, there is a public service from companies such as DigitalForge, Tel: 028 28983 or 086 081 9733; website www.digitalforge.ie/, which offers access by subscription (starting at one hour online). Inevitably, many more places than noted in the book are likely to have Wi-Fi.

BROADCAST RADIO (OVERSEAS)
Visitors from France, Germany, Spain and the UK should be able to receive domestic broadcasts, at night only, on the following Long and Medium Wave frequencies. Reception conditions vary greatly and cannot be relied on.
France: France Info on 1206, 1377 or 1404kHz, France Inter on 162kHz and Europe1 on 183kHz.
Germany: Deutschlandfunk on 1422kHz.
Spain: 1026kHz.
UK: Radio 4 on 198 and 756kHz, Radio 5 on 909kHz, Radio Wales on 882kHz, Talksport on 1089kHz and Radio Cornwall on 630kHz.

Emergency Services

IRISH COASTGUARD
The Irish Coastguard (IRCG), based on a Maritime Rescue Co-Ordination Centre (MRCC) in Dublin and Sub-Centres (MRSCs) at Malin Head and Valentia, manages the helicopter emergency service at four bases around the country, the Coastguard Stations, the Mountain and Cave Rescue Teams, the Community Rescue Boat Ireland Teams, a Pollution/Salvage Response capability and the supporting marine radio communications network. Of interest to the leisure sailor off this coast are:

Helicopter Emergency Service
IRCG manages its helicopter service using the Canadian Helicopter Corporation (Ireland) Ltd (CHCI), which supplies the helicopters, equipment and crews for each of the four bases at Sligo, Shannon, Waterford and Dublin Airports.

Emergency Coastguard Units
There are 54 Coastguard units, manned by 850 volunteers, based around the coast, which provide a search and rescue service. In the area covered they are based at:
County Kerry: Waterville and Dingle.
County Cork: Youghal, Ballycotton, Guileen, Crosshaven, Oyster Haven, Summercove, Old Head of Kinsale, Seven Heads, Castlefreke, Glandore, Toe Head and Baltimore, Goleen and Castletownbere.
County Waterford: Dunmore East, Tramore, Bonmahon, Helvick and Ardmore.
County Wexford: Kilmore Quay, Fethard-on-Sea.
Seventeen stations nationwide have general purpose boats. Along the coastline covered in this companion they are located at:
County Kerry: Dingle and Valentia.
County Cork: Castletownbere, Goleen, Toe Head, Old Head of Kinsale and Crosshaven.
County Waterford: Dunmore East.

Community Rescue Boat Ireland, (CRBI)
CRBI is based at the following locations:
County Kerry: Ballybunnion, Banna and Derrynane.
County Cork: Bantry, (Schull has applied to join).
County Waterford: Bonmahon and Tramore.

National Marine Communications Network
Radio transmitter/receiver sites are connected to manned control centres located in Dublin, Malin Head and Valentia. Within the scope of this book, vessels may communicate with:
• **VHF voice and DSC radio services**
Carnsore Point, Mine Head, Cork, Mizen Head, Bantry,

Valentia and Shannon. Channel numbers are given in the relevant chapters.
• **MF radio sites**
Valentia Island (1752 kHz) and Malin Head (1677 kHz).
• **NAVTEX transmitter sites**
Malin Head and Valentia Island.

RNLI STATIONS

The RNLI in Ireland rescued 1,119 people in 2007. The greatest number of callouts on this coast was to the Kilmore Quay lifeboat (35 callouts). The most frequent reason for callout was mechanical failure but there have been an ever-increasing number of calls to leisure vessels running out of fuel. RNLI stations are listed west to east along the coast covered by this book:
County Clare: Kilrush.
County Kerry: Fenit, Valentia.
County Cork: Castletownbere, Baltimore, Courtmacsherry, Kinsale, Crosshaven, Ballycotton and Youghal.
County Waterford: Helvick Head, Tramore, Dunmore East.
County Wexford: Fethard, Kilmore Quay.

Emergencies ashore

Ashore, the emergency number is 999 or 112 for Coastguard, Gardai (Police), Fire and Ambulance. A serious medical or other emergency at sea should be dealt with by the normal methods and routines.

Medical non-emergencies and treatment

If possible, it is best to visit a health centre or local GP during the working day, particularly if a diagnosis and medication is required. If a daytime visit is not possible, Ireland has an out-of-hours GP service which operates from 1800 to 0800 Monday to Friday, and on a 24-hour basis on Saturdays, Sundays and public holidays.
• In County Clare it is called ShannonDoc: Tel: 1850 212 999.
• In Counties Cork and Kerry it is called SouthDoc: Tel: 1850 335 999.
• In County Waterford it is called Caredoc: Tel: 1850 334 999.

Initially, an operator will take some details and then transfer the call to a nurse. Subsequently, a doctor will advise on how to proceed. This may just be a phone call or it may involve a visit to a designated surgery. A visit costs approximately €60 excluding medicines. By comparison, a visit to a local GP will cost approximately €50 per visit. Visitors are required to pay this money and claim it back later. It is essential to have adequate documentation for this claim, which the doctor should provide. Prescription drugs can only be purchased in a 'chemist' or a 'pharmacy', which may be found in most towns and large villages. Serious incidents will be treated at a nearby hospital. Local doctors, dentists, hospitals and pharmacies are listed in each section.

Ballycotton Lifeboat leaving harbour on an 'Open Day'

Useful information (for overseas visitors)

GAS (PROPANE AND BUTANE)

On this coast, it is important that gas, like diesel, does not become a factor in determining a passage plan. It is essential therefore for skippers to do a little research and pre-planning. A good place to start is Calor's marine website, which addresses some of the problems of obtaining gas abroad – www.calormarineshop. co.uk/marine_safety/gas_supplies_abroad.htm.

For those using Camping Gaz (a company operating world-wide, selling butane in light blue cylinders), there are many suppliers and, provided two canisters are carried, there should be few problems in maintaining a continuous supply. An imported canister should be easily exchangeable for a local canister.

Bottled gas is also supplied by Flogas and Calor-Kosan. These two companies supply propane (red cylinders) and butane (yellow cylinders) products, which are widely available from filling stations and small stores. However, even in the unlikely event that the physical connector is identical – connectors used in Norway, Spain, Portugal and Ireland are reportedly compatible – it is unlikely that an imported cylinder can be swapped for a local cylinder. In this case, a solution is to carry a Camping Gaz canister in place of the 'normal' spare and use it throughout the cruise by means of an adaptor. The boat's 'normal' gas is thereafter only used to cover the, hopefully short, periods when the Camping Gaz bottle is empty. In Waterford and Cork, it may be possible to have non-standard bottles refilled.

An adaptor for use with 901, 906 and 907 Camping Gaz cylinders is available for approximately €25 from Gaslow International Ltd, (Part number: 01-1665); Tel: +44 845 4000 600. Its brochure is also helpful – see www.gaslow.co.uk/pdf/GASLOW_2007_8pp.pdf.

Gaslow also manufactures adaptors and hoses for use with various European systems. Its Jumbo Adaptor (Ref: 01-1671) is used to connect a butane hose to Republic of Ireland cylinders. Price is approximately €25.

Also try Cavagna, Tel: UK +44 1332 875 878 or Italy +39 30 9663 111.

FUEL

Running out of fuel is cited by the RNLI in Ireland as an increasing cause of lifeboat callouts. Passage off the Atlantic headlands is not the place to have concerns about fuel remaining. Refuelling along this coast needs planning. If fuel is not to determine passage plans, a skipper needs to take some precautions along this coast. Harbours are well spaced and few have safe night-time entry. This pressurises arrival times and may increase the use of the engine. There are also few convenient fuelling berths and some of these may be well off the

Bottled gas connectors may need an adaptor

desired route. It is highly advisable therefore to refuel at every opportunity and to carry significant spare fuel. Alongside fuelling, from an installed pump, is possible at Kilrush, Fenit, Lawrence Cove, Kinsale and Cork.

There are many other refuelling sites but these either require a small road tanker next to an alongside berth or a symphony of spare containers, cooperative harbour staff, transport to the refuelling point, a dinghy ride with tens of litres of diesel and an intricate manoeuvre tipping large containers of fuel into a funnel with the inevitable spills. Always having ample spare fuel for 20 hours motoring will make for a more relaxed cruise.

The other issue is 'Green Diesel', which is widely available in rural South-West Ireland because of agricultural use. As with the UK's 'Red Diesel', EU laws have caused a change in the arrangements for leisure vessels from November 2008. In Ireland, 'Green Diesel' will continue to be available to leisure craft and Irish residents (tax payers) will be required to declare their usage to the taxman and adjustments will be made for the total amount used on the person's tax bill. The answer to the obvious question is 'yes'. Green Diesel is green, obviously green, and overseas visitors should be aware of the implications of returning to home ports, particularly in the EU, with green diesel in the fuel tank.

EQUIPMENT AND CREW

Cruising this Atlantic Coast calls for more self reliance than in more sheltered and populated cruising grounds. This is partly due to the exposure to the ocean but also because support and expertise in moments of need is likely to be anything but close at hand. Certainly, crews should be very confident in anchoring and mooring to buoys – the dominant means of securing in harbour.

As anchoring is frequently necessary, it is essential

to have anchors that are more than marginally fit for purpose. In some situations it is necessary to deploy two anchors and/or select an anchor type more suited to the bottom conditions. Use of a tripping line should be considered when the anchorage is likely to be foul.

When mooring to a buoy, a mooring hook (as opposed to a boathook) is recommended for ease of making the first connection. Reliance on a single boathook is not recommended.

LIFEJACKETS

The regulations concerning the wearing of personal flotation devices (PFDs) are taken very seriously in Ireland. The regulations, simplified, are these:
1. All persons on board any craft of less than 7m in length must wear a lifejacket.
2. The skipper is required to ensure that a lifejacket is carried for each person on board.
3. All persons under the age of sixteen must wear a lifejacket while on board except when alongside or at anchor.

PUBLIC VISITORS' BUOYS

In the late 1990s several coastal counties with government support laid mooring buoys at some of the more attractive locations to encourage visits by cruising yachtsmen. The buoys are still in place and are maintained on a 'best efforts' basis. In 2008 the buoys in Clare and Kerry were refurbished and it is expected that the buoys in County Cork will also be re-laid by the end of the same year. Originally it was intended that a small payment would be collected locally by a person named on a noticeboard near the landing place. The collection of this charge is not rigorously carried out and even the notices still refer to the old currency of Irish 'punts' (£). Visitors are encouraged to make an effort to pay the charge as it contributes to the maintenance and ongoing existence of the buoys.

MARINA AND MOORING CHARGES

Every effort has been made to include the most up-to-date information on marina charges for boats of varying lengths, although all harbours are likely to raise their fees each year to keep in line with inflation. The charges mentioned in the book are inclusive of VAT and generally refer to the peak season rates.

ELECTRICITY METERING ALONGSIDE

Many alongside berths providing electricity have adopted the use of prepayment meters.

The most common form of metering uses a swipe card. The cards have a kilowatt-hour (kW-h) value set individually by each marina. Any number of cards may be purchased. They are usually priced between €2 and €5. Each pontoon outlet has a prepay meter which is credited by pushing the card firmly in and then

withdrawing it. The success of the operation is recorded by the impress of three tiny dots on the card.

What the user needs to know

Inserting the card in the rain or with wet hands after handling wet ropes is likely to cause the card to fold and fail. The previous occupant of the berth may have charged the meter way beyond his usage and there may be plenty of credit left. Finally the meters are not always rigorously labelled to allow correlation with the berth. Try not to charge another berth's meter!

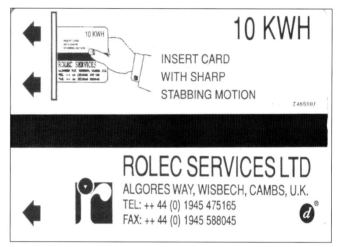
Electricity pre-payment card

BAREBOAT CHARTERING

There are just a few charter companies offering bareboat charter along this coast. Thankfully, they are all very helpful and knowledgeable. From west to east they are:
Dingle: Dingle Bay Charters;
www.dinglebaycharters.com
Baltimore: Baltimore Yacht charters;
www.baltimoreyachtcharters.com
Kinsale: Kinsale Yacht Charter;
www.kinsaleyachtcharter.com
Kinsale: Sovereign Sailing;
www.sovereignsailing.com/bbcharter.htm
Kinsale/Cork: Harbour Yacht Management;
www.harbouryacht.com/index.php

CUSTOMS

In normal circumstances, leisure craft from the EU need not contact customs upon arrival. Only vessels from outside the EU should contact customs on arrival. (Note that Jersey, Guernsey and the other Channel Islands and the Isle of Man are not part of the European Union).

The first contact should be with the nearest of the locations listed. The contact will be redirected to match the circumstances. Visitors should be aware that customs craft are likely to be encountered at sea and they should be given every assistance in executing their task. Drugs are high on their agenda since the prosecution in 2007 for the attempted import of €440M

The ubiquitous custom launch

of drugs near Dunmanus Bay and an even larger haul worth in excess of €500 million in the same area in November 2008.

Terminal Building, Rosslare Harbour,
County Wexford, Tel: 053 916 1310

Government Offices, The Glen,
Waterford, Tel: 051 862 100

Revenue House, Blackpool,
Cork, Tel: 021 602 7000

Marina House, Bantry,
County Cork, Tel: 027 53210

Government Offices, Spa Road, Tralee,
County Kerry, Tel: 066 716 1000

FOREIGN CONSULATES

Belgium
Cork: Dominic J Daly, Pembroke House, Pembroke Street, Tel: 021 427 7399.

Denmark
Cork: Mr Freddie Pedersen,
Combermere House, Glounthaune, Tel: 021 435 3051,
email: pedersenf@pedersen-eng.ie.

France
Cork: Ms F Letellier, 18 Mary Street, Tel: 021 431 1800.

Germany
Cork: Ronan Daly, Jermyn Solicitors, 1st Floor,
12 South Mall, Tel: 021 480 2700. Crohane, Fossa.
Killarney, County Kerry: Tel: 064 32628.

The Netherlands
Cork: G Van der Puil, Mainport, Monahan Road,
Tel: 021 431 7900.

Norway
Cobh: Mark Pearson, Jas Scott & Co, Westlands House Rushbrook, Tel: 021 481 1549.

Spain
Bantry: Maurice D O'Keeffe, Donemark House,
Tel: 027 50001.
Waterford: Iain R Farrell, Nolan Farrell & Goff,
Newtown, Tel: 051 872934.

Sweden
Cork: William H Sullivan, c/o Marsh Ireland Ltd,
12 South Mall, Tel: 021 427 6745.

LANGUAGE
The official language is Irish with English recognised as the second official language. A short dictionary of commonly occurring words is provided in the glossary on the Wiley Nautical website – www.wileynautical. com. Irish speaking regions are not limited to the far west corner of the country. Within 30km of Waterford there are coastal communities using Irish as their first language. Irish-speaking regions are known as 'Gaeltacht' where official signs are in Irish only.

CURRENCY, ATMS AND CREDIT CARDS
The € (Euro) currency, is shared by a large number of other European countries. ATMs are available where the size of population justifies them. Credit cards are widely accepted except in some upmarket restaurants. At the time of publication, the € exchange rate was $1.35 (US) and £0.90 (UK).

ABBREVIATIONS AND SYMBOLS

✈	Airport	⊠	Fish farm	⇌	Railway station
aka	Also known as	FV(s)	Fishing vessel(s)	✗	Restaurant
⚓	Anchoring	🛢	Fuel berth	SBM/ SPM	Single buoy/point mooring
⚓	Anchoring prohibited	⚓	Harbour master		
Ⓑ	Bank	Ⓗ	Heliport	SWM	Safe water mark
	Boat hoist	⇗	Holding tank pump-out	◀	Sailing club
✳	Boatyard	➕	Hospital	☞	Shore power
Ⓟ	Car park	𝒊	Information bureau		Showers
⚓	Chandlery	IDM	Isolated danger mark		Slipway
➕	Chemist/Pharmacist	🔲	Launderette	SCM	South cardinal mark
⊹	Church	Ldg	Leading	SHM	Starboard-hand mark
⦵	Crane	✦	Lifeboat		Supermarket
⊖	Customs office	Ⓐ	Marina	SS	Traffic signals
🞛	Direction of buoyage	NCM	North cardinal mark	Ⓥ Ⓥ	Visitors' berth/buoy
ECM	East cardinal mark	PHM	Port-hand mark	WPT⊕	Waypoint
⚓	Ferry terminal	PA	Position approx.	WCM	West cardinal mark
◂●◂	Fishing boats	⊠	Post office	⊕	Wreck, depth unknown
⊖	Fishing harbour/quay	◔	Public telephone	⛵	Yacht berthing facilities

BUOY COLOURS, LIGHTS AND FREQUENCIES

R	Red
G	Green
Y	Yellow
B	Black
W	White
BY	Black over yellow (north-cardinal)
YB	Yellow over black (south-cardinal)
BYB	Black-yellow-black (east-cardinal)
YBY	Yellow-black-yellow (west-cardinal)
BRB	Black-red-black (isolated danger)
FR	Fixed red
FG	Fixed green
Fl	Flashing light, period of light shorter than darkness. If followed by a number, this indicates a group of flashes e.g. Fl (3). Colour white unless followed by another colour e.g. Fl (3) G. Timing of complete sequence is given in seconds e.g. Fl (3) 10s – group flash three every 10 seconds.
LFl	Long flash i.e. period of light not less than two seconds.
Oc	Occulting light, period of light longer than the period of darkness.
Iso	Isophase light, equal periods of light and darkness.
Q	Quick flashing light, up to 60 flashes per minute.
VQ	Very quick flashing light, up to 120 flashes per minute.

Waterford buoy

Loop Head and lighthouse

Chapter one
Kilrush to the Blaskets

Loop Head is the start of this journey around the south and south-west coasts of Ireland. North of here is a very long stretch of hostile lee shore before the first refuge, which is 38M away in the Aran Islands or County Galway. The coast around Kilbaha gives a taste of the vertical splendour of the cliffs on the journey north of here. Journeying south is equally majestic. Once clear of the River Shannon – Ireland's main artery – the stark cliffs and mountains of the Dingle peninsula soon dominate the horizon.

Loop Head may have originally been called Leap Head. An Irish legend has it that Cúchulaiun (or Cuchullin, the Irish Achilles/Hercules – depending

on the storyteller) leaped from the head to flee the attentions of a boring/over-attentive woman/witch. As usual there are as many versions of the story as there are storytellers; an alternative version has it that the headland had the appearance of a wolf and was therefore named 'Lupshead'.

The remoteness of Loop Head is counterbalanced by the lively marine commerce based on the River Shannon. Unusually for this coast, buoys, lights and marks are plentiful, reflecting the numbers of large vessels that ply the river. Even so, there is ample sea room for all. A long established pod of Bottlenose dolphins reside in the Shannon estuary. Their contribution to the local economy is enormous. Their record for checking every arrival and departure is not as thorough as *Fungi*'s in Dingle (see page 54), but most boaters will spot them between Kilrush and Loop Head. Their sounds are unique (and loud) enough to transmit through the hull and be heard by off watch crew resting in bunks down below!

South of the Shannon estuary Brandon Mountain, the second highest peak in Ireland, dramatically dominates the scenery as it oversees Brandon and Tralee Bays, which are interesting destinations seldom visited by those on north-south passages.

West of Brandon Mountain, the coastline remains striking all the way to Blasket Sound, passing the Three Sisters, Sybil Point and the Blaskets themselves. Perpetually exposed to the Atlantic swell and the raw nature of the land, it is truly remarkable that the Blaskets supported human habitation for so long. Along the way, the marine life thrives with gannets diving, porpoises seeming to appear from nowhere and the occasional puffin flying by.

The passage to and from Dingle Bay has its

challenges, none more basic than at Kilrush where there is a sea lock, which may be a novel experience for many yachtsmen. The friendly and helpful staff at the lock will ensure a safe transit, although to be the first boat through the lock on free-flow may be the nearest thing to white water rafting that a helmsman will experience. This is followed immediately by a time critical passage using the strong tides through the mouth of the Shannon to the open sea, where full exposure to the Atlantic swell ambushes crew with unsteady sea legs!

Passage through Magharee and Blasket Sounds can be made comfortably with adequate planning. Both marinas along the route are particularly agreeable and the other anchorages are delightful in good weather, but the lasting memory will be of the dramatic sea cliffs backed by the majesty of Brandon Mountain on Dingle peninsula pushing out to sea at the western fringe of Europe. The distance from Kilrush to Dingle is 61M.

Paradoxically, the region is well populated compared to the coasts north and south of here. This is because of the relative proximity of significant centres of population at Tralee and Limerick, the large number

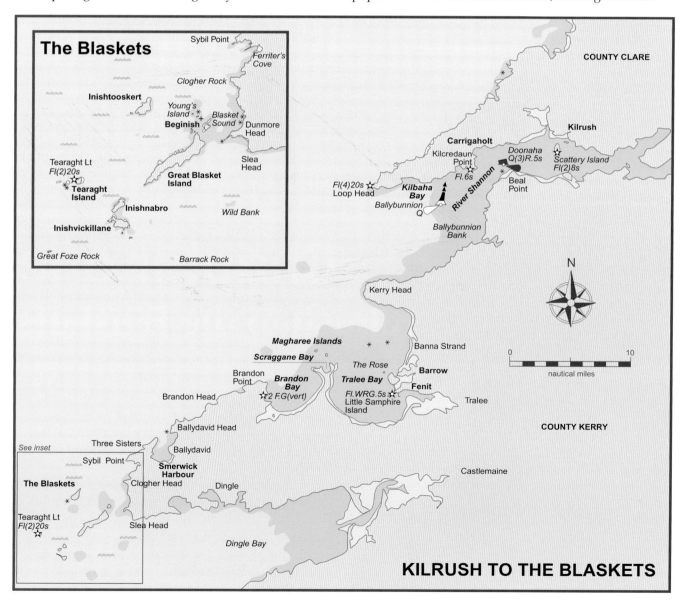

KILRUSH TO THE BLASKETS

KILRUSH TO THE BLASKETS – PASSAGE WAYPOINTS – WGS84 DATUM		
NAME	**DESCRIPTION**	**LAT/LONG**
Loop Head West	1.6M W of Loop Head	52°33'.65N 09°58'.55W
Loop Head South	1.4M S of Loop Head	52°32'.25N 09°55'.92W
Shannon Mouth	1M S of Kilcredaun Head	52°33'.80N 09°42'.57W
Kerry Head	2M W of headland	52°25'.00N 10°00'.00W
Tralee Bay	7 cables W of Fenit Approach	52°16'.00N 09°54'.16W
Magharee East	On 'Rose' transit in 10m	52°18'.90N 09°58'.20W
Magharee Sound	Mid Sound on 'Rose' transit	52°19'.32N 10°00'.74W
Magharee West	2 cables S of Gurrig Island	52°19'.32N 10°04'.29W
Deelick Point	½M N of point	52°18'.00N 10°10'.60W
Brandon Head	½M NW of headland	52°16'.97N 10°14'.90W
Pointanaminnam	½M N of headland	52°14'.68N 10°21'.38W
Sybil Point	½M NW of point	52°10'.96N 10°29'.46W
Youngs Island North	N end of Blasket transit	52°07'.22N 10°29'.61W
Blasket Sound South	S end of Blasket transit	52°05'.50N 10°30'.37W

of holiday resorts as well as the major gateway airport at Shannon.

FAVOURABLE TIDES

Off Kilcredaun Head for passage up the River Shannon, the flood tide commences 5 hours 55 minutes before HW Tarbert Island (approximately 5 hours 35 minutes before HW Cobh) and at Kilrush for passage out of the River Shannon, the ebb commences at 10 minutes after HW Tarbert Island (around 35 minutes after HW Cobh). However, these times may alter significantly depending on meteorological conditions and recent rainfall inland. Annual Tide Tables for Tarbert Island are available from the Shannon Foynes Port Company website: http://www.sfpc.ie.

Blasket Sound

Northward passage – commences 4 hours 30 minutes after HW Cobh.
Southward passage – commences 1 hour 55 minutes before HW Cobh.

Magharee Sound

Eastward passage – commences 5 hours and 50 minutes after HW Cobh.
Westward passage – commences 35 minutes before HW Cobh.

WEATHER INFORMATION BROADCASTS

This coast is served by the Valentia Coastguard transmitter above the Shannon on VHF Ch 28. An advisory announcement is made initially on Ch 16.

PASSAGE CHARTS FOR THIS CHAPTER

Admiralty Charts: AC2254 Valentia Island to River Shannon, 1:150,000.
Imray: C55 1:200,000. Includes plans for the following harbours in this chapter – The River Shannon, Kilrush and Fenit Island.

SAFETY INFORMATION

This section of the coast is managed by Valentia Coastguard, Tel: 066 947 6109.

ELECTRONIC AIDS TO NAVIGATION

Loop Head Lighthouse, AIS planned.
Ballybunnion NCM, AIS planned.
Inishtearaght Lighthouse, AIS planned.

COASTGUARD AIS STATION

Shannon (Knockamore Mt)
52°31'.44N   09°36'.35W   MMSI 002 500410.

The Blaskets; Inishtooskert – The Sleeping Giant in the evening haze

Kilrush

(Irish: *Cill Rois*, meaning Church of the Woods)
Approach waypoint: 52°36'.86N 09°32'.86W
(1M west of Round Tower on Scattery Island)
Entrance waypoint: 52°37'.65N 09°30'.21W
(Between the fairway buoy and No 2 PHM)

Kilrush Creek is an up-to-date, well-appointed, modern marina with plenty of visitors' berths located a few steps from the attractive market town of Kilrush, with its wide selection of shops and marine services. Proximity to Shannon Airport makes it an ideal candidate for a long lay up. Protection inside the sea lock is about as good as it gets.

NAVIGATION

Charts: Admiralty: AC2254 (Valentia Island to River Shannon). For more detail, AC1819 (Approaches to the River Shannon) covers the Shannon Mouth and AC1547 (River Shannon: Kilcredaun Point to Ardmore Point) or Imray C55.

Tides: MHWS: 5.0m, MHWN: 3.7m, MLWN: 1.7m, MLWS: 0.5m. Standard Port Tarbert Island, difference at HW: –00:10min.

These times can be altered in strong winds by up to 20 minutes. The anchorage at Kilbaha, just outside the mouth of the Shannon, is a good spot to await the tide.

The strong tides in the Shannon estuary can be used to great advantage. Conversely, tides should be avoided when they are unfavourable, not only because progress will be very slow, but also because the wind over tide can cause very turbulent seas in south-westerly winds against spring tides that can ebb up to 4kn.

Lights & Marks
Shannon entrance
• Loop Head Fl (4) 20s.
• Ballybunnion NCM Q.
• Kilstiffin PHM Fl R 3s.
• Kilcredaun Head lighthouse Fl 3s (conspicuous white tower, partly obscured between 224° and 247°T by adjacent hill to the north-east).
• Kilcredaun PCS buoy Fl (2+1) R 10s.
• Tail of Beal WCM Q (9) 15s.
• Carrigaholt PHM Fl (2) R 6s.
• Beal Spit WCM VQ (9) 10s.
• Beal Bar NCM Q.
• Doonaha PHM Q (3) R 5s.
• Corlis Point/Querrin Point leading lights Oc 5s on 046.4°T (Rear: Querrin Point is a conspicuous lattice mast).
• Rineanna Point lighthouse, Scattery Island, Fl (2) 8s, white sector 208° to 092°T.

www.irelandaerialphotography.com

Kilrush Marina and Boatyard, with Scattery Island in the distance

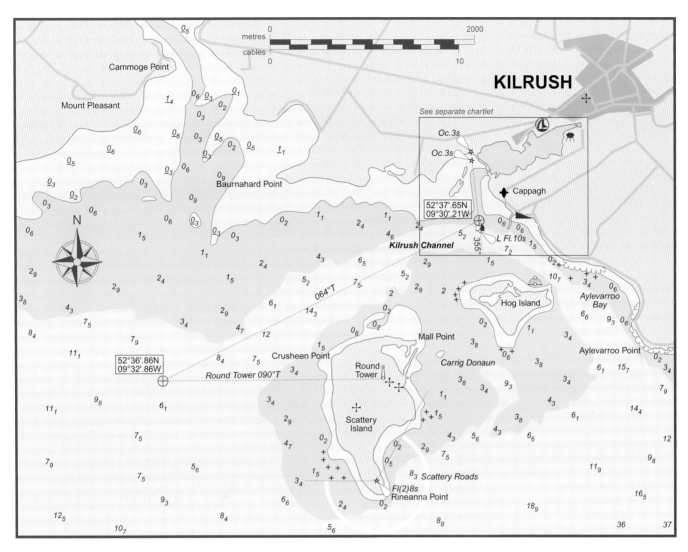

Kilrush entrance

- Marina Fairway Buoy L Fl 10s (red and white vertical stripes).
- Marina leading beacons/lights Oc 3s on 355°T.
- Four pairs of unlit lateral buoys.
- Sectored light at entrance Fl G 3s, green sector 065° to 091°T.
- Traffic signal RG (in front of lock building facing west).

Approaches: As might be expected for a seaway used by 200,000 tonne merchantmen, the approach to the Shannon is extremely well marked. Yachts have plenty of sea room to the west of the buoyed channel. Once past Kilcredaun Head and if making a daytime entry, it is worthwhile contacting the marina staff on Ch 80 or on the mobile phone number.

The Kilrush approach waypoint is on an unobstructed track of 069°T from Doonaha port-hand mark. The round tower on Scattery Island ahead stands clear of the skyline and is readily visible to the left of the twin chimneys of Money Point power station.

The small buoys for the entrance channel to the marina are unlikely to be visible from the approach waypoint. Until the buoyed channel is identified, use a base course of 064°T, steering above the north-west corner of Scattery Island in the Kilrush Channel. Be aware of the shoals to the south of this track, particularly when the town is neared. Stay in 5m and more.

Note 1: The lifeboat station, which had very visible

Kilrush approach waypoint 1M west of Scattery Island Round Tower, which stands clear of the skyline

Nearing the entrance waypoint. Note the port-hand mark in transit with the church tower

red doors at the time of writing, bears 061°T from the approach waypoint.

Note 2: Until arrival at the entrance waypoint, the fairway buoy should not bear north of east.

Eventually, the buoys in the entrance channel will become visible with the red of the port-hand buoys being much clearer than the green of the starboard-hand buoys against the shoreline. The fairway and No 2 buoys should be south of the most identifiable shoreline building – the lifeboat station. No 4 port-hand mark should become visible approximately in line with the church spire. (At the time this photo was taken, the fairway buoy was ashore for repairs.) Proceed to the entrance waypoint listed on page 26.

Pilotage: The buoyed entrance channel (initially 355°T on the leading beacons/lights at the north end of the channel) is dredged (approximately 3m at mean low water springs) to the lock gates. The lock can therefore be entered at all states of the tide. At the north end of the channel a hard turn to starboard is required to line up the lock portal.

Tao 3 leaving Kilrush and about to make a hard turn to port into the entrance channel

For daytime entry, confirm arrival from the fairway buoy with the marina staff on Ch 80 and clarify the state of the lock gates and traffic flow. It is inadvisable to enter the entrance channel until the outer lock gate is open, although there is room to turn, if necessary, outside the gates. Masts of outgoing yachts may be visible adjacent to the lock building (note the traffic light points west and is visible only at the north end of the entrance channel).

The lock is not manned 24 hours, but out-of-hours arrivals can berth in the lock overnight as can those waiting overnight for a favourable tide to leave. Otherwise, the lock operates every hour on the half hour from 0930 during daylight hours. It may be left open for free flow of traffic for a short time either side of high water, depending on the level of high water.

Entering Kilrush lock from seaward

Locking: Prepare fenders to protect the gunwale. Once inside the lock secure fore, aft and amidships by looping warps around the vertical rubber-clad chains. The rush of water when the levels are balanced is very strong and is capable of violently moving any boat. If alongside the north face of the lock, be aware of the proximity of the mast to the windows of the control room and avoid rocking the yacht.

If 'free-flow' is available, that is both lock gates are open simultaneously, ensure that the rate of flow of

water through the lock is fully appreciated and that the boat has enough speed through the water to maintain steerage if going with the flow or to make progress if working against it. 'Going with the flow' may feel like white water rafting compared to normal cruising speeds.

BERTHING

A berth will be allocated before leaving the lock. Proceed through the buoyed channel inside the marina, remembering to lower fenders from the locking positions. (There are two pairs of lateral buoys between the lock gates and the pontoons). The marina comprises 120 berths on three finger pontoons, and has depths of not less than 2.7m below chart datum. To find out about berthing availability ahead of time, contact the marina manager, John Hehir, on Tel: 065 905 2072 or 086 231 3870; VHF Ch 80; email: kcm@shannondev.ie; website: kilrushcreekmarina.ie/home.html.

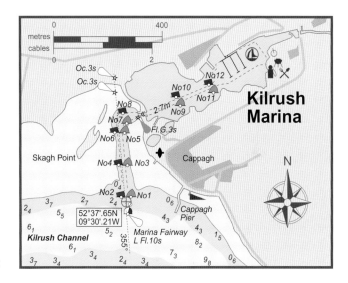

Berthing fees: Overnight rates are €2 per metre per night, plus €5 per night for electricity. There is a minimum charge of €24 per night.

Useful information – Kilrush

FACILITIES
Kilrush's sea lock has turned a muddy creek into an attractive, commercially successful marina. It is about to be further enhanced. The expansion includes a doubling of the size of the clubhouse, automation of lock gates, a breakwater, a new boatyard, a dinghy park, and a doubling of the berthing capacity.
Fresh water and electricity: On the pontoon.
Fuel: Diesel from an alongside pump in the boatyard opposite the marina. Petrol by can.
Launderette: Inside the secure area in the marina building (pay in reception).
Showers/toilets: Inside the

secure area in the marina building. Token-operated.
Rubbish disposal and recycling: Bins outside the marina building.
Gas: Bottled gas can be obtained from Kevin O'Brien, Henry Street, Tel: 087 203 9828, and Camping Gaz from Gleeson's, Henry Street, which also does bike hire, Tel: 065 905 1127.
Weather forecasts: Are available at the marina reception desk.
Boatyard: The boatyard is run by the marina, which approves the contractors permitted to work in the marina. Equipped with a 45 tonne boat hoist and a 1 tonne jib crane, the yard offers repair and

service facilities, including a slipway and open or covered standing/storage. Also available are small sail repairs, marine surveyors, shipwright and fibreglass as well as marine electrical and fitting services.

Each contractor has been vetted and has public and employer liability insurance. Owners may also carry out work themselves as may equipment vendors rectifying any items still under warranty.
Chandlery: Is limited. Try Central Sports & Leisure, Market Square, for ropes and some clothing, Tel: 065 905 2794, and Clancy's, Vandeleur Street, for hardware.

Communications/Internet: Mobile coverage is good. Wi-Fi and Internet access are available from K&K Computing in Frances Street, Tel: 065 905 1806.

PROVISIONING
Kilrush narrowly loses out to New Ross for having the closest supermarket to any marina on this coast. SuperValu is, at most, a 10-minute walk from the pontoons and is a good size with plenty of fresh food, Tel: 065 905 1885. Kilrush Farmer's Market is held every Thursday from 1000 to 1400 in the Market Square, Tel: 065 905 1047, while the main post office and banks can be

Useful information – Kilrush (continued)

found half way up Frances Street. Pharmacies include Kilrush Pharmacy, Tel: 065 905 1029, and Malone's Pharmacy, Tel: 065 905 2552, both of which are situated in Frances Street, as well as Burns in Henry Street, Tel: 065 905 1787.

EATING OUT

A walk from the marina up Frances Street, to the Market Square and along Henry Street, will reveal the majority of bars and restaurants in town. There are plenty of places to lunch or just snack. Recommended at lunchtime for food, drink and people-watching is Crotty's on Market Square, Tel: 065 905 2470. Patience is needed but customer turnaround can be relatively speedy and seating will ultimately become available. Inside Crotty's, take time to imagine how this 1914 building must have been when built. It won't tax the imagination; tiled and plank floors, original fireplaces and mirrors remain. There is an extensive collection of memorabilia on the walls. Of particular interest is that relating to Elizabeth Crotty who enjoyed considerable fame as a concertina player. Unfortunately, food is not served in the evening here and the choice of restaurants becomes quite limited for the size of town.

On Henry Street, try The Haven Arms, Tel: 065 905 1267, Taster's Diner, Kelly's Bar & Restaurant, Tel: 065 905 1811 (unmodernised and an eclectic mix of customers) and Silver House Chinese Restaurant, Tel: 065 905 2775. Near the marina is The Harbour Restaurant, Tel: 065 905 2836.

ASHORE

Kilrush is a planned town laid out to the design of Vandeleur, the local Dutch 'landlord'. A wide, straight street (Frances Street) leads up from the waterfront, lined with substantial shops, banks, bars and houses. The Market House is on the main square, with the Sessions House at the top of the street. Although Kilrush is a sizeable town, it is not big enough to attract the chain stores – each shop is individually owned. During working hours, the town buzzes with activity.

Nearby Scattery Island, once a sixth century monastic settlement founded by St Senan, is worth a visit by ferry for a stroll around its historic ruins. It has one of the oldest and tallest round towers in Ireland, and a lighthouse and battery at the southernmost point (no access to either). Uninhabited since 1978, there is an abandoned village in the north-east

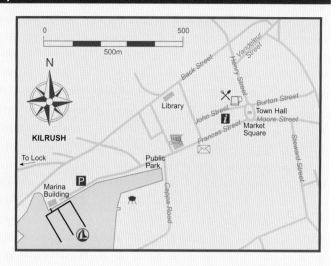

corner and the ruins of seven churches as well as a 'holy well'. The island was named after a dragon (*Cathach* in Irish, giving *Inis Cathach*). There is a small visitor centre on the island and guided tours are available free of charge. For ferry information, call Tel: 065 905 1327. Note that Hog Island to the north-east is privately owned.

Most visiting yachtsmen will have been approached by dolphins coming upriver, but for those with a more academic interest, the Shannon Dolphin & Wildlife Centre, Tel 065 905 2139, adjacent to the marina, has exhibits of skeletons of whales and dolphins and has sound recordings of the dolphins in the Shannon.

Vandeleur Walled Garden is also worth a visit. The Vandeleurs' home was Kilrush House. The walled garden protects the very delicate plants that manage to thrive in this temperate climate. 'Kilrush in Landlord Times' is a heritage display in the Vandeleur Centre. Open daily all year, Tel: 065 905 1760; website: www. vandeleurwalledgarden.ie.

TRANSPORT

Bus services: 336 Limerick-Ennis-Kilrush-Kilkee. Two to four buses per day every day.
Car hire: At Shannon Airport and Ennis (Liam Cleary, Kilrush Road, Ennis, Tel: 065 682 0942 – no delivery to Kilrush).

Taxi & minibus: Black's Hackney Service, Carnacalla, Tel: 065 905 1434; Joseph Carmody, Donogrogue, Killimer, Tel: 065 905 1325; John Flynn Minibus, Cappa Drive, Tel: 065 905 1489; Brendan McDermott, Cappa, Tel: 086 879 3456; Colie Tubridy, 2 Vandeleur Street, Tel: 065 905 2707; Seamus Kerrigan, Killimer, Tel: 065 905 3073.
Air: Easy access to Shannon Airport in one hour is possible by car or taxi and ideal for crew changes or laying up.

OTHER INFORMATION

Yacht club: The Royal Western Yacht Club uses the marina premises.
Police: Kilrush Tel: 065 908 0550.
Hospital: Mid-Western Regional Hospital Ennis, Tel: 065 682 4464.
Doctor: Frances Street, Tel: 065 905 1581/1374/1275/1470.
Dentist: Miriam Buckley & Niall McCarthy, Moore Street, Tel: 065 905 2888; Liam Jones Toler Street, Tel: 065 908 0080.
Tourist office: Kilrush Tourist Office, Frances Street, operates June to September, 1000-1300, 1400-1800 Monday-Saturday, 1000-1400 Sunday; Tel: 065 905 1577. Ennis Tourist Information Office operates all year round, Tel: 065 682 83 8366; email: touristofficeennis@shannondev.ie.

Shannon's dolphins celebrated by a statue on Frances Street

Carrigaholt near low water springs

Carrigaholt
(Irish: *Carraig an Chabhaltaigh,* meaning Rock of the Fleet)
Approach waypoint: 52°36'.00N 09°41'.00W
(6 cables due east of Carrigaholt Castle)

The village lies at the mouth of the Moyarta River and ½M north-west of a ruined MacMahon 15th century castle, which towers over the new pier. The remaining structure of this impressive five-storey tower house has been well-preserved. The new pier is sometimes referred to as Castle Pier for obvious reasons. The village also has another pier, which is situated in the village but dries out and has an awkward entrance. The newly laid moorings (2008) are out of the main tidal flow of the Shannon and therefore useful for awaiting a favourable tide. It is also well protected against westerlies but if an extended strong blow is expected, the much better protection and facilities of Kilrush and its marina are only 7M away.

NAVIGATION
Charts: No detailed chart. Use Admiralty AC1819.

Tides: MHWS: 4.9m, MHWN: 3.7m, MLWN: 1.9m, MLWS: 0.7m. Standard Port Tarbert Island, difference at HW: –00:35min.

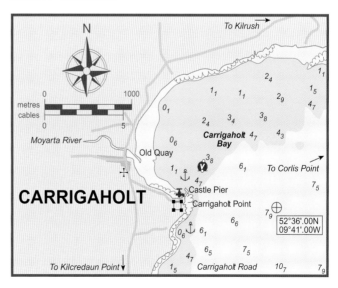

New or Castle Pier viewed from inside the old harbour

A large metal tide gauge faces the steps on the inside of Castle Pier under the ice facility.

Lights & Marks: As listed for Shannon entrance on page 26.

Approach: There are no obstructions to the entry except the unlit mussel farms between Corlis Point and Carrigaholt Bay, that is off the Shannon's north shore, half way to Kilrush and the shallows immediately south and south-east of Castle Pier.

Pilotage: From the approach waypoint, steer 295°T to the mooring buoys.

MOORING
Reportedly the public visitors' buoys at 52°36'.20N 09°41'.80W were replaced in late summer 2008 and there are now eight in place. (There had been concern of the safety of the previous buoys).

Land at Castle Pier. The road into the village from the root of the pier is obvious.

Useful information – Carrigaholt

FACILITIES
There is **fresh water** on Castle Pier (the tap has a threaded connection – no hose).

PROVISIONING
At the top of the access road to the Castle Pier is Sealyons fresh fish shop, Tel: 065 905 8222. Some supplies may be obtained from Keane's (see below).

EATING OUT
The Long Dock is a popular pub and restaurant. Although the 'Dining Pub' award dates from 2002, it

still receives consistently good reviews and when visiting at the colder ends of the sailing season, the large fire in the hearth is most inviting, Tel: 065 905 8106. At the time of writing, Fennell's Pub and Restaurant is not operating. Morrissey's village pub offers music while opposite is a fish and chip shop, Tel: 065 905 8041.

Carmody, Tel: 065 905 8038, and Keane's, Tel: 065 905 8102, are both pubs. In the peak season, Pat's Café, Tel: 065 905 8182, cum post office in the square sells 'tea shop' fare, including ice-cream, cakes, coffees and soft drinks.

ASHORE
Although farming and a little fishing are staple occupations for the local community, a number of day-trippers and caravanners from Limerick, who come for the excellent beaches in the area, are an additional source of income. The village has a workaday feel to it. The village square is its focal point and the facilities are all within 100m. It caters well for local needs. In 1588, sailors of the Spanish

New Pier and the Castle

Armada so enjoyed the hospitality here that they set fire to their ship in the bay to avoid having to set sail! As usual, live entertainment is readily available, particularly during the high season. The village has an annual oyster festival on May Bank Holiday Monday.

For those who were unlucky and missed the 200 strong pod of Shannon dolphins or need a more reliable view of them, Dolphinwatch, Tel: 065 905 8156, operates from the village using a licensed boat fitted with a hydrophone

to eavesdrop on dolphin conversations as they cavort around the boat.

Nearby: Three kilometres further south at Kilcredaun Point there is one of the six (three pairs) batteries that were built to protect the estuary against a Napoleonic invasion.

Rinevella Bay (4km) is a pebble/mud/sand beach with interesting tree stumps sticking up at low water – it was once a sunken forest.

TRANSPORT
Bus services: None.
Taxi: 'Jimmy' lives locally, Tel: 087 685 7752.

Kilbaha Bay near low water springs

Kilbaha Bay
(Irish: *Chill Bheathach*, meaning Birch Church)
Approach waypoint: 52°34'.00N 09°51'.00W
(4½ cables east by south of the pier)

Kilbaha is one of those pleasant surprises that occur when it is least expected. Kilbaha's obvious value, tucked in as it is behind the low hill to the west, is as an early respite from uncomfortable seas after a long passage south along the coast of County Clare. However, it should also be considered as a destination in its own right – its peacefulness is particularly enjoyable in settled, warm weather for a lazy lunch.

NAVIGATION
Charts: No detailed chart. Use Admiralty AC1819.

Tides: MHWS: 4.3m, MHWN: 3.3m, MLWN: 1.5m, MLWS: 0.5m. Standard Port Tarbert Island, difference at HW: –00:25min two days before neaps; –00:45min two days before springs.

Lights & Marks
• Loop Head Fl (4) 20s.

Approach: From the west, clear Dunmore Head (1½M south-west). From Kilcloher Head and the east, there are no offshore obstructions and a back bearing of 105°T on the masts on Knockamore Mountain above the Kerry shore, if visible, is useful.

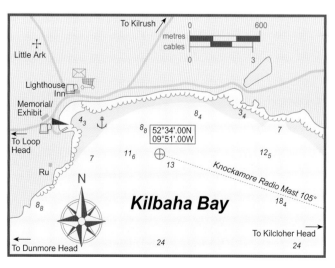

Kilbaha Pier near low water springs

Pilotage/anchoring: From the approach waypoint, steer 293°T and anchor outside the outermost buoys in the middle of the bay well clear of the rocky shores. Double check that holding is robust – the rocky bottom is known for poor holding.

Land at the pier or on the slip, although either will be problematic at low water springs (both the aerial photograph and the photo of the pier were taken within one hour of low water springs). Note that the bay is subject to swell and is only protected from westerly winds.

Useful information – Kilbaha Bay

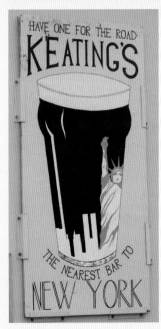

FACILITIES
Ashore there are very basic services centred on the two pubs. At the end of the pier access road is Keating's Bar (a large yellow building) which, with due lack of regard for Great Circle geometry, professes to be the 'nearest pub to New York'. The menu is brief but offers variety and is reasonably priced.

About 200m further round the bay, the Lighthouse Inn (the white building) does inexpensive bar meals and a back room also serves as the post office and small grocery, which has opening hours matched to those of the inn. Showers may be possible if guest rooms are unoccupied, Tel: 065 905 8358.

Both pubs have bench tables outside, facing the shore and overlooking the anchorage. There are no other services.

ASHORE
Ashore, the few facilities and local points of interest are all within easy strolling distance and, for those needing a greater challenge, for a 360° view of the panoramic scenery between Brandon Mountain and the Shannon and north to the Cliffs of Moher and County Connemara, a more bracing walk of 5km to Loop Head lighthouse is needed.

Opposite Keating's Bar, a small open-air exhibition and display provides a fascinating synopsis of some local history. Uniquely, one of these is the 'Little Ark'. In the 1850s, the local landowner forbade the Catholic priest to hold mass for his many hundreds of communicants on the owner's land. With admirable ingenuity, the priest acquired what amounts to a hut on a cart. Knowing that the landowner's rights end at the high water mark, he had his church taken to the shore each Sunday and held mass for his congregation who assembled along the beach. The Ark is now preserved in an annex to the local church, which is an easy 300m walk up the road alongside the Lighthouse Inn.

Back at the exhibit, there is concise information on the role played by Fenians locally in 1867 and the mystery of the 'yellow men', probably North African traders, who drowned and were buried nearby.

The pier is actively used for commercial fishing. For those heading north, the last 3M of the Shannon Estuary between Kilbaha and Loop Head gives a foretaste of the scenery about to be encountered.

TRANSPORT
Public transport is extremely limited. A community **bus** runs into Kilrush at noon on Friday and returns at 1530. Otherwise 'Jimmy', Tel: 087 685 7752, provides a local **taxi** service.

The Little Ark, dating back to the 1850s

Fenit Harbour looking west over Little Samphire Island to the Magharees, Scraggane Bay and on to Brandon Bay

Fenit (for Tralee)

(Irish: *An Fhianait*, meaning The Wild Place)
Approach waypoint: 52°16'.00N 09°53'.00W
(2 cables south of Little Samphire Island)

Fenit, a small village of 500 people, is 12km west of County Kerry's largest town, Tralee, in the beautifully panoramic Tralee Bay. Close to the small, well-protected marina is a comprehensive grocery shop, seasonal café and an exceptional pub/restaurant that, alone, makes it worth a visit. Fenit is an excellent base for day sailing to the beautiful anchorages off the North Kerry Coast.

Fenit Marina should not be overlooked for crew changes. Its position close to the railway and both Shannon and Kerry airports give it great flexibility.

NAVIGATION

Charts: Use Admiralty AC2739 or Imray C55.

Tides: MHWS: 4.6m, MHWN: 3.4m, MLWN: 1.6m, MLWS: 0.5m. Standard Port Cobh, difference at HW: Springs –00:57min; Neaps –00:17min.

Lights & Marks
• Little Samphire Island lighthouse: Fl WRG 5s. White sector 140°T to 152°T, which provides clearance between Mucklaghmore Island and the north-east limits of the Magharees. Green sector: 090° to 140°T

(safe water east of the Magharees).
• Samphire Island QR.
• Fenit Harbour Pier Head 2FR (vert).
• Marina entrance Iso R 6s to port, Iso G 6s to starboard.

Approaches: The clearest approach from all points seaward is in the white sector of Little Samphire Island lighthouse (see Lights & Marks above), that is, between Mucklaghmore Island (4.5M north-north-west) and the shallow patches north-east of the Magharee Islands. This track also avoids Illaunnabarnagh Island (4.2M north by west), the Rose (2M north by west) and Fenit Without (or Island) (1M north). **Note**: There is a rock (1.1m) in the white sector once south of Fenit Island – 9 cables north-north-west of the lighthouse.

Alternatively, if approaching from the west, use Magharee Sound if the weather and visibility is good. (Passage through the sound is described later in this chapter on page 40). Once clear of the extensive shallows east of the Magharees and the adjacent mainland peninsula, steer for Little Samphire Island (127°T).

In both approaches, note the two obstructions on the chart (both have a minimum depth of 5m) and the submerged rock (2.6m) in the midst of the shallows 1M north-west of Little Samphire Island. Arrive at the approach waypoint 2 cables south of Little Samphire lighthouse (which can be mistaken for a ship from a long distance in daylight).

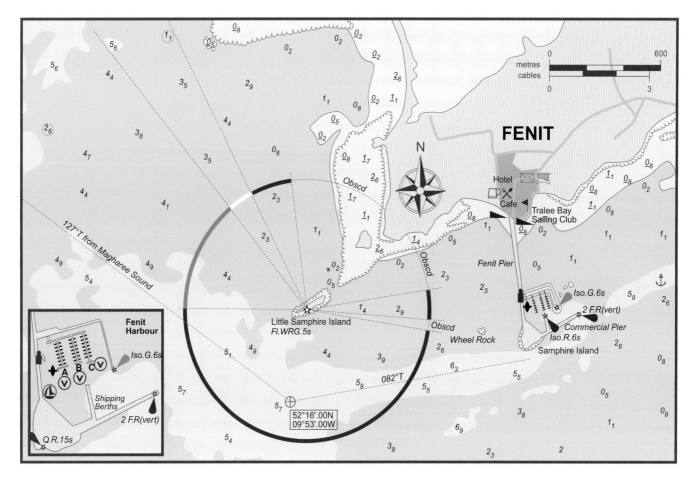

Scale:
metres 0 — 600
cables 0 — 3

Map labels include:
FENIT
Hotel
Cafe
Tralee Bay Sailing Club
Fenit Pier
Little Samphire Island Fl.WRG.5s
Obscd
Wheel Rock
Samphire Island
Iso.G.6s
2 F.R(vert)
Commercial Pier
Iso.R.6s
127°T from Magharee Sound
082°T
52°16'.00N 09°53'.00W

Fenit Harbour inset:
Fenit Harbour
Iso.G.6s
A B C
Shipping Berths
2 F.R(vert)
Q.R.15s

Pilotage: From south of Little Samphire Island, keeping in 5m, steer 082°T for a position ½ cable south of Samphire Island (St Brendan's statue). **Note**: The water shoals rapidly north of the line between Little Samphire and Samphire Island. Finally, steer east-north-east along the outer pier and turn into the marina entrance north of the outer pier. There is access at all tides and times and a night-time entry is possible.

BERTHING/MOORING

Telephone the harbour master/marina office during office hours (0900-1800 [21:00 in peak season]) to arrange for a security keycard, electricity cards, shower access code and a berth number. The harbour master, Michael O'Carroll, can be contacted on Tel: 066 713 6231

The lighthouse on Little Samphire Island

or 087 679 4079; VHF Ch 16 then working Ch 14; email: fenitharbour@eircom.net; website: www.fenitharbour. com/marina.html. The marina has 130 berths, including 15 visitors' berths, for vessels up to 15m, all in 3m, with one berth capable of taking boats up to 25m. Larger boats may use the fishing or commercial harbour. The pontoons are not labelled and the three major (A to C) and two minor (D and E) fingers have many identity plates missing. Visitors should berth on a hammerhead A13/14, B15/16 or C25/26 unless previously allocated a berth. Pontoon A-C berths are numbered counter clockwise.

Berthing fees: Overnight fees are €2.20 per metre per night.

In the off chance that there is no spare berth, a mooring buoy might be available from the sailing club.

The Currach

Also known as Curragh or *Naomhóg*, the currach is a traditional boat on the west coast of Ireland and is still seen all along the south-west coast. It was originally constructed using animal hide over a wooden frame. Nowadays, canvas sealed with tar is used instead of hide. It is very buoyant with a square stern and is virtually flat-bottomed, therefore making it ideal for heavy seas and shallow rivers. It could be sailed, pulled (the oars used these days are spade-like and square-edged) or now fitted with an outboard.

Historically, it is thought that currachs may have made the first transatlantic crossing. This hypothesis was tested by Tim Severin in 1978 when he successfully sailed to Newfoundland in a replica boat (see page 38). Lately they have been used for social racing. The 8m racing currachs are crewed by between one and four persons.

Fenit Marina

Useful information – Fenit

FACILITIES
Fresh water and electricity:
On the pontoon. Electricity
is by card (€1 or €5) in a
meter. The power sockets
are separate from the
meters and not all are
uniquely number paired –
be careful to use the card in
the correct meter.
Fuel: Diesel from alongside
'E' pontoon adjacent to the
marina office. Petrol, by can,
requires a trip to Tralee.
**Launderette and showers/
toilets:** In the marina

Tralee Bay Sailing Club

building. Access by code.
Rubbish: Disposal bins
are situated in the yard next
to the marina building.
Weather forecasts: Available
at the marina noticeboard
and reception desk.
Boatyard: Provides boat
repair, service facilities
and standing/storage.
The boat hoist is a 90 tonne
All Terrain crane.
Chandlery in Tralee:
O'Sullivan's Marine, Tel: 066
712 4524; Landers Outdoor
World, Tel: 066 712 6644;

Electric & Diesel,
Tel: 066 712 1530.
Communications: Mobile
phone coverage is good
but there is no Wi-Fi or
Internet access.

PROVISIONING
Parker's Londis general
store is small but
comprehensive. It includes
a post office and sells wine/
beer and Kosan gas. It is in
the village just beyond the
West End Bar, Tel: 066 713
6151. The nearest Camping
Gaz stockist is in Tralee.

EATING OUT
The West End Bar
& Restaurant (BIM
accredited), Tel: 066 713
6246, has been owned and
run by the O'Keeffes since
1885 and is less than 1km
from the marina. It has
different menus for the
bar and restaurant.
The restaurant, which
offers quality as well as
good value and service,
is highly recommended.
The bar is comfortable,
but a large television

screen rather dominates
the atmosphere.
Godley's Hotel & Pub
is a little further towards
the village. There is also
a seasonal beach shop
and café.
For those willing to step
a little further or summon
a taxi, the Tankard Pub
and Seafood Restaurant
(BIM accredited) is open
at lunchtime and in the
evenings. Receiving
recommendations from
both visitors and locals, it is
situated at Kilfenora, 4km
east of Fenit, Tel: 066 713
6164. Equally, a strong
local favourite is the Oyster
Tavern at Spa, Tel: 066 713
6102. Spa is 7km east of
the marina.

ASHORE
For those on the shortest
of visits, the story of St
Brendan the Navigator can
be found displayed on the
steps up to his statue which
surmounts Samphire Island
at the south-west corner of
the harbour and marina.
Taking a photograph of the

Useful information – Fenit (continued)

St Brendan showing the way west

4m bronze statue as he overlooks Tralee Bay is almost obligatory! St Brendan (AD484-577) was born a little north of the harbour. He is famous for the myriad of legends woven around his attempt to be one of the first Irishmen to emigrate.

Today's sailor may be interested to read about the 1976 attempt to verify the feasibility of St Brendan's journey (*The Brendan Voyage*, ISBN 0-349-10707-6). Tim Severin, in his leather hulled currach (see panel on page 36), sailed from Ireland to Newfoundland via Scotland, the Faeroes and Iceland. En route he demonstrated that many of the phenomena reported by Brendan can be accounted for by naturally occurring happenings. There are impressive views from the statue to Blennerville Windmill in the east on the outskirts of Tralee, past the Magharees to Brandon Mountain in the west and to Kerry Head in the north.

Not exactly entertainment, but most visitors will query the strange looking metal structures that accumulate on the outer pier and perhaps why the children's play area, opposite the West End Bar, has such huge colourful climbing frames. The answer lies in the fact that the harbour is the main port of loading for Liebherr container cranes, which are manufactured in Killarney. The parts are delivered to the old station yard opposite the Bar and eventually moved to the outer pier by tractors and self-propelled trailers. Freighters arrive about once a month, occasionally assisted by tugs. In the aerial photograph on page 35 a freighter is being loaded in the harbour entrance. The cranes are shipped to destinations worldwide.

Any shore leave from the marina means a short walk along the old railway pier, which connects Samphire Island to the village. The bridge also linked the harbour to the railway system in 1887 but the line from Tralee was eventually closed in the late 1970s. Tralee still has a railway station on the main rail network for a trip to Dublin and Cork. This is the last harbour close to a railway station until Cobh is reached.

A trip by taxi to Tralee (population 23,000) takes about 20 minutes and costs around €20. It is worth the effort to visit the Kerry County Museum, where there is a wealth of background on the people, harbours, places and history between here and the Kenmare River at the southern extremity of County Kerry.

Also nearby is Tralee Golf Club whose green fees, including the hire of clubs, are an eye-watering €225 per round – who said yachting is expensive? This was Arnold Palmer's first attempt at golf course design. Visitors can be accommodated midweek.

TRANSPORT
Bus services: 278 Tralee-Fenit – one a day on Friday.
Taxi: Bertie Carmody Tel: 087 261 0453/066 713 6191; McCarty's minicabs Tel: 087 250 4436.
Rail: Railway station in Tralee, Tel: 066 712 3533.
Air: Shannon (2hrs) Tel: 061 712 000; Cork (2hrs) Tel: 021 431 3131; Kerry (25mins) Tel: 066 976 4644.

OTHER INFORMATION
Sailing club: Tralee Bay Sailing Club has wonderful premises on a high promontory above the harbour. Contact Lorna Browne, Tel: 066 713 6119. The sailing club operates a sailing school.
Police: Based in Tralee, Tel: 066 710 2300.
Hospital: Based in Tralee, Tel: 066 712 6222.
Dentist: Based in Tralee, Tel: 066 712 7200.
Tourist office: Based in Tralee, Tel: 066 712 1288.

North Kerry Coast

Barrow

Approach waypoint: 52°18'.60N 09°52'.16W
(3 cables NE of Illaunnacusha in more than 5m)

This is a tiny inlet which leads to a large drying harbour less than 3km north of Fenit Marina as the crow flies. Historically, it was the entrance to the region's major port and was defended by Barrow Castle and Fenit Castle on either side of the very narrow entrance. Their ruins remain.

In extremely benign weather and calm sea state, it now provides a very small, tranquil and rarely used anchorage for the more adventurous boater with plenty of time to wait for a viable combination of tide and weather and who wishes to linger through a full tidal cycle. The tidal flow in the entrance is very strong, therefore a balance is needed between sufficient depth for entry and minimised tidal stream.

NAVIGATION

Charts: Use Admiralty AC2739.

Lights & Marks: None.

Tides (approx): MHWS: 4.6m, MHWN: 3.4m, MLWN: 1.6m, MLWS: 0.5m. Standard Port Cobh, difference at HW: Springs –00:57min; Neaps –00:17min.

It would be prudent to assume that the depth at the bar inside the entrance has only chart datum.

ANCHORING

The anchorage is north-north-west of Fenit Castle.

NEARBY

All there is in the immediate neighbourhood is the vast, beautiful expanse of Banna Strand stretching 9km to the north and Tralee Golf Club (see Fenit on page 38). Access ashore is very limited. Signs have been erected by the golf club which very heavily discourage non-golfers from crossing their links. Similar signs discourage access to the long walk back to Fenit along the seaward shore of Fenit Without (or Island). 'All there is', however, is really not an appropriate phrase in this anchorage because it is a place to appreciate from the cockpit and forget any thought of going ashore.

Barrow Harbour entrance looking south along Banna Strand

www.irelandaerialphotography.com

Magharee Sound and Islands

(Irish: *Oileain an Mhachaire.*

English: Seven Hogs)

Western approach: 52°19'.32N 10°04'.29W

(2 cables south of Gurrig Island)

Eastern approach: 52°18'.90N 09°58'.20W

(On 'The Rose' transit in 10m)

The Sound is the obvious and shortest route from the west to Fenit, but should only be used in settled conditions such as those depicted in the aerial photo. It is shallow in places and the sea needs little provocation to break vigorously on the islands and within the Sound, particularly in wind over tide conditions.

NAVIGATION – MAGHAREE SOUND

Charts: Use Admiralty AC2739.

Lights & Marks: None.

Tides (approx): MHWS: 4.6m, MHWN: 3.4m, MLWN: 1.6m, MLWS: 0.5m. Standard Port Cobh, difference at HW: Springs –00:57min; Neaps –00:17min.

The tides through the sound are strong (2-3kn) in springs. The east-going flood tide commences 5 hours 50 minutes after HW Cobh and the west-going ebb commences 35 minutes before HW Cobh.

Passages (general)

Strangers sailing east are likely to have difficulty unambiguously identifying the charted visual transit (see below) even in good visibility. Sailing west, the 'The Rose' transit may be easier to acquire and retain. In both directions, be aware of the islands off the mainland, (Illaunnanoon, Doonagaun and the half tide Illaundonnell). Least depth along the passage track is approximately 3.4m.

Passage from west to east: Gurrig Island is readily identifiable as the most westerly of the group. Commencing 2 cables south of Gurrig Island, head due east, staying clear of Illaunnanoon and Doonagaun Islands which lie 2½ cables off the mainland shore to the west of the entrance to Scraggane Bay. Clear Illauntannig (the large island facing Scraggane Bay) with more than a 5m depth and continue heading east until dissecting a line between Illaunturlogh (a small white/guano-capped island) and Rough Point on the mainland. At this point, try to identify the charted transit (106°T) – the south side of 'The Rose' in line with Fenit Castle (on Fenit Island) and Church Hill on the far side of Barrow Harbour. If the transit is acquired, continue on it until well east of Mucklaghbeg (the most easterly Magharee Island). Alternatively, use a back bearing, keeping the north of Gurrig just open of the south of Illauntannig (approximately 100°T) until well east of Mucklaghbeg to clear half tide Illaundonnell.

Finally, if headed for Fenit, alter course for a point south-west of Little Samphire Island, noting the two obstructions on the chart (both have a minimum depth of 5m) and the submerged rock (2.6m) in the midst of the shallows 1M north-west of Little Samphire Island.

Passage east to west is the reverse the above.

Magharee Sound looking south; Gurrig Island is at the bottom right. Little Samphire Island is visible in the distance (top left)

www.irelandaerialphotography.com

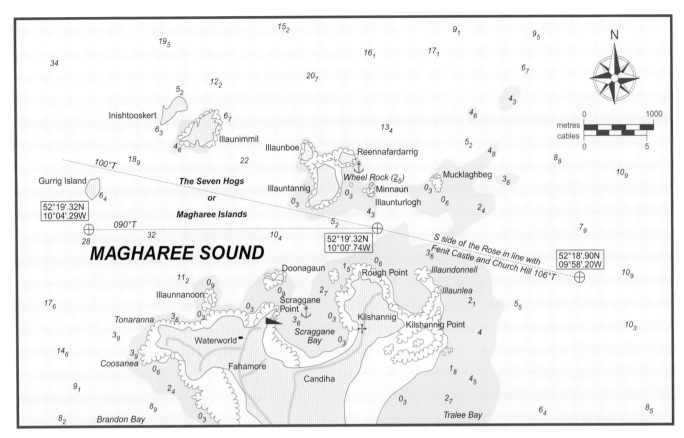

MAGHAREE ISLANDS ANCHORAGE

The anchorage is indicated on the chartlet above and is clearly visible centre left of the aerial photograph opposite. From the passage track described above, there is a channel going north between Illaunturlogh/Minnaun to the west and the shallows off Mucklaghbeg to the east. It is 300m wide and greater than 5m deep. Using the pilotage notes for the Sound, turn north when west of Illaunturlogh. Once the north shore of Mucklaghbeg bears south of east, turn north-west to the anchorage, which is east-north-east of the sandy beach and house. This anchorage has several small difficult-to-see buoys, some of which have floating ropes attached. It would be judicious to use this anchorage only in very settled weather such that the buoys and their attachments are clearly visible. Anchoring in deeper water to the east of the area may be less fraught.

This is not a place to have the mechanical sail disabled as the only local assistance might be the diving centre above Scraggane Pier! **Note**: Drying Wheel Rock (2.5m) lies south-west of the anchorage. Land on the beach.

ASHORE

With its name deriving from a corruption of *machair*, meaning a dune-like, low-lying raised beach, Magharee Sound separates the islands from the mainland. Inevitably eight islands (Gurrig Island, Inishtooskert, Illaunimmil, Illaunboe, Illauntannig, Reennafardarrig, Illaunturlogh and Mucklaghbeg) are needed to form the seven hogs, but only one is remarkable. Illauntannig (*Oileán t-Seanaigh*) has the remains of a monastic site with beehive huts and an oratory. There is a solitary house which is available as a holiday let in the summer. Oil lamps are used for lighting.

Proceeding north past Minnaun before turning north-west into the Magharees anchorage

Scraggane Bay (centre) with Brandon Bay beyond

Scraggane Bay

(Irish: *Cuan an Scragáin*)
Western approach: 52°19'.32N 10°04'.29W
(2 cables S of Gurrig Island)
Eastern approach: 52°18'.90N 09°58'.20W
(On 'The Rose' transit in 10m)

If there are divers in the crew then this is the anchorage they will appreciate. Nearby is Waterworld, the five star Dive Centre. Scraggane Pier is inside Scraggane Bay (the small horseshoe-shaped bay in the centre of the aerial photograph above) on its western shore.

NAVIGATION

Charts: Use Admiralty AC2739.

Lights & Marks: None.

Tides (approx): MHWS: 4.6m, MHWN: 3.4m, MLWN: 1.6m, MLWS: 0.5m. Standard Port Cobh, difference at HW: Springs −00:57min; Neaps −00:17min.

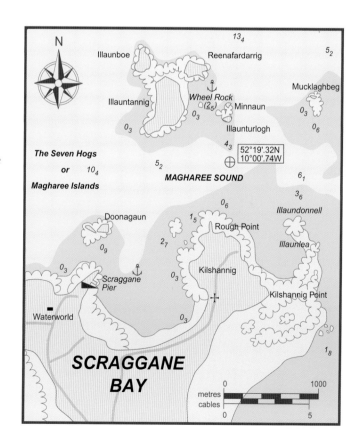

Scraggane slip and pier

Approach: Using the passage descriptions for Magharee Sound (appropriate to the direction of approach), turn south from the east-west leg to enter Scraggane Bay between Doonagaun Island and Rough Point (the shallows in the entrance to the bay extend 2½ cables west of Rough Point). This can be achieved by tracking due south of the west shore of Illaunboe (close north-west of the dominant Illauntannig), staying in 5m until abeam Scraggane Point.

ANCHORING
Head south-west towards the pier in the north-west corner of the bay, anchoring east-north-east of it in approximately 5m, north of the fishing vessel moorings. Note that this position may be exposed to swell. You can land at the pier or on the slip (the slip was refurbished in 2008). Protection is best in south-westerly winds.

Scraggane anchorage

Useful information – Scraggane Bay

FACILITIES
The only facilities close by are the leisure centre, bar and Islands restaurant attached to Waterworld.

Spillanes Bar, Fahamore

EATING OUT
Islands Restaurant, Tel: 066 713 9292, is in an elevated position above the pier and offers an airy ambience with good views. It is recommended for taking a leisurely lunch perhaps while the divers are away doing their thing.

Spillanes Bar and Restaurant (no reservations, evenings only), Tel: 066 713 9125, is a large establishment offering steak and seafood. It is 1km south on the east shore of Brandon Bay in Fahamore (*An Faiche Mór* meaning 'The Large Plain').

Further still, there is a bar, The Green Room, at Candiha on the southerly shore of Scraggane Bay or a wider choice in Castlegregory, which is 7km south.

ASHORE
Waterworld is a PADI five star Gold Palm Instructor Development Centre and also a 'National Geographic'

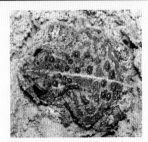
The Natterjack toad

Dive Centre. It capitalises on the clear waters, abundant sealife and remarkable geology of the area.

Apart from the Dive Centre, Scraggane Pier is 5km from Lough Gill, a shallow and relatively warm lake. Together with the adjacent sand dunes, this is a perfect breeding ground for the endangered natterjack toad, which may be heard more often than it is seen.

Brandon is tucked into Brandon Bay behind Deelick and Brandon Points

www.irelandaerialphotography.com

Brandon Bay
(Irish: *Cé Bhréanainn*)
Approach waypoint: 52°16'.10N 10°09'.20W
(ENE of pier head)

Brandon Bay is wide open to the north, admitting swell.
Also, strong winds with south in them fluke down the
mountain valleys to make conditions uncomfortable.
However, in lesser winds, it is reasonably sheltered
from the south-west and west. Indeed, shelter is
somewhat erratic; the local fishermen obviously
understand the problem and overwinter their craft in
Dingle, but even they lost six craft from their moorings
off the pier one stormy night.

NAVIGATION
Charts: Use Admiralty AC2739 or Imray C55.

Tides (approx): MHWS: 4.6m, MHWN: 3.4m, MLWN:
1.6m, MLWS: 0.5m.
Standard Port Cobh, difference at HW: Springs
−00:57min; Neaps −00:17min.

Lights & Marks
• Brandon Pier Head 2 FG on conspicuous support.

Approach: On the west side of Brandon Bay, Deelick
and Brandon Points are steep-to but Ballymore
Point (½M north of Brandon pier) has shallows
1 cable offshore. On the east side of the bay keep
3 cables off the point. Otherwise a direct route to
the pier may be taken.

ANCHORING
Anchor east of the pier in 5-6m.

Useful information – Brandon Bay

FACILITIES
This is not an anchorage for those looking for anything other than a restful stop-over and some sustenance en route or during a day sail from Fenit. The nearest store is 4km away in Cloghane, from where two buses (No 273) run every Friday to Tralee.

EATING OUT
There are three hostelries in Brandon: Murphys Pub is a pleasant bar overlooking the anchorage at the top of the pier. Expect snacks and possibly music, Tel: 066 713 8189.

O'Sheas Bar (run by the Mullalleys) is 200m from the pier and serves food all day in season, Tel: 066 713 8154.
Lastly, Tigh A'Chúinne is popular with the locals and offers basic pub food.

ASHORE
Do not confuse Brandon Bay/village with Brandon Creek (*Cuas an Bhodaig*), a small inlet west of Brandon Mountain which was the departure point for Tim Severin's 'Brendan' voyage (see Fenit on page 38) and featured on BBC's *Coast* programme in 2007.

Brandon anchorage

Smerwick Harbour's west shore. Looking south-west, the Three Sisters (right) lead on to Sybil Point and out to Inishtooskert and Inishtearaght. The low-lying land at the south-west of the harbour is clearly seen

Smerwick Harbour

(Ballydavid/Ballynagall)

Approach waypoint: 52°13'.20N 10°24'.10W
(Mid entrance in 50m)

Smerwick's 'signature' is the readily identifiable 'The Three Sisters' – three near identical cliffs that form the western headland of the harbour entrance. The harbour is difficult to summarise easily because, no doubt, in peak season and in settled weather it could be a glorious 'cruise' of its own. However, outside those conditions, it is neither a primary all-weather refuge nor a 'destination' harbour, although it would be extremely welcome in the very worst of Atlantic weather. It has several anchorages/moorings to select from to match the dominant weather conditions. The southern shore is quite flat terrain and therefore does little to reduce strong winds with south in them. Although the Three Sisters are a good defence against a north-westerly, the resulting swell eventually penetrates the harbour, making for discomfort.

Even a strong north-easterly will fluke down the valleys between Brandon Mountain and its offspring to cause uncomfortable conditions.

NAVIGATION

Charts: Use Admiralty AC2789B.

Tides: MHWS: 3.8m, MHWN: 2.8m. Standard Port Cobh, difference at HW: Springs –01:07min; Neaps –00:27min.

Lights & Marks
• Ballynagall Pier Fl R 3s.
• Radio mast with grey building at its base at Ardamore on the far shore when approaching the harbour from the north-west.

Approaches: Both headlands are foul in their own way and should be given a wide berth on entry into the harbour. This is not too much of a problem as the entrance is 1M wide. Outside the harbour, there is foul water for 2½ cables north of the middle Sister and 1 cable north of the eastern Sister (see photo above). Duncapple Island is 4 cables off the eastern headland and has a further obstruction 1 cable to its west (see photo below).

Smerwick Harbour's east shore looking north-east. Duncapple Island lies off the east shore of the entrance and Ballydavid Pier is centrally located

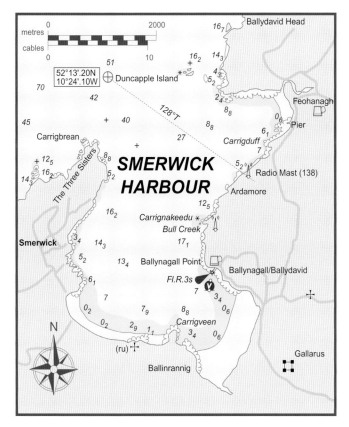

Pilotage: From the approach waypoint (see above), steer 128°T towards the radio mast (this mast has no protusions and a small grey building at its base). Another smaller mast is to the south. Inside the harbour there are no obstructions other that Carrignakeedu (½M south of the radio mast), which is foul 1 cable off the shore.

The harbour remains wide as it doglegs south to Ballydavid, sometimes referred to locally as Ballynagall.

MOORING / ANCHORAGE

In north-easterly winds: Try in the north-east corner of the harbour (Feohanagh), north of the radio mast. Anchor in 3m or more to avoid boulders. Beware fishing gear with floating lines! If in doubt, do not cross pairs of buoys and, in calm conditions, proceed slowly and inspect buoys before attempts at corrective action become useless. The mooring buoys south of Ballydavid may also be viable.

Ballydavid Pier

In north-westerly winds: Try in the lee of the Three Sisters on the west side of the harbour.

The low-lying land at the south-west corner of the harbour provides little protection and, furthermore, the bottom has been reported to be heavily weeded.

Ballydavid Pier: There is little water at low water at the end of the pier. Alongside berthing is not advised. Mooring buoys lying south of the pier are maintained by Kerry Council and should be comfortable in easterly through to south-westerly winds. Landing is at the pier or on the adjacent beach/slip, depending on the tide. Again, be wary of fishing buoys!

FACILITIES

Ballydavid has a small store, a post office and two pubs/restaurants (Begleys Pub and TP's), which are reliably open only in peak season. Without some very long walks, there is little of interest ashore that cannot be accessed better from Dingle where bicycles or taxis can be hired. The most popular spot, 2km south-east, is the 9th century Oratory at Gallarus (the only rectangular beehive not to have collapsed). Two buses per day run from Dingle (No 277) to Ballydavid on Tuesdays and Fridays.

Feohanagh, in the north-east corner of the bay, is the starting point for hikes to Brandon Creek and Brandon Mountain. For those in need of refreshment

The pier at Feohanagh

after the strenuous walks, there is either the 'Old Pier' restaurant, Tel: 066 915 5242, or the An Cúinne pub in the village, which serves snacks, Tel: 066 915 5222. This sleepy village valiantly took to its currachs on the night of 29 May 1944 to rescue the crew of *Badger Beauty*, a US Army Air Force B-17 that ditched five miles off Ballydavid Head. The crew were extremely lucky. First their bomb doors fell open in time to safely slow their landing, after which their dinghies were towed ashore and they were treated to local 'hospitality'. One crewman's recollection of the ditching is being somewhat inebriated on the back of a horse and cart heading towards Dingle. The event is commemorated by a plaque on the pub wall.

The Blasket Islands
(Irish: *Na Blascaodi*)

Southern approach waypoint: 52°05'.50N 10°30'.37W
(7½ cables S of Garraun Point)
Northern approach waypoint: 52°10'.96N 10°29'.46W
(½M NW of Sybil Point)

The Blaskets are a fascinating group of six uninhabited islands, the most westerly in Europe. The cruising yachtsman has two reasonable interests – safe passage through and around the islands and perhaps a landing.

Passage through Blasket Sound can be bedevilled by dangerous mid-channel rocks, fast tidal streams, overfalls, magnetic anomalies and poor visibility. With a little diligent planning, transit can be readily achieved safely in all but very bad weather. Rigorous seamanship standards will serve a skipper well in these waters.

For a visit, Great Blasket is the obvious choice because of its anchorage and the features ashore. The island is rugged and visitors need to be fit. Anchorages and landing on other islands are somewhat more adventurous than is normally encountered in the 'cruising' category. Local, up-to-date advice is recommended for adventurers going beyond Great Blasket, or alternatively, take an 'eco-tour' (€40) from Dingle on a modern high speed catamaran with an experienced guide. The tour will cover the other islands and point out the marvellous wildlife. These islands are wonderful in fair weather but should be avoided if there is any poor weather in the offing.

The Blaskets do not have the dramatic storybook appearance of the nearby Skelligs but are, nevertheless, a cornerstone of Irish heritage, especially in their role in preserving the Irish language. Lack of dramatic peaks translates into a humble amount of farmable land, but eventually it was not enough to sustain the population, which reached about 200 early in the 20th century. In 1953, the government evacuated the 120 remaining islanders and is now in protracted negotiation to make Great Blasket a national park. (The negotiations centre around ferry rights, the café, the fate of the Manx Shearwater and many other aspects that can influence the islands' future). The islands are used for grazing sheep and still have human habitation in the summer – Sue Redican has been in residence there for 20 years.

If a landing is prohibited by time or weather constraints, try to fit in a visit to the archive and, greatly revamped for the 2008 season, audio/visual presentation at the Great Blasket Centre (*Ionad am Bhlascaoid Mhóir*) at Dunquin on the mainland. In good weather, boats also leave from Dunquin (*Dún Chaoin*) for the 20-minute trip to Great Blasket. Landing is via dinghy until the planned new pier is complete. Contact Blasket Island Boatmen, Dunquin, Tel: 066 915 6455.

A pure form of the Irish language existed on Great Blasket Island for many years. It was preserved by the extreme geography and isolation of the island. The value of this resource was recognised early enough to allow the mostly illiterate islanders, with the help of academics, to record in both written and audio form a rich depository of knowledge of not only the language

Blasket Sound. Clogher Head and Sybil Head – top left – are easy to identify viewed from this altitude on a clear day. Finding the leading line from sea level is a much harder task. Dunmore Head is centre right opposite Garraun Point on Great Blasket

South of Blasket Sound on the charted transit. With good visibility, Clogher Rock is elusive

A closer view of Sybil Point and Clogher Rock

but also the traditions of a way of life that has been lost forever. The islanders had many useful words with no parallel in English. Irish schools use the autobiography of one islander – Peig Sayers – as a textbook.

NAVIGATION – BLASKET SOUND

Stromboli Rocks (1.8m) extend south-west off Dunmore Head, to reach half the width of the sound. Directly opposite Stromboli on the easternmost tip of Great Blasket (Garraun Point) is a rock (3.7m). Together they restrict the width of the sound at this point to 4 cables. For passage through Blasket Sound using visual bearings, visibility needs to be a reliable 6M.

Charts: Use Admiralty AC2790 or Imray C55.

Tides (approx): MHWS: 4.0m, MHWN: 3.2m, MLWN: 1.6m, MLWS: 0.8m. Standard Port Cobh, difference at HW: Springs –01:11min; Neaps –00:41min.

The north-going stream commences 4 hours 30 minutes after HW Cobh and south going at 1 hour 55 minutes before HW Cobh. The rate reaches 2-3kn at springs in the sound.

Lights & Marks: There are no lights. The primary leading line through the sound is the summit of Sybil Point in alignment with Clogher Rock on 015°/195°T. For the avoidance of doubt, the summit is the higher of the two peaks on Sybil Point and the one further from the point.

Approaches/Pilotage: From north to south: Giving Sybil Point at least ½M to clear the offlying rocks and islets allows a course of 180°T to join the transit north of Beginish and its northerly neighbour Youngs Island at the 30m contour. It is important to identify Clogher Rock as soon as possible and retain visual contact during the transit. Follow the transit on a course of 195°T.

From south to north, that is from Valentia and other points south: An intercept of the alignments of Inishtearaght lighthouse with the extreme south tip of Great Blasket (Canduff) with the Sybil Point leading line

gives a 2M run to the narrows. However, a newcomer to the area would need very sharp eyes to readily identify the transit from south of the sound. To compound the situation, magnetic anomalies occur in this area requiring magnetic compass bearings to be treated with caution. So, if augmenting visual navigation, ensure that paper chart, GPS and plotter positions are all set or corrected to the same datum, or that the differences, which may be up to 80m, are understood.

Note that a passage from Valentia to this intercept takes a track north of Coastguard Patch and south of Wild Bank, both of which can break in heavy weather. From the south, picking up the main leading line early on will enable you to clear Barrack Rock (8.2m), which is 2.3M south-east of Inishvickillane.

From east to north, that is from Dingle and Ventry: An east-west track ½M south of Slea Head in >30m, which is held until the transit is identified, will allay any temptation to turn early onto the westernmost of the Stromboli Rocks.

The southern approach waypoint is directly on the transit line (015°T). The transit should be strictly adhered to. North-going vessels should leave the transit only when north of Youngs Island.

Great Blasket (Irish: *An Blascaod Mór*)

Settled wind and moderate tide conditions are required for a rewarding visit to this 6km long island. In good conditions it is a pleasurable place for rambling, bird watching, exploring the ruined buildings and, should it be operating, relaxing with coffee and cake at the (seasonal) café. Many of the village buildings are still standing, albeit without roofs. The island is still grazed by goats, donkeys, sheep and abundant hares and rabbits. The latter have been somewhat threatened recently by the invasion of mink. Look out on the beaches for seals. This is one of Ireland's largest haul-out sites between September and December for pupping. Exploring beyond the village to gain a better view involves a climb to 200m and more.

North and north-west of Great Blasket there are two

passages west of Beginish used by local boats. The rocks are numerous and, legend has it, a retreating ship from the Spanish Armada made it through here unscathed. Legend also has it that two foundered. The unmarked channel is 1 cable wide and not recommended to visitors.

NAVIGATION

Charts: Use Admiralty AC2790.

Tides: As Blasket Sound, but note that eddies cause a tidal flow parallel to the strand which can reach 3-4kn.

Lights & Marks: None (Inishtearaght lighthouse is obscured).

Pilotage/Anchoring/Mooring: Use the pilotage given previously for Blasket Sound and then steer due west from the Blasket Sound transit to the anchorage off the strand. Anchor in 4m or secure to a mooring buoy (there is usually a couple free but check with one of the tourist boats that it is not required for a commercial ferry) and land on White Strand (*An Tráigh*). The anchorage is often subject to strong squalls and fast tides. Judge whether leaving a competent person on board for anchor watch would be prudent. Landing at the north end of the beach is good for dinghies. Note that, if needed, there is a slip and harbour marked on AC2790, but this refers to the more substantial landing place used by the dinghies from the commercial ferries.

ASHORE

Pending the debate on the status of the islands, the café is not operating. For the latest information ask at Dingle tourist office or marina.

The Blasket Princess ferrying day visitors to Great Blasket from Dunquin

Ferries moored off the Strand at Great Blasket

Inishnabro (Irish: *Inis na Bró*)

The magnificent scenery is the prime feature of this island. It is sometimes referred to as the 'Cathedral Rocks'.

Tearaght (Irish: *An Tiaracht*)

Tearaght, known to yachtsmen for its lighthouse, is the westernmost Blasket Island. Anyone cruising the islands should be extremely alert to the full extent of the rocks, particularly to the west and south of the island. The prime interest on the island is the Manx Shearwater. These birds spend northern winters in the southern hemisphere – it is outside the scope of this book to go into how the young, after they have been initially nurtured and then abandoned by their parents, manage to find their way to Brazil.

Having come this far, few will be able to resist a trip to the westernmost land on the European continental shelf: Great Foze Rock (*An Feo*) is 3.3M south-south-west.

Inishtooskert (Irish: *Inis Tuaisceart*, meaning Northern Island; also known as the Sleeping Giant)

Apart from a monastic ruin, the island also has the largest colony of storm petrels in Britain and Ireland.

Inishvickillane (Irish: *Inis Mhic Uileáin*, but sometimes referred to locally as Charlie Haughey's Island)

At the southern end of the Blaskets, this very attractive, privately-owned island hosts a single holiday home. The former owner (former Taoiseach Charles Haughey) solved the problem of anchoring and landing by flying in by helicopter. The house shares the island with a herd of red deer.

Beginish (Irish: *Beiginis*, meaning Small Island) and Youngs Island

Apart from a ruined house, it has large numbers of arctic tern and some common and roseate tern.

Youngs Island is immediately north of Beginish and visually merges with it from most viewing angles.

Cahersiveen and Valentia Island

Chapter two
Dingle to the Skelligs

So much of the recent history of this area derives from the key role it played in the first steps in transatlantic telecommunications. However, the technology has raced on and Valentia is currently struggling to keep even its role as a coastguard station now that the communications that consolidated its existence allow its role to be performed from elsewhere.

However impressive the cliffs along this stretch of coastline are, the magnet for yachtsmen must be the offshore islands – The Skelligs and The Blaskets. It is awe inspiring that humans lived for centuries here at the wild edge of Europe. To get the best out of these islands, first visit their mainland exhibitions respectively

in Portmagee and Dunquin (10km west of Dingle).

Remarkably, this part of the coast is rich in good shore facilities and refuges should the sea conditions delay a visit to the islands. Dingle and Cahersiveen have well protected marinas, excellent seafood restaurants and good stores. Improved facilities at Valentia are work-in-progress at the time of writing.

Crossing Dingle Bay, some of the crew will be admiring the magnificent scenery, as the green/brown hills (the unspellable Macgillycuddy's Reeks) rise higher and higher to the east-south-east (the Macgillycuddies were a local land-owning clan). However, this stretch of water is notorious for its short

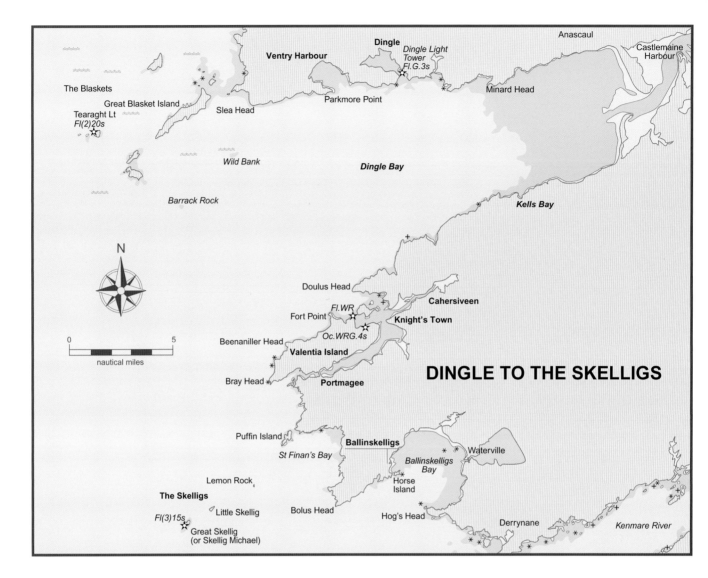

lumpy chop. The funnel mouth of the bay seems to focus the wave action, which produces seas out of proportion to the conditions – indeed it has made many an 'immune' person hang over the rail; this is one place on the coast to consider passing out the pills.

If it is uncomfortable here in benign conditions, consider the impact of bad weather hereabouts upon commercial fishermen – it is reckoned that local trawlers can make it to sea only 180 days a year (quotas permitting).

To ensure a skipper does not relax too much in settled conditions, bear in mind that Admiralty charts are still referred to the OSI datum, that the flood tide flows northwards and there are many magnetic anomalies to deflect the compass.

Suggestions for a one week Dingle Bay itinerary:

For those preferring to cruise 'shorter but often' it is worth considering a Dingle-based cruising circuit.

Day 1: Sail across to Kells Bay for a lunch and a visit to the recently opened gardens. After lunch sail to Valentia Harbour and cross Caher Bar to reach Cahersiveen Marina. Dine at QC's. (Note – spring tides improve the window for high water in the evening at Caher Bar).

Day 2: Leave Cahersiveen via Doulus Bay for a circumnavigation of Skellig Michael, returning to Portmagee and visit the Skellig Experience.

Day 3: Sail to Derrynane and stroll the beaches, visit Derrynane House or walk to Caherdaniel to have a drink at the Blind Piper.

Day 4: Sail to Valentia and take a mooring buoy or anchor off Reenard Point for a visit to O'Neill's Point Bar for the seafood.

Day 5: Sail to Great Blasket and anchor/moor off for a visit ashore (see pages 49–50 of chapter one). Catching the tide suitably for both directions through the sound, return to Ventry for a mooring buoy off the village.

Day 6: Return to Dingle.

Regrettably, Castlemaine Harbour, at the east end of Dingle Bay, is shallow and has strong tidal streams in its entrance as well as shifting sandbanks, thereby severely limiting suitability for yachts.

Cahersiveen. The barracks and the scenic view inland

FAVOURABLE TIDES

Blasket Sound
Northward passage – commences 4 hours 30 minutes after HW Cobh.
Southward passage – commences 1 hour 55 minutes before HW Cobh.

Between Valentia and the Skelligs
Northward passage – commences 5 hours 0 minutes after HW Cobh.
Southward passage – commences 1 hour 10 minutes before HW Cobh.

WEATHER INFORMATION BROADCASTS
This coast is served by the Valentia Coastguard transmitter at Valentia on VHF Ch 24. An advisory announcement is made initially on Ch 16.

PASSAGE CHARTS FOR THIS CHAPTER
Admiralty Charts: AC2254 Valentia Island to River Shannon, 1:150,000; AC2423 Mizen Head to Dingle Bay, 1:150,000; AC2495 Kenmare River, 1:60,000.
Imray: C56 Cork Harbour to Dingle Bay, 1:170,000 – includes plans for the following harbours in this chapter: Dingle, Valentia and Portmagee.

SAFETY INFORMATION
This section of the coast is managed by Valentia Coastguard, Tel: 066 947 6109.

OFFSHORE PASSAGE LIGHTS, MARKS AND ELECTRONIC AIDS TO NAVIGATION
Inishtearaght Fl (2) 20s, AIS planned.
Skelligs Rock Fl (3) 15s, AIS planned.
The Bull. Bull Rock Lighthouse Fl 15s. AIS planned.

COASTGUARD AIS STATION
Valentia (Kilkeaveragh Hill)
51°52'.03N 10°20'.06W   MMSI 002 500390.

DINGLE TO THE SKELLIGS – PASSAGE WAYPOINTS – WGS84 DATUM		
NAME	DESCRIPTION	LAT/LONG
Blasket Sound South	S end of Blasket leading line	52°05'.50N 10°30'.37W
Great Blasket South	S of Great Blasket # Inishtearaght	52°04'.10N 10°31'.00W
Dingle Approach	1.1M S of Light Tower in 30m	52°06'.20N 10°15'.51W
Valentia Approach	1M NW of Fort Point	51°56'.87N 10°20'.21W
Valentia NW	7 cables NW of NW Valentia	51°54'.34N 10°26'.45W
Great Skellig NW	½M NW of island	51°46'.40N 10°33'.50W
Great Skellig SW	6 cables SW of Washerwoman Rock	51°45'.40N 10°33'.50W
Puffin Island	1M W of island	51°50'.00N 10°26'.50W
Scariff Island	½M SW of island	51°42'.90N 10°15'.85W

Dingle Harbour on a sunny day. Smerwick Harbour can be seen in the distance

www.irelandaerialphotography.com

Dingle

(Irish: An *Daingean* meaning Fortress)
Approach waypoint: 52°06'.20N 10°15'.51W
(1.1M S of Dingle Light Tower in 30m)

Besides providing excellent protection against all weather and the best provisioning along this stretch of coast, Dingle's other main attraction is *Fungi*, the resident bottle-nosed dolphin; it would be astonishing if your arrival at Dingle Harbour wasn't noted (and, probably, recorded knowing the astonishing feats of these animals) by *Fungi*. He (reportedly male!) has been 'on station' since 1985 and now brings about 200,000 visitors a year to Dingle and several million euros. So, those small, and not so small, boats disobeying all the collision regulations in the harbour entrance are only trying to give their paying customers what they came to see.

NAVIGATION
Charts: Use Admiralty AC2790 or Imray C55/56.

Tides: MHWS: 4.1m, MHWN: 3.2m, MLWN: 1.6m, MLWS: 0.8m. Standard Port Cobh, difference at HW: Springs –01:11min; Neaps –00:41min.

The flood tide into the harbour commences 5 hours 30 minutes after HW Cobh and the ebb commences 1 hour 35 minutes before HW Cobh. The maximum rate in the harbour entrance is 2½kn.

Lights & Marks
• Eask Tower (unlit, 195m on cliff 8½ cables WSW of entrance, with a 'finger' pointing towards Dingle).
• Ruined Cairn (white – W side of entrance).
• Light Tower Fl G 3s (E side of entrance).
• Lough Tower/Hussey's Folly (unlit ruined tower at Black Point).
• Five SHMs (from seaward, all green) Fl (3) 5s, Fl 7s, Q, Fl 5s, Fl (2) 5s.
• Three PHMs (from seaward, all red) Q, Fl 5s, Fl (2) 5s.
• Leading beacons/lights; Oc 3s (White ◊ on a black pole).
• Sectored harbour light Oc WRG 4s; white sector 001° to 003°T.

Approach: The 'finger' on Eask Tower, high on its cliff, clearly indicates the general location of Dingle Harbour entrance between Reenbeg Point and Beenbane Point. The more southerly the approach the easier it is to acquire the entrance channel, which commences at the Light Tower. When approaching from the Blaskets/Slea Head and points north, stay at least ½M off to avoid Crow Rock (3 cables offshore between the harbour entrance and Eask Tower). Crow just covers at high water springs. Between Crow Rock and the entrance is Colleen-Oge Rock (1.8m), however, this will not be a problem if an east-going vessel has offed Crow and does not turn to port until the Light Tower is visible. Use of the Dingle approach waypoint ensures that passage from Slea Head can be achieved in depths in excess of 30m.

Once familiar with the local geography, there is a viable passage to and from Ventry between Colleen-Oge Rock and the mainland.

Pilotage: From the approach waypoint steer due north towards the Light Tower until the white, ruined cairn is abeam to port. Alter course to 318°T. Acquire and steer to pass close to Black Point starboard-hand mark. Around Black Point start to watch out for *Fungi* and the trip boats with their erratic movements. After Black Point starboard-hand mark follow the buoyed channel, assisted in the north-south dredged channel by the leading marks astern and/or by the sectored harbour light ahead. The channel between the open sea and the harbour is dredged to 2.6m and a night-time entry is possible.

BERTHING

The inner harbour has a small modern marina to port with all tides entry. It is partly separated from the commercial harbour to starboard by the old pier. Protection is near perfect here and the location is convenient if weather dictates a long stay. Historically and latterly, this sheltered harbour has been the foundation of Dingle's continued prosperity.

Make contact with the marina superintendent, Peter O'Regan, on Tel: 066 915 2889 (marina only) or 086 391 6049; VHF Ch M (Ch 16 in exceptional circumstances), during the working day to obtain an allocated berth; otherwise berth on a hammerhead. Dredged to 5m below chart datum, the marina accommodates 80 berths, including 20 visitors' berths, with more pontoons planned for 2009.

Berthing fees: Prices for an overnight stay are €2 per metre per night.

Dingle Light Tower

Dingle marina final approach with yacht masts in the marina to the left, the old pier ahead and the commercial harbour to the right

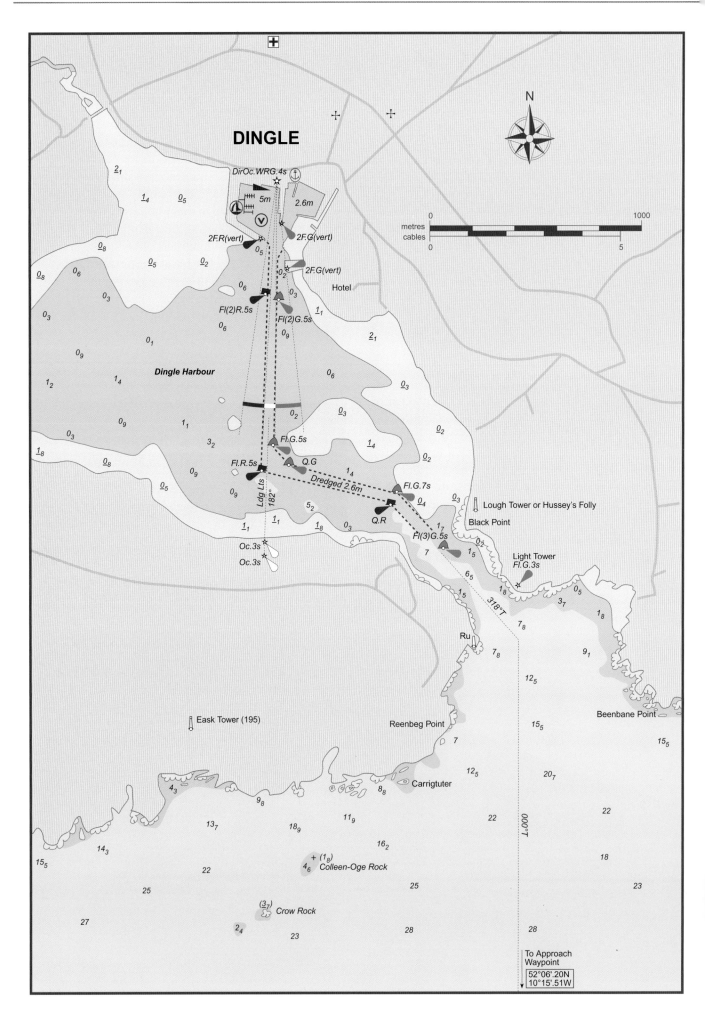

DINGLE

Useful information – Dingle

FACILITIES
Water: On the pontoons.
Electricity: On the pontoons by prepaid electricity card available from the superintendent, shop or Dive Centre.
Fuel: Multiples of 20 litres of diesel in cans via the superintendent, otherwise large quantities by road tanker from the slipway. Petrol can be obtained from local filling stations.
Gas: Camping Gaz at the marina shop.
Showers/toilets: Available at the marina centre, operating by token from the superintendent, dive centre or the shop.
Rubbish: Disposal is in a large skip adjacent to the marina centre. Where possible, use the recycling facility on the main or east piers.
Launderette: Part of Moran's Esso filling station (Mail Road – N86).
Weather forecasts: Posted daily outside the superintendent's office.
Chandlery: Small selection available at marina centre shop, otherwise O'Sullivans Marine at Tralee (50km), Tel: 066 712 4524.
Communications/Internet: Mobile coverage is good. No official Wi-Fi. There are two Internet cafés in Dingle – Dingle Internet Café on Lower Main Street, Tel: 066 915 2478, and The Old Forge Internet Café, Holyground (at the junction of Dykegate Street and Strand Street), Tel: 066 915 0523.
Boat hoist: None, but crane can be hired or it is possible to dry out at adjacent slip by arrangement.
Boatyard: None. Discuss specific requirements with marina superintendent.
Slipway: Adjacent to the marina.
Diving facilities: Available at the marina centre.

PROVISIONING
Grocery: Food stores include a Spar and a large SuperValu, Tel: 066 915 1397, 300m along the harbour (both will deliver to marina) as well as a Lidl

supermarket on the O'Conor Pass Road (less than 1km). Two other stores have usefully long opening hours: nearest the marina is the Highway Stores (opposite the tourist office), which opens until about 2300 for all the basics, and Moran's well-stocked delicatessen, behind the Esso filling station at the beginning of the Mail Road, opens earlier than all others.
Pharmacy: In Green Street and Main Street.
Banks and ATMs: Two banks on Lower Main Street.
Post office: Situated on Lower Main Street.

EATING OUT
You will find an extremely wide choice of good restaurants in Dingle and only the occasional bad one. There is no sure way to detect the bad except perhaps by avoiding those with very few local customers. Outside the immediate area of the marina, it is best to canvass local advice. Near the marina, the following recommendations are based on recent experience: Starting with breakfast, Harringtons is the only choice for the 'Jumbo Irish', or, for the strong willed, just a 'Full Irish'. Of course, a true bacon addict will find it hard to wait for Harrington's to open at 0900. In this case a trip to Moran's delicatessen, behind the filling station on the road to Killarney (Mail Road), will be rewarded with a superb bacon sandwich.

The advantage of an early breakfast is that lunch can be more fully appreciated. The restaurant at the top of the marina ramp is as far as you need travel to have a truly excellent fresh seafood lunch. Fish! is open from mid morning to late afternoon, Tel: 086 378 8584. The Marina Inn also offers good quality fare at lunchtime.

In the evening, Out-of-the-Blue (BIM accredited), Tel: 066 915 0811, is the place for fish, but booking in advance is essential. John Benny's, Tel: 066 915 1215, has excellent bar food and

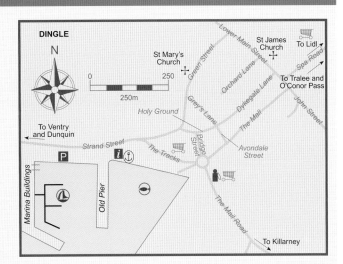

The Small Bridge pub, Dingle

Dingle is never understated

Useful information – Dingle (continued)

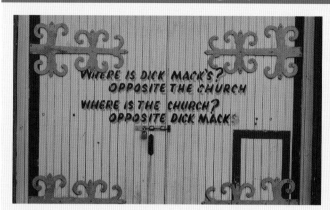
Dick Mack's – opposite the church

looks after its customers exceedingly well. Generally a table is found, however busy it appears. For late arrivals or just for a change, the Sarena Indian restaurant is excellent, Tel: 066 915 2961.

Also within sight of the harbour are the Waterside Restaurant, Tel: 066 915 1444, and James Flahive's bar.

A couple of 'Old Style' bars further into town are worth particular mention: O'Flaherty's and Dick Mack's.

ASHORE
The excellent, friendly local folk are very realistic. They recognise that fishing and farming can only partially support their community. The tourist is absolutely essential to a thriving Dingle and the town reflects this. The town is very lively beyond that of most towns of 2,000 inhabitants and there is a pleasant ambience here as the renovated blends with the new.

The old pubs appear to share counter space with the ironmongery of an old-fashioned hardware store, while drinkers settle in mazes of flagstone floored back rooms. An example of this is Dick Mack's, opposite the church, which had been a haberdashers and cobblers. No one bothered to clear the shoes, boots and tools when it was turned fully into a pub! Have a look at the pavement outside where plaques record the visits of 'celebrities'. Believe it if you will – Dolly Parton balanced

her way up the street after a few pints of non-alcoholic Murphy's. Another example is O'Flaherty's Bar in Bridge Street, Tel: 066 915 1983, which is basic with good *ad hoc* musical sessions. These pubs are a million miles from the production line 'Irish Theme Pubs' of Berlin, Barcelona and Brisbane.

The new is also well done as most sailors quickly discover. For example, the marina buildings are multi-functional, housing a café, chandlery, showers and a watersports centre. The staff in each are more than willing to help visitors and each other out when needed.

Local attractions include a swim with the dolphin – Jimmy Flannery Senior, Tel: 066 915 1967, rents wet suits (essential) and can arrange a boat, a fun fair at the east end of the harbour and an aquarium adjacent to the marina. Alternatively, you could watch a game of Gaelic football at the Gaelic Athletic Association Stadium or go to one of the traditional and folk music concerts held at St Mary's Church. On the other hand, you may prefer to watch a movie at the Phoenix Cinema in Dingle, Tel: 066 915 1222. The tourist office can also arrange horse-riding, golf, escorted tours, archaeological tours, diving courses, marine eco-tours as well as language and cultural interpretation.

The Blasket Islands: It may be the case that time, tide, magnetic anomalies, overfalls and weather will add up to work against

the possibility of a sail to the Blaskets. At Dunquin, a completely revamped hi-tec Great Blasket Centre (opened Easter 2008) allows the visitor to take a customised, virtual aerial tour of the Blaskets, which will partially compensate for an actual visit, but may also ensure that the most is gained from a subsequent landing.

TRANSPORT
Bus services: 275/281/284 Dingle – Tralee. Regular daily service.
276 Dingle – Ventry – Dunquin. Two per day Mondays and Thursdays.
277 Dingle – Ballydavid. Two per day Tuesdays and Fridays.
Taxis (Dingle): Kathleen Curran Tel: 087 254 9649; John Sheehy Tel: 087 239 9923; Cooleen Cabs Tel: 087 248 0008; Autocabs Tel: 087 988 0060.
Bicycle hire: Foxy John's, Main Street, Tel: 066 915 1316; Paddy's, Dykegate Street, Tel: 066 915 1606.
Rail: Trains at Tralee (50km).
Air: Shannon Airport is approximately 2½ hours away and will be closer once the tunnel under the River Shannon is completed (Autumn 2010). There are few destinations that cannot be easily reached from Shannon. A taxi carrying a crew of four is a reasonable proposition at a fare of approximately €200. Shannon taxis include JJCabs Tel: 087 234 9089, email: jjcabaa@jjcabs-tours.com; Doolin Cabs Mobile: Tel: 086 812 7049, email: doolincab@eircom.net.

A closer, perhaps better, proposition is to fly into Kerry airport which is less than an hour from Dingle. The number of destination airports is limited however. Typically the following routes are available: Dublin, Stansted, Luton, Manchester, Frankfurt (Hahn), Lorient.
Kerry Airport Taxis: John Brosnan Tel: 066 714 1184/087 260 1474; Dan Corcoran Tel: 064

36666/087 248 8757; James Courtney Tel: 086 389 514; Murt O'Sullivan Tel: 087 774 7858; Gerard Savage Tel: 087 258 3586/087 235 47874.
Car hire: Kerry Airport: Europcar Tel: 066 976 4733; Avis Tel: 066 976 4499; Hertz Tel: 066 976 3270. Tralee: Practical Car Rental, Ashe Street, Tel: 066 712 1124; O'Sullivan, Manor West, Tel: 066 718 1777; O'Connor Jos Clash, Rathass, Tel: 066 712 4782; McElligott's, Oakpark, Tel: 066 718 1911; Kerry Motor Works, The Mileheight, Tel: 066 712 1555; EU Car Rentals Ltd Tel: 066 718 0880.

OTHER INFORMATION
Marina superintendent: Peter O'Regan, Tel: 066 915 2889 (marina only) or 086 391 6049; VHF Ch M; email:1dingle@eircom.net; web: www.dinglemarina.com.
Harbour master: Brian Farrell, Tel: 066 915 1629; (Ch 16 for exceptional situations).
Bareboat yacht charter: Dingle Bay Charters, The Marina, Dingle, Tel: 066 915 1344/087 672 6100 or www.dinglebaycharters.com.
Police: Tel: 066 915 1522.
Hospital: Tel: 066 915 1455.
Doctor: Medical Centre Tel: 066 915 2225.
Dentist: Tel: 066 915 1527 (Brian Long).
Tourist office: Tel: 066 915 1188.

Fungi greets all

Dingle Bay Moorings

Ventry (Irish: *Ceann Trá*)

Approach waypoint: 52°06'.43N 10°19'.65W
(Mid harbour entrance in 30m)

Inside the harbour (*Cuan Fionntrá*) there is an impressive sweep of safe, sandy beach and, not so impressive, a large caravan park. It's no surprise that this is where many Irish families come on holiday and children are everywhere during the peak season. The small functional village of Ventry and its pier on the north side of the bay are useful nearby facilities.

The sheltered bay is very convenient as a quiet alternative to Dingle. The scenery is a relaxing combination of well-tended farmland near the shore backed by rolling hills leading to stark peaks inland or big skies to seaward. The bay is open to the south-east, otherwise it is well protected except when strong westerlies turn into squalls caused by Mount Eagle (516m high and 4km west of the harbour).

NAVIGATION

Charts: Use Admiralty AC2790 or Imray C55/56.

Tides (approx): MHWS: 4.1m, MHWN: 3.2m, MLWN: 1.6m, MLWS: 0.8m. Standard Port Cobh, difference at HW: Springs –1:11min; Neaps –00:41min.

Ventry pier and village

Marks: Chapel, just above the shoreline midway along Ventry Strand.

Approach: South-west entry: Reenvare Rocks project 1 cable south-east from Parkmore Point and a ledge continues ½ cable south. Stay in >20m for safety.
South-east entry: A shallow ridge extends 2½ cables south-west from the shore midway between Breagary (just west of Paddock Point) and Ballymore Point. The end of the ridge (2.9m) breaks in heavy seas.

Pilotage: From the approach waypoint enter the harbour midway between the shores on a course of 314°T to a local waypoint (52°07'.60N 10°21'.60W – 3 cables south of Ventry Pier), which is close south of Ventry moorings and anchorage. Coon Pier moorings are 6 cables south by west.

MOORING

Depending on the weather, choose a public visitor buoy, either off Ventry village in the north of the bay where there is a slip on the inside of the pier, or off Coon Pier in the south of the bay, where there is a slip overgrown with weed with a small beach beside it. There are two public visitors' buoys at Ventry and three public visitors' buoys at Coon. Anchoring is an alternative. Land at either pier.

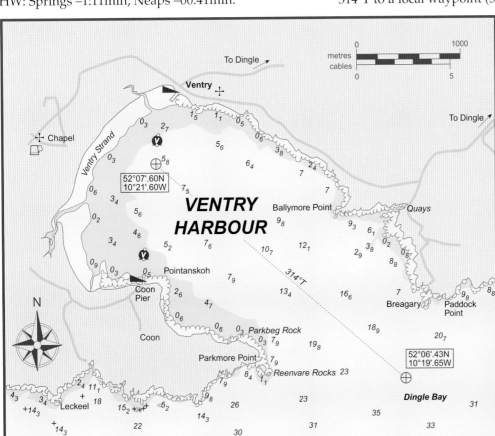

www.irelandaerialphotography.com

Ventry Harbour escapes the shadow of the clouds caused by Mount Eagle to the west

Useful information – Ventry

PROVISIONING
There are no marine facilities locally, but there is a small store for basic provisions and a post office in the village, Tel: 066 915 9060.

EATING OUT
You will find a small number of hostelries in Ventry village and nothing near Coon Pier. Quinn's Ventry Inn does bar food and has outside tables with a view of Ventry Harbour, Tel: 066 915 9949. Alternatively try Thady's 'Tigh an Bhidh' Seafood restaurant (and snacks), Tel: 066 915 9999, or Penny's Pottery Café, which is just west of the village, Tel: 066 915 9962. O'Shea's Pub is situated close to Ventry Strand, approximately half way between the two piers by road and 1½km from the village. The pub is owned by Gaelic footballing legend *Páidí Ó Sé* and features his sporting memorabilia, Tel: 066 915 9011.

TRANSPORT
Bus services: 276 Ventry – Dingle. One bus a day Mondays and Thursdays.
Taxi: Billy Kavanagh Tel: 087 655 3399.

Coon Pier with Ventry across the bay

O'Shea's Pub near Ventry Strand

Kells Bay (Irish: *Na Cealla*)
Approach waypoint: 52°02'.00N 10°06'.18W
(3 cables offshore in midbay)

Kells is a very small fishing village and picturesque holiday spot. The bay is wide and sheltered except in northerly through to easterly winds or if there is significant major swell in Dingle Bay. There is plenty of depth and a useful pier, which was rebuilt in 2008. For children (and adults!), it has a blue flag beach, exotic gardens and good walks. It is a splendid place to stop for lunch.

NAVIGATION
Charts: Use Admiralty AC2789 or Imray C56.
Tides (approx): MHWS: 4.1m, MHWN: 3.2m, MLWN: 1.6m, MLWS: 0.8m. Standard Port Cobh, difference at HW: Springs –01:11min; Neaps –00:41min.

Lights & Marks: None – Note that the mast above the shore is a transmitter, not a navigational aid.

Approach/pilotage: The approach is open and unobstructed. From the approach waypoint, steer directly into the harbour for a vacant mooring buoy.

MOORING
Four public visitors' buoys at 52°01'.65N 10°06'.28W. The buoys suffer severe treatment in winter storms; always check that their position is safe. Land at the pier.

www.irelandaerialphotography.com

Kells Bay in late afternoon sunshine. The newly refurbished pier can be seen in the centre of the photograph

Useful information – Kells Bay

FACILITIES
The pier was reconstructed early in 2008. Reportedly, it will have 3.6m at high water across the end. **Fresh water** is available (threaded tap).

PROVISIONING/ EATING OUT
In peak season, there is a shop and restaurant near the beach, while a strenuous 1½km walk away, on the main road above the village, is Pat's, incorporating a craftshop, **restaurant**, **food store**, **filling station** and **post office**, Tel: 066 947 7601. Caitin's pub is 3km distant in the opposite direction.

ASHORE
Kells Bay is the perfect place to relax and take in

the splendid ambience – even the caravan site is very discreet! Here trees push towards the shoreline and, on the moorings, the scent of pine actually dominates over the smell of the sea. The more active may walk the 'Golden Mile' (starting next to Pat's) for some excellent scenery and viewpoints towards the Dingle Peninsula.

Kells Gardens, Tel: 087 777 6666, opens to visitors in peak summer. It has a somewhat unusual 'Tree Fern' forest and other exotic plants. The current owners are attempting to restore the gardens to their full glory. Tea rooms are available.

TRANSPORT
Bus services: 279 Killarney-

Kells-Cahersiveen. Two per day Mondays to Saturdays. 280 Ring of Kerry Bus

– Kells-Cahersiveen-Sneem-Killarney. One way only and one bus per day in Summer.

Kells Gardens, Kells Bay

Knight's Town (bottom left) prior to the installation of the new breakwaters. The Blaskets can be seen on the far horizon

Knight's Town
(or Knightstown)
Approach waypoint: 51°56'.87N 10°20'.21W
(On Valentia Harbour leading beacons/lights, Doulus Head bearing 061°T, 1M to the narrows at Fort Point)

Valentia Island (Irish: *Bhéal Inse*, meaning 'Mouth of the Island') has scenic beauty, wonderful views across a wide horizon and huge value as a refuge, but its unique fame results from its century as a crucial communications hub between America and Europe.

NAVIGATION
Charts: The most detailed chart is AC2125; otherwise use Imray C56.

Tides: MHWS: 3.8m, MHWN: 3.0m, MLWN: 1.3m, MLWS: 0.5m. Standard Port Cobh, difference at HW: Springs –01:18min; Neaps –00:38min.

However, predictions based on local harmonic data will give times between 35 min and 1 hour after this. The tidal streams can reach 1½kn off Knight's Town.

Lights & Marks (west of Caher Bar)
• Fort Point lighthouse (white tower) Fl WR 2s. White sector 102° to 304°T, but in Dingle Bay is obscured by Doulus Head at 180°T.

• Geokaun Radio Mast FR.
• Harbour Rock ECM Q (3) 10s.
• The Foot ECM VQ (3) 5s.
• Reenard Point WCM VQ (9) 10s.
• Canganniv Spit ECM Q (3) 10s.
• Leading beacons/lights on 141°T. White sector 140° to 142°T: Front (red vertical on white triangular background) Oc WRG 4s, Rear Oc 4s (red stripe with triangular top on white background – see photo page 64).

Approach: The approach from the west is clear. The approach from the immediate north is determined by Doulus Head, but if arriving from Blasket Sound, refer to the relevant section in the previous chapter

Fort Point. Valentia's main entrance

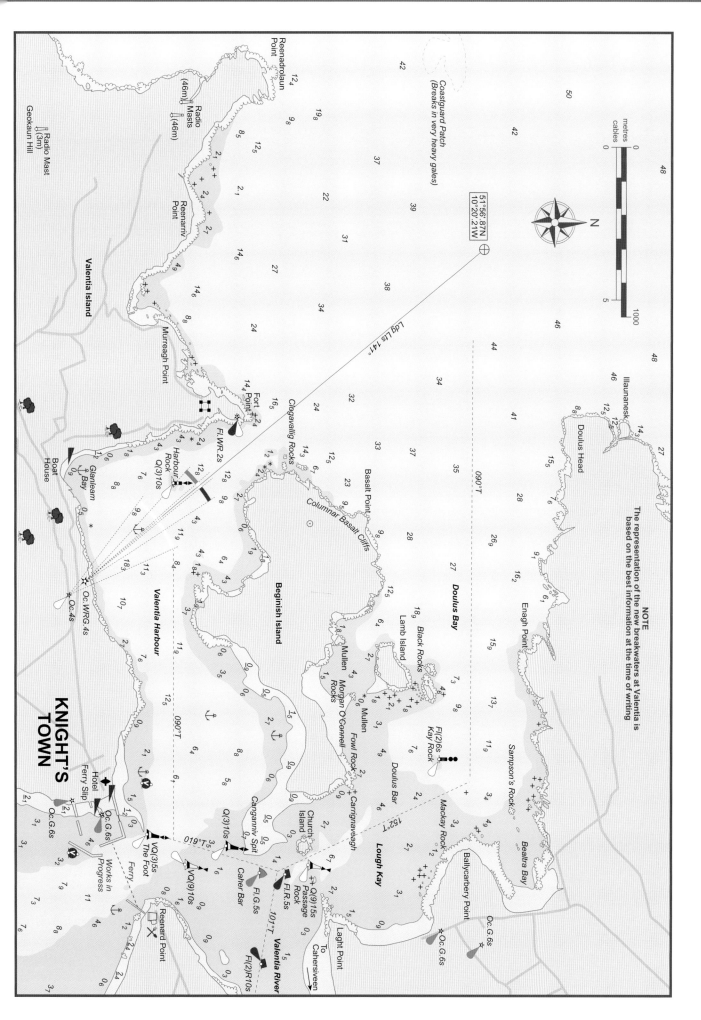

Valentia Harbour's leading marks

The Foot east cardinal mark, north-east of Knight's Town

on page 49. In calm conditions, the narrow (1 cable) entrance at Fort Point (also referred to as Cromwell Point) is no challenge but, in strong north-westerlies the seas often break spectacularly over the adjacent rocks, making the entrance appear very narrow indeed, in which case entry should be avoided. Acquire the leading marks/lights as soon as possible.

Pilotage: From the approach waypoint, steer (very accurately) 141°T on the leading marks or lights through the entry narrows. Identify Harbour Rock east cardinal mark and stay east of it; thereafter stay mid-water heading east. Least depth at entry at all times should exceed 5.8m, which occurs in the vicinity of Harbour Rock.

BERTHING

The harbour at Knight's Town is being redeveloped. It

is therefore imperative that only the latest information is used when visiting Valentia. Work commenced over the winter of 2007/8 on the first phase. The north and new south breakwaters were capped with concrete. In late 2008, work started on installing an L-shaped floating breakwater from the end of the north breakwater eastwards then southwards to a point east of the ferry pier and also from the end of the new southern breakwater straight eastwards. The harbour entrance is to be protected by a separate floating offset breakwater to provide shelter against the south-east fetch. The entrance to the harbour is to be located at the south-east corner and will be approximately 33m wide. The car ferry will continue to use the current slip until a new slip is funded and constructed outside the new harbour. Ultimately it is intended that the RNLI lifeboat will have an alongside berth and there will be up to 220 pontoon berths for recreational craft.

Knight's Town's quay before redevelopment

MOORING/ANCHORING

There are six public visitors' buoys north-west and six south-east of Knight's Town. Alternatively, anchorages may be chosen to suit the direction of the weather.

In westerly, southerly through to easterly winds: try Glanleam Bay 4 cables south of Fort Point in 4m. **In southerly winds**: 1 cable north-west of the village near the public visitors' buoys in 2.5m. **In northerly winds**: use the bay due north of Knight's Town and south of Beginish Island in 3m. **In north-easterly winds**: try south of Reenard Point in 5m.

Knight's Town's Clock Tower

Useful information – Knight's Town

FACILITIES
There is no convenient source of diesel. **Petrol** is available from Lynch's beyond Chapeltown, where there is also a **post office**, Tel: 066 947 6233.

PROVISIONING
Reidy's store has a small range of groceries.

EATING OUT
The Royal Hotel, Tel: 066 947 6144, ('royal' thanks to a visit by Queen Victoria) dominates the waterfront and has an admirable front garden which is perfect for watching the comings and goings on the water. The staff are friendly and excellent lunches are available in a spacious lounge. The traditional 'bacon and cabbage' is particularly good. Alternatively, try Knight's Town Coffee/ Sea Breeze Café, Tel: 087 783 7544, Boston's Bar & Restaurant, Tel: 066 947 6140, or Fuchsia Restaurant & Courtyard, Tel: 066 947 6051.

Reenard Point (opposite Knight's Town) has a better reputation for food. Here O'Neill's – The Point Bar and Seafood Restaurant, Tel: 066 947 2165, can be recommended.

At Chapeltown try The Ring Lyne Pub, Tel: 066 947 6103, for its bar food.

ASHORE
Frankly, Knight's Town is a rather unexceptional single street village, with little to commend it (except a large number of mooring buoys in safe water offshore) over its near neighbours, especially now that Cahersiveen Marina has a buoyed channel. There is a good selection of places of interest on the island but these involve a long walk or a taxi ride. Note that OSI uses the Valencia spelling.

Tetrapods, from 370 million years ago, the Vikings and early Christians all left traces of their sojourn here, but the island truly rose to fame because of the various transatlantic cables that terminated here. After four failed attempts, starting in 1857, it took Brunel's SS *Great Eastern* in 1866 to lay a successful cable and repair one of the failed cables before a reliable service was achieved. The terminal buildings were on a grand scale and many outsiders came to operate the station. The whole edifice was pretty incongruous in such a remote community. Operations finally ended in 1966.

Knight's Town was named after the local landowner, the 'Knight of Kerry'. The current incumbent is the 24th Knight of Kerry

– Sir Adrian FitzGerald, 6th Baronet (born 24 June 1940), who primarily resides in London. A great deal of credit is given to the then Knight of Kerry for successfully bringing the transatlantic cable facilities to Valentia.

Visitor attractions include the Knight of Kerry's former home at Glanleam, which is surrounded by 40 acres of sub-tropical gardens that are open to the public, Tel: 066 947 6176, as well as the Valentia Heritage Centre, Tel: 066 947 6411, and the Valentia Coastguard Station, Tel: (Administration) 066 947 6297.

Also worth visiting are the Grotto & Slate Quarry (which opened in 1816 and supplied slate to many famous buildings, including the Paris Opera), the tetrapod footprints on the rocks (the oldest animal tracks in Europe), and

Alan Ryan Hall's Sculpture Studio at the top of Market Street for innovative pieces.

TRANSPORT
Bus services: A bus service is available only at Cahersiveen.
Taxi: Jackie Sullivan Tel: 066 947 7183 or 087 616 9633.
Ferry: Pedestrian and car ferry to Reenard Point, Cahersiveen, Tel: 066 947 6141. Shuttle service March to October.

OTHER INFORMATION
Harbour master: The position of harbour master has been 'honorary' and has not been filled since 2006.
Dive centre: Valentia Island Sea Sports, Batchelors Walk, Tel: 066 947 6204.
Tourist office: The nearest tourist office is in Cahersiveen (seasonal), Tel: 066 947 2589.

O'Neill's Seafood Restaurant, Reenard Point

Cahersiveen

(Irish: *Cathair Saidhbhin*, meaning
Little Saidhbh's Stone Fort)
Approach waypoint: 51°56'.87N 10°20'.21W
(On Valentia Harbour leading marks/lights, 1M to the
narrows at Fort Point with Doulus Head bearing 061°T)

There is no doubt that Cahersiveen is worthy of a visit.
The passage upriver into a landscape of mountainous
terrain on a crystal clear day is utterly inspiring and
easy compared to the fraught navigation of recent
times. Furthermore the town is home to one of the best
restaurants in the region – QC's.

NAVIGATION

Measures have now been taken to simplify passage over
the 2M up the Valentia (or Caher or Fertha) River. Until
recently, only a series of difficult-to-see leading marks/
lights, both ahead and astern, identified the safe route
over the Caher Bar and up the river. Officially, these
have been augmented (note not replaced) by an isolated
danger mark, four cardinals and a dozen or so laterals.

Charts: No detailed chart. Use Admiralty AC2125 or
Imray C56.

Tides (approx): MHWS: 3.8m, MHWN: 3.0m, MLWN:
1.3m, MLWS: 0.5m. Standard Port Cobh, difference at
HW: Springs –01:18min; Neaps –00:38min.

Lights & Marks east and north of Caher Bar
• Kay Rock IDM Fl (2) 6s.
• Passage Rock WCM Q (9) 15s.
• Six PHMs Fl R – see chartlet for characteristics.
• Seven SHMs Fl G – see chartlet for characteristics.
• Marina entrance 2FG vert and 2FR vert.

Approach & pilotage
Approach over Caher Bar: The initial approach and
pilotage is identical to that for Knight's Town, from
where the entry to the Valentia River (for Cahersiveen)
is controlled by Caher Bar, which has 0.6m above chart
datum at its shallowest point. However, there is a
deeper (1.4m) channel across the bar. On a rising tide,
with sufficient depth over the bar, steer 019°T from
north of Foot east cardinal mark at Knight's Town to

Cahersiveen marina and town. The lateral buoys are downstream and the Old Barracks are adjacent to the road bridge upstream

www.irelandaerialphotography.com

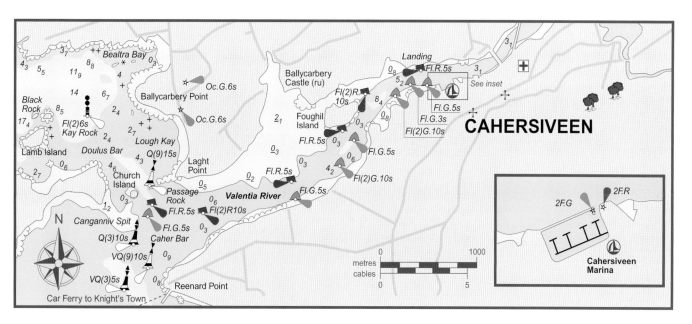

Main Street, Cahersiveen

leave Canganniv Spit east cardinal mark to port and
continue on to bring the first starboard-hand mark
(south-south-east of Church Island) close down the
starboard side. The sand bar immediately to port of
the track uncovers at low water. Turn onto 101°T and
follow the buoyed channel to Cahersiveen.

Approach over Doulus Bar: See photo on page 62.
The alternative approach is from the north via Doulus
Bay and Lough Kay, which is limited by Doulus Bar
at 2.4m above chart datum (2 cables south-east of Kay
Rock isolated danger mark). This route may need to be
assessed in the context of the prevailing sea state as the
bar is not fully protected by Beginish Island and its small
northerly neighbour Lamb Island. From the approach
waypoint, steer due east into Doulus Bay passing
Doulus Head to port and Black Rocks (north of Lamb
Island) to starboard. When Kay Rock isolated danger
mark is abeam (keeping ½ cable off in greater than 5m),
slowly alter course to 152°T to pass midway between
Passage Rock west cardinal mark and Church Island.
After leaving Church Island join the pilotage from Caher
Bar and follow the buoyed channel to Cahersiveen.

BERTHING

The tidal flow in the river is strong and, manoeuvring,
particularly into the inside berths in the marina, is best
delayed until slack water. Also the marina's inside
berths are remarkably tight for any vessel longer than
11m. For both these reasons, visitors should initially
use the north-east end of the long pontoon (the
south-west end has few cleats and is used for fuelling).
Accommodating 100 boats, including visiting
yachts, the marina has a minimum depth of 2.5m.
For more information on berthing at the marina
contact Kieran McCarthy (office), Tel: 066 947 2777 /
087 065 9089, or Patrick Foley, Tel: 087 672 1372; VHF
Ch M or 80; email: acard@eircom.net; website: www.
cahersiveenmarina.ie/index.htm.
Berthing fees: An overnight berth costs €2.50
per metre.

Cahersiveen Marina – the long pontoon upstream of the final lateral buoys

Useful information – Cahersiveen

FACILITIES

Water and electricity: Are available on the pontoons. Electricity is paid for by pre-payment card bought from the marina office.

Fuel: Diesel and petrol by cans arranged through marina staff or large quantities by road tanker from the west end of the long pontoon.

Showers/toilets: Available in marina building. Pay for key in the newly-built marina office.

Rubbish disposal and recycling: Bins provided within the marina. Recycling bins for the town are located in the central car park, 200m from the marina.

Launderette: Available locally at The Social Services Building or Bubbles laundry, 27 Church Street, Tel: 087 761 3098 or 087 676 5109.

Gas: Casey Cycles, New Street, Tel: 066 947 2474.

Weather forecasts: Forecasts are displayed daily on the office notice board.

Communications/Internet: Mobile coverage is good. No Wi-Fi in marina, but Internet access is available at the Internet Café on Main Street, which opens seven days per week.

Slipway: Truncated slipway at town pier.

Boatyard: The marina calls up boatyard services from Finnon Murphy who runs a full service boatyard with slipway, liftout facilities up to 28 tonnes and winter storage at Chapeltown on Valentia, Tel: 087 280 9861; website: www.murphymarineservices.com/services.html.

Chandlery: From Murphy's Boatyard – see above.

Future plans: A restaurant is planned for the new marina building.

PROVISIONING

Supermarkets: There are two small supermarkets (Spar, Main Street, and Centra, Church Street) in town; these are adequate for topping up supplies. The Centra store also includes a **post office**.

Larger EuroSpar and SuperValu supermarkets are on the Valentia Road. Most deliver to the marina. Dingle is the better option for a major revictualling.

Pharmacy: On Main Street.

Bank and ATMs: On Main Street (AIB) and Church Street (Bank of Ireland).

EATING OUT

The town offers many bars and restaurants. The Old Schoolhouse Restaurant, Tel: 066 947 3519, is a 2km walk west of the town. On the other hand, QC's Seafood Bar & Restaurant (BIM accredited) on Main Street, Tel: 066 947 2244, is close by and deserves its excellent reputation and critical accolades; it plays a large part in making Cahersiveen a 'destination' harbour.

There are five pubs in Main Street, including Keating's Corner House, the closest to the marina, Tel: 066 947 2107. Alternatively, others can be found in New Market Street, including Mike Murts hardware and bar, as well as in Rocky Road, New Street, West Main Street and Church Street. Many of them have bar food and offer live music.

ASHORE

Cahersiveen is the main shopping and bopping centre for the area. Traditional 'Social Dancing' (which officially includes Ceili and Set dancing) is very popular, as is more modern dancing. 'Disco' buses run to a timetable to places where there is no other public transport. Street markets take place on market days, attracting people from miles around. Traditional music also features strongly, culminating in the Celtic Music Festival held on the August Bank Holiday weekend (the first weekend in August).

The town itself has reminders of the influence of the Catholic Church – there are small squares adorned with religious statues.

'The Barracks' is one of the most photographed

Mike Murt's unorthodox window display

buildings in the area because it is so out-of-character. It was built in 1875 for the Royal Irish Constabulary. Its design is variously described as 'Schloss' and 'North West Frontier'. As usual, tales have been woven to explain the anomaly; the best of these concerns mixed-up plans for a fortress in India. The truth behind the design matters not because Cahersiveen has gained something unique, interesting and memorable. The building was a victim of the Irish Civil War and was burned down in 1922. It was restored 70 years later and now houses the Cahersiveen Heritage Centre and Exhibition describing the history of barracks, the Fenian Rising and the Iveragh Peninsula.

Over the bridge to the north of town lies the ruin of the 15th century Ballycarbery Castle.

TRANSPORT

Bus services: 279 Killarney-Cahersiveen; two per day Monday to Saturday.

280 Ring of Kerry Bus Cahersiveen-Sneem-Killarney; one bus a day and one way only during the summer.

Bicycle hire: Casey Cycles, New Street, Tel: 066 947 2474.

Car hire: Kerry Murphy Tel: 087 299 2523.

Taxi: McCarthy, Church Street, Tel: 066 947 2249.

Rail: Station in Killarney (60km).

Ferries: Valentia Island Car Ferry – at Reenard Point (4km). Note that despite local tourist literature, there is no ferry to Dingle.

Air: The nearest airport is Kerry Airport (60km).

OTHER INFORMATION

Yacht club: Atlantic Sailing Club, Tel: 086 858 7680.

Police: Tel: 066 947 2111.

Hospital: Tel: 066 947 2100.

Doctor: Tel: 066 947 2121/2434/3555.

Dentist: Tel: 066 9472411.

Tourist office: Cahersiveen Tourist Office (seasonal), Community Centre, Tel: 066 947 2589.

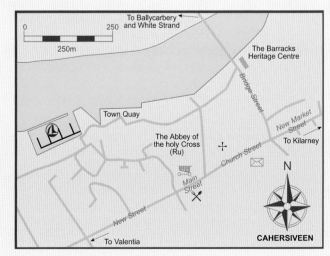

Portmagee
(Irish: *An Caladh*, meaning The Ferry)
Approach waypoint 51°52'.80N 10°25'.00W
(Mid channel – ½ M due E of S tip of Bray Head)

Portmagee is easy to pass by but that would be a great pity. Its facilities are few but those it has are excellent. Despite minor disturbance from tour boats and fishing vessels passing by in the main channel, once safely inside the dogleg entrance the harbour becomes a useful refuge.

NAVIGATION

Given the state of repair of the low bridge across the channel between Portmagee and Valentia, it would be amazing if it were ever brought back into service! Navigation from the open sea is therefore described below.

Charts: No detailed chart. Use Admiralty AC2125 or Imray C56 has an inset.

Tides (approx): MHWS: 3.8m, MHWN: 3.0m, MLWN: 1.3m, MLWS: 0.5m. Standard Port Cobh, difference at HW: Springs –01:18min; Neaps –00:38min.

Lights & Marks: The ruined signal tower on Valentia (Bray Head) is the only unambiguous mark.

Approach: At Bray Head, the seas in the entrance, particularly in strong south-westerlies, can be very boisterous as the waves and wind interact with the cliff faces and the multitude of islands on the mainland shore. The situation needs to be assessed long before committing to entry.

Pilotage: Navigation requires close attention once between Reencaheragh Point and Portmagee to avoid shallows and oncoming traffic. There is a charted depth of 5m to the public visitors' buoys. In general, the deeper water is to the north of the channel, except at Quay Brack.

From the approach waypoint, steer 058°T (mid channel and parallel to the Valentia shore). Midway between Skughaphort Reef and Reencaheragh Points, alter course to 110°T. Obstructions encroach towards the channel from the southern shore after 3 cables, but the main danger is to port – Anchor Rock (not named on the chart) lies 40m off the shore at Quay Brack and uncovers at low water. Abeam Quay Brack, come round to 065°T, which heads straight to the public visitors' buoys and avoids the shallows that extend well off the south shore.

If proceeding to the pier, stay on 065°T until abeam the islet on the starboard side (south of the visitors' buoys), then alter course to the pier.

www.irelandaerialphotography.com

Portmagee: The public visitors' buoys are in the small bay on the shore opposite the pier and adjacent small island. Skughaphort Reef and Reencaheragh Point lie at the bottom of the photograph

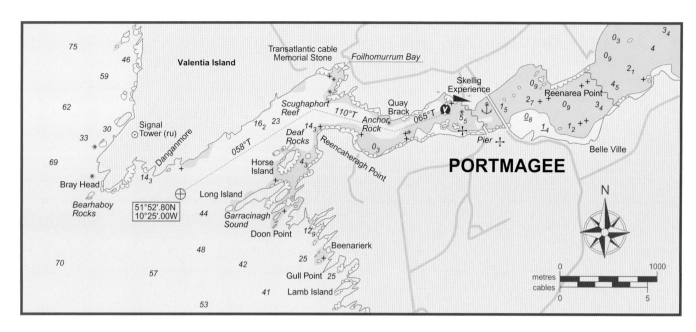

MOORING/ANCHORING

It is recommended to take one of the four public visitors' buoys – 3 cables west-north-west of the pier, noting that, although even westerly driven seas are well mellowed by the dog leg entrance, it may be prudent to take a buoy furthest from the shore in such winds. Land at the nearby slip on the north shore.

Alternatively, anchor in 5m off the pier, short of the bridge, clear of the underwater cable, the manoeuvring fishing boats and as far out of the fast flowing tidal current as possible.

Note: Although it is possible to anchor near the village, there is a lot to be said for the public visitors' buoys on the other side of the channel, 3 cables away. Firstly they are secure – the tide runs quite fast past the village. They are also tucked into a small bay off the main channel out of the way of the boat route to the sea where there is a lot of traffic. Furthermore, the view of the village and its mountain backdrop is wonderful from here. Finally, the access for a walk out to Bray Head and the transatlantic cable memorial is better.

Visitors' moorings at Portmagee

The downside of the buoys is that a trip to Portmagee means either a walk inland on Valentia to access the bridge or a dinghy ride that can be quite wet against the wind on the return journey.

Portmagee features viewed from the visitors' moorings

Portmagee village viewed from the 'Skellig Experience'

Useful information – Portmagee

FACILITIES
Water: Fresh water is available on the pier.
Showers: May be possible by prior arrangement with the Moorings Hotel.
Toilets: Public toilets (award-winning!) and some **glass/plastic recycling bins** are at the south end of the bridge. A manned alongside berth may be possible for short periods.
Launderette: Situated at Portmagee Community Centre, Tel: 066 947 7200.

PROVISIONING
Connell's Food Store and Post Office, Tel: 066 947 7101, holds a basic grocery stock sufficient for topping up.

EATING OUT
There is a small but good choice of two pub/restaurants; the Bridge Bar/Moorings Hotel, Tel: 066 947 7108, acknowledges and caters for the peak volume of customers with good quality meals in either a bar meal or restaurant format. Alternatively, the 'local' Fisherman's Bar & Skellig Restaurant, Tel:

066 947 7103, is very laid back and feels more like it is trying to work out why there are all these unknown people around in the summer months. However, it is very difficult to know what the locals are actually saying to one another because the accent/dialect/language can be impenetrable. The Skellig Mist café also has a good reputation and offers home-baked pastries, sandwiches, tea and coffee, Tel: 066 947 7250.

ASHORE
Apart from Irish and English, many other languages may be heard in Portmagee. People come in large numbers to 'The Skellig Experience', Tel: 066 947 6306, which sets out to describe the unique history of the islands and the fascinating people who managed to live on them despite the obvious deprivations. Many small boats take tourists from Portmagee to Skellig Michael to land for the real experience.
 Portmagee is what is often described as a well-kept

village with a pride in its appearance. Backed by the start of the Macgillycuddy's Reeks and fronted by the harbour, it leaves its visitors in no doubt that they are on holiday. It is just too easy to let hours slip by sitting on the harbourside benches overlooking the frequent bustling of the boats and the equally frequent weather changes as Valentia Island, opposite, interrupts everything the Atlantic throws at it.

TRANSPORT
Bus services: Community bus service only. A charter bus/**hire car** is available from Kennedy Bus Hire, Tel: 066 947 6183 or 087 264 8646.
Taxi: Taxi and bus service, Jackie Sullivan, Tel: 066 947 7183 or 087 616 9633.

OTHER INFORMATION
Police: Tel: 066 947 7102.

The telegraph cable memorial on Valentia Island. The entrance to Portmagee can be seen in the background

Horse Island and the western half of Ballinskelligs Bay

Ballinskelligs

(Irish: *Baile na Sceilg*, **meaning
Town of the Crag)**
Approach waypoint: 51°48'.85N 10°15'.20W
(8 cables ENE of pier on 20m contour line and
3 cables NE of Horse Island)

Provided the weather is predominantly west/north-west, this is a splendid location offering some protection, good hospitality ashore and a convenient spot for catching the boat ride to land on the Skelligs. It is a handy anchorage as long as there is no risk of a westerly strengthening and backing south but can be uncomfortable if heavy swell is entering the bay.

NAVIGATION

Charts: No detailed chart. Use Admiralty AC/LE2495 or Imray C56.

Tides: MHWS: 3.6m, MHWN: 2.8m, MLWN: 1.2m, MLWS: 0.5m. Standard Port Cobh, difference at HW: Springs –01:19min; Neaps –00:39min.

Lights & Marks: None. The pier, ruined abbey and ruined castle may be used for fixing.

Approach: The outer approach from the north and the Skelligs requires the rounding of the bold mass

of Bolus Head, while from the south, Hog's Head is accompanied by Pig's Rocks and drying rocks which extend a further 1½ cables north-west.

There is a drying bar between Horse Island and the mainland; do not be tempted to enter here. The approach to the pier and anchorage is from the north-east of Horse Island! Give Bullig, a drying rock (0.5m) 1 cable east of Horse Island, a wide berth to arrive at the approach waypoint.

Note: Bay Rock (1.2m) lies 8 cables due east of the ruined castle on the promontory north of the pier.

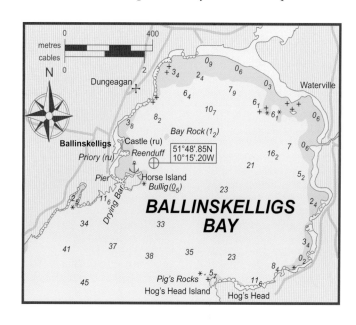

Horse Island

Local moorings off Horse Island

Pilotage/Anchoring: From the approach waypoint steer 255°T for the pier, tracking along the north shore of Horse Island, 1 cable off.

Either anchor in 3-5m, staying mid Horse Island for maximum southerly protection or, if conditions permit, berth alongside the pier, where fishing vessels have priority. Dinghies may land at the pier or at the adjacent slip.

Useful information – Ballinskelligs

FACILITIES
There are just a few houses in the near vicinity of the pier, which is 1km south of the village crossroads.

PROVISIONING
There are no facilities for yachtsmen, but there is a small **store**, **newsagents**, **Internet** access point and **post office** in the village opposite Cable O'Leary's bar.

EATING OUT
Near the crossroads is the beach café (Café Cois trá), which sells teas and snacks, Tel: 087 296 5874. About ½km north of the crossroads is Cable O'Leary's welcoming pub, Tel: 066 947 9104, while a little north of that, at Dungeagan, is Cill Rialaig Gallery & Seasonal Café and Restaurant, Tel: 066 947 9277.

ASHORE
Currently Ballinskelligs is an under-visited destination, probably because it receives scant attention in sailing publications and it is on a very minor road off yet another minor road, somewhere at the edge of the tourist map. Waterville, its dominant neighbour across the bay, on the other hand, is in the mainstream on the 'Ring of Kerry'. Ballinskelligs is on the 'Skellig Ring' and so, until it is 'discovered', there is plenty of sea room and it gives the feeling of being off the beaten track.

The Siopa Cill Rialaig Gallery could be fairly termed unique. It is an artists' co-operative with a difference. Artists apply to stay as guests and, when accepted, pay for their stay by leaving pieces to be sold. The buildings are thatched and also house a café with outstanding and inspirational views.

There is some debate about the provenance of St Michael's Priory (Augustinian – 13th century). One version is that the monks of Skellig Michael retreated here, when extraordinarily bad weather in the 12th century drove them from their offshore sanctuary. The ruin, which dates from the 15th century, is the first on the foreshore when heading towards the village from the pier.

Further north, on the spit, are the ruins of Ballinskelligs Castle, which was built in the 16th century as a Tower House to defend the village.

TRANSPORT
Bus services: Nearest bus is in Waterville.

OTHER INFORMATION
Ballinskelligs Watersports at Dungeagan offers tourist and diving trips to the Skelligs, Tel: 066 947 9182; www.skelligboats.com.

Ballinskelligs Castle

The Skelligs

The Skelligs rise sheer from the ocean. Without the wind and the smell of the sea they could be the backdrop for the opening sequence from the latest 'Lord of the Rings' film. Skellig Michael (or Great Skellig) is the larger of the two Islands. Little Skellig is the other.

Skellig Michael is vast compared to its similarly named monastic counterparts on the English and French sides of La Manche. Two hundred metres high and 12km offshore, its 6th century monastery sets the standard for self imposed hardship for the monks that lived here. The monks lived and worshipped in weatherproof, beehive-shaped dwellings, or clochons, and two oratories on the lower of the two island peaks, 640 stone steps from sea level. They reserved the higher peak as a hermitage. They were self sufficient as they fished and tended small gardens. The site is exceptionally well preserved, partly due to its isolation and partly to the robustness of the design of the beehives. After 1,500 years the beehives' continued integrity is truly impressive. The colony, which numbered about 12 monks at any one time, lived on the island for 600 years until a really adverse change in the weather (a little ice-age) caused them to move to the Augustinian Priory at Ballinskelligs on the mainland.

Because the monastic settlement existed here throughout the 'Dark Ages', there remained a core of Christians who became missionaries throughout Europe

Skellig bird life

Amazingly, Little Skellig's gannets share their home with many other species. Combined with Puffin Island, off to the north-east, and Skellig Michael's bird population, there are plenty of opportunities for bird watching. Puffins are supposed to be common but may be suffering a downturn in numbers as their appearance is now a remarkable event. The ocean mariner's favourite, the Manx Shearwater, breeds here during the very short time it spends ashore anywhere. Storm petrels can be spotted in large numbers as can fulmar, kittiwake, razorbill and guillemots. There are also peregrine and chough.

after the fall of the Roman Empire. Skellig Michael retained its religious associations and, in the 1500s, it became a popular place of pilgrimage.

In the 19th century, commerce intruded to build a lighthouse and so the island became inhabited again, at least until the lighthouse was automated in 1987.

Skellig Michael, which became a UNESCO World Heritage Site in 1996, is one of those places that has to be experienced in person. Regrettably, the weather and schedules may conspire to make a visit impossible, in which case a visit to the 'Skellig Experience' at Portmagee is recommended, which may partly compensate for the disappointment, Tel: 066 947 6306; website www.skelligexperience.com.

Little Skellig is totally different; it has a character peculiarly its own. The gannet rules Little Skellig. They nest everywhere they can and provide a spectacular diving display for the onlooker. Needless-to-say, landing is not on the agenda.

Visiting: Without doubt, the best way to visit Skellig Michael is to take a half day trip with one of the local boatmen. This will give 1½ hours ashore without any worries about what the Atlantic may be doing to a yacht.

For those that must, a landing by dinghy (negotiated in advance with the staff on the island using VHF Ch 9) is appropriate, leaving the boat standing off with a competent crewman. Strong surge and scend at the quay, even on calm days, require very experienced dinghy handling.

NAVIGATION

Many yachtsmen will want to circumnavigate the Skelligs, in which case, beware of Washerwoman Rock which lies 3 cables south-west of Skellig Michael and has underwater rocks north of it!

www.irelandaerialphotography.com

Skellig Michael in the foreground is attended by Washerwoman Rock (bottom right). Its old and new lighthouses are clearly visible

Kenmare River

Chapter three
Kenmare River

Kenmare River (which is really a bay) offers something for most types of yachtsmen. There is plenty of sea room when sailing between the various anchorages, a wide range of tricky harbours to intrigue the navigator and isolation to suit a wilderness seeker. Those short of time heading the 8M straight across the mouth of the bay can still make a visit to the jewel of Kenmare River – Derrynane Harbour. Many rightly include Sneem on their itinerary – not for its reputation as a favourite stop on the Ring-of-Kerry tour, more for its peaceful wooded, safe harbour. Beyond these two harbours, visitors are rare.

At the mouth of the estuary, the Kenmare River is signalled by the imposing Scariff and Deenish Islands to the north and The Bull and The Cow to the south. The only sign of human habitation on these islands nowadays is the lone cottage on Deenish, which was built in 1908 by Patrick Curran who raised 10 children on the island. The building is now used to store supplies for the island's livestock. The mainland has predominantly rocky shores and sea cliffs. Further upriver the foreshores are mostly muddy sands backed by low and well-cultivated fields, giving the air of rural serenity. The river valley is framed by a striking

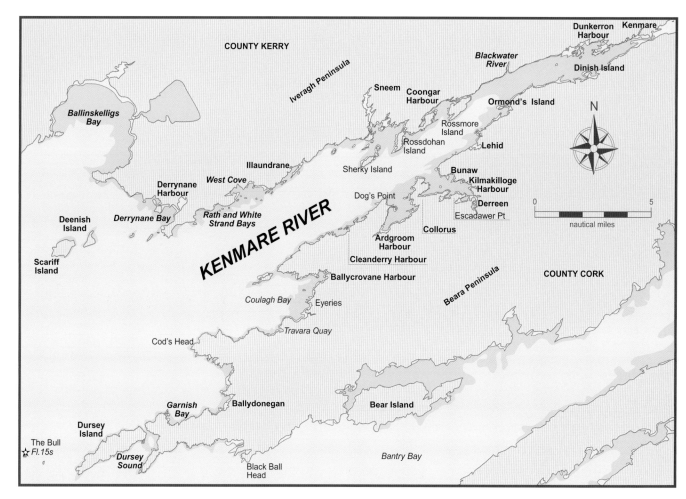

COUNTY KERRY

Ballinskelligs
Bay

Iveragh Peninsula

Sneem

Coongar
Harbour

Dunkerron
Harbour

Kenmare

Blackwater
River

Dinish Island

Ormond's Island

Rossmore
Island

Rossdohan
Island

Lehid

Illaundrane

West Cove

Sherky Island

Bunaw

Kilmakilloge
Harbour

Derrynane
Harbour

Dog's Point

Derreen

Deenish
Island

Derrynane Bay

Rath and White
Strand Bays

KENMARE RIVER

Escadawer Pt

Collorus

Ardgroom
Harbour

Scariff
Island

Cleanderry Harbour

Ballycrovane Harbour

Beara Peninsula

COUNTY CORK

Coulagh Bay

Eyeries

Travara Quay

Cod's Head

Garnish
Bay

Ballydonegan

Bear Island

Dursey
Island

The Bull
Fl.15s

Dursey
Sound

Black Ball
Head

Bantry Bay

N

0 — nautical miles — 5

backdrop which is mostly stark mountain and, on a good day, pastel sky. The Macgillycuddy's Reeks, which include the highest peak in Ireland, lie to the north on the Iveragh peninsula and the Caha range lies to the south on the Beara Peninsula. Together they firmly enclose the bay. It is so unpopulated here that encountering even a small town such as Kenmare in peak tourist season can be quite a shock after a few days cruising the coast and can create a feeling of metropolitan hustle and bustle. The population around the shores of the bay has recently grown to 7,000.

In these harbours and anchorages the only man-made noises that come close to being intrusive are the fish farm service craft and the overhead aircraft in the transatlantic corridors 10km up, but these are unlikely to drown out conversations.

When fishing rights were granted in the 19th century, a landowner in the Kenmare area managed to get the English Parliament to pass an Act which changed the name of the Kenmare Estuary to the Kenmare River, giving him the fishing rights from Kenmare to the open sea. Disputes about this status roll on; the

The lone house on Deenish Island

Sneem's visitors' buoys from the Garinish moorings

legislation is still in place and continues to provide employment for lawyers.

With such a wide choice of anchorages, it is wise to identify any particular objectives. As Kenmare River aligns with the prevailing south-westerly wind and is wide open to the Atlantic, each choice requires a back-up plan should weather and sea conditions deny access to the planned destination. The choice of where to go has to be balanced against where not to be if the weather worsens.

Lit Aids to Navigation are rare in Kenmare River. Fishing floats in the middle of harbour entrances are not uncommon. For these reasons night entry into harbours, even Sneem, is not recommended for strangers.

Provisions and services are not conveniently available at any of the harbours – it would be prudent to visit Kenmare River in a well-stocked boat.

OVERVIEW BY HARBOUR (CLOCKWISE)

Derrynane Harbour is a scenic harbour that is worth a visit in its own right. It is the one Kenmare River overnight destination for those with insufficient time to explore further into the bay or needing a harbour well-situated for the Skelligs. It is a navigational challenge, but a well-protected anchorage with beautiful sandy beaches.

Sneem is a blissful harbour in wooded surroundings with interesting side trips for those not under time pressure – to the nearby picturesque village and the sophisticated Parknasilla Hotel. Sneem would be a good choice if weather-bound for a few days.

Kenmare, the largest town in the bay, offers good facilities but has severe tidal restrictions. It is a busy, attractive town and a tourist hotspot for the many nationalities that visit the west of Ireland.

Tuosist Parish (Kenmare to Kilmakilloge Harbour): Confusingly for the visitor, this area (the County Kerry part of the Beara peninsula) on the southern shore of the Kenmare River, may be referred to as Tuosist Parish rather than the individual village/hamlet name. Bunaw in Kilmakilloge Harbour has the benefit of O'Sullivan's

pub on the harbour. The seafood (especially the mussels) has received a number of positive visitor reports. The other Kilmakilloge attraction is Derreen Gardens at the head of the harbour, which has its own nearby anchorage.

Kilmakilloge and Sneem harbours lie opposite each other half way up the bay and, between them, provide comfortable moorings/anchorages for most wind conditions. Neither offer full facilities.

Ardgroom to The Bull (Beara Peninsula, County Cork): This area has a most impressive collection of archaeological sites, including Stone Circles and Ogham Stones. Regrettably, these harbours are either very cluttered with mussel and fish farms or are very exposed to the Atlantic sea conditions. Ballycrovane has the most routine entrance of all these harbours.

Throughout the bay there are several other isolated anchorages offering solitude and self reliance.

TIDES

There is a singular aspect to the tide at this point of the coast; the flood tide around Ireland and the UK divides at The Bull, going north along the west coast of Ireland and east along the south coast. The ebb does the reverse. This causes a few idiosyncrasies in this area. There is no definitive data published on this phenomenon; local charts are devoid of tidal diamonds and there is no Admiralty tidal atlas. In summary, the situation is as follows:

Tides run north (flood)/south (ebb) in the sounds between inside Scariff, Deenish and Moylaun Islands (up to 1.5kn in springs). The tide runs directly in and out of Kenmare River and is generally weak except off headlands and pinch points. The flood tide runs from north of The Cow and east along both sides of Dursey Island, causing a south-going stream through the Sound, which, in turn, generates significant eddies in Dursey Sound.

Tides flow strongly past Dursey Head and turbulence may be expected between Dursey and beyond The Cow. In particular, avoid the area around Lea Rock (1 cable south-west of Dursey) and The Calf nearby. Favourable tides occur as follows:

Dursey Sound
Northward passage – commences 1 hour 35 minutes after HW Cobh.
Southward passage - commences 4 hours 50 minutes before HW Cobh.

Between Scariff, Deenish, Moylaun and Two Headed Islands.
Northward passage – commences 5 hours 5 minutes after HW Cobh.
Southward passage – commences 1 hour 20 minutes before HW Cobh.

Approaching Dursey Sound from the south

In Kenmare River
In-going flood – commences 5 hours 5 minutes after HW Cobh.
Out-going ebb – commences 1 hour 20 minutes before HW Cobh.

WEATHER INFORMATION BROADCASTS
This coast is served by the Valentia Coastguard transmitter above Bantry Bay on VHF Ch 23. An advisory announcement is made initially on Ch 16.

PASSAGE CHARTS
Admiralty Charts: AC2423 Mizen Head to Dingle Bay, 1:150,000; AC/LE2495 Kenmare River, 1:60,000.
Imray: C56 Cork Harbour to Dingle Bay, 1:170,000. C56 includes one panel covering Sneem, Ardgroom and Kilmakilloge.

Exploring the Kenmare River requires the support of Admiralty Chart AC/LE2495, which has several larger scale plans covering Dursey Sound, Ardgroom/ Kilmakilloge, Sneem, Ballycrovane and the Upper Kenmare River (notably excluding the last mile to Kenmare town quay!). This chart complements Admiralty Folio SC5623 by abutting the northernmost equivalent scale chart in that pack. It is also useful for the north and south approaches to Kenmare River. The chart should be used with caution because no survey data dates from after 1900 and the chart is referenced to OSI not WGS84. This means that satellite derived coordinates must be corrected 0.02 minutes southwards and 0.03 minutes eastwards before they are plotted on the paper chart. This is significant in many instances in Kenmare River!

Be sure to have access to the latest Notices to Mariners for AC/LE2495 as there have been several changes to lights & buoys (particularly the navigation marks in the Upper Kenmare River).

SAFETY INFORMATION
This section of the coast is managed by Valentia Coastguard, Tel: 066 947 6109.

COASTGUARD AIS STATION
Bantry (Knockgour Hill)
51°38'.40N 10°00'.11W   MMSI 002 500380.

LIGHTS
- The Bull. Bull Rock lighthouse Fl 15s.
- Maiden Rock SHM, Fl G 5s.
- Bat Rock SHM, Fl G 5s.
- No 1 (Illaunmoylan) SHM, Fl G 5s.

Maiden Rock starboard-hand mark

KENMARE RIVER – PASSAGE WAYPOINTS – WGS 84 DATUM		
NAME	DESCRIPTION	LAT/LONG
Scariff Island	½M SW of island	51°42'.90N 10°15'.85W
Dursey Sound North	Mid entrance	51°36'.80N 10°09'.70W
The Bull	1¼M SW of The Bull	51°35'.00N 10°20'.00W

www.irelandaerialphotography.com

Derrynane Harbour: Bunavalla Pier serves the north-west corner of the harbour while the old pier is just visible in the north-east corner. The 'Ring of Kerry' road threads along the side of the mountain

Derrynane Harbour

Approach waypoint: 51°45'.00N 10°10'.05W
(On the leading beacons/lights, 7 cables out)

Derrynane (Darrynane on Admiralty charts) encapsulates the uniqueness of a South-West Ireland cruise in one harbour and is not to be missed. The Atlantic, the offshore islands, the rudimentary pilotage, rocks nearby that have never been called less than 'scary' by new visitors and glorious scenery at the seaward end of the 'Ring of Kerry' all combine to make this a harbour thoroughly worth all the crucial planning and orientation! The reward is a well protected anchorage surrounded by sandy beaches and close to good hospitality but few facilities. With trip boats, fishing boats as well as a windsurfing and canoeing school, Derrynane can seem very busy at the peak of summer.

NAVIGATION

Charts: No detailed chart. Use Admiralty AC/LE2495.

Tides (approx): MHWS: 3.6m, MHWN: 2.8m, MLWN: 1.2m, MLWS: 0.5m. Standard Port Cobh, difference at HW: Springs –01:19min; Neaps –00:39min.

Lights & Marks

• Derrynane leading beacons/lights Oc 3s.
• Derrynane Harbour PHM pillar.
• Derrynane Harbour SHM pillar.
• Odd Rock beacon.

Approach: The approach waypoint is positioned to be readily reached from the north-west and also from the south and east using the deep water channel between

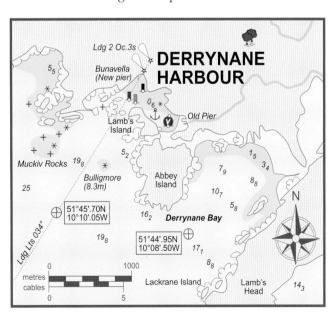

It is absolutely essential to identify the leading marks correctly

Moylaun and Two Headed Islands. It allows an initial cautious approach on the leading beacons/lights course (034°T), avoiding drying Bulligmore Rock (0.3m) to the east of track and the Muckiv Rocks to the north-west, until the leading beacons/lights are unambiguously identified (as shown in the photo sequence).

It is absolutely essential to identify the leading marks correctly. The mountainous backdrop approaching from the west (see photo above) descends to a rock-strewn shoreline with few distinguishing features at this distance. This makes identification extremely difficult.

Further confusion is possible because there is a large grey roof interceding between the upper and lower leading marks. The roof and vegetation in the vicinity may delay the upper leading mark becoming visible. Also, fittings on the new pier may be misinterpreted.

Entry pilotage: Once located on the leading beacons/ lights, the track must be held unerringly until close upon the port-hand mark at the entrance to the harbour. Note particularly (see photo below) the unusual construction and the unique character of the port-hand

Hold the leading marks unerringly until close upon the port-hand mark

Approaching the port-hand mark – about to alter to starboard. The starboard-hand mark on Lamb's Rock is now clearly visible

mark and also that the house and new pier are NOT part of leading beacons. The rocks shown on the left of the photo at the bottom of the opposite page will get extremely close. This is the main reason that entry or departure is not advisable in a heavy swell, especially from the west or south-west.

Be alert to traffic leaving the harbour, which will

Passing the port-hand mark

appear with little warning from behind Lamb's Island to the right of the photo above.

Inside the harbour: A hundred metres past Middle Rock to starboard, alter course to starboard from the leading marks just before the port-hand mark (see between the yacht's stays in the photo above) and steer 030°T until clear of Lamb's Rock starboard-hand mark. From here head south-east towards the moorings. Keep south of Odd Rock Beacon (just visible in the photo above half way between the two marks).

Departure pilotage: Unusually, the adrenalin will be required again for departure. It will be generated firstly by the need to be constantly alert to the danger of being trapped inside the harbour by an increasing sea-state and, secondly, the entrance/exit channel is easy to confuse with an unsafe adjacent channel to the east! It is always important to keep the transit marks in line astern.

MOORING/ANCHORING

The public visitors' buoys may be found in the south-east corner of the harbour at approximately 51°45'.60N 10°08'.80W. Alternatively, anchor nearby.

The old pier in the north-east of the harbour

Useful information – Derrynane Harbour

Caherdaniel is a small village 3km east along a beautiful winding country lane.

FACILITIES/PROVISIONING
Caherdaniel has a Texaco filling station, which also stocks gas. In addition, it has a small grocery shop (Freddy's), a Friday market in the village hall (1000-1200 June to September) and a Sunday market near the Blind Piper pub (1200-1800 May to October), where fresh oysters and locally smoked salmon can be bought. For more information contact Jane Urquhart on Tel: 066 947 5479. Approximately 2km further along the N70 main road is O'Carrolls Cove Beach, Tel: 066 57171 (see White Strand Bay on page opposite).

EATING OUT
From Bunavalla Pier in the north-west corner of the harbour, there is a very strenuous 3km walk uphill to the Scariff Inn. Its restaurant claims 'the best views in Ireland'. They are truly panoramic, encompassing The Skelligs to The Bull and Dursey Island. The menu features stews, curries, 'bacon and cabbage' and local seafood salad. It is best to time a visit outside the peak Ring-of-Kerry tourist traffic times.

Keating's Bar (just up the lane from the old pier in the north-east of the harbour) is popular for a drink, soup and sandwiches. Derrynane House has a good cafeteria 1km east of the old pier.

In Caherdaniel, the Blind Piper pub/restaurant, Tel: 066 947-5126, is very popular and is spoken of enthusiastically for its garden, food and live music (at weekends). Freddie's Bar in the village also offers groceries.

ASHORE
A boat for the Skelligs leaves from Bunavalla Pier (for more details call John O'Shea on Tel: 087 689 8431), while canoes, dinghies and windsurfers can be hired at Derrynane (Old) Pier from Helen Wilson who runs Derrynane Sea Sports, Tel: 066 947 5266/087 908 1208.

Derrynane House was the home of Daniel O'Connell, 'The Liberator', who won Catholic emancipation at the turn of the 19th century and is a national hero (see page 106). The house is now a National Monument and part of a National Park. The interesting gardens include South American Fern Trees.

Caherdaniel village

The mile-long Blue Flag Derrynane Beach borders Derrynane Bay and is popular for surfing, walking and swimming as the shallow water warms rapidly.

Abbey Island and Lamb's Island form the south shore of the harbour. The 13th century ruined abbey in the north-east corner of Abbey Island is particularly worth exploring. Access is across the spit of land that separates the bay from the harbour. Abbey Island is named after Derrynane Abbey – said to have been founded by St Finan.

TRANSPORT
John Paul O'Sullivan's **taxi** service is on hand to ease the distance from the harbour to the various locations, Tel: 087 318 3337.

OTHER INFORMATION
Refuges: If Derrynane proves impossible, an alternative refuge is essential. Nearby destinations towards Valentia are generally exposed to the west/south-west but consider Ballinskelligs behind Horse Island. Passage through Dursey Sound under the cable car has limitations (see later on page 104). Study of the Kenmare River anchorages, starting with Sneem, will help to identify at least one appropriate harbour.

Derrynane Sea Sports

Minor anchorages between Derrynane and Sneem

In this first section covering Derrynane to Sneem, it helps if the reader is clear about the various geographical points labelled 'Lamb's Island/Rock/Head' etc on this part of the coast. To clarify the situation and for the avoidance of any doubt, Lamb's Rock is in Derrynane Harbour and the harbour starboard-hand mark is built on it. There are two 'Lamb's Islands'. The larger forms the south-west shore of Derrynane Harbour. The smaller and lower (34m high and conical) island is south-east of Lamb's Head in the main Kenmare River and 2M south-east of the first Lamb's Island.

Kenmare River is well endowed with anchorages that will have appeal to some sailors but cannot be said to be essential for a full appreciation of this coast. Safe navigation into the following anchorages often calls for settled conditions and clear visibility of hazardous obstructions. Entry near low water is therefore preferable, subject to keel depth and sea state. There are no facilities at the locations unless otherwise stated.

Derrynane Bay. With only two hours before high water springs, much of the magnificent sweep of sandy beach is covered

Derrynane Bay
1M north-north-west of Lamb's Head
Approach waypoint: 51°44'.95N 10°08'.50W
(Midway between Lamb's Head and Abbey Island)

Derrynane Bay is a useful temporary anchorage in offshore winds. The shores are largely foul. At first sight, this may appear to be a very attractive simple alternative to Derrynane Harbour (across the sand spit to the west), but the bay has a three star (out of five) reputation for surfing, which is not usually compatible with comfortable anchoring. In the event of a secure anchoring, access to facilities involve a beach landing and then proceed as for Derrynane Harbour (see pages 79–80).

Pilotage: From the approach waypoint, run in on 020°T for approximately 3½ cables and, to clear the obstructions, it is best to anchor south-east of the derelict abbey (north-east corner of Abbey Island), where the depth will be 8-10m.

Rath Strand and White Strand Bays
1½ and 2½M north-east of Lamb's Head

The next two sandy bays to the north-east are not labelled on AC/LE2495. However, they are separately identified by OSI. The more westerly is Rath Strand Bay and, just to the north-east, White Strand Bay. Both bays have several rocks awash at low water. Rath Strand accommodates the huge Wavecrest caravan site with its camp shop, while White Strand Bay has some potential as it is convenient for the road and advertises 'O'Carroll's Cove – Ireland's only Beach Bar & Restaurant'.

O'Carrolls Cove

West Cove
3½M north-east of Lamb's Head
Approach waypoint: 51°45'.42N 10°03'.50W
(On SW-NE leading marks; 1½ cables east of the south shore of Illaunroe in 20m depth)

West Cove is a tiny anchorage, well protected by the surrounding reefs. It can accommodate a very small number of yachts in 1.5m above chart datum. There are two entrances but the entry from the south-west is the less ambiguous and is based on substantive leading beacons/lights. The surroundings are a mixture of rocky foreshore and sandy beaches. It is a delightful anchorage for shallow draught vessels in very settled conditions.

NAVIGATION
Charts: No detailed chart. Use AC/LE2495.

Tides: MHWS: 3.5m, MHWN: 2.8m, MLWN: 1.2m, MLWS: 0.5m. Standard Port Cobh, difference at HW: Springs –01:13min; Neaps –00:33min.

Lights & Marks
• NE-SW leading beacons/lights Oc 2s.
• NW-SE leading beacons/lights Fl 2s.
• Limpet Rocks beacon Fl R 3s.

Pilotage/Anchoring: From the approach waypoint, only proceed (course 045°T) if the leading beacons/lights have been clearly identified. These are 1¼M to the north-east. Good visibility is therefore essential as are the right light conditions. The track is narrow and shallow, leaving Grey Island very close to port – the room for error is small. The turn to port onto the second set of leading marks is taken when the beacon on the shore (east of the quay and cottage in the trees)

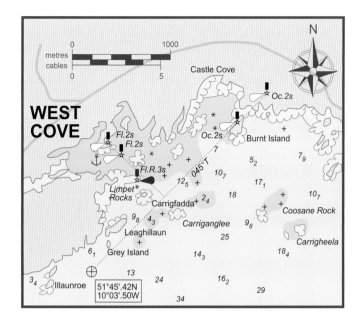

is just open of the Limpet Rocks beacon (this beacon is not part of the leading line). Clear Limpet Rocks and soon bring the beacon on the shore in line with a mid-distance post. The course for the leading beacons/lights between the shoreline beacon and the post will be approximately 315°T. When 20m short of the post, turn to port and proceed on a west track to find an anchorage.

ASHORE
One incentive to visit here is Jane Urquhart's bread, cakes and quiches. Her bakery is five minutes up the path from the pier, Tel: 064 947 5479. Otherwise, Castle Cove hamlet is 2½km by road. It has the Black Shop pub and O'Leary's small store and filling station.

Illaundrane
6M north-east of Lamb's Head
Approach waypoint: 51°46'.25N 09°59'.60W
(3½ cables S of the entrance between Illaunsillagh and Leaghcarrig)

This isolated anchorage behind a long low profile island is well sheltered. There are no navigation marks and the entrance requires avoidance of rocks awash at low water. The main reason a skipper will evaluate whether entry to this anchorage is safe and worth the risk is the prospect of anchoring in the midst of a secluded area known for otters, seals and abundant marine life in the relatively shallow water. **Note**: Illaunsillagh looks like two islands on the chart. Leaghcarrig is a small version of Illaundrane. There are no facilities at all nearby.

West Cove's rocky entrance

Sneem. Two approaches are described below, either side of Inishkeragh, the island in the foreground. The yachts in the centre of the photograph are moored on the visitors' buoys. The other yachts are moored in the bay north-west of Garinish Island. Sneem village can be seen 3km up river

Sneem
(Irish: *An tSnaidhm*, meaning The Knot)
and Parknasilla
Approach waypoint (South): 51°46'.50N 09°57'.00W
Approach waypoint (East): 51°47'.18N 09°53'.10W

Sneem's moorings are popular with many visitors primarily for their beautiful surroundings. Sneem is also a characteristically well-kept picture postcard village with a wide selection of pubs, restaurants, shops and, surprisingly, many sculptures. The 3km to the village (either by dinghy – limited to half tide – or by road) from Oysterbed Quay in the north-west corner of the harbour is a minor price to pay for the setting but it does make provisioning and fuelling very inconvenient. It is best to arrive well stocked and top up from the village only if necessary. Nevertheless, it is the one village on the Kenmare River of a reasonable size with a deep-keel anchorage nearby. (Kenmare is bigger/livelier but its quay dries, making access difficult). It is an attractive refuge with alternative anchorages close at hand to suit the weather. It also provides a good range

of options ashore for those weather-bound days when passage out of Kenmare River into the Atlantic would not be prudent.

NAVIGATION
Charts: AC/LE2495 has a useful large scale inset. Imray C56 has an inset covering Sneem and the adjacent anchorages.

Tides (approx): MHWS: 3.5m, MHWN: 2.8m, MLWN: 1.2m, MLWS: 0.5m. Standard Port Cobh, difference at HW: Springs –01:15min; Neaps –00:30min.

Lights & Marks
• Sneem Harbour – light beacon. Fl 5s on Carrignarone (Seal Rock).
• Unlit Beacon (3 cables ENE of Carrignarone).

Pilotage: When approaching from the south in settled weather, it is safe to take a direct route between Inishkeelaghmore (a grassy rock) and Sherky Island (the large island in mid bay) and then Potato Island and Inishkeragh. From the southern approach waypoint,

Entering between Sherky/Inishkeragh and Rossdohan Islands, heading towards the Parknasilla Resort

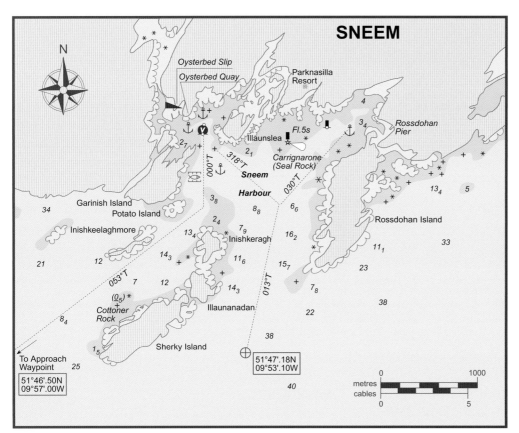

with a pointed tower) on 013°T. Keep the lit beacon on Carrignarone (Seal Rock) close on the port bow. When north of the final island to port (Inishkeragh), identify the north-east point of Garinish Island and when it bears 318°T, alter course to port and steer close east of the point, leaving it clear by 75m and leaving Illaunslea to starboard. Proceed to the anchorage or mooring buoys described below.

The alternative anchorage north-west of Rossdohan may be reached by steering 030°T from the Garinish Island turn just described. Steer between Carrignarone and Rossdohan Island, keeping in depths greater than 5m until a favourable anchorage is found. The unnamed beacon east of Long Point will be off to the north-west.

identify Inishkeelaghmore and Sherky Island. Proceed between them favouring Inishkeelaghmore. This will avoid Cottoner Rock, which dries (0.5m) and is 1½ cables off the north-west shore of Sherky Island. Charted depth is not less than 10m as far as Potato Island. Once past Potato Island and the adjacent rocks, the north-east corner of Garinish Island will come clear when it bears 000°T. It is safe to steer to the north-east corner of Garinish Island, keeping clear of the mussel farm, the north-east limits of which are indicated by an unlit yellow buoy. Proceed to the anchorage or mooring buoys described below.

The alternative entrance is between Sherky Island/Illaunanadan/Inishkeragh and Rossdohan Island. Steer from the eastern approach waypoint towards the clearly identifiable Parknasilla Resort (a large building

MOORING
There are three convenient and very popular public visitors' buoys between Oysterbed Quay and Illaunslea (51°48'.71N 09°53'.57W). They are well spaced and yachts will anchor in and around the mooring buoys. **Note**: Oysterbed slip is 50m west of the pier and is not immediately visible from the moorings.

ANCHORING
There are four possible anchorages:
• Between Illaunslea and the pier close to the mooring buoys described above.

Also off Oysterbed Quay are the anchorage and private moorings to the north-east of Garinish Island

Oysterbed slip is 50m west of the quay

- Outside the moorings north-east of Garinish Island in 2.5m; 51°48'.60N 09°53'.80W.
- South of Illaunslea in 6-9m.

All three are convenient for landing at Oysterbed slip or quay (depending on the state of the tide).

- North-west of Rossdohan Island in 5m; 51°48'.65N 09°52'.00W.

The latter is nearer to the Parknasilla Resort (see panel opposite) and a landing may be made at the picturesque Rossdohan Quay. However, this location is far more exposed to weather from the east around to the south-west. The pier at Rossdohan is suitable for dinghy access but there are no facilities anywhere nearby.

The Parknasilla Resort

The Parknasilla Resort, in the north-east corner of the harbour, had been a four star Great Southern Hotel and Restaurant. George Bernard Shaw wrote *Pygmalion* here and Robert Graves, who lived in the Bishops House in the grounds, wrote *I Claudius* here. There is a very pleasant walk through the rock gardens. The hotel was completely renovated in 2007/2008 and re-launched as The Parknasilla Resort. The hotel, spa and 12-hole golf course came under new management. It remains open to non-residents if capacity allows. It has its own small quay just to the south-east, which can be approached by dinghy (if arriving by dinghy go south about Illaunslea). Non-residents, in smart-casual attire, may have refreshments, lunch or dine in the Pygmalion restaurant, where booking is essential. It also offers, at a price, a full range of facilities, including swimming, a spa, golf and gardens, Tel: 064 75600.

The newly renovated Parknasilla Resort

Useful information – Sneem

Sneem is a village with two village greens – North Square and South Square separated by the chasm of the river. For the avoidance of doubt, South Square is the easterly one and North Square the westerly one.

Provided the dinghy is comfortable, quiet and capable, do not be put off the long river trip into Sneem. The alternatives are a rather uninteresting walk, partly along the N70, or calling a taxi. The river scenery and wildlife is marvellous – seals do travel all the way up the river. Tie up at the quay, which is still 300m from the village, and make sure there is enough depth (and fuel) for the return trip.

A dinghy exploration of the many islands and the passages between them through lush greenery is very rewarding, although, in such tranquil surroundings, it would be nobler to row. The water is extremely clear; the bottom can be easily seen. In season, seals are abundant around Sneem Harbour and Potato Island is noted for them.

FACILITIES

Water is available from a domestic style tap on Oysterbed quay. There is no indication of the water's provenance, but there are several large houses in the vicinity which support the hope that the water has not stood for too long. For everything else, a trip to Sneem is necessary.

Green and white **diesel** are readily available from McCartney's garage, Tel: 087 231 5015, Christian's Mace shop or Sneem House. However, the convergence of enough containers to make the exercise worthwhile and transport from and to the quay make refuelling here unnecessarily complicated. For a **launderette** go to O'Sullivan's in the village, Tel: 087 132 4466.

PROVISIONING

Christian's Mace shop, Tel: 064 45116, is the obvious choice for buying provisions if only because it is the nearest store to the quay. It also offers a taxi back to the pier. The range of groceries is limited, but will meet basic needs

Other shops include O'Sullivans the butcher, Daybreak stores & Deli, The Bakery (and wine and cheese delicatessen),

Useful information – Sneem (continued)

South Square, Sneem village

Burn's grocer, a pharmacy and a hardware shop.

The market takes place every Tuesday, 1100-1400 (June-September). For more information contact Jill House on Tel: 066 947 5312.

EATING OUT

Sneem has several coffee shops: The Village Kitchen just west of the bridge can be particularly recommended, although there are many other good places to eat.

The Blue Bull, Tel: 064 45382, on South Square also has a very good reputation. Its menu changes for the evening, so local crab may be had for a light lunch, with a choice of seafood or the more reasonably-priced traditional dishes (for example, 'bacon and cabbage' €12) being served in the evening. While waiting for the food to arrive, it is interesting to examine the photographs on the walls showing Sneem in times gone by.

Other restaurants worth investigating include family-run O'Sullivan's Sacre Coeur Restaurant, off North Square, Tel: 064 45186 evenings only, again specialising in seafood. There is also the Stone House restaurant on North Square, Tel: 064 45188, serving seafood and steaks.

There is no shortage of pubs, most of which have live music. On North Square try Restlers Inn, Tel: 064 45398, or Danny O'Shea's bar, which has a balcony overlooking the river and countryside – perfect for a fine evening. On South Square, pubs appear in quick succession: O'Sullivans – Sneem House (also supplies groceries, wines and fuel), Riney's Bar (doubles up as a newsagent and sweet shop) Tel: 064 45225, Murphy's Bar and The Blue Bull.

ASHORE

Sneem, the village, is quite distinct from Sneem, the moorings, known to yachtsmen. It is one of the most cosmopolitan of villages. The park-keeper is English, a German runs the tourist office, barmaids are Australian and Polish workmen can be seen racing off in fishing boats. At certain times of the day, coaches on the Ring-of-Kerry circuit congregate here and temporarily let loose a large number of tourists. In the evenings, the streets are less populated and a quiet stroll is possible, serving a secondary purpose – menu reading. In a country where house colours are far from reserved, Sneem must be able to claim to have the gaudiest colours anywhere.

Sneem does nothing to promote that it is the birthplace in 1852 of the founder of the UK's security services – a real person who became the inspiration for one of the most famous fictional characters of film ever. William Melville left Sneem for London and became a 'Peeler'; a policeman. He rose through the ranks to become a member of the Special Branch and, eventually, he joined Military Intelligence and, consequently, 'disappeared'. It is said that he became the first 'M', now known by filmgoers as James Bond's spymaster. There is no monument to him in Sneem and there was controversy when the County Museum (named after Irish rebel leader Thomas Ashe) in Tralee hosted an exhibition featuring Melville.

Sneem, however, does admit to being the hometown of one of the Republic's presidents – he merits a statue. The village green hosts a sculpture of former President Cearbhall Ó Dalaigh and a statue of Steve Casey, known as 'Crusher'. He was a world champion wrestler from 1938 to 1945.

TRANSPORT

Bus services: (Summer service operates from the last week in June to the end of August. No services on Public Holidays.) 270 Sneem-Kenmare.

Summer – not Sundays. Winter – Fridays only.

280 Ring of Kerry. Serves Sneem but only to Killarney – no return service.

Taxi: There is a taxi service available from and to the pier, courtesy of the Christians who run the Mace shop on South Square, Tel: 064 45116. Other taxis are operated by Jimmy Casey, Tel: 064 45324, and Teddy McCarthy, Tel: 064 45143/087 231 5011.

OTHER INFORMATION

Doctor: Sneem Health Centre (Drs Patrick and Diane Malone) is on South Square, Tel: 064 45102; Home Tel: 064 45133.

Fresh water on the quay

'Crusher' Casey's statue

Minor anchorages between Sneem and Kenmare

COONGAR, RIVER BLACKWATER AND DUNKERRON

Heading north, Maiden Rock starboard-hand mark will be identifiable close by Rossmore Island. Pass Coongar harbour and keep to port of the starboard-hand mark to avoid Maiden Rock, which breaks impressively when challenged by the remnants of the Atlantic swell. Church Rocks foul the Beara shore here.

North of Maiden Rock, aquaculture starts in earnest. From Rossmore Island eastwards to Ormond's Island and then north-east to Hallissy Rock, the waters are heavily obstructed by mussel farms, pot buoys and buoys with floating lines between them.

The Iveragh shore is comparatively free of fishing buoys. It also has the wider channel and cleaner shore for passing Lackeen Rocks (2.4m), which lie mid river 2.8M upstream from the starboard-hand mark. Ease a course towards the River Blackwater anchorage. Beyond the Blackwater, continue to hug the coast (not forgetting to admire the striking Dromore Castle on the shoreline). When Carrignaronebeg beacon bears 086°T / Reennaveagh Pillar bears 139°T turn and steer east along latitude 51°51'.00N. Continue due east leaving the beacon 1 cable to port until 1 cable north of Bat Rock starboard-hand mark.

Alter course to 073°T for Dunkerron.

Dromore Castle

Coongar
Approach waypoint: 51°48'.60N 09°49'.10W
(4 cables S of the middle of the entrance)

Coongar has a heavy concentration of mussel farms. It has no navigational marks or facilities and has little to recommend itself to the cruising yachtsman.

The 10M River Blackwater is known for its salmon and trout fishing

Pilotage: From the waypoint, proceed due north, keeping to the centre of the harbour.

Anchoring: Anchor in 9-10m where the bridge between Rossmore Island and the mainland comes into view to starboard. Beware that once the bridge does come into view, the depth reduces rapidly.

River Blackwater
Approach waypoint: 51°50'.75N 09°44'.75W
(2½ cables S of the pier)

The River Blackwater is very shallow once within the river proper. The pier is not recommended because of shallows and lack of turning space. The favoured anchorage is outside the entrance in approximately 5m, which provides good shelter from a westerly wind. The area has neither navigational marks nor facilities.

Dunkerron Harbour
Approach waypoint: 51°51'.28N 09°39'.50W
(3½ cables N of Dinish Island)

Dunkerron is a delightful large but shallow lagoon dotted with tree-covered islets. This far upriver it avoids the worst of the swell. Seals are usually plentiful around the harbour. It also makes a less restrictive point of access to Kenmare, which is 6km away.

Charts: AC/LE2495 has a useful large scale inset.

Tides: MHWS: 3.9m, MHWN: 3.0m, MLWN: 1.4m, MLWS: 0.5m. Standard Port Cobh, difference at HW: Springs –01:17min; Neaps –00:27min.

Dunkerron and Dinish Island are useful anchorages downstream of the shallow channels leading to the head of navigation at Kenmare. In the foreground are anchorages either side of Dinish Island. The Dunkerron anchorage is in the gap between the islands off the opposite shore

access to Templenoe Pier north-north-west of the anchorage is available at high water for access to Templenoe village (1½km west) where there is Pat Spillane's pub and a post office.

Access to the other pier, which is 4 cables north-east of the anchorage, is also limited to high water. However, this pier is part of the adjacent Dromquinna Hotel complex. At the time of writing, this hotel is not operational and is up for sale by auction. Until the future of the hotel and its pier are clarified, it would be wise to treat access, robustness and the potable quality of its fresh water with caution.

Lights & Marks
- Bat Rock SHM Fl G 5s.
- No 1 (Illaunmoylan) SHM Fl G 5s.

Pilotage/Anchoring: From the approach waypoint steer 015°T to enter the anchorage between Illaungowla and Dunkerron Island West. Clear the Cod Rocks (North and South), which are clean, to port and then, to starboard, the Fox Islands and their offlyers, including 'The Boar', which extend west underwater by half a cable.

Depth restricts the anchorage to 1 cable west of Fox Islands in 3m, north-west of The Boar. Dinghy

Templenoe Pier

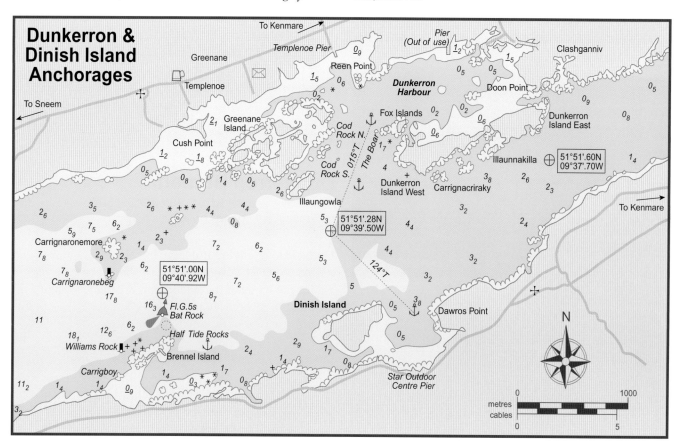

Kenmare Town and Quay

Approach waypoint: 51°51'.60N 09°37'.70W
(Due S of the E point of Dunkerron Island East in just over 2m)

Kenmare Quay sits at the head of Kenmare River. Kenmare Town, with a population of only 1,800, is the largest community on the river. It is an attractive market town with a wide range of facilities and diversions in a striking setting. Unfortunately, the last mile to the quay is extremely shallow and a great impediment to those keen to visit. The size and quality of the villas lining the north shore on the approach are testament to Ireland having the second largest per capita income in the European Union. In essence, Kenmare is therefore a very pleasant but optional destination as its attractions for the yachtsman can be satisfied elsewhere along the coast.

NAVIGATION

Charts: Kenmare Quay (also referred to as Kenmare Pier) at the head of the Kenmare River is disadvantaged by the absence of chart detail (the inset on AC/LE2495 extends only as far as No 1 starboard-hand mark one mile short of the quay). The final part of the passage is poorly covered by published charts and pilots (which is ironic, given that the town site was gifted to Sir William Petty as a reward for completing the mapping of Ireland).

In addition to No1 starboard-hand mark, there is a pair of lateral buoys to the north-east to assist routing to the quay. Most of the harbour dries at low water. However, a deep keel yacht can stay afloat at low water off the quay (below the bridge in a pool scoured deep by the outflow of the River Roughty) but the quay itself, and hence access to the town, will be dry for approximately three hours.

A visit over high tide is a possibility however – high water occurs near noon at neap tides, making it a pleasant day run from one of the deeper harbours down the bay. Alternatively, if the objective of the visit is to see as much wildlife as possible, a visit at the bottom of a spring tide may be better. If time or tide does not permit a waterborne visit, the alternatives are a bus trip from Glengarriff (see Bantry Bay) or anchoring in Dunkerron Harbour and using Templenoe Pier.

Tides (approx): MHWS: 3.9m, MHWN: 3.0m, MLWN: 1.4m, MLWS: 0.5m. Standard Port Cobh, difference at HW: Springs –01:17min; Neaps –00:27min.

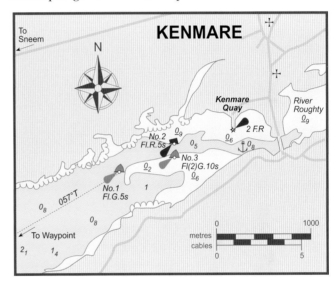

Kenmare Quay

The final mile to Kenmare between Buoys 2 and 3

Lights & Marks
- No 1 (Illaunmoylan) SHM Fl G 5s.
- No 2 PHM Fl R 5s.
- No 3 SHM Fl (2) G 10s.
- Kenmare Pier 2FR vert.

Approaches/Pilotage and Anchoring: From the approach waypoint, a course of 057°T leads to No 1 starboard-hand mark (off the north shore), at which point the depth is charted as being 0.2m above chart datum. This is borne out in practice between the buoy and the pier and is therefore prudent for planning purposes on a first visit. With an eye on the sounder to help keep off the shallows to the south, head between the pair of lateral buoys. From No 2 and No 3 buoys, head towards the south side of the harbour, all the time using the sounder to stay in the deeper water. The deeper water in the anchorage is amid the mooring buoys away to the south-east from the pier head.

Kenmare Quay

Useful information – Kenmare Town and Quay

FACILITIES
There are no marine services to speak of, although there are filling stations for road **fuel**. **Wi-Fi/Internet access** are available at LiveWire, Rock Street (off Main Street), Tel: 064 42714, and Kenmare **Post Office** on Henry Street, Tel: 064 41490.

PROVISIONING
SuperValu, Tel: 064 41307, on Railway Road and a wide range of **food shops** make this a useful place to top-up supplies during a visit ashore. SuperValu will arrange to deliver to the quay. The Farmer's Market is held at An Cro, Bridge Street (off the Square), 1000-1800 Wednesday-Sunday and seven days a week during July and August. For more information

contact Vince on Tel: 086 312 8262. McSweeneys on the Square sells **hardware** while also on the Square is the Bank of Ireland. Alternatively, there is an AIB on Main Street. Both **banks** have **ATMs** and foreign exchange facilities.

EATING OUT
As most of the pubs and restaurants are condensed into such a small area, it will not take long to complete a circuit of Henry Street, Main Street, Shelbourne Street and the Square to settle on a suitable choice. Published reviews by extremely faddy diners indicate that Kenmare's restaurateurs are well versed in accommodating unusual requests, but upmarket dining here does not have

the same competitive pressure to maintain standards as it does in Dingle or Kinsale.

ASHORE
The town is ½M north of the harbour. The approach over the hill gives a splendid view down Henry Street, with its colourful array of swinging shop signs. Henry Street and adjacent Main Street both lead down to 'The Square', as it is described on most maps. Between them these roads host most of the town's banks, pubs, restaurants and the post office. The town is very tourist focussed and serves as a main stopover point for tours of the 'Ring of Kerry' and the 'Ring of Beara'. If it looks a little too organised, that is because it is. It was

planned and laid out by Sir William Petty in 1670. The Pettys later evolved into Lansdownes – see later on pages 97–98. For older members of the crew, Kenmare's individual shops will be a reminder of how towns used to be before the ubiquitous chain stores arrived.

The English name is said to derive from the Viking name for 'Head of the Sea', via a translation through the Irish – 'Ceann Mara'. Kenmare's Irish name is An Neidín meaning 'The Little Nest'.

Local attractions include Kenmare Stone Circle. This is large with 15 stones. It can be reached at the end of Market Street at the side of the tourist office. The quay is a popular spot for visitors despite its

Useful information – Kenmare Town and Quay (continued)

distance from the town, partly because Seafari runs its popular seal-watching trips from there.

Lacemaking was introduced as a famine relief project and after the decline in popularity of lace to trim clothing, the tradition was preserved by nuns, the Sisters of St Clare, in the local convent. Lacemaking continues nowadays outside the convent and devotees of this intricate craft can be seen at the Lace & Design Centre in the Heritage Centre, Tel: 064 42978.

TRANSPORT
Bus services: Summer service operates during the last week in June to the end of August. No services on Public Holidays.
252 Cork-Skibbereen-Bantry-Glengarriff-Kenmare-Killarney. Daily summer service only.
270 Sneem-Kenmare, daily. Summer only. Winter – Friday only.
270 Kenmare-Killarney. No weekend service in winter.
282 Kenmare-Ardgroom-Castletownbere. Summer only. No Sunday service. (The 280; Ring of Kerry bus does not serve Kenmare).
Rail: At Killarney – 50 minutes by bus, 25 minutes by car.
Taxi: Kenmare Taxi Service Tel: 087 614 7222; Finnegan Tel: 064 41491 or 087 248 0800.

Bike hire: Finnegans, on the corner of Shelbourne and Henry Street, Tel: 064 41083.
Air: Kerry airport is approximately one hour by car.

OTHER INFORMATION
Police: Police, Marine and Mountain Rescue: Tel: 064 41177.
Doctor: Rory and Bernadette O'Driscoll Tel: 064 41333; Denis O'Connor Tel: 064 41003; Vincent Boland Tel: 064 41303; Rose Crushell Tel: 064 41515; D Waterhouse Tel: 064 45204; Health Centre Tel: 064 42414.
Dentist: Gerard McCarthy Tel: 064 41650; Con O'Leary Tel: 087 237 1893; Dental Clinic Tel: 064 41042.
Hospital: Kenmare Community Hospital Tel: 064 41088.
The tourist office: The Tourist Office and Heritage Centre, Tel: 064 41233, are open in the summer next to the courthouse on the Square. Members of staff are particularly helpful and go to great lengths to answer queries from those arriving in their town by sea.
Specialist shops: Kenmare has several antique and craft shops, including galleries exhibiting paintings, silverware and ceramics by local artists.

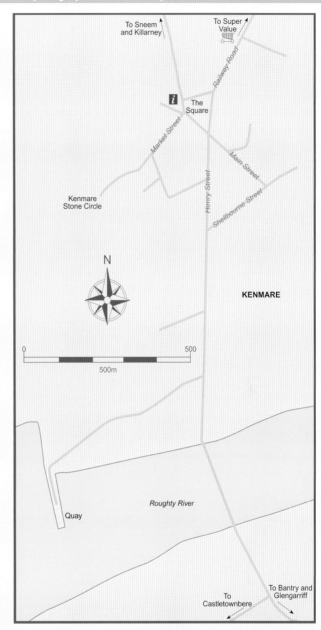

Henry Street, Kenmare

Minor anchorages in Tuosist Parish

The south-east shore of Kenmare River in County Kerry is known as Tuosist Parish. From just outside Kenmare, it stretches 12 miles west along the Beara Peninsula to the County Cork border, at Ardgroom Harbour. The backdrop to the south is the Caha Mountains and across the bay there are superb views of the Macgillycuddy's Reeks, the highest peaks in Ireland. Ashore, there are many archaeological treasures in a setting of lakes, ancient woodland, rivers and waterfalls. The flora has a sub-tropical flavour with abundant wild flowers and ubiquitous rhododendrons.

Dinish Island
8½M north-east of Kilmakilloge, opposite Dunkerron Harbour

There are anchorages east and south-west of Dinish Island. Both are visible in the aerial photo of Dunkerron Harbour (page 90). The eastern anchorage is convenient for a landing at the recently-built Star Outdoors Centre's privately-owned pier (located at 51°50'.72N 09°39'.09W), while the south-west anchorage is simply that, an anchorage with no facilities.

Charts, Tides and Lights & Marks: are as for Dunkerron earlier in this chapter on pages 89–90.

Dinish Island (East) anchorage
Approach waypoint: 51°51'.28N 09°39'.50W
(3½ cables N of Dinish Island)

From the south-west, pass Bat Rock starboard-hand mark and then from the Dinish/Dunkerron approach waypoint north of Dinish Island, steer 124°T for ½M.

From Kenmare, arrive at Kenmare approach waypoint; steer 230°T for 1M.

Anchor midway between Dinish and Dawros Point in 3-4m (approximately 51°50'.96N 09°38'.87W). Here there is some protection from all winds except those with any north in them. It is also a useful place to wait for the tide to Kenmare Quay. Land the dinghy at the pontoon alongside the pier (there is no charge for this).

ASHORE
The Star Centre is privately run. Always contact the office if wishing to use its facilities on Tel: 064 41222. Close to high water it may be possible to go alongside (with prior agreement). Facilities include fresh water on the pier (with a hose end) and showers in the admin block.

There are no shops in the vicinity but the sailing centre incorporates Con's Seafood restaurant and bar. It is on the upper floor of the complex, which provides magnificent views across to Dinish Island, Kenmare River and the mountains beyond. The restaurant is open from mid-April to October and last orders are at 2100. There is also a fish and chip van in the summer months.

Dinish Island (East); The Star Sailing Centre (centre) lies on the mainland shore beyond the eastern tip of Dinish Island

Dinish Island (West). Bat Rock starboard-hand mark and the view across Kenmare River from the anchorage

Dinish Island (West) anchorage
Approach waypoint: 51°51'.00N 09°40'.92W
(0.8 cables N of Bat Rock SHM)

The anchorage is well protected from the south.
From the south-west: At the approach waypoint north of Bat Rock starboard-hand mark, proceed on a course of 134°T for 3 cables.

    From the north-east: At the Dinish/Dunkerron approach waypoint, north of Dinish proceed on a course of 234°T for 8 cables to the anchorage.

    Anchor 3 cables east of Brennel Island and 4 cables south-east of the Bat Rock starboard-hand mark in 4-5m.

Ormond's Island
(4M north-east of Kilmakilloge,
opposite the River Blackwater)
Approach waypoint: 51°49'.25N 09°46'.00W
(½ M due W of Hog Island)

Ormond's Island lies just off the Beara shore of Kenmare River. The anchorage is on the south side of the island protected by Hog Island to the south-west. There are no facilities. At the east end of the anchorage is Coomagillagh Quay. Unfortunately, the approach to this harbour is teeming with fishing pots and floating lines between pots. It is difficult to imagine why the risks would warrant the use of this harbour by strangers, especially as there is little shelter against the prevailing westerly/south-westerly winds. Enter between Hog Island and the rocks on the west tip of Ormond's Island.

www.irelandaerialphotography.com

Lehid Harbour – only for curiosity

Lehid Harbour
(2M north-east of Kilmakilloge Harbour,
opposite Coongar Harbour)

Lehid anchorage is in a 3m deep pool that is denied open access to the sea at low water. The 'harbour' is therefore of very limited interest.

    It has a narrow entrance between rocky obstructions, and for entry a calm sea is essential. Ashore, there is nothing for a very long way!

www.irelandaerialphotography.com

Ormond's Island anchorage

Kilmakilloge Harbour – plenty of sea room and four anchorages. Bunaw Quay is visible (centre)

Kilmakilloge Harbour

Approach waypoint: 51°47'.00N 09°50'.70W
(3½ cables offshore in 30m depth)

Kilmakilloge encompasses four distinct anchorages (listed west to east): Collorus is south of the entrance and is dominated by mussel farms. It has no facilities but offers protection from southerly/south-westerly winds and access to Ardgroom Stone Circle. Bunaw to the north has some limited facilities, including a good pub and excellent seafood. Escadawer Point has no facilities but is very attractive and offers protection from southerly/south-westerly winds.

Derreen is at the far eastern end of the harbour (for the gardens and Lauragh village, which has a shop and pub).

NAVIGATION

Charts: AC/LE2495 has a useful large scale inset as does Imray C56.

Tides (approx): MHWS: 3.5m, MHWN: 2.8m, MLWN: 1.2m, MLWS: 0.5m. Standard Port Cobh, difference at HW: Springs –01:15min; Neaps –00:30min.

Lights & Marks

• Bunaw leading line; black pole with yellow bands. Front, on pier head, Oc R 3s, Rear Iso R 2s.

Approach: The entrance to the harbour lies between Laughaun Point to the north-east and the unnamed south-west shore, 3 cables north-west of Collorus Point. Laughaun Point should be given a very wide berth (3 cables) as there are obstructions extending southwards from the point, 4 cables beyond Collorus Point. In the middle of the harbour is Spanish Island, which consists

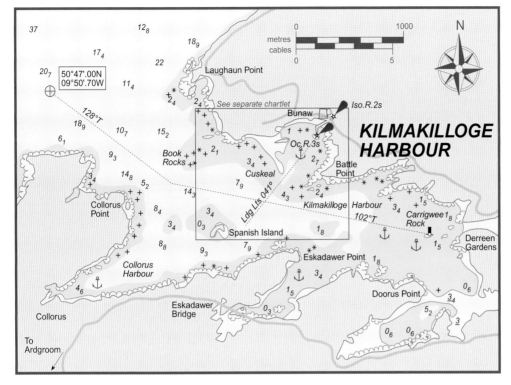

BUNAW PILOTAGE/ANCHORING

From a position off Collorus Point and south of Book Rocks, steer north of Spanish Island (102°T) to avoid the mussel farm, and pick up the Bunaw leading marks/lights (041°T), which will clear rocks on either side of a 1 cable wide entrance to Bunaw. Anchor in 5m±1m on the leading beacons/lights. Dinghy landing is at the quay. Bunaw is exposed to strong southerly winds. It can be very choppy.

ESCADAWER POINT PILOTAGE/ANCHORING

This anchorage is in a small inlet on the south shore. It is reached by continuing on 102°T until the nearest point of Escadawer Point bears 245°T, which clears the mid-harbour shallows (1.8m). Alter course to starboard and steer 230°T to enter the inlet. Anchor in 4m south of Escadawer Point. Beware of rocks extending north-east of the point when entering or exiting.

DERREEN PILOTAGE/ANCHORING

Derreen can be reached by continuing on 102°T from north of the Spanish Island mussel beds to the far end of the harbour, anchoring in 4m west or south-west of Carrigwee Rock for Derreen Gardens (and House). Dinghy landing for Derreen is possible just south of the house. (Carrigwee did not have a beacon at the time of writing).

ASHORE

Collorus: There are no facilities nearby but this anchorage is closer to Ardgroom Stone Circle than is Pallas Pier in Ardgroom Harbour. Ardgroom Stone Circle is also known as Canfie Circle. The site is off the road between Ardgroom and Kenmare. It is a little north of Ardgroom village and uphill over rough ground. It is one of the best-preserved Bronze Age relics in the area (see photo on page 98).

Bunaw: As Kilmakilloge Harbour, particularly to its south-east, is dense with mussel farms, it is no surprise that O'Sullivan's alluring pub on Bunaw Quay, Tel: 064 83104, has such a good reputation for dishes of mussels that are local, fresh and a match for any Brittany harbour.

Derreen Gardens: The Derreen Gardens were begun in 1870 by the 5th Marquess of Landsdowne

of grass-topped boulders, but from a distance the island looks very much like a beach on the far shore.

Pilotage: From the approach waypoint, steer 128°T for the north of Spanish Island. This favours the south shore of the entrance at Collorus Point and avoids Book Rocks which are a further foul area extending 2 cables offshore from the north-east shore opposite Collorus Point. There is also a shallow patch extending 1 cable to the north-west of Spanish Island towards the approach.

COLLORUS PILOTAGE/ANCHORING

Collorus anchorage is reached by turning to starboard once past Collorus Point (passing between the starboard shore and Spanish Island) and keeping 2 cables off the shore on a south-west bearing. Anchor in 6m. The serried lines of mussel floats are grey in colour and would not be visible in other than crystal clear conditions. There are also unassociated fishing pots cluttering the open channels.

The extensive aquaculture north of Spanish Island

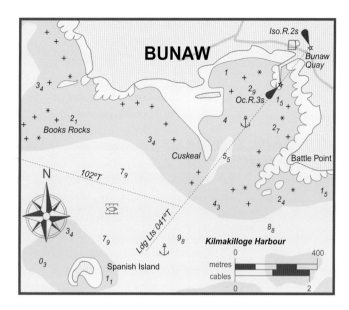

Bunaw leading line/lights

(Henry Petty-FitzMaurice), who was the sixth generation descendant of Sir William Petty, the founder of modern Kenmare (see page 91). Between 1883 and 1888, Lansdowne was Governor General of Canada and went on to become Viceroy of India from 1889 to 1894. He nurtured the 90 acres of gardens for 60 years. Thanks to the moderating effect of the Gulf Stream, the gardens thrived and now offer the visitor an opportunity to see such exotic plants as tree ferns, azaleas, rhododendrons, eucalyptus, giant blue gum, bamboo and even a 43m Red Cedar, Tel: 064 83588. A preview is available online: www.anothermovie.co.uk/2007/derreen/derreenpages/derreen.html.

Lauragh, a tiny village with a church, pub, post office and a small shop, is 1km south. Bus service 282 operates from Lauragh Church. There are no buses on public holidays. Services are Kenmare-Ardgroom-Castletownbere (Monday to Saturday during summer) and Ardgroom-Kenmare and back, Fridays only in winter.

Canfie (Ardgroom) Stone Circle

Ardgroom Harbour
Approach waypoint: 51°46'.50N 09°53'.63W

At first sight this is another appealing and well-sheltered harbour, half way down the Beara shore straddling the county boundaries of Cork and Kerry. However, the harbour is accessed using multiple transits, which a stranger should assume to be difficult to distinguish. Furthermore, the extensive aquaculture here overwhelms all of the harbour's benefits. Regrettably, it has to be said that the harbour should only be approached by experienced navigators in mild weather at the correct state of the tide, under engine in a vessel with good manoeuvrability. Its shores are well forested and it is protected by a long spit of land jutting out from its west side called Cus. This provides excellent shelter for Pallas Harbour and the anchorage/pier at Reenavaud Quay, which is in the north-west corner of the harbour.

Argroom, where mussel farms dominate

Tides (approx): MHWS: 3.5m, MHWN: 2.8m, MLWN: 1.2m, MLWS: 0.5m. Standard Port Cobh, difference at HW: Springs –01:15min; Neaps –00:30min.

Lights & Marks
The charted transits and leading marks are:
1. From the approach waypoint steer 135°T between Dog's Point and Carravaniheen Island to a black beacon on Halftide Rock. Turn to port before Halftide Rock onto the second transit.
2. The next leading beacons are white with the front beacon on Black Rock and the rear on the shore. This leading line clears the bar (2.4m) on 099°T. Once past the bar, be prepared for a turn to starboard.

NAVIGATION
Charts: AC/LE2495 has a useful large scale inset. Imray C56 has an inset covering Ardgroom.

3. Pick up a stern transit on 026°T. The front beacon is on Yellow Rock and the rear one on the shoreline. The beacons have black bands. This leading line clears the rocks and shallows south of the bar. If the leading beacons/lights are lost, there is deeper water to the east, provided the Yellow Rock beacon bears between 206°T and 195°T.

Proceed to the quay between the floats and the shore, keeping at least 2 cables off the latter (in more than 5m).

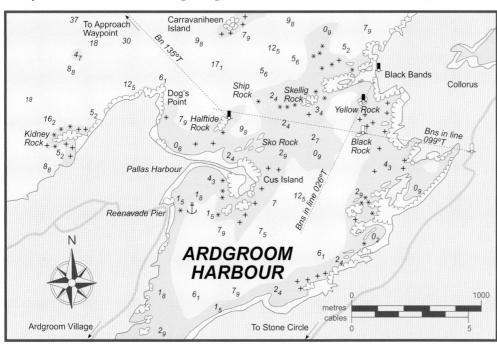

Useful information – Ardgroom Harbour

FACILITIES
There are no marine services nearby. Ardgroom village at the south-west corner of the harbour is a 3km walk from Pallas. It has most village amenities, including a highly recommended bar and restaurant, the Village Inn, run by the Mullins family, Tel: 027 74067.

Harrington's **general store** incorporates the **post office**, local arts and crafts, an **Internet** café, taxi service and **road fuel**, Tel: 027 74003.

ASHORE
The major attraction in the vicinity is Ardgroom Stone Circle, which is as easily

visited from Collorus in Kilmakilloge Harbour.

TRANSPORT
Bus services: From Ardgroom post office. Services are as for Lauragh on the previous page. Also Harrington's has an early morning minibus running to Cork

every day except Thursdays (booking essential).
Taxi: A local taxi is run by John O'Shea, Tel: 087 671 3372, or call Harrington's shop.

Minor anchorages on the south-east coast

Coulagh (Eyeries) Bay, Ballydonegan Bay and Garnish Bay are rock-strewn bays that face the prevailing south-westerly winds and should be avoided if bad weather or sea conditions from that direction are forecast. Harbours in these bays can be dangerous.

The narrow entrance and extensive aquaculture; Cleanderry Harbour

Cleanderry Harbour

Approach waypoint: 51°44'.90N 09°55'.85W

Cleanderry lies between Ardgroom Harbour and Coulagh Bay. The nearest village is Ardgroom, which is a steep climb and a long haul on foot. Cleanderry is largely given over to aquaculture, which means occasional noise from the service boats. It has an extremely narrow entrance (7m) with rocky obstructions and is exposed to the south-west at high water. The rough quay at the northern end of the harbour has no facilities and is largely occupied with machinery. It is not recommended as an anchorage.

Ballycrovane Harbour

Approach waypoint: 51°42'.40N 09°59'.00W
(3½ cables NW of Eyeries Island; S of Reen Point)

For those wanting to sample the rawer nature of the Beara Coast under the Slieve Miskish Mountains, Ballycrovane has more to offer than the other minor anchorages nearby. Firstly, there is a degree of all-round protection; the anchorage is tucked in behind a promontory to the south-west, leaving just a small southerly entrance open to the sea. Secondly, there are several archaeological points of interest ashore – particularly Ireland's tallest Ogham Stone.

The terrain ashore is rugged and sparsely populated except in nearby Eyeries village.

NAVIGATION

Charts: AC/LE2495 has a useful large scale inset.

Tides: MHWS: 3.5m, MHWN: 2.8m, MLWN: 1.2m, MLWS: 0.5m. Standard Port Cobh, difference at HW: Springs –01:16min; Neaps –00:36min.

Lights & Marks
• Illaunnameanla (Bird Island) PHM beacon Fl R 3s.

Approaches: When making to/from harbours in upper Kenmare River, there is a shortcut into Coulagh Bay between Kilcatherine Point and Inishfarnard, but calm seas are needed as the 70m channel is foul with rocks and shallows on either side, not to mention a large number of fishing buoys. Depths should exceed 7m throughout. Inishfarnard is an abandoned island that once supported more than 20 people. It has a large marine farm off its south-east shore. Once through the narrows, visually acquire the beacon on Illaunnameanla, which can be easily identified at this point – later on the entry track, it will

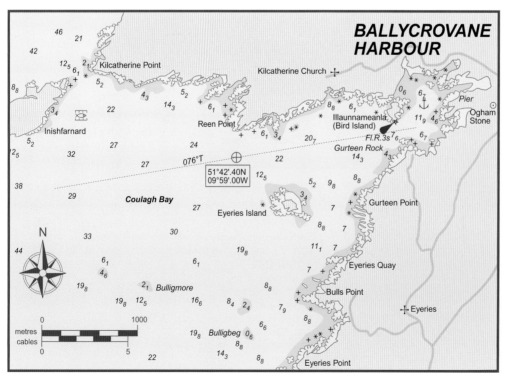

www.irelandaerialphotography.com

Ballycrovane: A harbour for those blessed with settled weather and a little time. The anchorage is bottom right

be difficult to distinguish against the background. Join the entrance track by steering for Miskish Mountain (approximately 150°T).

When making to/from the mouth of Kenmare River be aware of the obstructions that extend a mile south-west from Inishfarnard. Bridaun and Bridaun Beg are two islets off the south-west tip of Inishfarnard. Bulligabridane covers and uncovers (1.2m) 2 cables west-south-west of Bridaun outside the 10m contour. Stickeen Rock (1.5m) lies ½M south-west of Bridaun.

Pilotage/Anchoring: The entrance track to Ballycrovane, once inside Coulagh Bay, is on a course of 076°T passing between Reen Point and Eyeries Island towards the lit beacon on the south tip of Illaunnameanla – a small island, close against the north shore of the bay. At all times up to the beacon depths should exceed 10m. The sharp-eyed may notice that this course heads directly towards the Ogham Stone hidden in the verdant backdrop. After the beacon, turn slowly to port, keeping in greater than 5m until steering 000°T and anchor in the

old harbour where moorings are laid in depths of 3-5m.

Landing at the new pier/slipway is best for good access to the Ogham Stone.

FACILITIES
There are no facilities immediately ashore. It is a 3km walk to Eyeries, which is a sizeable village with two bars (O'Shea's and Causkey's – the latter serves food) and two grocery stores – one at each end of the village. The nearer, Mary Harrington's, Tel: 027 4700, doubles up as a post office and will deliver to the harbour. The other, O'Sullivan's, Tel: 027 74016, has Flogas, white and green diesel and petrol. There is also a health centre adjacent to the post office. The local speciality is a soft cheese that is widely exported; Milleens Farmhouse Cheese is available in both stores.

Beacon on the south tip of Illaunnameanla at entrance to the anchorage

Ballycrovane Pier

Ireland's tallest Ogham Stone

Eyeries village, near Ballycrovane Harbour, in August sunshine

ASHORE

The main attraction at Ballycrovane is the nearby Ogham Pillar Stone, the largest in Ireland at over 5m. The inscription translates as '(The stone of) the son of Deich the descendant of Torainn'. There is a fee to visit the stone.

Along the road to the north-west is Kilcatherine church, which is a ruined 7th century church on an ancient monastic site and named for St Caithighearn. Legend has her as 'The Cat Goddess': note the cat-like carving over the archway. Nearby, the 'Hag of Beara' is an exposed rock formation which has as many legends associated with it as people asked to tell them (see page 106).

Kilcatherine church

Eyeries is a picturesque village that overlooks Coulagh Bay and nestles at the base of the highest peak in the Slieve Miskish mountain range, which forms the backbone of the peninsula. It has been the location for the shooting of several films.

Transport: A bus to/from Eyeries and Castletownbere from Ballycrovane operates on Wednesdays, Tel 027 52727. For taxis from Castletownbere contact Martin Shanahan on Tel: 027 70116/086 246 1877.

Eyeries Quay

Eyeries Quay is included here mainly to clarify some of the ambiguity of naming various harbours and islands. Eyeries Quay is 1km north-west of the village, 2km south-west of Ballycrovane Harbour and 1¼km north-north-east of Eyeries Point. It is only suitable for very small craft such as dinghies. It is a wonderful spot to watch otters playing on the shoreline against a backdrop of Eyeries Island, a small, flat island with many rocky outcrops, and the beautiful scenery of Coulagh Bay. However, it is not a place for a yacht. The quay (located at 51°41'.94N 09°57'.90W), which dries, is not marked on AC/LE2495.

Travara Quay, Ardacluggin/Urhan

Approach waypoint: 51°40'.80N 10°01'.00W
(5 cables WNW of the harbour entrance)

This is another quay which is included to try to eliminate potential confusion. The pier is located between Ardacluggin and Urhan/Urhin at 51°40'.62N 10°00'.06W. To the south, an additional harbour wall can be clearly seen. This is the quay at Travaud Strand. Only Ardacluggin is named on AC/LE2495. This harbour is 5km south-west of Eyeries by road.

The harbour is wide open to the west and the associated swell. It is also badly maintained and there are no shore side reasons to recommend this harbour. Sharks may be encountered offshore here.

Travara: A working harbour in rugged country

Ballydonegan Pier

Ballydonegan

Approach waypoint: 51°37'.77N 10°04'.00W
(1 cable S of Bird Rock)

Ballydonegan is a small caravan holiday village that has few facilities. The main beach and pier below the village is backed by flat pasture. The pier is bounded by rocks and the bay is totally exposed to the south-west. This is the nearest harbour to Allihies village (2km inland).

Allihies, up to the 1930s, was a small copper mining village which now shows off its cottages in a multi-coloured pastel array contrasting incongruously with the natural scenery. The mine spoil still persists on the beach at Ballydonegan. The Copper Mine Museum is worth a visit. The Mountain Mine Man Engine House, located on the mountain above the village, has recently been conserved by the Mining Heritage Trust of Ireland.

Garnish Bay

White Strand approach waypoint:
51°37'.25N 10°07'.50W
Carrigduff South approach waypoint:
51°37'.15N 10°07'.35W

Garnish Bay is useful as a temporary anchorage and is convenient if waiting for passage through Dursey Sound. Garnish (or Garinish) Island and Long Island are a pair of closely spaced islands off Garnish Point. They shelter White Strand Quay, a drying harbour tucked in between Long Island and the mainland. Here there is a pier/slipway on both Long Island and the mainland. A reef lies across the entrance to the harbour. Immediately south-east of Long Island is a beacon on a rock called Carrigduff. Garnish Bay is surprisingly susceptible to swell even close to the shore. It provides protection from winds from south-west to east.

There are no facilities nearby.

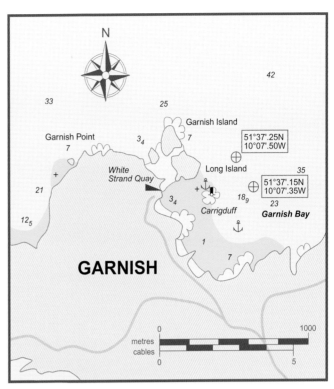

NAVIGATION

Charts: There is no detailed chart. Use AC/LE2495 for the approach.

Tides (approx): MHWS: 3.5m, MHWN: 2.8m, MLWN: 1.2m, MLWS: 0.5m. Standard Port Cobh, difference at HW: Springs –01:16min; Neaps –00:36min.

Lights & Marks
• Carrigduff beacon.

Pilotage/Anchoring: The preferred anchorage is in the bay between the beacon and Long Island, as close to shore as the fishing pots and buoys will allow, in 5m. A beach landing is possible, but improvements to the pier in 2008 may make that accessible. Use the White Strand approach waypoint, keeping to 225°T (south-west) while favouring the Long Island shore. If conditions dictate, anchor in the bay south-east of Carrigduff to have less lee shore. Use the Carrigduff South approach waypoint.

Garnish Bay; Carrigduff Beacon

Dursey Sound looking north

Dursey Sound

North entrance approach waypoint:
51°36'.80N 10°09'.70W
South entrance approach waypoint:
51°36'.41N 10°09'.35W

Dursey Island is 6½km in length with a population of just nine. It is clearly identifiable by the signal tower on the summit and is connected to the mainland by cable car (the only such in Ireland) over Dursey Sound.

Dursey Sound, in the right conditions, is the obvious passage between Kenmare River and Bantry Bay. The distance saved is significant, but the greater value is the rare experience of successfully negotiating a channel with a dangerous rock in midstream while having calculated with certainty that the top of the mast will clear a cable car full of people just over 20m above mean high water springs and avoiding the lobster pots. Whichever direction the passage, the dangling cable car will seem desperately close to the yacht's rigging – this is a good place to test even the most confident/competent skipper's nerve.

The right conditions involve taking a favourable tide and avoiding the turbulent waters that can occur at the north entrance.

Hope to transit Dursey Sound near high water slack in benign wind and swell conditions, but as someone once said 'Hope is not a strategy'. Forget 'Hope', good planning and preparation are essential.

NAVIGATION

Charts: AC/LE2495 has a useful large scale inset that charts the Sound immediately north and south of the narrows. SC5623.2 or Imray C56 will be needed for the approach from Bantry Bay

Tides (approx): MHWS: 3.4m, MHWN: 2.6m, MLWN: 1.2m, MLWS: 0.3m. The south-going stream commences 4 hours 50 minutes before HW Cobh. The north-going stream commences 1 hour 35 minutes after HW Cobh. Standard Port Cobh, difference at HW: Springs –01:15min; Neaps –00:35min.

Spring rate north and south is approximately 4kn.

Lights & Marks: None.

Approaches: Dursey Sound presents itself quite differently depending on whether passage is north to

Heading south on the western side of the Sound as the cable car crosses the turbulent waters off the eastern shore

www.irelandaerialphotography.com

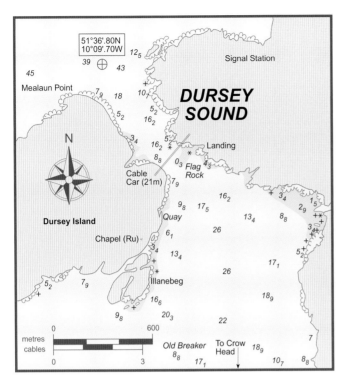

south or south to north. These are described separately below. In both cases, the motor should be used and it is highly recommended that all crew wear lifejackets. Under the cable car, the channel will narrow to less than 70m. It is advisable to have the sails configured such that the engine can always keep the vessel under control in unforeseen wind changes.

Approach (North to South): The sea in the northern entrance can become very disturbed as a result of recent strong northerly/north-westerly winds or swell. The cliffs are also sufficiently high to cause some fluky wind changes through the Sound. Approaching from mid-entrance (northern approach waypoint), the channel and the cable car come into view from a reasonable distance off, where there is still 30m under the keel.

Pilotage (North to South): Edge to the west shore of the channel long before the cable crossing and use eyes and the 10m contour to maintain a track close to the west shore. Immediately south of the cable car, Flag Rock is mid channel and only 0.3m below chart datum. It may be that allowance must be made for traffic in the opposite direction which, just south of the cable car,

would place a north-going vessel closer to the rock.

Once the sound widens out, stay in the middle to avoid back eddies and follow a dogleg well clear of Crow Head, Crow Island and into Bantry Bay.

Approach (South to North): Stay well clear of Cat Rock, Crow Island and Crow Head. Keep to the middle of the sound to avoid eddies. Arriving from Bantry Bay into the calm waters of the sound, which is well sheltered from strong northerly/north-westerly winds, will give a false sense of security. The waters at the northern exit can produce very disturbed seas, out of proportion to the swell experienced in Bantry Bay. This only becomes apparent when seeing the white water crash on the rocks on the lee shore to the north. These seas have been described, typically, as 'daunting', but they attenuate rapidly once clear of the entrance to the sound.

Pilotage (South to North): See photo on page 78. It is extremely late before the camouflage of the hillsides reveals the cable car crossing and the channel through the sound. With a favourable tide and numerous pot buoys, it can be quite enervating identifying features leading to the correct course. The charts show several apparently unique features, however, in practice these merge well into the landscape and none are dependable for use by a stranger.

Give Bull's Forehead (west of Crow Island) a wide berth and steer to close Illanebeg, an island on the Dursey shore, south of the channel. From Illanebeg, keep to the Dursey shore all the way past the cable car. Staying too far off will increase the influence of the set of the tide, which is on to Flag Rock.

A spring tide showing its strength through Dursey Sound

The northern entrance to Dursey Sound in very quiet seas

Places and people in the Kenmare River

The Hag of Beara

The Hag of Beara is also known as *Cailleach Bhéarra*, meaning 'a wise woman dwelling on the Beara Peninsula'. One version of the story has her leaping from the summit of Knockatee in Tuosist to Hungry Hill in Bantry Bay. Another version describes her as the 'Shaper of the Land'; she did this by sliding down rocks! Yet another has her living seven lives, then being petrified into rock to await the return of her husband 'Manannan Mac Lir', the God of the Sea. The Hag can be found in Kilcatherine, near Ballycrovane, alongside one of the oldest church sites in Ireland. This has a subterranean monks' cell, an ancient cross, and, over the doorway, a cat's head gargoyle.

The Old Hag of Beara

Daniel O'Connell (1775-1847)

Daniel O'Connell

Derrynane is dominated by the legendary Daniel O'Connell ('The Liberator'; 1775-1847), who lived at Derrynane House when he felt unable to support (or participate in the suppression of) violent rebellion.

Daniel O'Connell was a Kerryman and a Paris and London trained lawyer. He was a devoutly non-violent egalitarian, campaigning for Catholic and Jewish emancipation in Ireland. Frequently declaring allegiance to the British Crown and denouncing violent methods, he worked from inside the 'system' to bring about change. His major achievements include amending the parliamentarians' oath of allegiance to eliminate elements offensive to Catholics.

O'Connell also campaigned for Irish independence but with the retention of Queen Victoria as Head of State. He is now honoured by a statue which dominates the eponymous O'Connell Street, Dublin, where he became the first Catholic Lord Mayor since the Reformation. His principles are crystallised in his phrase – 'The altar of liberty totters when it is cemented only with blood'.

Derrynane House

Castletownbere and Bear Haven looking east

Chapter four
Bantry Bay

Bantry Bay is a 20M long drowned river valley (ria) with cliffs and rocky shores at its mouth yielding to sheltered stony, wooded shores at its head near Bantry. The bay is exposed to westerly winds and swell.

There are few dangers in the open bay provided the occasional oil tanker, the extensive (and increasing) marine farms and the obstructions off Whiddy and Bear Islands are avoided.

Marine mammals abound. Harbour seals haul-out in large numbers. Their sites are predominantly located on the northern shore from Adrigole eastwards and the Gerane Rocks off Whiddy Island. Glengarriff Harbour has by far the largest concentrations. Whales and dolphins are frequently seen off the outer headlands.

Bantry Bay is the largest mussel-producing bay in Ireland, with salmon farms, a dozen oyster farms and over 50 mussel farms mainly concentrated in the upper bay.

Leahill Quarry is the largest quarry in Ireland. It is only too visible on the north shore between Adrigole and Glengarriff. The output of good quality roadstone is exported using ships of up to 75,000 tonnes. Over 100 vessels a year have called at the quarry.

The oil terminal at the north-west of Whiddy Island provides storage both for the Irish strategic reserves and output from offshore oil-fields. Oil and refined products are pumped ashore from tankers that moor on the single point mooring (SPM) via a pipeline along the sea-bed to the tanks. The tanks have a capacity of one million tonnes. The SPM handles tankers up to 320,000 tonnes. Smaller vessels berth at the jetty on the south-west of the island. Approximately one to two ships a week call at the terminal. Other vessels re-fuel here.

NAMES AND PLACES
The stranger should be wary of the repetitious use of place names and their variance in spelling on charts, almanacs and locally-produced maps. The most common of these are as follows:

Bere or Bear: Bere/Bear Island, Bear Haven and Castletownbere.

Castletown Bearhaven or Castletownbere: The town and its harbour are referred to in the text as Castletownbere (partly to ease distinction from Castlehaven in chapter seven on page 180).

Garinish or Garnish: There are two islands with the name Garinish in Bantry Bay (and two in Kenmare River). Garinish West is a small island, 200m off the shore, midway between Glengarriff and Adrigole, north of Sheelane Island.

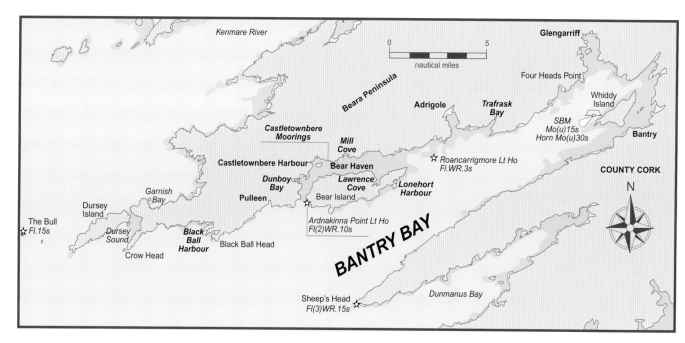

Garinish Island in Glengarriff Bay is widely referred to by its Irish name Ilnacullin (with a variety of endings …en, …ing etc) or as Garnish Island.

SUGGESTED ITINERARY FOR A SHORT VISIT TO BANTRY BAY

• After passage, arrive at Lawrence Cove during the working day. Here it is easy to refill fuel and water, shower, launder and recharge the batteries. Eat on board and enjoy the view of Hungry Hill.
• Depart for Glengarriff to arrive early. Take a visitors' buoy, tour the gardens on Ilnacullin and visit town.
• Next day, go by bus to Kenmare and Killarney.

The mountainous roads reveal stunning scenery.
• Sail to Bantry and take a visitors' buoy, visit Bantry House and Gardens. Eat in town.
• Sail out of Bantry, taking the south entrance if conditions permit, to arrive midday at Adrigole. Pick up a mooring buoy and go ashore for a shower and a visit one of the bars in Drumlave.
• The following morning, pick up a mooring buoy at Castletownbere for lunch and some reprovisioning, followed by a night at anchor in Dunboy Bay.
• Leave Bantry Bay.
Twenty five visitors' moorings are distributed throughout the bay.

Setting pots in the creeks off Dunboy Bay

TIDES

Within the bay tidal rates are unremarkable and only significant (up to 2kn) off outer headlands, such as Black Ball Head, and at the pinch points at the narrow west entrances to Piper Sound and Bantry Harbour.

The tidal streams for craft leaving Bantry Bay for the north are more problematic. For passage north, the choice is either to go around The Bull or through Dursey Sound. The latter is by far the shorter and more interesting route, but must be taken with a favourable tide and in the absence of a heavy westerly/north-westerly swell, which produces turbulent water at the north entrance of Dursey Sound.

The flood tide originates from north of The Cow and runs east along both sides of Dursey Island causing a south-going stream through Dursey Sound.

Tides flow strongly (3kn) past Dursey Head and turbulence may be expected between Dursey and beyond The Cow. In particular, avoid the area around Lea Rock (1 cable south-west of Dursey) and The Calf nearby.

In Dursey Sound

Northward passage – commences 1 hour 35 minutes after HW Cobh.
Southward passage – commences 4 hours 50 minutes before HW Cobh.

WEATHER INFORMATION BROADCASTS

This coast is served by the Valentia Coastguard transmitter in Bantry Bay on VHF Ch 23. An advisory announcement is made initially on Ch 16.

PASSAGE CHARTS FOR THIS CHAPTER

Admiralty Charts: AC2423 Mizen Head to Dingle Bay, 1:150,000. AC/LE2495 Kenmare River, 1:60,000. SC5623.2 The Bull to Glandore Harbour.
Imray: C56 Cork Harbour to Dingle Bay, 1:170,000.
Plans for harbours included in this chapter:
Castletownbere, Glengarriff and Bantry.

As might be expected of an old Royal Navy base, Bantry Bay is well covered by the Admiralty charts in Folio SC5623, which provides coverage south and east of Piper Sound. The folio uses a WGS84 Datum, theoretically eliminating coordinate adjustments. However, caution is advised because other, particularly

local, publications have not necessarily been updated to reflect the revised datum. This means that WGS84 satellite derived coordinates may be plotted directly on these charts but other Lat/Lon coordinates may need to be corrected 0.03 minutes northwards and 0.03 minutes westwards before they are plotted on the paper chart. Even when data is purported to be based on WGS84, it has not always been done correctly. Importantly this applies to close-quarters situations such as small minor harbours.

Be sure to have access to the latest Notices to Mariners for SC5623. There have been several changes to depths in Bantry Bay as a full geological survey started in 2008.

SAFETY INFORMATION

This section of the coast is managed by Valentia Coastguard, Tel: 066 947 6109.

COASTGUARD AIS STATION

Bantry (Knockgour Hill)
51°38'.40N 10°00'.11W   MMSI 002 500380.

MAJOR LIGHTS

• The Bull, Fl 15s.
• Ardnakinna Point lighthouse Fl (2) WR 10s, white sector 348° to 066°T.
• Sheep's Head, Fl (3) WR 15s, white sector 017° to 212°T.
• Dinish Island leading lights Dir Oc WRG 5s, white sector: 024.0°T to 024.5°T.
• Roancarrigmore lighthouse Fl WR 3s, white sector 312° to 050°T.

Sheep's Head

BANTRY BAY – PASSAGE WAYPOINTS – WGS84 DATUM		
NAME	DESCRIPTION	LAT/LONG
Dursey Sound South	Mid Entrance	51°36'.41N 10°09'.35W
Crow Head	1M SW of Crow Head	51°34'.00N 10°10'.50W
The Bull	1¼M SW of The Bull	51°35'.00N 10°20'.00W
Sheep's Head	1M NW of headland	51°33'.20N 09°52'.00W
Three Castle Head	1½M W of headland	51°28'.75N 09°52'.61W
Mizen Head	½M SW of headland	51°26'.50N 09°50'.00W
Fastnet SW	7 cables SW of rock	51°22'.85N 09°37'.00W

Minor harbours in Outer Bantry Bay

There are three minor anchorages that are included here for completeness. They may appeal to those seeking solitude but cannot be said to be essential for a full appreciation of Bantry Bay. Each has significant access limitations.

Black Ball Harbour

Approach waypoint: 51°35'.40N 10°03'.40W
(Due W of Black Ball Head and 2 cables SSW of White Ball Head)

Black Ball Harbour

This anchorage is fully exposed to south-westerlies and any swell can reflect off White Ball Head to the north of the entrance to cause a very disturbed sea. Entry should only be attempted in very settled weather.

NAVIGATION

Charts: Black Ball is the only harbour in this section that is not depicted on the larger scale charts in SC5623. AC/LE1840 is needed for detail.

Tides: MHWS: 3.4m, MHWN: 2.7m, MLWN: 1.2m, MLWS: 0.6m. Standard Port Cobh, difference at HW: Springs –01:15min; Neaps –00:35min.

Lights & Marks: None.

Pilotage: From the approach waypoint steer 052°T, keeping in 10m until the entrance; stay closer to the north shore than mid channel to avoid Black Rock (½ cable offshore).

Pulleen Harbour

Approach waypoint: 51°36'.75N 09°58'.25W
(30m contour – 2 cables SW of entrance)

This anchorage is fully exposed to southerlies and to swell in outer Bantry Bay, which refracts into the harbour. This inlet is only suitable for very small craft. There are many fishing pots. Before navigators had access to modern technology, it was not unknown for Pulleen to be mistaken for Piper Sound, which is understandable when viewing from a distance. By the time the error was noticed, the ship was on a lee shore with no escape.

NAVIGATION

Charts: Pulleen is included on SC5623.7 (1:30,000) or use AC/LE1840.

Tides: Approximately as Black Ball Harbour above.

Lights & Marks: None.

The entrance to Pulleen Harbour

www.irelandaerialphotography.com

Lonehort Harbour at the eastern end of Bear Island

Lonehort Harbour
Approach waypoint: 51°38'.18N 09°47'.55W
(20m contour)

Lonehort Harbour lies at the east end of Bear Island on its southern shore. It is protected from the south-west by Leahern's Point. It is the most sheltered of the outer bay harbours; entry requires great attentiveness – involving a 180° turn past a dangerous reef and following a shallow (1.8m or less) channel that is approximately 35m wide. Reports by strangers of groundings are not uncommon. From the anchorage it is possible to access Rerrin village with its very limited facilities (see Lawrence Cove on page 122).

NAVIGATION
Charts: Use SC5623.7.

Tides (approx): MHWS: 3.3m, MHWN: 2.5m, MLWN: 1.2m, MLWS: 0.4m. Standard Port Cobh, difference at HW: Springs –01:00min; Neaps –00:30min.

Lights & Marks: None.

Pilotage: The spit forming the south-east shore of the anchorage slopes into the sea and subsequently forms a (mostly) submerged reef. Only the west end of this reef is uncovered at low water. The photo below shows the entrance and the exposed reef 45 minutes before low water springs. The entrance channel lies immediately west of the reef. To the south of the entrance is another rock off Bear Island shore. Stay north of this during the approach to the entrance channel. Finally, turn east-north-east to anchor in 2.7m at the east end of the cove.

Lonehort Harbour entrance looking west. The spit forming the south-east shore of the anchorage descends into the sea (right of photo). The west end of this reef is visible

Bear Haven

The second largest natural harbour in Ireland was, up to the 19th century, the domain of smugglers and fishermen. In the 19th century the harbour was fortified and became a key asset for the Royal Navy. Following Irish Independence and up to 1938, Bear Haven remained one of the British 'Treaty Ports' in the Irish Free State, that is a UK sovereign base retained by the Royal Navy – the modern equivalents being the UK bases on Cyprus.

Bear Haven is a natural harbour. Its western entrance (Piper Sound) is narrow and faced by cliffs, overlooked by Ardnakinna Point lighthouse – a fine 60m high structure which looks out over Sheep's Head to the south and the Atlantic to the west. Roancarrigmore lighthouse stands on an island at the east entrance, where both the island and immediate mainland foreshore are gently sloping. Within the haven, there is a variety of moorings and anchorages:

• Dunboy is a peaceful, isolated anchorage in a wooded bay with a great historical legacy.
• Castletownbere town anchorage is right in the midst of a very busy harbour focussed on developing its fishing role.
• Castletownbere moorings are close to good basic facilities and give easy access to the town but without the noise and disturbance of the commercial harbour.
• Mill Cove is for those with very shallow keels that prefer solitude.
• Lawrence Cove Marina on Bear Island is an essential 'pit stop' for major refuelling, watering or if a walk-ashore berth is required.

www.irelandaerialphotography.com

Piper Sound looking south-south-west from Castletownbere

NAVIGATIONAL DATA COMMON TO BEAR HAVEN DESTINATIONS

Charts: SC5623.7 provides coverage from Piper Sound in the west to Roancarrigmore in the east. A larger scale chart SC5623.6A provides coverage from Piper Sound to Minane Island, which is useful for greater detail of Dunboy anchorage and Castletownbere anchorage and moorings. The equivalent standard chart is AC/LE1840A/B. Imray C56 also has an inset.

Tides: MHWS: 3.2m, MHWN: 2.6m, MLWN: 1.2m, MLWS: 0.4m. Standard Port Cobh, difference at HW: Springs –00:48min; Neaps –00:12min.

The strongest tides flow at 2kn (flood and ebb) through the west entrance at Ardnakinna Point; some turbulence may be expected. The ingoing tide commences 5 hours 50 minutes after HW Cobh. The outgoing tide commences 25 minutes before HW Cobh.

In the east entrance the flood runs east to west (and the ebb west to east). The two opposing streams meet near George Rock isolated danger mark.

Lights & Marks: Bear Haven
• Ardnakinna Point lighthouse Fl (2) WR 10s; white sector 348° to 066°T.
• Colt Rock beacon PHM.
• Piper Sound No 1 SHM QG.
• Piper Sound No 2 PHM QR.
• Dinish Island leading lights Dir Oc WRG 5s; white sector 024.0°T to 024.5°T.
• Walter Scott SCM Q (6) + L Fl 15s.
• Privateer Rock SCM.
• Sheep Island NCM Q.
• Hornet Rock SCM VQ (6) + L Fl 10s.
• Bardini Reefer (Carrigavaneen) NCM Q.
• George Rock IDM Fl (2) 10s.
• Carrigavaddra SCM (unlit).
• Roancarrigmore lighthouse Fl WR 3s; white sector 312° to 050°T.

NAVIGATION – PIPER SOUND – THE WESTERN ENTRANCE TO BEAR HAVEN
Approach waypoint: 51°36'.00N 09°56'.30W

Approach: The approach to Piper Sound is between Fair Head to the west and Ardnakinna Point lighthouse. In the daytime, the Dinish Island leading lines through Piper Sound on 024°T are barely distinguishable from Ardnakinna. The close up photo on page 113 may help to pick them out. Be aware that if the leading marks are not visible, there are no obstructions to a mid Sound track until six cables north of Ardnakinna Point. Acquire the leading line before the depth decreases to 15m to pass Harbour Rock (3.7m) safely.

Dunboy anchorage is to port just before Colt Rock beacon (see separate description on page 114). Pass

Piper Sound from Bantry Bay – the western entrance to Bear Haven

A close-up of Dinish Island leading marks

NAVIGATION – THE EASTERN ENTRANCE TO BEAR HAVEN
Approach waypoint: 51°39'.00N 09°43'.00W
(an aerial photo can be found on page 107)

The eastern entrance is approached south of Roancarrigmore lighthouse. From the approach waypoint, a course of 269°T passes close south of George Rock isolated danger mark where the entrance to Lawrence Cove Marina is to port (see separate description). At the isolated danger mark, alter course to pass north of *Bardini Reefer*'s north cardinal mark and then south of Hornet south cardinal mark. A little before Hornet south cardinal mark, the entrance to Mill Cove is to starboard (see separate description on page 120). Beyond Hornet south cardinal mark the western entrance is as described above (in reverse).

No 1 starboard-hand mark (opposite Colt Rock) to arrive at No 2 port-hand mark. The commercial harbour entrance is directly ahead on 010°T (see separate description on page 117). At No 2 port-hand mark, alter course to pass close south of Walter Scott south cardinal mark. The Castletownbere mooring buoys in the bay east of Dinish Island are to port (see separate description on page 118). At Walter Scott south cardinal mark, alter course to pass close south of Hornet south cardinal mark to the eastern entrance to Bear Haven (see below).

Walter Scott south cardinal mark and Privateer Rock Perch (right)

Roancarrigmore lighthouse overlooks the eastern entrance to Bear Haven

Dunboy Bay

Entrance waypoint: 51°38'.00N 09°55'.00W
(1 cable SE of Colt Rock and No 2 PHM # front leading
mark on Dinish Island)

Dunboy Castle (*Caisleán Dhún Baoi*) was a stronghold
of the clan chief O'Sullivan Beare and protected Bear
Haven. O'Sullivan Beare took taxes from the fishing
fleets along the nearby coasts when they sheltered in
the harbour. It was also a centre for the import/export
trade to and from the Continent. The castle has been a
ruin since 1602 when an English force destroyed it.

Close by is Dunboy House (aka Puxley's Castle).
Originally a Victorian Gothic mansion, it was the
home of the Puxley family. Their story provided the
inspiration for Daphne du Maurier's novel *Hungry
Hill*. It was razed by the IRA in the 1920s. The setting
is undeniably beautiful – this was not lost on one
five star hotel chain. A €60 million restoration has
been undertaken and the result is the new 'Capella
Dunboy Castle Hotel'.

Approach: As Piper Sound (see aerial photo on page 112).

Pilotage/Anchoring: From the entrance waypoint, steer
for midway between Colt Rock (foul 50m south) and
the point of land to the west (foul 50m in all directions).
To stay clear of the mid-harbour drying rock (1.5m),
do not stray more than 100m north and keep Colt
Rock north of east at all times. The drying rock may

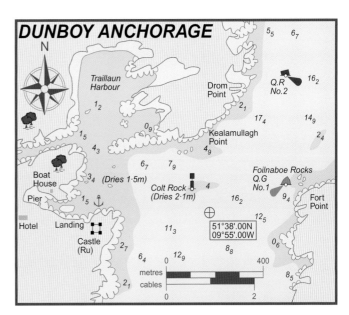

Colt Rock beacon in the evening sun

Dunboy Bay anchorage viewed from the Dunboy Castle ruins, with a close-up of the drying rock

www.irelandaerialphotography.com

Dunboy Bay from Pipers Sound

be marked with a red/orange buoy (the photo below, taken at low water springs, shows the buoy 'high & dry' on the rock). Anchor in 3-5m ½ cable north of the ruined castle inside the point.

Land at the small beach for a visit to the Dunboy Castle ruins. A public road leads from the beach past the new hotel to the main road. There are no facilities nearby and it is a long walk to the main highway; the anchorages' attraction is the glorious surroundings.

Castletownbere
(Irish: *Baile Chaisleáin Bhéarra*)

Castletownbere, which is also known as Castletown Bearhaven, has a very small population (around 900), but gives the impression of being a much bigger. The name Beara is said to come from the eponymous Spanish wife of Owen Mór, a son of the King of Munster. They met when he was recuperating in Spain from battle injuries in the second century AD. Castletownbere has a long relationship with Spain based on fishing rights.

Castletownbere's commercial harbour

O'Sullivan Beare made a lucrative living from these.

The commercial harbour is protected by Dinish Island, which projects into Bear Haven and is now connected to the town by a low bridge. It is primarily an industrial estate. About 1km further east is Minane Island. Between the two islands are the visitors' buoys described below.

Over 100 fishing vessels are based in Castletownbere, which is being continually developed. The current improvements include the construction of an additional 120m of quay, dredging the harbour, and the removal of the Perch Rock to create a deeper and wider entrance channel. The dredged material will be used to land-fill on Dinish Island where a new fish auction hall will be built. It is therefore understandable why, officially, 'the harbour is not suitable for pleasure craft'.

The town is unprepossessing but the square is worth visiting, with its brightly painted shops, often with elaborately painted names, cafés and opportunities for alfresco dining.

NAVIGATION
Lights & Marks
• Cametringane Spit PHM QR.
• Castletownbere leading lights/marks Oc 3s; white sector 005° to 015°T.
Note: Perch Rock beacon has been removed but not the rock – check Notices to Mariners for further changes.

The fishing industry still dominates in Castletownbere

Castletownbere: the entrance to the commercial harbour

Pilotage: From Piper Sound, alter course at No 2 port-hand mark to pick up the inner leading line/lights on 010°T. The entrance narrows to 36m where Perch Rock beacon used to be. Pass close to the port-hand mark off Cametringane Spit.

From the east, at Walter Scott south cardinal mark, alter course to due west and pick up the inner leading line/lights as above.

BERTHING/ANCHORING

If intending to go alongside, it is recommended to inform the harbour master, Peter Murphy, Tel: 027 70220; VHF Ch 14, 16. There is usually space to tie up between the berthed fishing vessels and the ferry pier for landing crew. More usually, however, anchor in the vicinity of the lifeboat and take the dinghy ashore.

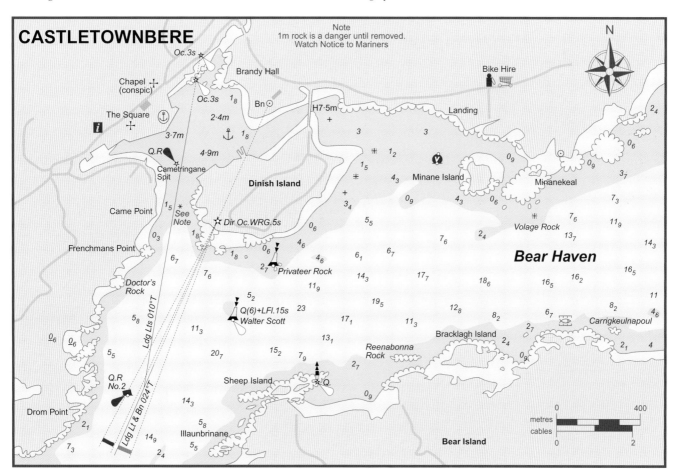

Castletownbere anchorage is on the 'town' side of Dinish Island. The visitors' buoys are banished to the other side of the island (centre right) but usefully sited for replenishing stores at the nearby shop/garage

Castletownbere mooring buoys
Dinish/Minane Islands

A far more restful environment is provided by the four yellow public visitors' buoys between Dinish and Minane Islands (laid 2½ cables east of Dinish Island at: 51°38'.95N 09°53'.40W). If the objective is to top up provisions and a small quantity of diesel or petrol, then the nearby Centra store is very convenient (large quantities of diesel are better acquired from Lawrence Cove Marina – see page 122). Beware the shoal (0.9m) west-south-west of Minane Island.

NAVIGATION

Pilotage from Piper Sound: At No 2 port-hand mark, alter course to starboard (054°T), proceed close south-east of Walter Scott south cardinal mark, and then to the mooring buoys ¾M beyond on a course of 047°T. Pass ½ cable south-east of Privateer Rock (which, south of Dinish Island, may be marked by a south cardinal mark), staying parallel to Dinish Island's south-east shore.

Pilotage from the eastern entrance: The main obstruction is Volage Rock, 2 cables south-east of Minane Island. Along with the shoal patch west-south-west of Minane, it means giving Minane a very wide berth if heading towards the moorings from the east. When safe to do so, head for Dinish Island and obtain a back bearing on Walter Scott south cardinal mark of 227°T. Alter course to 047°T and proceed as above to the mooring buoys.

Land on the nearby beach, from where a track leads up to the main Castletownbere to Bantry Road. A notice at the top of the track suggests that payment (in Irish Punts – £s) for the moorings is made to 'Aden McGunn' contactable by a telephone number that in 2008 connected with the hospital. Hopefully the situation will be clarified for future users of the moorings.

FACILITIES IN THE IMMEDIATE AREA

A Centra store/Texaco filling station, Tel: 027 70820, is close (500m) to the Minane mooring buoys. It incorporates a hot food counter, Flogas, bicycle rental – Tel: 086 128 0307, a mini-market and supplies road fuel and green diesel (by can).

The Cottage Heights restaurant is particularly convenient for the mooring buoys, being only 300m west along the road from the path down to the buoys, Tel: 027 71743.

Useful information – Castletownbere

FACILITIES
Fresh water: Available on the quay.
Gas: Camping Gaz is stocked by Harrington's, Tel: 027 70011, on Main Street.
Launderette: O'Shea's Launderette on Main Street.
Marine engineers: Harbour Engineering, Dinish; Tel: 027 71300 or 087 239 5498.
Outboard motor servicing: O'Donoghue's on the Square, Tel: 086 601 5227.
Chandlery: Limar (Lili Zwaan), between the Square and the pier, Tel: 027 70830.
Electronics: Barry Electronics, The Square, Tel: 027 70016.
Boat hoist: On Dinish Island, but primarily used by fishing vessels.
Internet access: Is available at the Beara Action Group on the square (€1.50 for 15 minutes).

PROVISIONING
In addition to the Centra store near the moorings (see above), a SuperValu store, Tel: 027 70020, can be found in the centre of town at The Bridge (opposite the ferry pier).

The nearby Orpen's fresh fish shop receives many plaudits, especially for its crab, langoustine and scallops – very useful to those who do not object to cooking in the close confines of a boat. An AIB bank with ATM is situated on the Square; the post office is in Main Street.

EATING OUT
There is no shortage of restaurants, bars and cafés in Castletownbere, but new businesses and closures occur frequently.

The Square is especially pleasant if the weather permits outside dining, where the choice includes: Breen's Lobster Bar, specialising in seafood delights, Tel: 027 70031, O'Donoghue's, also serving seafood, Tel: 027 70007, and O'Shea's Bar, Tel: 027 70600. The Copper Kettle

MacCarthy's grocery and bar in the Square

Café is very popular with the locals. MacCarthy's Bar (and grocery) is much photographed for its elaborate, highly-painted exterior and its star role in the eponymous novel. The pub, part grocery store and part bar, is a 'must see'. It also provides free Wi-Fi, Tel: 027 70014.

A walk from the ferry pier west along Main Street passes most of the other establishments: Murphy's Restaurant is recommended although it offers a limited menu – family style, Tel: 027 70244. Other options consist of Jack Patrick's, Tel: 027 70319, Golden Coast Chinese Restaurant, Tel: 027 71111, Olde Bakery Café / Restaurant, West End, Tel: 027 70869, and Cronin's Hide-Away family restaurant, West End, Tel: 027 70386.

ASHORE
The 'Call of the Sea Visitor Centre' relates the town's maritime and industrial history. Although it is currently closed, it may reopen in 2009.

Outside the town to the west there is an impressive stone circle at Derreenataggart (2km). Also an unexcavated ringfort can be seen at Teernahillane. To the south-west are what remains of the original Dunboy Castle – see Dunboy Bay anchorage on pages 114–115.

If the tranquillity of this coast has failed to totally

relax the crew then they may like to try 'Dzogchen Beara', which is a Buddhist Retreat Centre high above the entrance to Pulleen Harbour, Tel: 027 73032. They welcome all, with or without belief of any kind.

TRANSPORT
Bus services: Summer services operate from June to August. Sunday service on Public Holidays.
236: Cork-Bantry-Glengarriff-Adrigole-Castletownbere. Every day – summer service. Mondays, Wednesdays, Fridays and Sundays – winter service.
282: Kenmare-Ardgroom-Castletownbere. July/August only. No Sunday service.
O'Donoghue's: Bantry-Glengarriff-Castletownbere. Thursdays. Tel: 027 70007/70677.
Harringtons: Cork-Castletownbere. Not Thursdays. Tel: 027 74003/087 267 8388. Booking essential.
Taxi: AD Hackney Tel: 087 284 5796/086 346 2718; Shanahans – Atlantic Cabs Tel: 027 70116 or 086 246 1877; Beara Cabs Tel: 087 649 4796 or 086 085 7232.

OTHER INFORMATION
Police: Castletownbere, Tel: 027 70002.
Hospital: Castletownbere, Tel: 027 70004.
Tourist office: Castletownbere, Tel: 027 70054.

Only the Leprechaun was late turning up to see what the police were taking an interest in!

Mill Cove

Approach waypoint: 51°38'.82N 09°52'.00W
(1 cable ESE of Hornet SCM – 3½ cables W of
Bardini Reefer NCM)

Mill Cove is a small shallow (2m) anchorage, which offers shelter in northerly winds but no facilities, except the golf clubhouse. Aquaculture occupies a huge area immediately outside the entrance, extending well to the east of Hornet south cardinal mark.

Pilotage: From the approach waypoint, steer east of the outer limit of the fisheries. The entrance is delineated by Illaunboudane (1.5m and foul 50m all around) close to the east shore (Shore Point). To the west is Corrigagannive Point, which is foul for ½ cable east. Anchor inside the entrance as dictated by depth. The quay outside the cove is Defence Department property despite the large number of fishing pots on it! Landing, if required, is at the beach adjacent to the clubhouse on the eastern side of the quay.

Lawrence Cove

Approach waypoint: 51°38'.90N 09°49'.68W
(1 cable S of George Rock IDM)
Entrance waypoint: 51°38'.30N 09°49'.30W

Lawrence Cove Marina is a small, hospitable and really useful serviced facility which provides sheltered alongside berthing, diesel and refuge where no other alternatives exist for many miles. To get the best from this berth, it is advisable to make early contact by telephone and obtain clear instructions on where to berth using an up-to-date pontoon diagram. Do not delay telephone contact until the approach, not only because it requires attention but also the mobile phone coverage is, unusually for Ireland, poor here. Once secured alongside, plan to buy tokens for and use the showers and launderette during 'social hours' to improve the possibility of having someone on hand if difficulties are encountered.

NAVIGATION

Charts: Use SC5623.7 or Imray C56.

Tides: MHWS: 3.2m, MHWN: 2.6m., MLWN: 1.2m, MLWS: 0.4m. Standard Port Cobh, difference at HW: Springs –00:48min; Neaps –00:12min.

In the main haven, opposing flood tides run towards George Rock isolated danger mark from both directions (east and west). The ebb does the reverse.

www.irelandaerialphotography.com

Lawrence Cove Marina and Rerrin village. Hungry Hill is top left. Lonehort Harbour, Roancarrigmore lighthouse and Adrigole are to the top right

Approaching Lawrence Cove. A turn to starboard at the point (right of photo) will bring the marina into full view

Hungry Hill – the inspiration for Daphne du Maurier – and the 'rusty cylinder' mentioned in the approach pilotage

Lights & Marks

- *Bardini Reefer* (Carrigavaneen) NCM Q.
- George Rock Isolated Danger Mark Fl (2) 10s.
- Roancarrigmore Lighthouse Fl WR 3s – in the red sector.

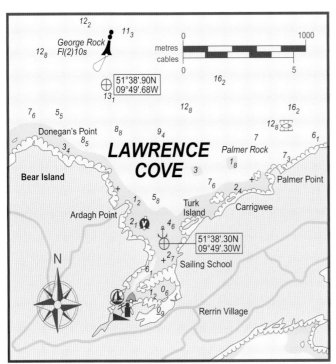

Approach: From the west, keep a sharp lookout for fishing pots to arrive at the waypoint. Turn to starboard onto 159°T. This course passes close to Ardagh Point and the four public visitors' buoys to a position just off the next headland and the entrance waypoint (see above).

From the east, the shore of Bear Island is obstructed between Palmer Point and the harbour. Palmer Rock (1.8m) is 1½ cables off shore and another rock (1.8m) lies off Turk Island. The simplest way to avoid these is to use the western approach waypoint (see page 120) and turn to port so as to approach the entrance waypoint (see page 120) from due north.

Pilotage: From the entrance waypoint, stay within 50m of the shore to the east. Look out for a small island with a large rusty cylinder on it. Leave it to port to enter the marina. The least depth en route to the long pontoon is 2.5m. Night-time entry is not advised.

BERTHING

The marina can accommodate 40 yachts on two north-easterly/south-westerly pontoons. Depths in the marina are not less than 3m below chart datum.

The long pontoon and fuelling berth (outboard)

The deepest water is to be found on the long pontoon but, when manoeuvring, stay away from the shallow patch marked by an orange buoy at the eastern end of this pontoon. Keep clear of the fuel berth during office hours. For berthing availability call the marina in advance on Tel: 027 75044; email: lcm@iol.ie; website: www.lawrencecovemarina.com.

Berthing fees: Overnight fees are €2 per metre per night.

MOORING/ANCHORING

For those not requiring an alongside berth, there are four public visitors' buoys in 3m outside the main harbour area south of Ardagh Point. Alternatively, anchor in 4m to the west of Turk Island.

Idyllic sail training. West Cork Sailing's *Jessy* manoeuvring near the Lawrence Cove mooring buoys at Ardagh Point

Useful information – Lawrence Cove

Shore facilities at the marina

FACILITIES
Fuel: Alongside diesel from the fuelling berth on the long pontoon at the bottom of the shore ramp. No petrol, gas or chandlery.
Fresh water and electricity: On the pontoons. €5 per night for electricity.
Showers and launderette: Situated in the marina building, both are token-operated. Showers cost €2 per token and for the washing and drying machines, allow €6-10.
Rubbish disposal and recycling: Chargeable and only small quantities. Unfortunately, the nearest recycling plant is, impractically, at the west end of the island.
Boatyard: Has a 14-ton boat hoist and slip. It offers hull cleaning/anti-fouling and open standing/storage.
Communications: Mobile phone coverage is very poor. There is a public telephone outside the office. No Wi-Fi, Internet access or weather forecasts.

PROVISIONING/ EATING OUT
In Rerrin village, there is a small **shop/post office**, a **bar** and a **restaurant** which, under new management, opens weekends and everyday in peak season. However, it's advisable to have a few back-up meals on board just in case the restaurant is closed. A craft shop at the marina stocks a wider and better selection of wine than the village store. The nearest convenient **supermarket** can be accessed easily from Castletownbere mooring buoys.

ASHORE
Bear Haven separates Bear Island (Bere Island or *An tOileán Mór*) from the mainland. The permanent population of the island is about 200. Two car ferries serve the island. The western ferry crosses from Castletownbere slip. The eastern ferry runs from the 'Pontoon' pier in Lough Beal, next to the golf course (4km east of Castletownbere), to Ballinakilla or Rerrin, the only village on Bear Island. Tiny Rerrin is a 10-minute walk from the marina. It has very limited facilities.

Rerrin/Lawrence Cove is not so much a 'destination' harbour, more a very welcome oasis. Bear Island, which is 3km x 7km, has some minor attractions such as the relics from its military past. These sites are: Martello Towers, one of which has recently been restored and opened as a Heritage Centre, standing stones and the Millennium Cross. The battery above Lonehort Bay is now under consideration for renovation as it has significant relics such as guns, mountings and a fort. An occasional military camp is staged on the island in the summer. The Beara Way Walk follows waymarked paths through superb scenery and provides views of the bay and the hills of the Beara Peninsula to the north. A diversion from a walking tour around these sites is the hotel bar at Ballinakilla (midway along the north shore of the island, 3km from Lawrence Cove, Tel: 027 75018). Best of all though, on a warm summer night, is relaxing in the cockpit, from where the view of Hungry Hill across Bear Haven is utterly magical. ('Hungry Hill' may sound familiar because it was the title of a Daphne du Maurier novel about the local copper-mining barons of the 19th century. It was subsequently filmed in 1947 in black and white with an all-star cast and is occasionally shown on daytime television).

TRANSPORT
There are no taxis or buses on the island.

OTHER INFORMATION
Medical: Bear Island Public Health Nurse Tel: 027 75008 or 087 220 4974.

Rerrin village store

Adrigole

(Irish: *Eádargoil*, meaning Between Two Inlets)
Approach waypoint: 51°40'.51N 09°43'.22W
(Midway in the entrance narrows)

Adrigole Harbour is beautiful and well sheltered, except for the occasional squall fostered by the presence of Hungry Hill (682m), which rises due west and dominates the landscape. It is a very picturesque location and quiet except for a little background noise from the nearby road, which is the main road from Castletownbere to anywhere.

NAVIGATION

Charts: No detailed chart, use SC5623.5, AC/LE1840 or Imray C56.

Tides (approx): MHWS: 3.3m, MHWN: 2.6m, MLWN: 1.1m, MLWS: 0.5m. Standard Port Cobh, difference at HW: Springs –00:45min; Neaps –00:25min.

Adrigole at high water looking east. Orthon's Island takes centre stage in the bay. Trafrask Bay can be seen in the background

Lights & Marks
• Roancarrigmore lighthouse Fl WR 3s.
• Carrigavaddra SCM (unlit).
• Sheep's Head, Fl (3) WR 15s;
white sector 017° to 212°T.
• Sailing Centre pier light.

Approach: **From the south-west**: Between Bear Haven and the approach waypoint are several dangers. Keep 1 cable south of Roancarrigmore to clear its offlyers.

In particular, drying Doucallia Rock (1.2m) is 1.3M south-south-west of the Adrigole entrance and can be hazardous, especially if a turn north is made too soon after passing Roancarrigmore lighthouse. Bulliga Ledge (3.7m) lies ½M south-south-west of the entrance and Roancarrigbeg Rocks are north of Roancarrigmore.

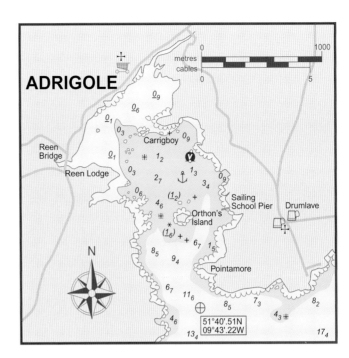

The inshore route and the western side of the harbour entrance are heavily populated with mussel beds.

From the east: Passage is clear of dangers from south of Shot Head.

Pilotage: The entrance narrows to 1.8 cables, after which the channel is to the east of Orthon's Island on a north-east track in not less than 5m. (There are rocks to the west of the island). There may be pontoons/floats off Orthon's Island's shore.

MOORING/ANCHORING

Either take one of the seven public visitors' buoys to the north-east of Orthon's Island or, alternatively, anchor in 3-5m to the north or north-west of the island or between the pier and the island in 4m. The yellow visitors' buoys seem more than able to cope with the demand. Landing is easiest at the privately-owned West Cork Sailing Centre pier.

The Adrigole public visitors' buoys are positioned at 51°41'.11N 09°43'.25W.

Orthon's Island, Adrigole. Track to the right of the pontoon towards the pier

Useful information – Adrigole

FACILITIES

Gail and Niall MacAllister, Tel: 027 60132, run the West Cork Sailing School and the pier. They welcome visiting yachts. **Showers** in their building are 'on the house' (during working hours and if not needed for classes). **Fresh water** is available as is advice on obtaining **diesel** (in cans). A **recycling** facility for glass and cans is ½km from the pier.

PROVISIONING

The **shop** is 2km to the west. Known locally as 'Peg's Shop', Tel: 027 60007, it also provides very limited **postal** services.

EATING OUT

Opposite the church in Drumlave (up the road from the quay, turn right (east) at the main road; a total distance of 1km) are Thady's Bar, Tel: 027 60008, and Murphy's Bar, run by Annie Murphy. Both are good basic bars known for musical get-togethers.

The Glenbrook Bar and Coffee Shop is to the west, near Peg's Shop. It has music on Fridays and is a favourite haunt of Gaelic football supporters, Tel: 027 60004.

ASHORE

Adrigole has a population of less than 500 and few services. The parish is spread thinly along the main road around the head of the inlet.

Orthon's Island lies centrally inside Adrigole harbour off the slip and pier. It is one of the main seal haul-out sites in Bantry Bay.

TRANSPORT

Bus services: For more information on bus services see Glengarriff on page 128. 236 Cork/Bantry-Glengarriff-Castletownbere. O'Donoghue's: Bantry-Glengarriff-Castletown. Harringtons: Cork-Castletown (booking is essential).

Taxi: Shanahans – Atlantic Cabs Tel: 027 70116 or 086 246 1877. Beara Cabs Tel: 087 649 4796/086 085 7232.

West Cork Sailing's pier

Trafrask Bay

Approach waypoint: 51°40'.44N 09°40'.77W
(3 cables NW of Shot Head)

There is a single public visitor's buoy (51°40'.83N 09°40'.27W) in a cove 2M east of Adrigole (see aerial photograph of Adrigole). This may suit those travelling westwards as either a quiet overnight stop or for lunch. The only reason to avoid the cove going east is because the single buoy may well be taken and that would mean backtracking to Adrigole. Pilotage is direct and simple into the middle of the cove. Landing is at the adjacent slipway.

ASHORE

The Sugarloaf Bar is ¾km inland. It serves some bar food at weekends, has a small grocery store (which includes a wine and beer section) and a filling station. Road fuel is available as long as the shop or bar is open, Tel: 027 60187.

Trafrask is the geographical link to the Sullivan family who, famously, experienced one of the most tragic family losses of WW2. The five Sullivan brothers joined the US Navy. The boys elected to serve on the same ship, the USS *Juneau*, which was torpedoed during a particularly ferocious battle at Guadalcanal in November 1942. Four died instantly when *Juneau* exploded, the fifth died, after five days in a liferaft, as a result of a shark attack. This tragic story directly influenced the US Navy's policy of separating serving siblings. It also provided inspiration for the more recent film *Saving Private Ryan*. The connection with Trafrask is based on the emigration of the brothers' great grandfather to the USA in 1849.

A single visitor buoy is available in Trafrask Bay

www.irelandaerialphotography.com

Illnacullen (Garinish) Island is at the entrance to Glengariff Harbour

Glengarriff
(Irish: *An Gleann Garbh*, meaning Rough Glen)
**Approach waypoint: 51°43'.80N 09°32'.28W
(2 cables W of Gun Point and 3 cables SE of
Garinish/Illnaculen)**

Glengarriff Harbour is a large sheltered inlet strewn
with attractive wooded islands and surrounded by
lush green hills. It is unanimously recommended by
all the guide books and rightly so! The harbour is
absolutely delightful with innumerable numbers of
seals, two exotic gardens, elegant houses half hidden in
the undergrowth around the shores, not to mention the
protection given from a south-westerly blow up Bantry
Bay. However, there are two Glengarriffs; the other
Glengarriff is the village, which has been designed
to meet, just, the needs of 'mass' tourism. The main
street is a ribbon development of B&Bs, restaurants,
cafés, souvenir shops and pubs. There are a few gems,
which are listed below, and a small food shop with a
good wine selection. The weather-bound sailor also
has excellent public transport a short dinghy trip away.
Buses go to Kenmare, Castletownbere and even Cork.
More frequent buses go to Bantry town. In view of the
relatively exposed moorings there, this is the preferred
way of visiting Bantry.

George Bernard Shaw, Thackeray and Sir Walter
Scott all admired Glengarriff. Thackeray couldn't find

words to describe Glengarriff: 'Within five miles around
the pretty inn of Glengarriff there is a country of the
magnificence of which no pen can give an idea'. Less
often quoted is his comment about the supposed vulgar
attitude of fellow tourists.

NAVIGATION
Charts: SC5623.4, AC1838 or Imray C56 (inset).

Tides (approx): MHWS: 3.4m, MHWN: 2.6m, MLWN:
1.1m, MLWS: 0.5m. Standard Port Cobh, difference at
HW: Springs –00:45min; Neaps –00:25min.

Lights & Marks: Upper Bantry Bay (none in Glengarriff)
• Sheelane S PHM Fl (2) R 6s.
• Coulagh PHM Fl R 3s.
• League SHM Fl (3) G 6s.
• Gerane North SHM Fl G 3s.
• Gerane West WCM Q (9) 15s.
• SBM (aka SPM) Mo (U) 15s
Morse letter 'U' – 'dot dot dash'.
• Carrigskye IDM Fl (2).

Outer approach: On the outer approach from the west,
leave the single buoy mooring (SBM), north-west off
Whiddy Island with its 530m protection zone, and
Carrigskye isolated danger mark to the south of track.
Sheelane South and Coulagh Rocks port-hand marks
identify the north shore. Stay well off Four Heads Point,
Cowdy Point and Big Point.

Before Gun Point and the approach waypoint, the shores are lined with mussel farms. Thankfully, these are all tucked in to the shore, well out of the main channel, and are predominantly marked by lit yellow buoys. There are no reliable visual bearings at this point. Keep 1 cable off both shores.

Pilotage: After Gun Point, the track is 030°T towards the gap between Ship Island and the east shore of the harbour. Ship Island is the easternmost off-island

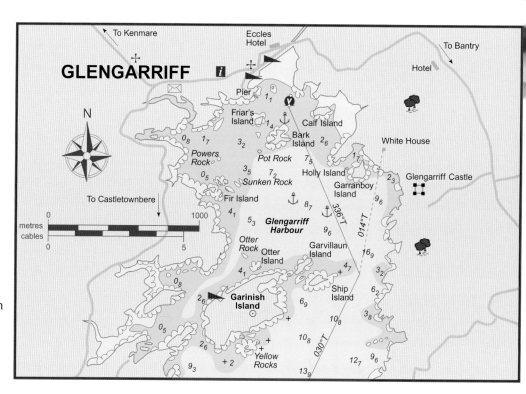

White house set into the hill beyond Ship Island

of Illnacullen. Steer to pass closer to the mainland shore than Ship Island, which has offlying shallows out to 1 cable east. As the gap is neared, a large white house set into the hill to the north will become clearer. When Ship Island is abeam and the house bears 014°T, alter course to 336°T and proceed towards the east of Bark Island.

Do not be tempted to go west of Ilnacullen as the channel is narrow and rocky, and an electricity cable crossing has a height clearance of only 15m.

Passing east of Ship Island and its many seals

At the north end of the harbour is a wide selection of moorings and anchorages (centre). The pier is busy with ferry boats. The slip, adjacent to the main road, is more convenient for the village (top right)

MOORING/ANCHORING

Six yellow public visitors' buoys are laid off Eccles Hotel, to the north-east of Bark Island, 51°44'.90N 09°32'.30W, or alternatively there are two yellow buoys south of Bark Island. These are more convenient for Illnacullen, but far from the town landing.

Options for anchoring are a) south of Bark Island in 7-10m or b) north-east of Bark Island in 3m.

Landing: There is a very visible slip directly in front of the Eccles Hotel, but a more useful slip is about 100m west. Another 100m further west is the pier, which is heavily used by commercial traffic, although an overnight stop outboard of a fishing boat may be negotiable. Both slips are on an inlet that is extremely shallow. The bottom adjacent to the slip is foul and the use of strong wellies would be preferable.

The tranquil moorings at Glengarriff off the Eccles Hotel

Useful information – Glengarriff

FACILITIES

Fresh water: Can be drawn from a domestic tap where the roads to Kenmare and Castletownbere divide.

Showers: Are available at the Eccles Hotel, Tel: 027 63003, (€12 for 15 minute room rate – several may shower).

Launderette: The village launderette is in Main Street, Tel: 027 63931.

Fuel: Road fuel (in cans) and Kosan are found at the filling station adjacent to the moorings.

Rubbish: Can be disposed of in the Tidy Town bin behind the Shamrock Store/Spinning Wheel after first identifying yourself as a visiting sailor. The store also sells **Camping Gaz**.

Communications: Wi-Fi access is available at the Glengarriff Park Hotel and free for customers. Internet access is possible 0900-2200 (€2/15min) at the Black Cat opposite Casey's Hotel on Main Street.

PROVISIONING

The Spar supermarket on Main Street has a good but limited selection of **groceries**, beer and wine, Tel: 027 63346, and also incorporates the **post office**. The filling station store (QuikPik), adjacent to the Eccles Hotel, has a hot food counter and a range of basic provisions, Tel: 027 63849. There are no banks, but the Spar and The Spinning Wheel have **foreign exchange** facilities.

EATING OUT

Glengarriff does not claim the culinary heights sought by Kinsale or Dingle and eating out here can be indifferent. Most of the restaurants are situated on Main Street, and places listed below in italics have had good reports, although it's best to seek recent personal recommendations before committing to a restaurant: *Casey's Restaurant*, Tel: 027 63072; *Blue Loo Bar*, Tel: 027 63167, which serves great salmon sandwiches at lunchtime; *The Martello Restaurant*, Tel: 027 63860 – offering French and Irish cuisine, it is family run and has an early bird menu; Cottage Bar & Restaurant Tel: 027 63226; The Spinning Wheel Café Tel: 027 63347; Bernard Harringtons/ Maple Leaf Bar Tel: 027 63021; Rainbow Restaurant/Hawthorn Bar Tel: 027 63449/63315.

Adjacent to the slipway are The Old Church Café, Tel: 027 63663, and *Eccles Hotel* Tel: 027 63003.

ASHORE

The main attraction for the tourist are the gardens on Garinish Island. Ashore, the form 'Ilnacullin' is mostly used instead of Illnacullen on the Admiralty chart and other variants. It is a contraction of *Oileán an Chulinn*, which is Irish for 'Island of Holly'. These gardens were designed by Harold Peto for Annan Bryce, a former Scottish MP for Inverness. The features include a colonnaded Italianate garden, a Grecian Temple, a walled garden and a Martello Tower hidden in the trees. The gardens flourish thanks to the Gulf Stream and the protection of the surrounding hills. Bryce died in 1923 before the gardens reached maturity but his family continued his work until 1953. The island is now publicly owned and maintained by Heritage Ireland, Tel: 027 63040. Open March to October – times vary. Adult fee €3.70. Facilities provided include toilets, restaurant/tearooms and self-guiding trails.

A dinghy tour of the harbour en route to Illnacullen (Garinish Island) will be an attractive proposition, especially at low water when there are larger numbers of seals hauling-out, particularly on Garvillaun and Ship Islands (the two islands off the east and north-east side of Illnacullen). Otters are rare but can be seen in the harbour. It is essential not to disturb seals and other wildlife. Although the local tourist boats can closely approach the seals, they are ignored because they are 'familiar'. Dinghies, on the other hand, are rarer and the seals may panic. For Illnacullen, use the official landing point, midway along the north of the island. There is a stony beach at low water, and otherwise a slip. Secure opposite to where the small ferries dock. The boathouse and slip on the north-east side are private.

Local attractions: Worth a visit is the somewhat unusual Bamboo Park, Tel: 027 62570, with its exotic collection of tree ferns, bamboos and palms. The park is a little east of the Eccles Hotel. Glengarriff Woods Nature Reserve encloses a native oak forest a little to the west of the village. There are walks to suit all constitutions.

TRANSPORT

Bus services: Summer services operate from the last week in June to the end of August. No services on Public Holidays. 236 Cork-Bantry-Glengarriff-Adrigole- Castletownbere. Every day (summer service). Mondays, Wednesdays, Fridays and Sundays (winter service). 252 Bantry-Glengarriff-Kenmare-Killarney. Daily summer service only. O'Donoghue's: Bantry-Glengarriff-Adrigole-Castletownbere. Thursdays. Tel: 027 70007 or 027 70677. Harringtons: Cork-Glengarriff-Adrigole-Castletownbere. Not on Thursdays. Tel: 027 74003 or 087 267 8388. Booking is essential.

Taxi: Glengarriff Cabs and Coaches, Main Street, Tel: 087 973 0741; Pat Somers' Limousine Service, Main Street, Tel: 027 63397; Harrington's Coach & Hackney Service, Tel: 086 105 0828; Billy Downey's Cabs, Tel: 087 297 1837.

OTHER INFORMATION

All locations are on Main Street.

Police: Tel: 027 63002.

Doctor: Glengarriff Medical Centre opens daily, Tel: 027 63300.

Tourist office: Tel: 027 63084.

The gardens on Garinish Island

Bantry
(Irish: *Beanntraí*)

North approach waypoint: 51°42'.52N 09°28'.80W
(1 cable N of Whiddy Point East)

West approach waypoint: 51°40'.00N 09°31'.50W
(On the entrance transit, 3 cables offshore in 10m)

Bantry is a busy modernised town and the region's commercial centre. In summer the centrepiece, Wolfe Tone Square, hosts street entertainers and craft markets. Bantry makes few concessions to the visiting yachtsman. The inner harbour dries and the main anchorage and moorings are a step along the Cork Road towards the graveyard. This anchorage is prone to a south-westerly wind as it is funnelled around the headland, making for a potentially choppy dinghy trip to and from the shore. Glengarriff is an alternative haven, from where a regular bus service travels to Bantry.

Apart from the extensive range of shops, the other big local attraction is Bantry House and Garden for its furniture and tapestry collections, the magnificent views from the gardens and the 1796 French Armada Exhibition.

NAVIGATION

Entrances: There are two entrances to Bantry Harbour. The primary entrance is to the north of Whiddy Island and then east of Horse Island and the two Chapel Islands, through a buoyed, lit channel. The western entrance is advised only in settled seas with 3M visibility and at high water.

Charts: Use SC5623.4, AC1838 or Imray C56 (inset).

Tides: MHWS: 3.2m, MHWN: 2.4m, MLWN: 1.1m, MLWS: 0.4m. Standard Port Cobh, difference at HW: Springs –00:45min; Neaps –00:25min.

Tides are weak at approximately 0.5kn to the north-east of Whiddy Island, but can reach 1.5kn at springs in the narrow part of the western entrance.

Lights & Marks: Upper Bantry Bay
- Sheelane South PHM Fl (2) R 6s.
- Coulagh PHM Fl R 3s.
- League SHM Fl (3) G 6s.
- Gerane North SHM Fl G 3s.
- Gerane West WCM Q (9) 15s.
- SBM (aka SPM) Mo (U) 15s.
- Carrigskye IDM Fl (2).

The northern entrance to Bantry Harbour is around the north-east corner of Whiddy Island – in the centre of the photograph

www.irelandaerialphotography.com

Lights & Marks: Bantry Harbour
- Horse SHM Fl G 6s.
- Gurteenroe PHM Fl R 3s.
- Chapel SHM Fl G 2s.
- Fundy SHM Fl (2) G 10s.

Lights & Marks: Western Entrance
- Whiddy Point West Fl Y.
- Whiddy Jetty Fl (3) G 15s.

Approach from the north and Glengarriff: From the north coast of Bantry Bay, clear Sheelane South and Coulagh Rocks port-hand marks, the League and Gerane North starboard-hand marks, the single point mooring (also referred to on some charts as single buoy mooring {SBM}) and Carrigskye isolated danger mark to arrive at the approach waypoint. Alternatively, if arriving from Glengarriff, keeping Carrigskye isolated danger mark close to starboard before turning for the approach waypoint will clear Carrigskye Islet and Castle Breaker (3.8m). **Note:** the single point mooring has a 530m protection zone and, more substantively, a 100m floating hose which lies low in the water.

Pilotage from the north: There are a large number of mussel farms in the north approach to Bantry Harbour. These are generally well marked by lit yellow buoys

Horse starboard-hand mark

– as a precaution, keep 2 cables off all islands. From the approach waypoint, steer 119°T to arrive north-east of Horse starboard-hand mark. Alter course to 192°T. This course will leave Gurteenroe port-hand mark close to port. It marks the west edge of the shoal extending from Gurteenroe Point and, incidentally, a mussel farm. On the same course, leave Chapel starboard-hand mark to starboard. This buoy identifies the east

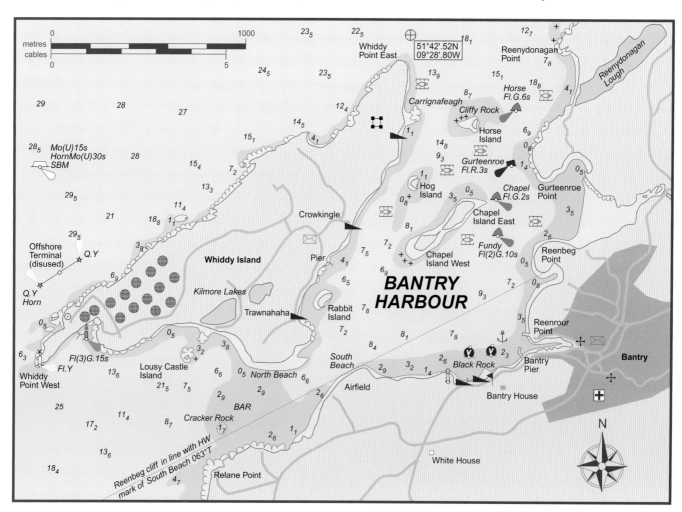

edge of the shoal extending from the north-east end of Chapel Island East. Fundy starboard-hand mark was introduced 1.8 cables south in 2008, which is consistent with altering course at Chapel starboard-hand mark to around 180°T for the west of Bantry Pier.

Approach from the west: Whiddy Island has several obstructions to the west – The Gerane Rocks all lie north of the west cardinal buoy. Cracker Rock (1.7m) and a bar (with depth of 2m) are the main dangers.

Pilotage from the west: Approach Relane Point (south-west of the entrance narrows) on a heading of 063°T. Keep the high-water mark on South Beach (seaward edge of airfield) in line with the cliff on the south side of Reenbeg Point (distant rounded hill) to clear Cracker Rock. Off Blue Hill (a 33m heavily-wooded hill west of the airfield and South Beach) edge to port and stay around 100m off the beach, keeping in a 5m depth of water.

MOORING/ANCHORING

Moor on one of 12 orange visitors' buoys laid approximately east-west outside of all other moorings between the pier and the graveyard (€6 per night – payable by depositing it at the sailing club, opposite their slip near the entrance gate to Bantry House, or at the harbour office). The moorings are administered by the Harbour Commissioners, whose offices are next door to the tourist office on Wolfe Tone Square, Tel: 027 51253/53277. Land at the sailing club slipway. It is also possible to land at either the pier or the slipway below the graveyard,

From the burial ground at the bottom of the photo, the main road from Cork follows the shoreline into the centre of Bantry town

however both of these are used commercially and therefore subject to frequent traffic. The sailing club is a 1km walk from the town. **Note**: Extensive works are planned for 2009 to build a new Ro-Ro slip north of the graveyard.

Anchoring off the pier is possible but there is considerable traffic and the bottom is prone to fouling the anchor. Alternatively, anchor outside the mooring buoys. Beware of Black Rock if manoeuvring close in to the shore.

Bantry slip and burial ground – 1km west of Wolfe Tone Square

Useful information – Bantry

FACILITIES
Road fuel can conveniently be obtained from the filling station close to the pier but, impractically, **green diesel** has to be transported 1km from out of town.

Available on the pier are limited **rubbish disposal** facilities and **fresh water**. Alternatively, fresh water as well as **showers** can be had at Bantry Bay Sailing Club, when open. For **laundry**, go to Rosie's Launderette, Tel: 027 55501, which is situated in Bridge Street. **Wi-Fi** is available at Vickery's Inn in New Street, while **Internet** access is provided by fast.net in Bridge Street, Tel: 027 51624.

PROVISIONING
There are several **supermarkets** close to the centre of town and a Spar shop that shuts at 2200, which also has the advantage of being nearer to the landing places. The larger stores are: SuperValu, New Street, Tel: 027 50001; Centra, Chapel Street, Tel:

027 51247; Mace, Main Street, Tel: 027 50219. **Market Day** is the first Friday of each month. Two **pharmacies** are situated on the Square: Coen's Tel: 027 50531 and O'Sullivans Tel: 027 50113. **Banks**: Both the Bank Of Ireland and the AIB are in Wolfe Tone Square and have ATMs and foreign exchange facilities.

EATING OUT
A good selection of pubs may be found concentrated on New Street, Barrack Street and The Square. To single one out of many, try Murphy's Bar and shop on New Street for a touch of Old Ireland.

The majority of restaurants are located along the southern side of the quay and in the Square. Beyond here only El Gitano Tapas Bar in New Street is worth a mention. There will be something to satisfy most appetites and budgets. The Snug is highly recommended. It has received Bridgestone

Wolfe Tone's statue

Bantry: Wolfe Tone Square

Useful information – Bantry (continued)

Bantry House and Garden

awards consistently from 2000 to 2008. It is cosy, intimate and has a simple but comprehensive menu. Be prepared to perch where space permits, Tel: 027 50057. Other restaurants include O'Connors (BIM accredited), Tel: 027 50242, The Waterfront – family dining and reasonably priced – Tel: 027 53933, and Eastern Tandoori, Tel: 027 56800. Some only open at weekends (The Mariner and De Barra's).

ASHORE
Bantry House, the seat of the Earls of Bantry, is the main attraction for visitors, Tel: 027 50047. The entrance is conveniently close to the visitors' moorings. Dating from the early 1700s, it attracts a variety of reactions. Some are pleased that the renovation has been kept to a minimum, thereby preserving a little more semblance of how it would have been in days gone by. Others are disappointed

by that same lack of renovation. For those of neither opinion, the exhibits are interesting, especially the tapestries and portraits displayed in exotically-decorated rooms. It also incorporates a coffee shop.

The well-kept gardens are stepped and marble statues prevail. With a little climbing, stunning views over the house, harbour and distant hills will be revealed. (An even better view can be had from the viewpoint at the summit of the road past Sheskin – 1½km south-south-east out of town).

A failed 1796 French invasion known as the 'French Armada' is illustrated in a small exhibition in the adjacent grounds and worth a visit. It describes the attempt by Irish Nationalist Wolfe Tone and French Admiral Hoche to invade – see separate panel on page 134.

The town also boasts a three-screen cinema which is tucked in next to the Marine Hotel on

the quay, Tel: 027 55777; website: www. cinemaxbantry.com.

TRANSPORT
Bus services: Summer services operate from the last week in June to the end of August. No services on Public Holidays.
236: Bantry-Glengarriff-Adrigole-Castletownbere. Every day in summer. In winter a bus runs to Glengarriff on Mondays, Wednesdays, Fridays and Sundays.
236: Cork-Bantry. Daily service (also: 252 Cork-Skibbereen-Bantry in summer only).
252: Bantry-Glengarriff-Kenmare-Killarney. Daily summer service.
255: Bantry-Durrus-Ahakista (Kitchen Cove)-Kilcrohane. Twice each way on Saturdays only (this route is along the north shore of Dunmanus Bay).
O'Donoghue's: Bantry-Glengarriff-Adrigole-Castletownbere. Thursdays. Tel: 027 70007/70677.

Harringtons: Cork-Bantry-Castletownbere. Not Thursdays. Tel: 027 74003 or 087 267 8388.
Bantry Rural Transport, 5 Main Street, Bantry, Tel: 027 52727.
Taxi: Liam Ward Tel: 027 61476/086 855 6189; Ken McGuirk Tel: 086 086 0860; Buddy's Cabs Tel: 027 51503; Bishop's Tel: 086 882 8176. Daytime service: CallACar Tel: 027 52373; George Plant Tel: 027 50654; Mal's Cabs Tel: 027 51488.
Bicycle hire: Nigel's Rent-a-Bike Tel: 027 52657.
Air: Cork airport is approximately 1½ hours by car.

OTHER INFORMATION
Harbour master: Tel: 027 53277.
Police: Tel: 027 50045.
Hospital: Tel: 027 50133.
Doctor: Tel: 027 50405.
Dentist: Mark Foley, William Street, Tel: 027 51424, and S O'Luasa, The Square, Tel: 027 50027.
Tourist office: On Wolfe Tone Square, Tel: 027 50229.

People and events around Bantry Bay

Marine Farms

Bantry Bay plays a significant role in Ireland's farmed seafood industry, which is worth well in excess of €100M, with shellfish worth €63M of this total.

Approximately 4,000 tonnes of mussels are harvested annually in Bantry Bay. Increasingly the mussels are processed before export. The typical mussel farm uses 'stocking' nets suspended from long lines, strung between flotation barrels.

Two salmon farms operate in the bay, one producing organic salmon. There is an abalone (large, edible sea snail) farm on Bear Island. Sea urchins' seed is nurtured and supplied to a co-operative of growers in both Bantry and Dunmanus Bays. The seed is brought on in conditions close to those that would occur naturally. Production is principally for export to France. Approximately four tonnes of oysters are harvested annually.

Maërl (calcified red seaweed nodules which grow unattached on the seabed) is dredged east of Bear Island. It is used in agriculture as a grassland fertiliser in animal feeds and in cosmetics. The processed seaweed is widely exported.

Mussel farms in upper Bantry Bay are mostly marked by yellow buoys

O'Sullivan Beare

O'Sullivan Beare was the local Clan Lord who lived in Dunboy Castle. When English forces defeated an Irish/Spanish allied force at Kinsale, he marched for 20 days with 1,000 soldiers to Leitrim to join the remnants of the rebellion. Only 35 men made it all the way. Many of the others left the march to settle in places along the route. In his absence, the English destroyed Dursey Castle in 1602. Dunboy Castle was also destroyed after a siege in the summer of 1602. The 58 survivors of the two-week siege were executed in the nearby market square and the power of the O'Sullivan clan was broken.

The Battle of Bantry Bay (1689)

A French fleet arrived in Bantry Bay in 1689 to bolster support for James II against William of Orange and successfully landed 1,500 men with money, arms and ammunition. An inconclusive battle between the French and the Royal Navy followed, taking place off Sheep Head and Bear Island. James II was subsequently defeated at the Battle of the Boyne in 1690.

Wolfe Tone and Richard White (1796)

In 1796, French Admiral Hoche, accompanied by Wolfe Tone, an Irish patriot, with a fleet of 50 ships carrying 14,000 troops, attempted to invade in Bantry Bay. They hoped to inspire a rebellion, banish the English and install an Irish Republic. Although Richard White of Bantry had a loyal, well-trained militia ready to repulse the invasion, bad weather overtook events and the French lost 10 ships. It was 1982 before divers found the wreck of the *Surveillante* off Whiddy Island. It is now a national monument and, where possible, the ship and its contents are being recovered, preserved and exhibited.

Bantry remembers both men: Wolfe Tone is commemorated by a statue in the Square and Richard White by Bantry House (he went on to become the first Earl of Bantry).

UK Sovereign base – Bear Haven Treaty Port

Following Irish Independence, one of the practicalities that had to be dealt with was the relocation of large strategic military bases. Bantry Bay, with its commanding location near the North Atlantic, 10° west of London, was not a facility that could be moved overnight. The Royal Navy was given until 1938 to leave its base at Bear Haven. Originally, the failed French Armada in 1796 had spurred the fortification of the harbour but as the enemy and technology changed, the value of the base, with its deep, sheltered anchorages, grew. During WW1 Bear Haven was used by the British and Americans to protect the Atlantic sea lanes. It was obvious that the loss of the Royal Navy base just before the start of WW2 would contribute to the losses of convoy ships heading for Europe. Among the appellants calling for retention of the base was Winston Churchill, but to no avail. The harbour was returned to Irish sovereignty in 1938. The strategic loss was replaced when Britain occupied Iceland in 1940 and established a Royal Naval base there.

The *Bardini Reefer*

Anyone passing through Bear Haven cannot fail to see the sunken wreck of the *Bardini Reefer* marked by its north cardinal buoy. The *Bardini Reefer* was a fishing factory ship that suffered a fire and sank. It now rests very obviously on the bottom. At high water masts and an inner funnel flue show several metres above the water.

The *Bardini Reefer* partly submerged in Bear Haven

Dunmanus Bay

Chapter five
Dunmanus Bay

Dunmanus Bay is a cul-de-sac for connoisseurs. It is rarely visited by road or by sea as it is not on the well-publicised visitor itineraries for either. Historically, many east and south coast cruising sailors have thought twice of travelling west of Mizen Head for fear of being trapped by the weather. Visitors' numbers are further reduced as many, in fact most, craft head directly across the mouth of the bay for the secure havens of Bantry Bay and Long Island Bay. Furthermore, the Imray chart does not have an inset for any harbour in this bay. It is almost as if there is a concerted effort to conserve the bay for those 'in-the-know'. This is a great pity because a night at anchor in Kitchen Cove on a beautiful summer evening would be balm for any troubled spirit. One notable exception to this attempted concealment is the British Admiralty, which considers the bay worthy of two full size charts in a Leisure Folio and three harbour inserts on yet another sheet. This may be a legacy of anchoring Royal Navy patrol boats here in WW1. Some other connoisseurs have discovered the bay; divers and gardeners. Divers appreciate the clear water due to the lack of tidal movement. Gardeners can anchor close to some of the most popular garden sites in South-West Ireland. The climate in the bay has resulted in three of Cork's most visited gardens hugging its shoreline – for more details see later in this section on page 143.

Inland from the entrance to the bay between the rocky cliffs of Sheep's Head (Muntervary) and Three Castle Head, Dunmanus Bay changes its aspect gradually over its length to a photogenic pastoral idyll lined with meadows. Its distinction is that it has a history more to do with copper mining than fishing and agriculture, but nature has done a very efficient job of obscuring the little remaining evidence of this along the shoreline. Sheep's Head sports a prominent light, giving guidance only into Bantry Bay. Three Castle Head has no light but, when approached from the south-west in daylight, a distinctive ruined castle in a dip short of the headland is its 'signature'. There are no navigation lights in the bay so a night passage is inadvisable.

The Atlantic swell penetrates well into the bay and will cause breakers, particularly on Carbery Island; anchoring decisions therefore need to be carefully considered.

Three Castle Head

This chapter is structured somewhat differently to the other chapters to more concisely describe the self-contained nature of Dunmanus Bay and its harbours. Vessels making a passage across the entrance of the bay (between Sheep's Head and Three Castle Head) should refer to the passage information in adjacent chapters.

Another oddity of the bay is that the combination of agricultural run-off, little tide and summer temperatures make the bay susceptible to algae growth.

There are only three small villages along the north side of the bay – Kilcrohane, Durrus and, more by way of a hamlet, Ahakista, whose anchorage is known as Kitchen Cove. The only other area of heavy population is on the Carbery, Cold and Furze Islands, which abound with seals. Another peculiarity of the area is the numerous aspects that depend on the enthusiasm of a small number of individuals. Well-liked attractions can disappear as individuals move on (by way of an example, Ahakista's unusual 'tin pub', whose closure in January 2008 was widely lamented, has since reopened).

Off the coast on 23 June 1985 Air India Flight 182 from Montreal to London was completely and instantly destroyed by a bomb. Wreckage was initially found by the cargo vessel, *Laurentian Forest*. There were no survivors. Over 200 Canadian citizens died in Canada's largest terrorist atrocity. As a memorial Canada has erected the Air India monument, in beautifully manicured gardens a short walk north of Ahakista Pier.

The population hereabouts is still at approximately 15% of its pre-famine level. It is only conjecture that the unpopulated shores of Dunmanus Bay influenced the choice of landing place for the €440m drugs haul in 2007 at Dunlough Bay (Three Castle Head) and the regular appearance of the customs launch ever since. It should be evident from this preamble that a vessel must be fully provisioned when visiting Dunmanus Bay (and have no reason to attract a rummage by the gentlemen in their high-speed, grey craft).

The harbours in the bay have, to a very large degree, common navigational and local information. Where appropriate, further information is given on the individual harbours.

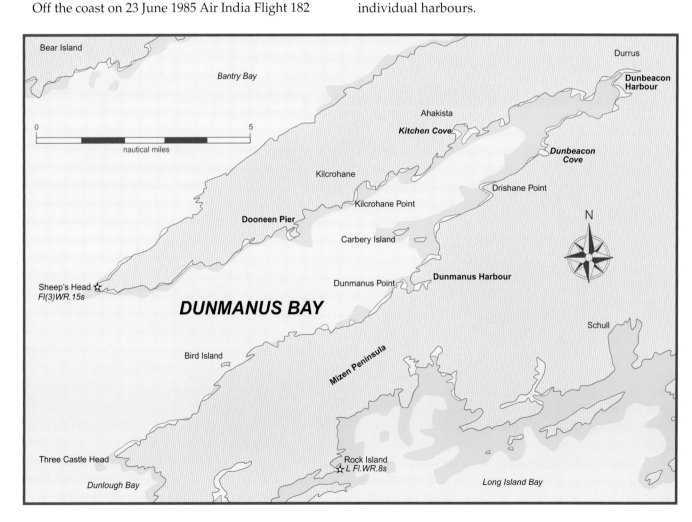

WEATHER INFORMATION BROADCASTS
This bay is served by the Valentia Coastguard transmitter at Mizen Head on VHF Ch 04. An advisory announcement is made initially on Ch 16.

SAFETY INFORMATION
This section of the coast is managed by Valentia Coastguard, Tel: 066 947 6109.

COASTGUARD AIS STATION
Mizen (Mt Gabriel)
51°33'.36N 09°32'.59W   MMSI 002 500370

COMMON NAVIGATION DATA FOR DUNMANUS BAY
Charts: Use Admiralty SC5623.8 & SC5623.9, SC5623.6B for Dunbeacon Harbour, 6C for Kitchen Cove, 6D for Dunmanus Harbour. The alternative standard chart is AC/LE2552. There were many changes to the charts in 2007. Check the latest Notices to Mariners.

Tides (approx): MHWS 3.3m, MHWN 2.5m, MLWN 1.0m, MLWS 0.3m. Tidal streams are negligible.

Standard Port Cobh, difference at HW: Springs −01:00min; Neaps −00:30min.

Lights & Marks
The only light is Sheep's Head, Fl (3) WR 15s; white sector 017° to 212°T. Dunmanus Bay is not illuminated by Sheep's Head light. The lighthouse was installed in 1968 to improve navigation for large oil tankers making their way to the oil terminal on Whiddy Island in Bantry Bay.

Lord Brandon's Tower, midway between Kilcrohane and Ahakista, serves as a useful mark. (It was built, circa 1847, as a famine relief project).

Approach to the bay: Both Sheep's Head and Three Castle Head are clean beyond 1 cable except for (North) Bullig (6m), 2 cables west of Sheep's Head, and South Bullig (4.5m), 4 cables south-west of Three Castle Head. The usual precautions should be taken concerning tidal streams at headlands.

Pilotage in the bay: Rocks extend 3 cables west-south-west of Carbery Island. Passage east of Carbery Island is fraught and not recommended.

Useful information – Dunmanus Bay

Kitchen Cove and Dunmanus Harbour are the two substantive havens in Dunmanus Bay and warrant a visit as part of a comprehensive cruise of Southern Ireland. These harbours are described in full on pages 139 and 144 respectively. There are also minor piers and anchorages that are included here to assist skippers to assess their usefulness, should the need arise.

A comprehensive hardware store can be found in Durrus, but fuel is not readily obtainable locally.

EATING ASHORE
There are restaurants only in Durrus and Kilcrohane. All three villages have pubs, some of which may serve food. It is safest to assume that eating on board is the surest option in Kitchen Cove. There are neither pubs nor restaurants on the south shore.

TRANSPORT
Bus services: 255 Bantry-Durrus-Ahakista (Kitchen Cove)-Kilcrohane: Twice each way on Saturdays. **Taxi:** O'Mahoney's Cabs, Kilcrohane, Tel: 027 67095/086 856 9159.

Panorama of Dunmanus Bay from the ruined tower above Dunbeacon Cove. Dunmanus Bay extends to the Carbery Islands and Sheep's Head

Anchorages along the north shore

Dooneen Pier
Approach waypoint: 51°33′.84N 09°43′.30W
(2½ cables E of pier in 30m)

Dooneen Pier, marked as 'Lndg' on the chart, is an old, decaying, stone pier with widely spaced rotten timber pile facings. It is included here for information only and is not recommended. It has landing steps.

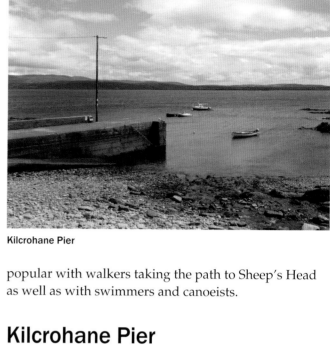

Kilcrohane Pier

Approaching Dooneen Pier

Pilotage: The bottom rises rapidly as the pier is approached – anchoring should be left to a skipper's discretion.

ASHORE
There are no facilities here or for several kilometres now that the nearest pub has closed. The environs are very popular with walkers taking the path to Sheep's Head as well as with swimmers and canoeists.

Kilcrohane Pier
(Irish: *Cill Crochain*, meaning The Church of Crochan)
Approach waypoint: 51°34′.48N 09°41′.40W
(2½ cables E of pier)

Kilcrohane Pier, marked as 'Lndg' on the chart, gives access to the village facilities and a well-known garden.

Pilotage: The bottom rises rapidly as the pier is approached – anchoring must be at a skipper's discretion. If going ashore, consideration should be given to leaving a competent person behind on anchor watch.

ASHORE
A lane from the pier leads up to Kilcrohane village, 1½km away. O'Mahoney's is a comprehensive emporium where Frank tries to answer 'yes' to most customer requests by holding stock geared to match the seasonal visitor's needs. The shop sells Kosan, diesel and petrol as well as combining grocery, post office, restaurant, café and wine bar, Tel: 027 67001.

The shore side garden, Cois Cuain, is nearby – see page 143 for details.

There are also several pubs to choose from, including The Bay View Inn, Tel: 027 67981, and Eileen Fitzpatrick's Bar, which serves sandwiches and bar snacks, Tel: 027 67057.

www.irelandaerialphotography.com

Kilcrohane looking east at high water springs. The pier is tucked in north of Kilcrohane Point (right). Moored boats lie off Cois Cuain gardens at the bottom of the photo

www.irelandaerialphotography.com

The approach to Kitchen Cove from the south with Owen's Island in the centre. The photo was taken at high water springs

Kitchen Cove
(Ahakista village)
Approach waypoint: 51°35'.44N 09°38'.17W
(2½ cables SW of Owen's Island)

Possibly the only reason that this harbour does not receive more visitors is the 22M round trip to the mouth of the bay. This is a great pity as it offers as many attractions as several other 'favourites' on this coast along with excellent shelter, being protected from all winds except southerlies, in a beautiful tranquil setting. Like so many things in life, the best things speak for themselves and do not need long adjective-filled descriptions. Kitchen Cove is one such place, despite the shrill cacophony made by the oystercatchers on Owen's Island.

NAVIGATION
Harbour chart: Use Admiralty SC5623.6C or AC/LE2552.

Approach: From the south, the 11M direct track from clear of South Bullig off Three Castle Head to Kitchen Cove is unobstructed. From Bantry Bay and points north, round Sheep's Head and keep 2 cables offshore. This will clear all dangers and approximates to the 30m contour to beyond Pointabulloge (1M south-west of the approach waypoint).

Pilotage: From the approach waypoint, steer 017°T for ½M. Stay in a 5m depth until 1 cable short of the pier. Rocks encroach from the shore to virtually encircle the inner harbour, helping to add to the protection. The deepest water at the entrance is at the mid point of the gap in the surrounding rocks. However, one such rock dries (0.2m), but is marked by a pole topped with a well-worn flag. This is immediately to port of the entry track and must be given due respect.

Alternative pilotage: The passage north of Owen's Island, the islet guarding the entrance to the cove, is flanked by rocks and has a least depth of 2.6m. Strangers are advised against entering here.

The inner harbour is ringed by rocks. The drying rock immediately to port of the entry track is marked by a pole (viewed from inside the harbour)

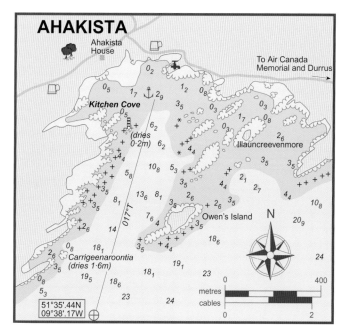

The Air India memorial

Ahakista's Tin Pub

ANCHORING/BERTHING

Anchor in 3m south of Ahakista Pier. The pier has less than 0.5m at its outer end.

ASHORE

Ashore there are two pubs. A short walk south is the well-known Ahakista Bar (The Tin Pub – see page 136) which opens at 1600, Tel: 027 67203. Arundel's Pub overlooks the harbour and has an excellent garden which slopes down to the shore, giving a beautiful view of the moorings, Tel: 027 67033. The Air India Memorial Garden is a short walk north of the pier (see page 136). Wi-Fi is available from DigitalForge in the harbour. Fresh water can be obtained, on a hose, midway along the pier.

Kitchen Cove, Arundel's Pub and pier

Dunbeacon Harbour

(For Durrus village)

Approach waypoint: 51°36'.00N 09°36'.00W
(2 cables ESE of Reen Point)
Entrance waypoint: 51°36'.30N 09°34'.30W
(1 cable north of Twopoint Island)

Positioned at the head of Dunmanus Bay, this is a large shallow bay with many islets and much mussel farming. It is very convenient for landing at the new pier, 1½km from Durrus, which is the nearest to 'busy' that occurs in the area. It is also well situated for access to two of the gardens on the bay. Despite its distance 'inland', the harbour has a windswept feel, exposed as it is to the south-west along the length of Dunmanus Bay.

NAVIGATION

Harbour chart: Use Admiralty SC5623.6B or AC/LE2552.

Approach: Upper Dunmanus Bay has several obstructions that need attention before closing the harbour entrance. A submerged rock (1.7m) 2½ cables off the north shore and two obstructions (4 to 5m) off the south shore leave a 2½ cable-wide channel for passage.

Dunbeacon Harbour. To the south of Mannion's Island the harbour is taken up with extensive mussel farming

The charted leading line for this passage depends on clear and unambiguous visibility (over approximately 10M) to Three Castle Head. Taking bearings over that distance may not be dependable. It may be better, in near zero tide conditions, to do a running fix backed up by GPS. Try using the Promontory (Old) Fort – a ruined tower abeam the obstructions. Once clear of the obstructions, the track to the entrance waypoint is uncluttered in at least a 10m depth.

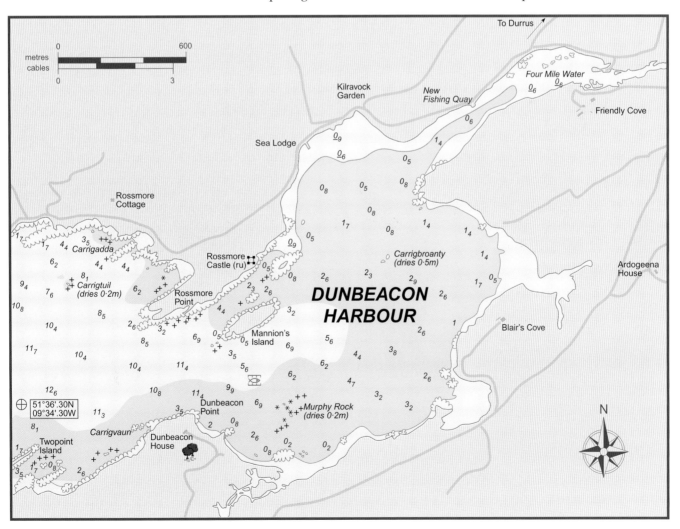

Mannion's Island

Entrance pilotage: The entrance is between Rossmore Point (to the north) and Dunbeacon Point (to the south). There are no charted leading beacons into the harbour. Always stay north of a line with Twopoint Island open of Dunbeacon Point to clear Murphy Rock (in fact a group of rocks), which fouls the south side of the harbour. From the entrance waypoint, steer on 078°T to be midway between Dunbeacon Point and Mannion's Island, keeping in more than 5m until south of Mannion's Island (Mannion's Rock is foul to its south-west for ½ cable). A large house on the far shore may be used as a guide. Keep north of the marine farms. Three cables north-east of Mannion's Island lies Carrigbroanty Rock, which dries (0.5m). North of Carrigbroanty, the water shallows to less than 2m in general.

ANCHORING
Anchor east of Mannion's Island in 2-4m and clear of marine farms or berth at high water alongside the new pier to the north-east. Time alongside will be determined by a least depth of approximately 0.5m between Carrigbroanty Rock and the pier.

Useful information – Durrus village (Irish: *Dubh Ros*, meaning Black Headland) or Dúrras

Five roads meet in the compact village, which has a small but good selection of services for such a little place.

FACILITIES/ PROVISIONING
The Londis **mini-market** sells **Kosan gas** and includes a hot food counter.

Wiseman's hardware store stocks **Camping Gaz**, Tel: 027 61070.

EATING OUT
The Good Things Café, Tel: 027 61426; website: www. thegoodthingscafe.com, is dedicated to all things culinary and even a non 'foodie' will appreciate this café and restaurant, which is conveniently situated between the new pier and the village. The café's Porter Cake is memorable.

Four hostelries also providing a range of food are: The Long Boat, Sheep's Head Bar & Restaurant, Tel: 027 62822, Ross's Bar and O'Súlleabháin's (O'Sullivan's), which is a fine example of a traditional pub, Tel: 027 61155.

ASHORE
Durrus has two public gardens which capitalise on the temperate climate; the two-acre Carraig Abhainn Gardens and the Kilravock Gardens – see page 143.

Durrus village crossroads

O'Súlleabháin's, Durrus village

Anchorages along the southern shore

Dunbeacon Cove

Approach waypoint: 51°35'.58N 09°35'.28W
(2 cables west of ruined fort and the midpoint
of Mount Gabriel radomes at 142°T)

This anchorage, for very small craft, has little to recommend it except in settled weather or as a refuge in an easterly blow. There are no facilities nearby.

Pilotage/Anchoring: From the approach waypoint, steer 135°T to anchor in 4-5m. Note that Carriglea Rock (3.2m) and its northerly offlyers obstruct the anchorage to the south and south-west.

Dunbeacon Cove

Ruined fort outside Dunbeacon Cove

Dunmanus Bay Gardens
The best time to visit the gardens is during the two-week period in June when a large number of gardens in West Cork and Kerry are open to the public. Together they are promoted as a 'Trail'. See www.westcorkgardentrail.com/ for details. At other times, the gardens open generally by appointment.

Cois Cuain, Kilcrohane, Tel: 027 67070/087 212 6290. Cois Cuain is a two acre garden located on the shoreline. It has appeared regularly on television. Inevitably, it features salt and wind resistant plants but also rare plants from the Southern Hemisphere. Open by appointment (€5); website: www.aseasidegarden.net.

Kilravock Gardens, Durrus: Tel: 027 61111/087 816 1526. Kilravock is a two acre garden on the Kilcrohane Road out of Durrus, south of the pier. It has Mediterranean and Southern Hemisphere areas, which have received international attention. Open by appointment (€6); website: www.kilravockgardens.com.

Carraig Abhainn Gardens, Durrus: Tel: 027 61070. This is a woodland garden with its own natural waterfall and millstream. Unusual bridges and statues augment the sheltered environment. Open daily (Sundays by appointment) (€5); website: www.carraigabhainngardens.com.-

Kilravock Gardens, Durrus

Dunmanus Castle, Dunmanus Harbour with Kilcrohane on the far side of the bay and Hungry Hill (in Bantry Bay) in the distance

Dunmanus Harbour

(Irish: *Dhun Manais*)

Approach waypoint: 51°32'.89N 09°39'.94W
(½M – 353°T from Dunmanus Castle)

The south shore of Dunmanus Bay is rugged cliff face most of the way between Three Castle Head and this delightful haven due south of Carbery Island. The anchorage is sheltered except from the north.

The afternoon sun illuminates Dunmanus Castle at the south end of the harbour. The landing quay is behind the small island in the harbour

www.irelandaerialphotography.com

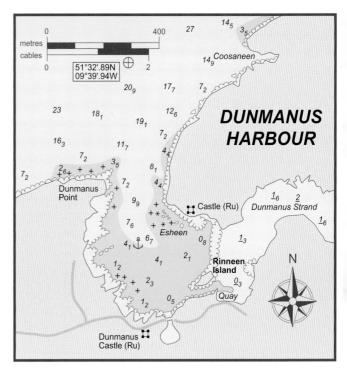

Harbour chart: Use Admiralty SC5623.6D or AC/LE2552.

Marks: There is the very conspicuous ruin of Dunmanus Castle at the south of the bay.

Pilotage/anchoring: From the approach waypoint steer 173°T. The entrance is less than 1 cable wide at its narrowest point, the prime culprit being the confusion of rocks spreading from the east shore. Anchor in 4-6m, clear of moorings. Landing is at the quay in the southeast corner of the bay, hidden behind Rinneen Island.

There are no facilities nearby.

The Fastnet Rock lighthouse and Cape Clear Island

Chapter six
Long Island and Roaringwater Bays

The Fastnet Rock lighthouse is iconic to the sailing community. It stands guard over Long Island Bay, where watersports activities take high priority. Ferries scuttle between the islands for those without the benefit of their own boat; sometimes carrying many individuals and groups with impossible amounts of equipment for pulling fish from the sea or for photographing rare birds or sea creatures.

Within a short distance, a comfortable harbour can be found whatever the weather and with a little planning most facilities can be come by. With such a water-focused community, the visitor is guaranteed a warm welcome here. Crookhaven and Schull are both 'destination' harbours and should not be missed. They buzz with activity on the water, particularly in the school holidays and especially during 'Calves Week', which initially sounds like a corny parody of 'Cowes

Week' but does have substance based on the three Calf Islands that dominate the middle of the bay. The first week of August in the bay is not the place to be for a quiet cruise as very large numbers of sailors of all types descend on Schull and the nearby harbours. Both harbours have well-marked, deep entrances, with public visitors' buoys to provide simple reliable mooring and easy access to the villages. They appear on many cruisers' 'most visited' list and deservedly so.

A wide selection of day anchorages along the Mizen Peninsula offer quiet secure havens in beautiful surroundings. Clear Island is an intriguing destination if the right weather and sea conditions can be found. It is a bird watcher's heaven but can be a helmsman's hell if North Harbour is very busy.

The area, despite its relative proximity to Cork, is surprisingly unvisited from the shore side, all of the

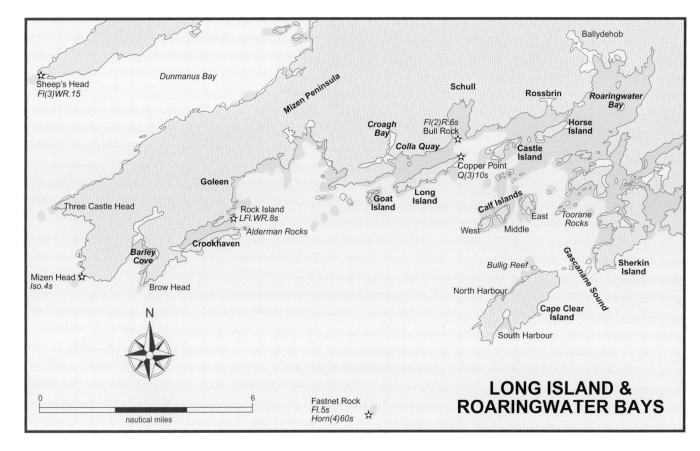

LONG ISLAND & ROARINGWATER BAYS

locations either being an island or on a minor road.

Those sailing in a generally easterly direction will notice more navigational aids which reflects the greater number of craft using these waters compared to further west. In the event of an incident, do not feel too bad; in 1985, even Prime Minister Haughey once sailed his motor cruiser onto the rocks below Mizen Head and had to be rescued by the keepers and the Baltimore lifeboat.

BOATYARDS
As previously mentioned, this area is densely used for recreational watersports and ferry borne traffic. There are four boatyards in the bay to support this activity, two of which, DT Marine and Rossbrin Boatyard, are situated around Schull. DT Marine's services include boat, engine and electrical repair and maintenance as well as boat storage, Tel: 028 28652/086 173 2021.

Rossbrin Boatyard has a 16 tonne liftout capability, a covered workshop and winter storage. It provides a wide range of marine services, including boat and engine repair and maintenance. An agent for a number of marine engine manufacturers, the boatyard can be contacted on Tel: 028 37352; website: www.rossbrin-boatyard.com.

At the eastern end of the bay, Oldcourt on the River Ilen is home to a further two boatyards – Donal O'Donovan's Oldcourt Boats and Hegarty's.

Oldcourt Boats, Tel: 028 21249 or 087 232 4151, has a 26m pontoon for visiting or waiting boats, a slipway that can handle up to 40m in length, a 70 tonne travel hoist which can handle 21m yachts with up to a 6m beam, hull and mechanical repairs and outdoor and indoor storage. Pilotage up the river from Baltimore can be arranged if required. A full winter maintenance service is available, covering engine, electrics, hull etc. The boatyard focuses on 'timber' restoration. Electronics, sails and rigging are subcontracted.

Hegarty's Boatyard, Tel: 028 22122, has a tracked slipway with a winched cable, mobile crane and does hull and mechanical repairs. It is the smaller of the two yards at Oldcourt. It specialises in building new wooden boats.

Other support facilities include Fastnet Sails – Christophe Houdaille manufactures new sails and carries out repairs, Tel: 028 35753 or 086 176 2377. The nearest large chandlery is CH Marine at Skibbereen, Tel: 028 23190, but first try Schull Watersports at the root of Schull pier, Tel: 028 28554.

ORIENTATION
There can be confusion over the naming of the bay for strangers planning a first visit. The charts (and OSI maps) clearly separate Long Island and Roaringwater Bays. Both agree that Roaringwater Bay is limited to the very shallow waters east of Horse Island and north of Skeam Islands. However, in the *lingua franca*, 'Roaringwater Bay' is used both by the locals and marketeers to describe the wider geographic area, including Long Island Bay. Who can blame the latter for stretching a point; Roaringwater Bay sounds far more exciting than Long Island Bay and does

Oldcourt Boatyards. Oldcourt Boats is to the east (left) and Hegarty's Boatyard is to the right of the inlet. The village pub can be seen in the trees to the right

www.irelandaerialphotography.com

attract the attention of many visiting sailors. To dispel a myth many may have, the name is nothing to do with a raging Atlantic penetrating far inland; Roaringwater refers to the name of the river that descends from Mount Kid (300m), which is 6km to the north and trickles uninterestingly into the north-east corner of the bay. With so many islands scattered across the bay, it is intriguing that the waters to the west – Long Island Bay – were named on the chart after only one of them.

Many will be tempted to 'Round the Fastnet'; the best photography is to be had after noon, when the sun will better illuminate the tower. Apart from the Fastnet lighthouse, the other unmissable landmark in the bay is 400m above sea level. Mount Gabriel, north of Schull, is surmounted by two large radomes which house and protect radar antennas used for tracking aircraft crossing the Atlantic out to about 18°W. They are Monopulse Secondary Surveillance Radars (MSSR), which mean they send pulses of radar out and receive replies that uniquely identify the aircraft, its speed and altitude. The radar's computers use this data to generate details of every aircraft's track and transmit that data to air traffic controllers in Shannon, London etc. The radomes are also quite useful as a fixing mark for several harbours, when visibility allows.

FAVOURABLE TIDES
Coastal Passage
Off Mizen Head for eastward passage – commences 4 hours 20 minutes before HW Cobh.
Off Cape Clear Island for westward passage – commences 1 hour 55 minutes after HW Cobh.

(There is no advantage in entering the bay for those making passage along the coast. Off the Fastnet, assume 2kn at springs. Around Mizen Head, the spring rate can reach 4kn).

Rounding Mizen Head into Long Island Bay

Gascanane Sound

Southward passage – commences 55 minutes before HW Cobh.

Northward passage – commences 5 hours 20 minutes after HW Cobh.

(Passage through Gascanane Sound between Sherkin and Cape Clear Islands is a popular way to enter Long Island Bay from the east. As Gascanane Sound experiences tidal rates up to 3kn, passage should be made at slack water or with the tide. This passage is fully described on page 157 as one of the approaches to Schull).

Long Island Channel

Eastward passage – commences 6 hours before HW Cobh.

Westward passage – commences at HW Cobh.

(Long Island Channel, between Long Island and the Mizen mainland, is a popular route between Schull and the west. Here the spring rate can reach 1½kn).

WEATHER INFORMATION BROADCASTS

This coast is served by the Valentia Coastguard transmitter at Mizen Head on VHF Ch 04. An advisory announcement is made initially on Ch 16.

PASSAGE CHARTS FOR THIS CHAPTER

Admiralty Charts: AC/LE2424 Kenmare River to Cork Harbour, 1:150,000; AC2184 Mizen Head to Gascanane Sound, 1:30,000; AC/LE2129 Long Island Bay to Castlehaven, 1:30,000; SC5623.2 The Bull to Glandore, 1:150,000.

Imray: C56 Cork Harbour to Dingle Bay, 1:170,000. Plans for harbours in this chapter cover Schull and Crookhaven.

SAFETY INFORMATION

This section of the coast is managed by Valentia Coastguard, Tel: 066 947 6109.

ELECTRONIC AIDS TO NAVIGATION

Mizen Head: DGPS on 284kHz.
Fastnet: AIS planned.

COASTGUARD AIS STATION

Mizen (Mt Gabriel)
51°33′.36N 09°32′.59W   MMSI 002 500370.

The 1979 Fastnet Race and Betelgeuse Tragedies

The biennial Fastnet Race starts in Cowes immediately after Cowes Week, the course rounds the Fastnet Rock and finishes in Plymouth. The first winner (of seven competing yachts in 1925) was the *Jolie Brise* sailed by EG Martin. Three hundred and three yachts entered the race in 1979. Initially conditions were very kind, but midway through the race there were reports of a 'great fury', with winds going from 30kn to 60kn in a matter of seconds. Fifteen sailors died. Eighty-five boats finished the race and 16 boats sank. The major lessons learned were the need for all participants to carry a trysail and a radio. A few years later, electronic navaids were allowed. Entrants also had to pre-qualify. The organiser, the Royal Ocean Racing Club, was eventually cleared of any blame. The Baltimore Lifeboat played a crucial role in saving life over those few days! The Fastnet Race continues to be one of the world's most fiercely competitive offshore races. The year 1979 was an *annus horribilis* in maritime County Cork.

That year the *Betelgeuse* explosion in Bantry Bay was still fresh in locals' minds. The large crude carrier was two-thirds of its way through discharging 10,000 tonnes of crude oil when cracking sounds were heard, followed by a massive explosion that killed the crew and jetty workers. Fifty people died and only 27 bodies were recovered. The remains of the jetty are still visible off Whiddy Island.

The Fastnet Memorial on Cape Clear Island

LONG ISLAND AND ROARINGWATER BAYS – PASSAGE WAYPOINTS – WGS84 DATUM		
NAME	DESCRIPTION	LAT/LONG
Mizen Head	½M SW of headland	51°26′.50N 09°50′.00W
Fastnet SW	7 cables SW of rock	51°22′.85N 09°37′.00W
Fastnet SE	½M SSE	51°22′.85N 09°36′.00W
Baltimore approach	4 cables S of entrance	51°27′.90N 09°23′.48W

www.irelandaerialphotography.com

Crookhaven. The Alderman Rocks and Black Horse Rocks occupy the south side of the entrance. Rock Island light is opposite on the mainland side. The village is half way along the peninsula

Crookhaven

(Irish: *An Cruachán*)
Approach waypoint: 51°28'.60N 09°41'.00W
(8 cables due E of Rock Island lighthouse)

Crookhaven is fun! Step ashore and from that moment feel part of the scenery. Acceptance is immediate (or at least once the mooring fee is paid for the very convenient mooring buoys) and it is virtually impossible not to fall into conversation with someone, resident or visitor. A quick scan of the view reveals that Crookhaven has had several histories, but this is not yet another rainbow-painted picture postcard village. Ask a question about the stone quarry, Fastnet, the Watch Towers or Rock Island lighthouse and their stories will be told, sometimes several differing versions; the over-riding feeling is that the residents are looking to the future not the past.

Crookhaven is not large. It is maybe 1km to the outskirts, where the village church rests on a promontory. From here there are excellent views along the inlet and down onto the moorings. Whether as a destination in its own right or as a convenient stopoff for those on a coastal passage, it is highly recommended.

For anyone planning to stay a while, the walks to Barley Cove and Brow Head will be rewarding. The harbour is only uncomfortable in strong easterly winds that blow in directly or westerlies that skip over the low land at the other end of the harbour.

NAVIGATION

Charts: Use Imray C56 or SC5623.10 and SC5623.11 for the approach, but note carefully, when rounding Mizen Head and heading towards Crookhaven, do not be tempted to solely use Admiralty Chart SC5623.10. For an unfathomable reason, given the amount of white space to the west of the chart, it does not extend eastwards to the Alderman Rocks (see photo above) at the east end of the Crookhaven peninsula. SC5623.10 shows only the western shore of Alderman Sound, indicating adequate depth for the average yacht but not showing the rocks to the immediate east. Although the sound is used by locals, it is not recommended to strangers. The photo on page 150 shows the view north from the edge of SC5623.10. It's a very inviting shortcut that should be resisted.

Tides: MHWS 3.3m, MHWN 2.6m, MLWN 0.9m, MLWS 0.3m. Standard Port Cobh, difference at HW: Springs –00:57min; Neaps –00:33min.

Lights & Marks
• Mizen Head Iso 4s 313° to 133°T.
• Fastnet lighthouse Fl 5s.
• Rock Island lighthouse L Fl WR 8s.
White sector in the bay; Long Island north shore to 281°T.
White sector in the harbour 348°T to north shore.
• Alderman Rocks (Black Horse Rocks) NCM (unlit).

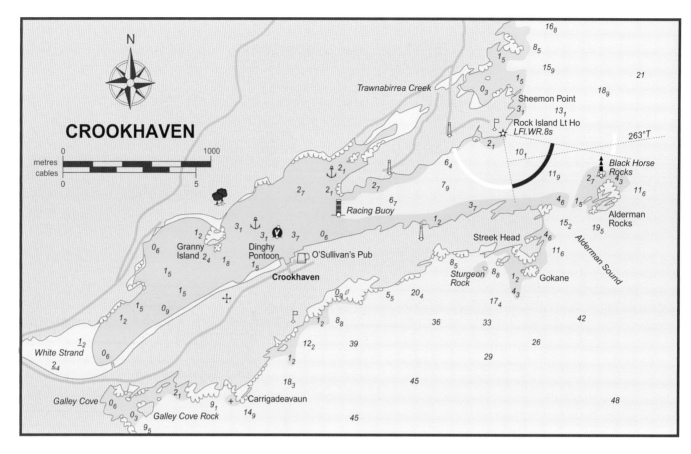

Approach: From the north-west, round Mizen Head with offing appropriate to the sea conditions (tidal stream maximum is 4kn at springs). Keep making south to clear Brow Head. Remain 2 cables south of Streek Head and 1 cable off the Aldermans. A depth of 30m is a good safety guide without adding too much distance.

The approach from the east-north-east (Schull and Long Island Channel) is unobstructed locally.

From the south-east, beware of Bullig Reef ½M north of Cape Clear Island if using Gascanane Sound (see Schull approaches for more information).

Pilotage: From the approach waypoint, steer 263°T to a point 1 cable due south of Rock Island lighthouse,

passing 1 cable north of Black Horse Rocks north cardinal mark. Steer a course to the middle of the narrowest part of the entrance (where there is an uncharted, small racing buoy). The sailing school is very active, particularly in the school holidays. Expect to encounter fleets of small sailboats helmed by children! Proceed to a mooring or anchorage.

MOORING

There are numerous yellow public visitors' buoys and spherical red visitors' buoys owned by Crookhaven – all chargeable. The nearest buoys to the shore are those immediately off O'Sullivan's pub. The public buoys are a little further away from the

Rock Island lighthouse viewed through Alderman Sound

Approaching the moorings at Crookhaven with the uncharted racing buoy (centre)

village. The charge (€15) for all buoys is collected at O'Sullivan's, Tel: 028 35319.

ANCHORING

There are several anchorages as indicated on the chartlet; try either the entrance to the Rock Island inlet if there is east in the wind or to the east of Granny Island if there is west in the wind. There is a dedicated seasonal dinghy pontoon, but if that is not available land at the jetty/harbour outside O'Sullivan's, which has steps and is particularly close to the shop.

Mooring off O'Sullivan's pub

Useful information – Crookhaven

FACILITIES
Fresh water: On the pier.
Fuel: Diesel can be obtained (in vessel's own cans) from O'Sullivan's.
Communications: Wi-Fi is available without charge on the moorings and weather forecasts can be acquired at O'Sullivans if a broadcast has been missed.
Boat services: If boat repairs are needed, refer to the 'boatyards' section at the beginning of the chapter on page 146.

PROVISIONING
A limited range of **groceries**

'Boys will be boys' in Crookhaven

is available from the shop in O'Sullivan's pub but, to be blunt, this is the end of the supply line for food and choice is limited. It is worth talking to the bar staff if the shop is closed and the need is urgent. However, to say it plainly, this is one place where eating ashore needs no debate.

EATING OUT
The Crookhaven Inn, Tel: 028 35309, doubles up as an excellent restaurant that is listed as one of the 100 best restaurants in Ireland. Under the ownership of

Emma & Freddy Olsson, it definitely comes into the 'must return to' category of restaurants. It is extremely popular with those who live in the area. Added to that it is not expensive and the staff are remarkably helpful.

O'Sullivan's pub, Tel: 028 35319, has a relaxed atmosphere and its outdoor tables afford a good view of the harbour (see photo above). The pub also excels with its seafood at lunchtime. A third pub, The Welcome Inn (or Nottages), opens in peak season at about 2100 for the locals who would otherwise be squeezed out of O'Sullivan's by us visitors.

Last but not least is The Harbour restaurant, Tel: 028 35963, next to O'Sullivan's. Alternatively, if eating alfresco on the harbour wall appeals then The Rustler Char & Grill take-away van will provide.

ASHORE
Twenty-first century Crookhaven lies within 100m of the dinghy

pontoon. In its time the harbour has been an important revictualling stop for transatlantic shipping, a gritstone quarry for England's roads, a Marconi Signal Station and a major shellfish exporter. Like Morse Code, these have now passed into history and Crookhaven is doing an excellent job focusing on the tourist industry.

It's amazing how such a small place – it has a population of less than 50 in the winter – can create such an ambience, which derives mainly from the enthusiasm and professionalism of the local businesses. Children play happily with water, sand and boats while parents supervise from the tables outside the pub.

TRANSPORT
There is a community bus, but this is not the place to come if the plan is to leave by road.

www.irelandaerialphotography.com

Goleen. This aerial photograph clearly shows the narrowness of the harbour at the outer quay, the reef extending from the northern shore and, to the right, the green mast (centre right) and the church spire (bottom). The main road from Schull enters bottom left

Moorings along the Mizen Peninsula

Goleen
(Irish: *An Góilín*)
Approach waypoint: 51°29'.60N 09°42'.00W
(Due E of the Green Mast – 1½ cables offshore)

Goleen is the local commercial centre for the tip of the Mizen Peninsula. Its attraction to a visitor is mainly the picturesque, narrow, rocky harbour, which winds inland and eventually dries. This is a harbour for those making a comprehensive cruise around the bay.

NAVIGATION
Charts: No detailed chart. Use Admiralty SC5623.11.

Tides (approx): MHWS 3.3m, MHWN 2.6m, MLWN 0.9m, MLWS 0.3m. Standard Port Cobh, difference at HW: Springs –00:57min; Neaps –00:33min.

Lights & Marks: The church spire and an uncharted green mast (the very sturdy remains of the Voss windmill) are the most useful marks.

Approach: Goleen is in the north-west corner of Ballydivlin Bay, which has many obstructions to avoid. The entrance to Goleen is not easily acquired.
   From the south: Spanish Point is foul for ¾ cable. Once clear, steer north with an offing of 1½ cables and bring the green mast into transit with the church spire. The entrance to the harbour should now become apparent to the west-north-west. Continue to the approach waypoint.
   From the south-east: Drying Bulligmore (0.9m) limits the course of approach to approximately 290°T.

Heading north 1½ cables off, the harbour entrance appears just after the transit of the mast and the church spire

From Schull: North-east of a line between Bulligmore and Goleen there are many rocks and islets, but a course from south of Castle Point through Barrel Sound is possible, in which case the turn to Goleen should not be made until clear of Amsterdam Reef (0.3m), 2½ cables south-west of Amsterdam Rock (1.2m).

Pilotage: The outer end of the new quay is clearly visible as a concrete slab from outside the entrance. It is best to ascertain if there is space available at the quay before entry and, where possible, avoid entering when there is outgoing traffic. Approach the quay, keeping to the south side of the entrance to steer clear of outcrops of rock that extend well off the north shore. Close to the quay, turning space is very limited. Entering stern first is recommended.

BERTHING

Alongside berthing is possible for approximately two yachts. The quay is exposed to the south-east.

The quay at Goleen can be very congested

Useful information – Goleen

FACILITIES
Road fuel (petrol and diesel in cans) is available from O'Meara's in the village. The Church of Ireland church on the Crookhaven Road is now deconsecrated and houses a **sailmaker** – Fastnet Sails, Tel: 028 35753 or 086 176 2377.

PROVISIONING
Sheehan's QuikPik **mini-market** and a **McCarthy's Butchers** (open only two days a week) provide the possibility of a top-up of provisions.

EATING OUT
The Heron's Cove restaurant (BIM accredited) receives excellent reviews and is conveniently situated at the drying end of the harbour, Tel: 028 35225.

In the village, at the other end of the spectrum is Richie's fast-food take-away and four bars to choose from: The Lobster Pot, Tel: 028 35366; The Fastnet Bar, Tel: 028 35355; O'Meara's Bar, Tel: 028 35146 and Norma's. The latter is disguised behind an unmarked door on the crossroads diagonally opposite O'Meara's.

ASHORE
Goleen village is one of those places that receives only faint praise, but the harbour is a delight.

TRANSPORT
Bus services: 237; Cork-Clonakilty-Skibbereen-Schull-Goleen. Three buses a day every day.

Goleen. The drying inner harbour and the Heron's Cove Restaurant

Croagh Bay, Colla Quay, and Long Island (*Inis Fada*) Pier

Croagh Bay approach waypoint: 51°29'.78N 09°34'.86W
(Due S of anchorage in mid Long Island Channel)
Colla/Long Island approach waypoint:
51°30'.15N 09°33'.75W
(S and N of anchorages in mid Long Island Channel)

All three adjacent anchorages lie between the mainland Mizen shore and Long Island. Coney Island, which is a privately-owned holiday retreat, is to the east of Croagh Bay. Refer to the chart on page 158 (Schull). Nearby, to the east of Coney Island, lie Colla and Long Island quays, which are the termini for the year round Long Island ferry. Long Island is still inhabited, but the population is down to eleven. These anchorages are protected quiet places away from the crowded (for these parts) environs of Schull and are perfect for a long lunch stop to soak up the scenery, wait for the tide or just a tranquil night. There are no facilities here.

Colla and Long Island. Colla, top, and Long Island pier attract many day visitors

NAVIGATION

Charts: Use Admiralty SC5623.11.

Tides (approx): MHWS 3.2m, MHWN 2.6m, MLWN 1.1m, MLWS 0.4m. Standard Port Cobh, difference at HW: Springs –0040min; Neaps –0015min.

The flood direction is north through Man of War, Goat and the other inter-island Sounds, turning east through Long Island Channel towards Schull and beyond across the north shores of Castle and Horse Islands. The ebb is the reverse of this. Approximately, the east-going flood tide commences at HW Cobh –0600 and the west-going ebb at HW Cobh, reaching 1½kn at springs.

Long Island with Schull Harbour top right

Lights & Marks

- Copper Point (aka Long Island Point) Q (3) 10s.
- Cush Spit NCM Q.
- Bull Rock Fl (2) R 6s.
- Goat Island beacon (unlit).

Approach: From the west the approach is as for Schull (see page 156) using the unlit beacon on Goat Island Little and Man of War Sound. From the east stay north of Cush Spit north cardinal mark and keep in mid channel.

Pilotage/anchoring: Enter Croagh Bay on a northerly track using the western half of the entrance to avoid obstructions extending 2 cables west of Coney Island – Esheens Rocks (1m) and the shallows (2.1m) to their west. Anchor off the farm buildings on the western shore.

For Colla Quay or Long Island Pier, a simple visual selection of an anchorage is adequate.

There are no facilities here, although Wi-Fi coverage is available from DigitalForge.

Colla Quay is very popular with divers

Rossbrin Cove

(Irish: *Ros Broin*, meaning Bron's Headland)

Approach waypoint:
51°30'.61N 09°32'.00W
(On the Schull leading line/lights 2 cables SE of Bull Rock Perch)

Rossbrin Cove. Horse Island is at the top of the photo. The castle ruins are the dark shape on the right of the entrance. The boatyard slip can be seen bottom right

www.irelandaerialphotography.com

Rossbrin Harbour is a large drying inlet 3M east of the entrance to Schull. The Cove, at the entrance to the harbour, is not only a quiet anchorage but also useful as a waiting area for shallow draught vessels crossing Horse Island Bar into Roaringwater Bay. The harbour is home to Rossbrin Boatyard.

NAVIGATION

Charts: Use Admiralty SC5623.12.

Tides (approx): MHWS 3.2m, MHWN 2.6m, MLWN 1.1m, MLWS 0.4m. Standard Port Cobh, difference at HW: Springs –00:40min; Neaps –00:15min.

Lights & Marks
• Bull Rock Perch Fl (2) R 6s.
• Rossbrin Castle Ruin.

Approach: Rossbrin is approached from the west as for Schull, using the same waypoint.

The approach from the east is across a sand bar, named 'Horse Ridge' on charts, which dries (0.3 to 0.6m) and is therefore only passable on the top of a suitable tide and not recommended to strangers for this reason.

Pilotage: Castle Island Spit acts as a bar on the southern shore of Castle Island and Horse Island Channels. Least depth is 0.6m. Keep to the north side of both channels.

On the flood above half tide, from the approach waypoint steer 073°T, checking the depth regularly to stay in 3m above chart datum.

ANCHORING

Anchor due south of Rossbrin Castle in 3m or less. Edge into the cove towards the moored local boats as far as draught and the moorings will allow, but this will still be somewhat exposed out in the channel. Nevertheless these are very pleasant surroundings if a quiet night at anchor is wished for.

FACILITIES

Rossbrin Boatyard, Tel 028 37352 – see details under 'Boatyards' at the beginning of this chapter on page 146. Note the harbour dries (0.9m) so local advice will be required for access to the boatyard by water.

Moorings in the entrance to Rossbrin Cove, below Bron O'Mahoney's Castle

Bull Rock Perch

www.irelandaerialphotography.com

Schull. Copper Point, bottom centre, leads north to Bull Rock and the harbour. The pier is at the top left of the harbour. Mount Gabriel dominates the scene from 400m above the village

Schull

(Irish: *Skull*, meaning School, after
a monastic college)
Approach waypoint: 51°30'.61N 09°32'.00W
(On the Schull leading line/lights 2 cables
SE of Bull Rock Perch)

Schull is a busy, sophisticated, village with a large comfortable anchorage – a truly fine harbour. There is an emphasis on sailing and boating in all its forms in Schull. The sailing activity peaks in the first week of August when 'Calves Week' takes place (see page 145). Casual visitors should avoid the harbour at that time. Protection is excellent except in strong southerly winds, when it is best to decamp to Long Island Channel or even Crookhaven.

NAVIGATION

Charts: Be aware of the Admiralty chart enigma – if approaching from the west, the SC5623.11 chart doesn't fully cover Schull, missing the last ½M at the top of the harbour and therefore the actual position of the visitors' moorings (see page 158). However, approaching from the south-east, SC5623.12 offers complete coverage of the harbour, but still misplaces the visitors' buoys. Imray C56 covers the whole harbour.

Tides: MHWS 3.2m, MHWN 2.6m, MLWN 1.1m, MLWS 0.4m. Standard Port Cobh, difference at HW: Springs –00:40min; Neaps –00:15min.

Lights & Marks
• Schull leading marks/lights Oc 5s 346°T leave Bull Rock to port.
• Bull Rock Fl (2) R 6s (also known locally as 'The Perch').
• Copper Point (aka Long Island Point) Q (3) 10s.
• Cush Spit NCM Q.
• Amelia SHM Fl G 3s.
• Mount Gabriel Radomes in alignment with Copper Point 355°T clears Calf Island West.

Approaches: A popular approach from the west is via the protected waters of Long Island Channel, between Long Island and the Mizen shore. Goat Island Little has an unlit beacon on its southern tip to help identify Man of War Sound to the west of it and Goat Island Sound to the east of it. These are the usual passages to gain access to Long Island Channel. Man of War Sound is cleaner than Goat Island Sound, which has Goat Island protruding into it from the west and Sound Rock, which dries (1.8m), from the east.

In Long Island Channel steer mid channel leaving Coney Island to port and Cush Spit north cardinal mark to starboard. Cross the transit of Copper Point and Bull Rock to pick up Schull leading marks at the approach waypoint. Bull Rock in the harbour entrance may be passed on its west side, if preferred.

The alternative approach from the west staying south of Long Island takes a course to the midpoint between Long Island and Calf Island West. Just after Copper Point bears due north, the Mount Gabriel and

Bull Rock from the south at low water springs

Schull leading lines camouflaged amid the clutter of the north shore

Copper Point transit occurs. Alter course to a little east of north to arrive 2 cables off Amelia starboard-hand mark. Proceed past Copper Point (to port) to the Schull approach waypoint using the harbour leading line/lights. Only at Copper Point should the depth be less than 20m.

The main approach from the SE is using Gascanane Sound, which separates Sherkin Island and Cape Clear Island. Carrigmore Rocks sit inconveniently in mid-sound. The western half of the Sound is further fouled by Gascanane Rock which dries (1.8m). Fortunately, the east half of the Sound is 3 cables wide and not less than 30m deep.

Gascanane Sound Waypoints

Gascanane South: 51°26'.67N, 09°26'.84W
(4 cables south of the channel).
Gascanane North: 51°27'.43N, 09°26'.84W (1½ cables west of Crab Rock – Northern entrance to the Sound).

When rounding Illaunbrock, the island off the SW of Sherkin Island, keep at least ½ cable off and steer due north. Local traffic should note that the southern waypoint on the chartlet is conservative and designed to facilitate passage planning to/from both east and west.

Passage should always be made with the tide which flows approximately NW/SE at up to 3kn. The commencement of the streams is given at the beginning of this chapter on page 148. Be careful to lay off course appropriately to compensate and to avoid being carried onto Crab Rock to the north-east or the Carrigmore Rocks to the north-west. Once clear north of the Carrigmores, it is safe to turn to the north-west towards the south-west corner of Calf Island West, staying 1 cable off the latter. Note that Bullig Reef extends ½M off the north shore of Cape Clear Island, due south of Calf Island East. Overshoot Calf Island

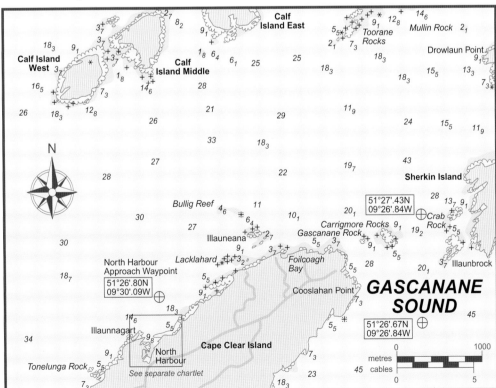

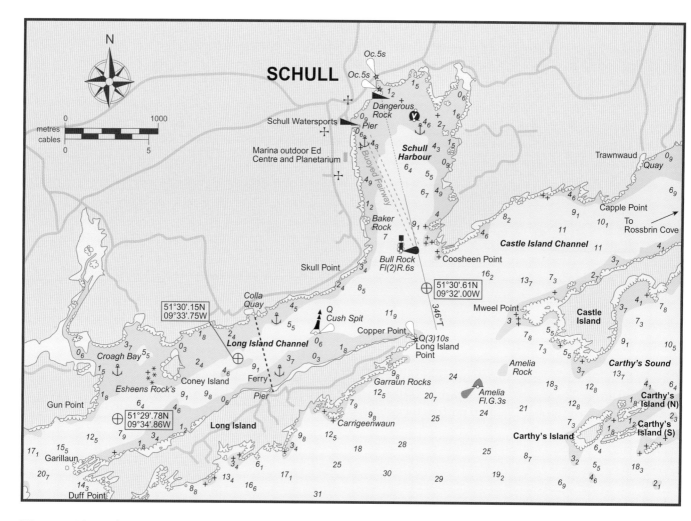

West to pick up the Mount Gabriel with Copper Point transit, or in insufficient visibility, track north along the west side of Calf Island West in greater than 20m. Head due north to arrive 2 cables west of Amelia starboard-hand mark and proceed as above.

Pilotage: From the approach waypoint steer 346°T along the leading marks until well inside the harbour and then proceed to the chosen mooring. The leading marks can be very difficult to acquire in the daytime as they are camouflaged by the surrounding buildings. In the photo on page 157, they are central below the gap in the trees and the pink house with the three dormer windows in the roof. A slip descends to the water (left to right) immediately in front of the front leading mark. Inside the harbour, keep clear of the buoyed fairway to the pier, which is heavily used by commercial traffic.

MOORING/ANCHORING

There are 12 public visitors' buoys in the north-east corner of the harbour. A night's mooring costs €10, which should be paid to Schull Watersports at the root of the pier. Note that, nearby, an underwater rock has been reported approximately 1.5 cables south-east of the front leading beacon. It is indicated on chart SC5623.12. (The very large buoys east of the pier are for fishing vessels – keep clear of these).

Otherwise, anchor south-east of the pier in 3m. The holding has been described as 'variable', which is not surprising given the popularity of the harbour and the associated amount of cast-off equipment that is likely to be there! Avoid anchoring in the fairway between the harbour entrance and the pier. The fairway is defined by four port and four starboard lateral buoys (small with a pennant).

Landing is at the dinghy pontoon on the pier or the sailing centre slipway.

Note that a temporary alongside berth may be had on the fishing vessel pier.

Landing at the slipway at the root of the pier. Schull Watersports may be found in the large white building (centre)

Useful information – Schull

Schull's main street in 'Calves Week'

The simplest way to explore Schull village is to take the foreshore walk from the pier to the sailing centre and from there walk up to Colla Road. Turn right and arrive at the top of Main Street with the An Tigin Bar opposite. It is then all downhill along Main Street back to the harbour past most of the facilities.

FACILITIES
Water: Fresh water is on the pier.
Showers: May be taken in the sailing centre (€2.50) but only during mid morning and mid afternoon.
Fuel: There is no fuel available locally but large quantities can be obtained from Carbery Oils, Tel: 028 23890.
Rubbish: Can be disposed of at the sailing centre.
Gas: Camping Gaz and Kosan are sold at the Eurospar in the village.
Chandlery: May be found from Simon Nelson at Schull Watersports, which is situated at the root of the pier, Tel: 028 28554.
Boat services: If boat repairs are needed, refer to 'Boatyards' at the beginning of the chapter on page 146
Communications: Wi-Fi coverage is available from DigitalForge, Tel: 028 28983.

PROVISIONING
In the village, there are small supermarkets (Centra and Eurospar), an **Internet** café, **pharmacy**, **post office** and **launderette**. Schull has a Sunday Market, 1000-1400 April through to Christmas. An **ATM** is available at the AIB **bank**.

EATING OUT
There is a very large number of eating, drinking and snacking establishments in Schull and, as with most major holiday hotspots, it is easy to eat in a restaurant on the 'chef's night off'. Ask local advice before committing. The choice of restaurants and cafés include: New Haven (most frequently recommended by locals – Tel: 028 28642) and the Waterside (for finer dining – Tel: 028 28203) on Main Street. The fresh fish shop on the quay has a good reputation and incorporates a seasonal restaurant and take-away, Tel: 028 28599. Notable pubs are Bunratty Inn (known for its bar food), and for yachties, The Courtyard and Newman's.

ASHORE
Schull has a lively, welcoming atmosphere and is a cosmopolitan village with interesting individual stores and facilities, including health food shops, a chocolatier and vegetarian restaurants. A small selection of marine books can be found in Chapter One on Main Street.

The village mainstays, apart from commercial fishing, are second homes, holiday cottages and the many marine activities – including diving, angling and sailing. There is a fine watersports centre, Fastnet Marine & Outdoor Educational Centre, Tel: 028 28515; website: www. schullsailing.ie, at Schull. As an alternative, if a day ashore is planned, visit the Schull Planetarium on Colla Road, Tel: 028 28315/28552. Times vary – see the website www.westcorkweb.ie/ planetarium/detail.html.

TRANSPORT
Bus services: 237 Cork-Clonakilty-Skibbereen-Schull. Three buses a day every day.
Taxi: Tel: 028 28320 or 086 854 3631.

The popular Bunratty Inn

Ferry: A seasonal ferry runs to Cape Clear Island.

OTHER INFORMATION
Harbour master: (Seasonal and not a full time role), Tel: 086 103 9105.
Rescue service: A tremendous amount of effort has gone into establishing the Schull Community Inshore Rescue Service, which is awaiting Coastguard assessment to allow it to become one of only two Community Rescue Boats in County Cork. It will operate in conjunction with the Goleen Coastguard boat and the RNLI from Baltimore.
Doctor: Schull Medical Centre Tel: 028 28688.
Dentist: Tel: 028 27636.
Tourist information: '@ Your Leisure' on Main Street, Tel: 028 28600. Schull has its own excellent website – see www.schull.ie.

Schull: Foreshore Walk

Cape Clear Island
(Irish: *Oileán Chléire*)

The rugged, sparsely-populated island is a detached part of the West Cork Gaeltacht, or Irish-speaking area. It is a place of individuality and scenic beauty. Despite a fearsome reputation for its winter weather, it has one of the highest records of sunshine hours in Ireland. There is no doubt that Cape Clear Island is well worth a visit. Choosing which of its two very different harbours is the first challenge.

South Harbour
Entrance waypoint: 51°25'.00N 09°30'.13W
(1M due S of the anchorage)

South Harbour is extremely exposed to any weather with a southerly component. On the other hand this harbour is an absolutely delightful sun-trap in settled weather with no swell. It is by far the most relaxed way of spending time on the island and ideal for those with children or looking for a peaceful anchorage or a swim.

NAVIGATION
Charts: No detailed chart. Use Admiralty SC5623.12, AC2184 or AC/LE2129.

Lights & Marks: None.

Tides (approx): MHWS 3.2m, MHWN 2.6m, MLWN 1.1m, MLWS 0.4m. Standard Port Cobh, difference at HW: Springs –00:40min; Neaps –00:15min.
   Cape Clear Island interrupts, face on, the flood tide

South Harbour anchorage in late July – this would be considered busy for these cruising grounds

heading east. The part of it deflected south by Cape Clear is further deflected by Blananarragaun, a small bill aligned north-south at the south-west entrance to South Harbour. Whenever a tide is flowing, there will be an eddy induced off this bill. On the flood it is anticlockwise – the reverse on the ebb.

Approach: Approach from the west is constrained by the Fastnet Rock (4M to the south-west) and the tidal eddies associated with Blananarragaun at the harbour's south-west entrance (see above). The approach from the east is clear except for a rock ½ cable off the tip of the south-east entrance to the harbour.

Pilotage/Anchoring: From the approach waypoint, steer due north and anchor mid-bay in 5-8m. Land at the steps along the quay furthest from the buildings on the east shore. There are no lines, rails or eyes permanently attached to the quay – improvised 'crampons' are needed to secure lines until the first dinghy passenger is safely landed on the steps. A long dinghy painter is needed. Although there is a stony beach on the east side of the harbour, it is too rocky and slippery for landing other than at high water.

Cape Clear Island. South Harbour, top right, is quieter and simpler to moor in than North Harbour, if sea conditions permit

www.irelandaerialphotography.com

The Fastnet Rock light, which replaced Cape Clear's original lighthouse

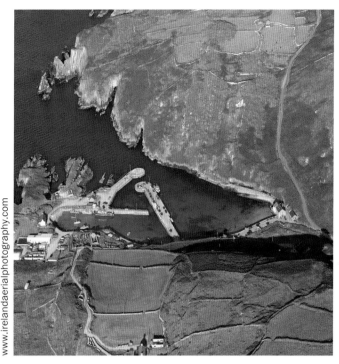

Cape Clear Island North Harbour. Deep keel yachts berth on the inside 'bulb' of the outer pier

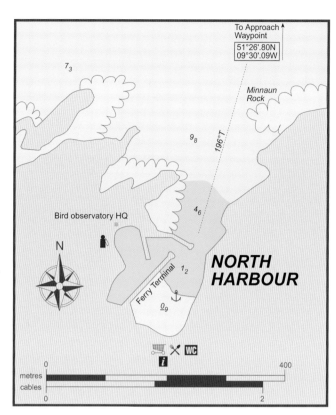

North Harbour

Approach waypoint: 51°26'.80N 09°30'.09W (3½ cables from the outer pier end bearing 196°T. This position is also due south of the east side of Calf Island Middle)

North Harbour bustles in summer! Ferry traffic is heavy. All types of watercraft continually arrive and depart and tourists congregate around the harbour as they await their ferry departure.

Arriving from the sea, the entrance is not easily acquired and once inside the harbour, space is extremely tight! It is advisable to ascertain if there is space available inside and, where possible, avoid entry when there is outgoing traffic. It is possible to see the deep keel berth from outside the harbour. If there are three or more masts, come back another time. Calm conditions are needed, particularly for those unfamiliar with the entrance. This is a very small, partly-drying harbour. There is little room to manoeuvre and none to swing. Vessels require good astern steerage capability. Those able to take the ground fare better as they may dry out on a gently sloping bottom. North Harbour is well protected except in strong northerlies.

NAVIGATION

Charts: No detailed chart. Use Admiralty SC5623.12, AC2184 or AC/LE2129.

Tides (approx): MHWS 3.2m, MHWN 2.6m, MLWN 1.1m, MLWS 0.4m. Standard Port Cobh, difference at HW: Springs –00:40min; Neaps –00:15min.

The flood and ebb flow along the north shore of Clear Island. The NE flood commences approximately 4 hours 45 minutes before HW Cobh. The SE ebb commences at approximately 1 hour 15 minutes after HW Cobh.

Lights & Marks: None.

Approaches: Approaching from the west and north-west there are no obstructions.

The approach from the east and north-east is fouled by Bullig Reef, which extends ½M off the north shore of Cape Clear Island, due south of Calf Island East. Stay in water deeper than 20m until unambiguously west of the west side of Calf Island East before turning south-south-west towards the approach waypoint. During this approach do not close the Cape Clear Island shore rapidly – stay in greater than 20m until the waypoint is reached. The shoreline is very rocky out to 2 cables.

Approaching North Harbour near low water springs. The harbour is remarkably free of vessels on an early June day

The entrance and Minnaun Rock viewed from the outer pier head

determined by a rock which is approximately 1.8m below the lowest low water springs.

Others that are able to may take the ground in the inner harbour towards the shop/café, leaving the frequent ferries plenty of room to manoeuvre.

Harbour master: The harbour is run by one of the ferry owners, who is often away from the harbour on his craft. He may therefore not be able to advise on conditions in the harbour instantaneously.

Pilotage: From the approach waypoint, steer 196°T towards the end of the outer breakwater. This takes the track very close to Minnaun Rock to port! Break off this course only when close to the entrance, which is just 30m wide. At times, 'keep pots' will be positioned off the rocks to port.

BERTHING

Deep keels can be accommodated only on the south face of the outermost pier (see photo right) – rafting will be necessary for all but the first visiting yacht. Shore lines are also needed from rafting yachts to avoid the 'raft' moving to block the entrance to the western arm of the harbour. Space is very limited; typically three yachts can be comfortably accommodated. Very long warps (25-30m should be adequate) are needed for shore lines even if rafting is not necessary.

The depth on the outer pier berth is reportedly

Deep keel berth; long mooring lines are essential on the outer pier

A fine July day boosts the harbour traffic. Two obscured yachts are berthed on the outer pierhead, with a third berthed alongside an inactive ferry. Another yacht has taken to the ground in mid harbour

Useful information – North Harbour (Cape Clear Island)

Cotter's Bar

FACILITIES/ PROVISIONING

Siopa Beag (The Co-op Tel: 028 39145) will supply **diesel** and **petrol** (in cans) from the small industrial yard near the outer pier during the working week. **Fresh water** is available from a domestic-type tap on the outer pier. As usual with most off-islands, **rubbish disposal** is discouraged.

There is a small **grocery** within the café adjacent to the tourist office.

EATING OUT

For such a small community, Cape Clear Island has a good selection of eateries, but assume pubs and restaurants are open during the summer only until proven wrong.

The harbourside café and restaurant, under new management, are run by Neil O'Regan and his very enthusiastic staff (see photo opposite). Throughout the day the menu is changed to reflect the time of day. Breakfast and lunch are augmented at the weekend (Thursday-Saturday) by dinner, with an interesting, competitively-priced menu. The café serves teas, coffees, sandwiches, and, on Fridays, pizzas.

Ciaran Danny Mike's pub, Tel: 028 39153, at the brow of the hill separating North and South Harbours, has excellent views over South Harbour. Bar or restaurant meals are available in a friendly atmosphere with a fine outside beer garden. Cotter's Bar, just up the hill from North Harbour, offers bar food and Thai food every Wednesday, Tel: 028 39181/086 409 9664. There is a summer 'Chip Van' on North Harbour.

ASHORE

The climb out of the North Harbour area is very steep but exceedingly rewarding in good visibility – excellent for a panorama photo because a single shot could not do justice to it.

The island hosts Irish language residential courses during the college holidays. With only around 150 residents, there is negligible road traffic, but the population swells unimaginably when a rare bird is spotted and the 'twitchers' descend on the island. This is not an unusual occurrence because the southerly location provides a refuge for many a migrating or, simply, lost bird. The birding community has its oldest observatory close to North Harbour.

Nearby, the hills are sprinkled with Megalithic stones, a 12th century church ruin and the 14th century O'Driscoll Castle – Dún an Óir (Gold Fort). The Heritage Centre, which opens June to August, is a museum of all things local, including the 1979 Fastnet Race disaster.

In a country that hosts the Blarney Stone (see page 214), what else but an International Story-telling Festival happens every August? It attracts huge audiences.

The Fastnet Rock lighthouse was built to replace the Cape Clear lighthouse, the remains of which can still be clearly seen on the middle summit. This great height was its downfall. One night in 1847, it was obscured by fog/low cloud, causing the *Stephen Whitney* to mistake Rock Island lighthouse for Clear Island lighthouse when making landfall from the USA. Altering course based on that assumption, she promptly ran on to Calf Island West, killing at least 90 people.

Club Cléire, Tel: 028 39119, is the island's social centre and is in the same building as the store on North Harbour. It has traditional music on summer weekends.

TRANSPORT

Ferries: *Cailín Óir* (*Golden Girl*) to Baltimore and Crookhaven, Tel: 028 39159/41923; 086 346 5110. *Naomh Ciarán II* to Baltimore, Tel: 028 39153, 087 268 0760, 087 282 4008. Karycraft to Schull, Tel: 028 28278, 086 237 9302.

OTHER INFORMATION

Medical: A nurse can be contacted on Tel: 028 39109. The nearest doctor is on the mainland.
Tourist office: Open during the summer only, it doubles up as a craft and souvenir shop, Tel: 028 39100.

North Harbour: Staff at the welcoming café, restaurant and shop

www.irelandaerialphotography.com

Roaringwater Bay and the Sound. The Sound leaves Baltimore Harbour, bottom right. At Turks Head, the River Ilen heads east. Hare Island is centre left. Ballydehob Bay can be seen in the distance. The passage to Clear Island is bottom left

Roaringwater Bay

Roaringwater Bay (as defined by Admiralty charts and OSI), the River Ilen and also the access channels to them both through The Sound at Baltimore are all rock strewn and shallow. They are also heavily obstructed with vast mussel farms that have narrow navigable channels between them. The mooring cables at the ends of these channels may be unmarked. Within its bounds, there is little by way of must-see destinations. Pilotage notes for the area are rife with dire warnings about the need for local knowledge when navigating through these waters. Indeed, local charter companies have either banned or severely limited passage through The Sound to the north of Baltimore Harbour and the other routes through the bay.

Having established these negatives, it is a perfectly pleasant location with countless low-lying islands and remote anchorages. From the road, there are high lookout points along the many peninsulas penetrating into the bay, affording magnificent panoramas which put all the regional iconic features into context – Lot's Wife, Cape Clear Island, the Fastnet Rock, Mizen Head and the peach-coloured Kilcoe Castle, now owned by the actor Jeremy Irons. This is undoubtedly an area that is very satisfying to explore by road. On the other hand, the local industries comprise quarrying and aquaculture

and, although this is probably one of the most attractive industrial estates that can be entered by sea, there are many other places along the coast where equally challenging navigation leads to moorings that are utterly different to anything found elsewhere in Europe and are far more rewarding.

Inevitably, these comments will provoke some yachtsmen, quite rightly, to investigate for themselves, in which case, the most straightforward and safest access is using Carthy's Sound, entering south of Horse Island and north of the Skeam Islands. (For readers who want to take an initial look at the more intricate passages, there are the local ferries that run between Baltimore – The Sound and Cape Clear Island). Failing that, good local information is needed. A suitable starting point

Kilcoe Castle and the abundant marine farming in Roaringwater Bay

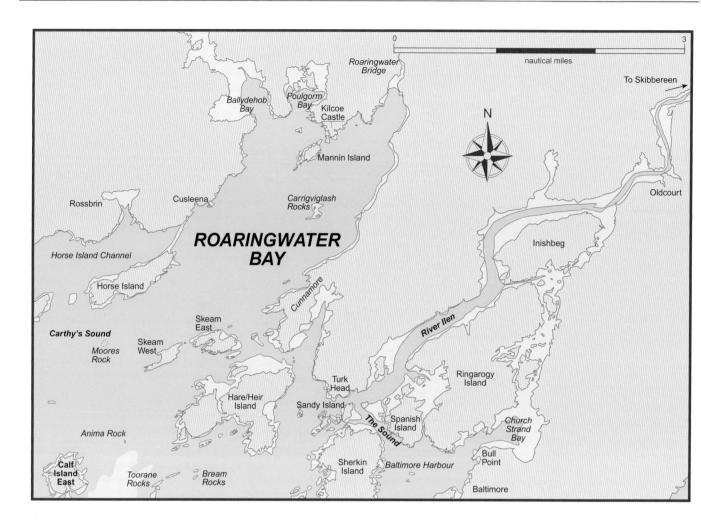

for balanced advice is Diarmuid Minihane, the harbour master at Baltimore. He also charters out small boats. Other sources of advice in Baltimore are the sailing club (on the harbour) and Glenans Sailing School (at the old railway station buildings towards the lifeboat station).

The main centres of population are Ballydehob and Skibbereen. Both involve long dinghy journeys near high water. If Skibbereen is a wished for destination, it is accessed much more easily by bus from Baltimore.

There are two boatyards at Oldcourt with very comprehensive facilities. If their services are needed, it is best to also seek their advice on passage to them!

NAVIGATION

Charts: Admiralty chart SC5623.12 has adequate coverage of the navigable parts of Roaringwater Bay (but upper Ballydehob Bay and the village are omitted). SC5623.14 has a good chart of the River Ilen. Regrettably the inset on SC5623.13 illustrating The Sound cuts off at the point of most interest, that is before the East-West split for Hare Island and the River Ilen.

Tides (approx): MHWS 3.2m, MHWN 2.6m, MLWN 1.1m, MLWS 0.4m. Standard Port Cobh, difference at HW: Springs −00:40min; Neaps −00:15min.

Lights & Marks: None.

Routes through Roaringwater Bay

The Sound: Is reached by crossing the shallows of Baltimore Harbour. For planning purposes, the least depth in the harbour towards The Sound is 2.5m, provided Wallis Rock and Lousy Rocks are given a wide berth. The Sound, between Sherkin Island and Spanish Island, is deep and straight. Beyond the north of The Sound, the River Ilen heads north-east (see bottom photo on page 167) and the passage to Roaringwater Bay and Long Island Bay heads west. Given the intricate navigation and shoals, passage early on a rising tide will expose as many rocks as possible. The flood (north to south) tide in The Sound commences HW Cobh +05:45 and ebb (south to north) at HW Cobh −00:25.

The Sound is heavily used by ferries and commercial craft going purposefully to and from the boatyards and the islands. While it is important not to obstruct their progress, do not be pressured into standing into danger.

South of Hare/Heir Island to Cape Clear Island and the West: This is an intricate passage. There are no navigation marks. It requires the unambiguous identification of featureless islets and islands (see photo on page 165). The route twists and turns and obstructions lie close to or in the channel.

Particular dangers include:
a) An unnamed rock which covers and uncovers at 51° 29′.74N 09° 24′.42W. (100m north-east of Sandy Is).

Roaringwater Bay with Long Island Bay in the distance

b) Mealbeg covers and uncovers. It lies ½ cable south of Turk Head.

c) An unnamed submerged rock north-west of The Catalogues, impeding the turn south toward Drowlaun Point.

d) Two unnamed rocks situated 1 cable south of Two Women's Rock.

e) A dangerous rock, 2½ cables south-south-west of Two Women's Rock in the fairway.

f) Mullin Rock, 2½ cables north-west of Drowlaun Point in the fairway.

g) Bream Rocks and Greymare Rocks obstruct the passage between Hare Island and Toorane Rocks.

North of Hare/Heir Island – *Inis Uí Drisceoil*: This is the most intricate passage of all. The least depth across the route is 0.3m, requiring half tide before most vessels may attempt to pass. At half tide many rocks cover. Great care is essential.

East of Calf Island East: Implicit in this route, which is primarily to facilitate passage from Gascanane Sound or The Sound to Carthy's Sound, is the safe passage to the west of both Anima Rock (0.1m) and Toorane Rocks (½M in length on south-west – north-east alignment). There are no local navigation marks, but two alternative clearing lines

are given on the chart:

a) Using a chapel against the hillside on Cape Clear Island and a small islet (Illauneana) off its north shore requires excellent light conditions and certainty that the correct features have been identified – quite a challenge for a stranger. This transit passes Anima Rock 1 cable to its west – good reason to be sure that this transit is unambiguously identified.

b) The other transit (Barnacleeve Gap bearing 336°T) is based on a very distinct cleft in the mountain top on the east slope of Mount Gabriel. This transit requires visibility of > 6M. As Mount Gabriel can be seen from virtually everywhere in the bay, it will be evident early on before committing to this passage, if there is adequate visibility. Both transits join Carthy's Sound.

Carthy's Sound: Carthy's Sound is wide (2½ cables between Moores Rock and Horse Island), deep and unambiguously marked by the Amelia Rock starboard-hand mark at the entrance. Take a track closer to the Castle/Horse Island shores in greater than 5m above chart datum.

ANCHORAGES

Some potential anchorages are:

East of Horse Island: 4 to 6 cables south of Cusleena. There are no facilities nearby.

River Ilen looking east. The river meanders, centre and left of photo, off to Oldcourt and Skibbereen. The piers at Cunnamore and on Hare Island show in the foreground

Oldcourt Boats on the River Ilen

Ballydehob Bay: The anchorage is south of the quay on the west shore of the peninsula leading to Reen Point. This is the nearest anchorage to Ballydehob but still demands a 1½M dinghy trip, although some craft may be able to take the ground at an alongside berth at Ballydehob Quay. Alternatively, land at the nearby quay and walk 3km to Ballydehob, partly along the busy N71 trunk road.

Poulgorm Bay: Is suited to shallow draught craft and is a little further from Ballydehob.

Hare Island East anchorage: Is between the mainland and the island – there is good access to the pier on Hare Island and another at Cunnamore. There is a highly rated restaurant on Hare Island (Island Cottage restaurant Tel: 028 38102), but booking is essential as only six people can be accommodated. The anchorage extends south towards Two Women's Rock.

River Ilen: River Ilen boatyards, Tel: 028 21249 or 087 232 4151, at Oldcourt offer alongside berths. Speak to either boatyard about the possibilities. There are few facilities at Oldcourt; the quiet village bar has a very pleasant garden and buses pass to and from Baltimore and Skibbereen. Alternatively, Skibbereen is a 3M dinghy ride upriver. The river is undergoing public works improvements.

The limiting depth in the River Ilen is 1m above chart datum. The flood commences HW Cobh +05:45 and ebb at HW Cobh –00:30. Local advice is to journey upriver in the two hours before local high water.

ASHORE – BALLYDEHOB

Ballydehob is a busy village, whose services include shops, a filling station, launderette, hardware store and, most importantly, refuse bins. Among the places to eat is Annie's Restaurant, which has an interesting arrangement whereby orders are taken from clients while they drink in Levi's pub opposite, Tel: 028 37292. There is also Duggans Restaurant and the Wok Inn Chinese Restaurant, Tel: 028 25222, along with several bars.

Ballydehob is the native village of Dan O'Mahony, who was world wrestling champion in the 1930s and invented the eponymous 'whip'. He is commemorated by a statue and a bar named 'The Irish Whip'.

Skibbereen

Ballydehob Bay. The village, bottom left, is at the head of the bay. Kilcoe Castle, on its peninsula, can be seen in the distance

www.irelandaerialphotography.com

Timoleague, Argideen River, Courtmacsherry and, in the far distance, Old Head of Kinsale

Chapter seven
Baltimore to Kinsale

This 40-mile stretch of the Cork coast is the ideal sailing ground, having well-spaced, attractive, protective harbours and stopovers, ample navigational challenges, a scenic coastline and plenty of wildlife. As an added bonus most facilities can be found at both ends of the area. There is something for every type of cruiser on this coast!

It is difficult to avoid discovering the history of this region. There will be stories of the O'Driscoll clan, religious wars and the Resident Magistrate (RM).

Other tales are hidden by the sea; one such is the wreck of the *Kowloon Bridge* off The Stags in 1986. Sister ship to the infamous *Derbyshire*, she is still the largest wreck in Europe.

This is a very popular part of the coast for many visitors, who typically make landfall in Kinsale or Baltimore to refresh both boat and crew after a long crossing. Many of the 'destination' harbours of County Cork are concentrated along or near this coastline. A typical out-and-back itinerary is Kinsale to Glandore to Baltimore to Crookhaven, near Mizen Head, returning via the Fastnet Rock, Castletownshend and Courtmacsherry before making passage round the Old Head of Kinsale to Crosshaven in Cork Harbour.

In addition, five minor anchorages are included in this chapter for completeness. They may appeal to those seeking solitude or a stop-over for lunch, but cannot be said to be essential for a full appreciation of the area. Each has significant access limitations. None has facilities ashore.

FAVOURABLE TIDES

Off Cape Clear Island for eastward passage – commences 4 hours 20 minutes before HW Cobh.
Off Kinsale for westward passage – commences 1 hour 50 minutes after HW Cobh.

WEATHER INFORMATION BROADCASTS

This coast is served by the Valentia Coastguard transmitter at Mizen Head on VHF Ch 04 in the west and at Roche's Point on Ch 26 in the east. An advisory announcement is made initially on Ch 16.

The Old Head of Kinsale

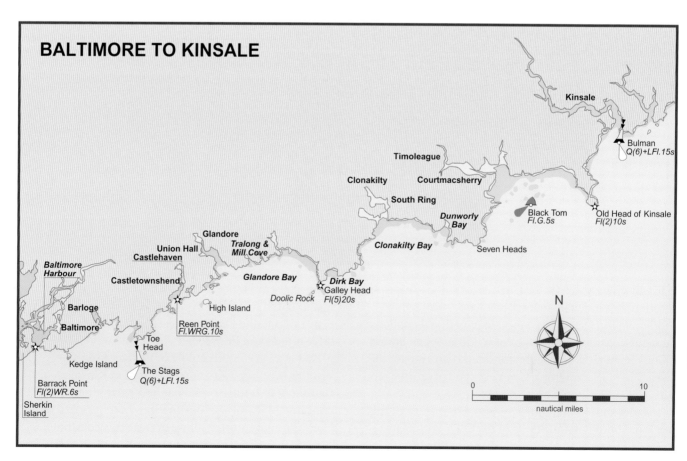

BALTIMORE TO KINSALE

Kinsale

Bulman
Q(6)+LFl.15s

Timoleague

Clonakilty   Courtmacsherry

South Ring

Black Tom   Old Head of Kinsale
Fl.G.5s   Fl(2)10s

Dunworly
Bay

Glandore   Clonakilty Bay

Tralong &   Seven Heads
Mill Cove

Union Hall
Castlehaven

Baltimore
Harbour   Glandore Bay   Dirk Bay
          Galley Head
Castletownshend   Doolic Rock   Fl(5)20s

Barloge   High Island

Baltimore   Reen Point
          Fl.WRG.10s

          Toe
          Head   N

Kedge Island   The Stags
          Q(6)+LFl.15s

Barrack Point
Fl(2)WR.6s   0   10

Sherkin   nautical miles
Island

BALTIMORE TO KINSALE – PASSAGE WAYPOINTS – WGS84 DATUM		
NAME	DESCRIPTION	LAT/LONG
Fastnet SE	½M SSE of rock	51°22'.85N 09°36'.00W
Cape Clear	7 cables S of Cape Clear	51°24'.50N 09°31'.00W
Baltimore approach	4 cables S of entrance	51°27'.90N 09°23'.48W
Kedge Island	¼M S of island	51°24'.00N 09°20'.80W
The Stags SCM	2 cables S of buoy	51°27'.40N 09°13'.70W
Galley Head	1M S of headland	51°31'.00N 08°58'.00W
Old Head of Kinsale	1½M SSE of headland	51°35'.00N 08°31'.00W

PASSAGE CHARTS

Admiralty Charts: AC/LE2424 Kenmare River to Cork Harbour, 1:150,000; AC/LE2129 Long Island Bay to Castlehaven, 1:30,000; AC/LE2092 Toe Head to Old Head of Kinsale, 1:50,000; AC1765 Old Head of Kinsale to Power Head, 1:50,000; SC5623.2 The Bull to Glandore, 1: 150,000; SC5623.3 Glandore to Ballycotton Bay, 1: 150,000.

Imray: C56 Cork Harbour to Dingle Bay, 1:170,000. Plans for harbours in this chapter cover Baltimore, Castlehaven, Glandore, Courtmacsherry and Kinsale.

SAFETY INFORMATION

This section of the coast is managed by Valentia Coastguard, Tel: 066 947 6109.

ELECTRONIC AIDS TO NAVIGATION

Fastnet   AIS planned.
Old Head of Kinsale   AIS; MMSI 992501107.

COASTGUARD AIS STATIONS

Mizen (Mt Gabriel)
51°33'.36N 09°32'.59W   MMSI 002 500370.
Cork (Airport)
51°50'.91N 08°27'.63W   MMSI 002 500360.

The wreck of the *Kowloon Bridge*

In itself this wreck, dating from 1986, is notable in that, at 300m long, it is the largest wreck in European waters. All the crew were saved. Normally that would end the story but this wreck had a huge political significance in that she was the sister ship to the *Derbyshire*, which vanished in the Far East with the loss of all hands. The *Kowloon Bridge* sank during one of the enquiries into the sinking of the *Derbyshire*. It was thought that cracking faults caused both ships to sink. It took until 2000 for the matter to be settled to the satisfaction of the families of the *Derbyshire* crew, whose perserverence in seeking the true cause of the sinking was vindicated. Bulk carrier design was modified as a direct result of these sinkings. The rate of loss of bulk carriers in the 1970s was 15-20 per year. This is now much reduced. Recently, a new controversy has started as the value of the wreck and its cargo of iron ore, based on global metal pricing, exceeds the cost of salvage, resurrecting the prospect of a major salvage operation, renewed pollution and the loss of a prime diving site. A final curiosity is that official lists of lights and marks describe the Stags south cardinal mark as the *Kowloon Bridge* south cardinal mark.

The *Kowloon Bridge*

Galley Head

Baltimore Harbour panorama. From right to left: The harbour entrance is overlooked by Lot's Wife, Sherkin Friary, Sherkin Pier and, in the distance, Baltimore village

Baltimore Harbour

Approach waypoint: 51°27'.90N 09°23'.48W
(½M S of Loo SHM)

Baltimore Harbour is a virtually landlocked shallow haven that features two interesting but very different ports of call. Baltimore village is an interesting tourist magnet and a useful stop for topping up fuel, water and provisions. Across the harbour to the west is the peaceful and almost car-free Sherkin Island with its O'Driscoll Castle, friary, hotel and lone pub. In a nutshell choose Baltimore to 'do' and Sherkin to 'be'. Note that the first week in August is exceptionally busy and space is at a premium – see 'Calves Week' in chapter six on pages 145 and page 156.

There are two entrances to Baltimore Harbour. The south entrance is deep and the obstructions are well marked. All references in this section are made with regard to the south entrance. The north-west entrance (The Sound) is unmarked and needs careful navigation, making it difficult enough to be off limits for some charter company yachts. For more detail on The Sound see chapter six pages 166–167.

Five miles east of the main harbour entrance along the coast is Barloge, from where Lough Hyne, a unique saltwater nature reserve, can be visited. This anchorage is described later in this chapter on page 179.

Entering Baltimore Harbour. Barrack Point lighthouse (left) and Lot's Wife Tower (right) form the southern portal to the harbour

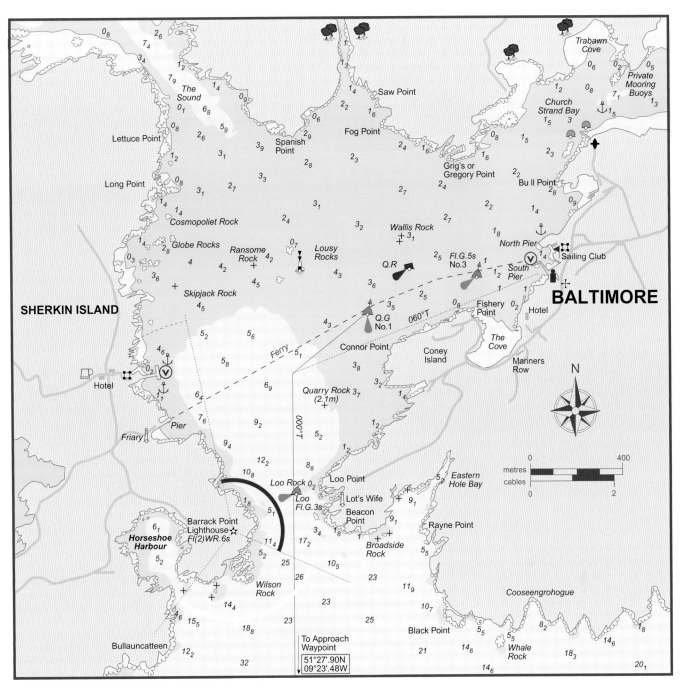

NAVIGATION

Harbour charts: Use Admiralty SC5623.13, AC3725 or Imray C56 (Inset). Use Admiralty SC5623.12 & .14, AC/LE2129 or Imray C56 for the approach.

Tides: MHWS 3.5m, MHWN 2.9m, MLWN 1.4m, MLWS 0.6m. Standard Port Cobh, difference at HW: Springs –00:25min; Neaps –00:05min.

The flood stream enters Baltimore Harbour from both The Sound and from the south entrance. These streams combine and head north-east into Church Strand Bay. The ebb is the reverse. The flood begins at HW Cobh +05:45 and ebb just after HW Cobh.

Lights & Marks
• Barrack Point lighthouse Fl (2) WR 6s.
White sector 294° to 138°T.
• 'Lot's Wife' on Beacon Point. A white conical pillar.

• SHMs: Loo Rock Fl G 3s, No 1 QG, No 3 Fl G 5s.
• Lousy Rocks SCM.
Not lit but a conspicuous perch by day.
• Wallis Rock PHM QR.
• The Stags SCM Q (6) + L Fl 15s (also sometimes referred to as the 'Kowloon Bridge SCM').

Approach: From the west, a track more than 2 cables off the south-east coast of Sherkin Island will clear all obstructions, including Wilson Rock in the south-west of the entrance channel.

The approach from the east is determined by a shallow wreck (1.8m) off the south shore of Kedge Island. To clear the obstructions in the south-east of the entrance do not let Barrack Point lighthouse bear less than 300°T before turning to the west-north-west.

Sherkin Island
(Irish: *Inis Earcáin*)

Sherkin Island is a delight. The main shoreside attractions are the 'quirkiness' of life on the island, invigorating walks and the Franciscan friary, which is gradually being restored. The ruins of *Dún na Long* (Fort of the Ships) Castle are just that and not preserved in any way. Both antiquities are 15th century and are situated close to the pontoons/anchorage. Protection is excellent in north-westerly/westerly winds with some scend in south/south-easterlies.

Sherkin overview. The visitors' pontoon projects offshore at the bottom of the photograph. Boats are moored around the pier. Horseshoe Bay is at the top of the picture, with the hotel at the bottom right

NAVIGATION

From the approach waypoint steer due north, keeping Loo starboard-hand mark very fine on the starboard bow and staying in depths exceeding 20m. This track clears Wilson Rock and, subsequently, the rocks under Barrack Point. From Loo starboard-hand mark steer 315°T and gradually close the Sherkin Island side of the harbour. The pontoon, partly constructed from an old hulk, is very visible to the north of the pier.

ANCHORING/BERTHING

Either anchor near or berth on the pontoon. For those that anchor, there is a €2 charge for a dinghy landing on the pontoon. The pontoons are easy to access.
The Pier: The south side of the pier is used 10 times a day by the Baltimore ferry. The slip, also on the south side, is used in the working week by the landing barge. The north side of the pier has a rock to the west end but otherwise has sufficient depths to go alongside. It is occasionally used for temporary mooring by local boats. Vertical berthing lines are secured to the sheer pier face, which has built-in steps. The pier is ½km from the pub and hotel and is also subject to the wash from the ferry.
Alternative anchorage: Horseshoe Bay is just outside the main harbour entrance to the west of Barrack Point and is favoured by some for a peaceful stopover. There is a good view of it from the hillside reached by a path south-west of the friary.

The O'Driscolls

The O'Driscoll clan ruled the area of West Cork around Baltimore. Their income was from fishing and piracy. They defended their realm by building nine castles, some of which are still standing. After much renovation, the early 17th century *Dun na Sead*, the 'Fort of the Jewels', in Baltimore village, is in a good state of repair. Others include *Dun na Oir*, the 'Fort of Gold', on Cape Clear and *Dun na Long*, the 'Fort of the Ships', on Sherkin Island.

A small island on which sit the ruins of Clohane Castle lies in the middle of Lough Hyne. The last of the clan chiefs, Sir Fineen O'Driscoll, died penniless here in 1629, supposedly having exchanged his lands in return for a title. Quite how this fits with surviving the ravages of the Battle of Kinsale is difficult to fathom.

Sherkin Island pier and Franciscan friary

Sherkin Island's visitors' pontoon. Above to the right are the ruined castle, the Islander's Rest Hotel (green) and the Jolly Roger pub (white)

Useful information – Sherkin Island

FACILITIES/EATING OUT
The seasonal pontoon is owned by the Islander's Rest hotel, Tel: 028 20116/086 241 9923. Charges are €20 up to 12m, €25 up to 15m and €30 thereafter, including electricity. **Fresh water** and **electricity** can be located on the pontoon but no rubbish disposal facilities have been installed on the island. There is one **toilet** ashore, which is shared with the restaurant. **Showers** may be possible by arrangement

with reception. Breakfast is served from 0900-1100, while all other meals are served from 1200-1930. There are currently plans to redevelop the hotel.

After all the walking and sightseeing, there will be a warm welcome at the Jolly Roger pub, 50m above the hotel. There is in fact a very interesting, and somewhat confusing, ebb and flow between the hotel and the Jolly Roger. At one moment the pub may be deserted

and the lounge bar in the hotel will be very busy, while a short time later the reverse is true. Also, taking an early evening siesta and stepping out after 2100 for a very late session seems to be routine. Look out for special concerts at the hotel. They are very popular with folk from the mainland and additional late night ferries are laid on to cope with the demand.

ASHORE
Above the pontoon are the remains of the castle. A little further on is the hotel and pub. Further afield, there are several sandy beaches, magnificent views and a profusion of wildlife (as well as abandoned cars and houses).

The ongoing conservation work commenced on the friary in 1986.

Baltimore
(Irish: *Baal an Tí Mhóir*, meaning Great House of Baal [a Celtic God])

Baltimore is a bustling village dominated by its harbour. Frequent ferries, fishing vessels, cruising yachts, sailing schools and the main village facilities all congregate on the tiny area around the harbour. It is also a very popular destination for day visitors and second-home owners, and can get particularly busy at weekends. Baltimore has yet to develop its full potential in marine leisure and is struggling with the pressures on the fishing industry. It would greatly benefit, among other things, from a larger improved visitors' pontoon with a breakwater, a pedestrianised harbour and a nearby chandlery. Nevertheless it is an excellent option as a landfall harbour from England, France and Spain, although it remains more of a pit-stop than a destination. Protection is mainly excellent, but a very strong north-westerly to south-westerly wind

can make berths on the west side of the village very uncomfortable. In such conditions move north-east past the lifeboat slip to Church Strand Bay.

NAVIGATION
There are numerous obstructions in this shallow harbour. Only one is likely to trap an ordinarily judicious navigator. This is Quarry Rock (2.1m) on the direct line between Loo starboard-hand mark and No 1 starboard-hand mark. Delaying the starboard turn to Baltimore by 1 cable on the entry track overcomes this concern.

From the approach waypoint steer due north, keeping Loo starboard-hand mark very fine on the starboard bow and staying in depths exceeding 20m. This track clears Wilson Rock and, subsequently, the rocks under Barrack Point. The Sherkin Island moorings are off to the north-west. At Loo starboard-hand mark, continue north for at least 1 cable before turning slowly to No 1 starboard-hand mark to avoid Quarry Rock. A check on the point of turn is the majority of the harbour

Lifeboat Station
Wallis Rock PHM
NO3 SHM
Dún na Séad Castle

A stranger arriving in Baltimore may have difficulty distinguishing local features

buildings coming clear of Connor Point at 060°T. Keep No 1 starboard-hand mark close to starboard to stay well south of Lousy Rocks south cardinal mark. Identify Wallis Rock port-hand mark and, north of the moored boats, try to identify No 3 starboard-hand mark whilst steering 070°T.

BERTHING/MOORING/ANCHORING

There is a choice of berthing on the pontoon, mooring on a visitor's buoy or anchoring. However, the choice is not as straightforward as might be expected for an obviously marine-centric place. If in doubt seek help from the harbour master, Tel: 087 235 1485, who is always willing to help.

Mooring: The easiest solution is to take one of the visitors' buoys. Phone the harbour master on the above telephone number to be allocated a buoy (by number). Situated in deeper water north of the piers, these buoys are usually large and mainly fitted with pickup buoys. The village is a short dinghy ride away. Land inside the harbour on the steps or slipway or at the small dinghy pontoon behind the yacht pontoon.

Berthing alongside: The pontoon (summer only) is very convenient for all of Baltimore's facilities. Unfortunately, it is very small (20 berths – more in good weather) but, based around an old hulk, is in great demand by those stopping for a quick meal, shower, drink, water fill or repairs etc. It is also surrounded by shallow water (around 1.5m above chart datum at low water springs); there may be adequate water alongside, but low water springs can give vessels with average keel depths some difficulty when approaching the pontoon. In summary, persistence, luck and negotiation skills are all needed to get alongside, but it can be done and will improve the crew's rafting knowledge.

Berthing fees: Overnight costs are €20 up to 10m, €25

Baltimore's piers and visitors' pontoon. The visitors' pontoon is connected by a footbridge to the newly refurbished South Pier.
Ferries constantly bustle to and from the inner harbour

for 10 to 12m and €30 for 12 to 15m. Day visits are €10 upwards.

Anchoring: Anchoring can be problematic too because the area off the pontoon to the north side of the buoyed channel, south-west or north-east of the visitors' buoys, is usually crowded and the holding dubious. The other close-by anchorage, to the north of the North Pier, can also be difficult because of commercial boat traffic nearby.

All of these locations are susceptible to bad weather from the west, in which case it is best to proceed a little to the north-east past the lifeboat slip to Church Strand Bay to anchor. Here the access to shore is either onto the beach, which can be fouled by weed, or a long dinghy trip back to the harbour.

Useful information – Baltimore

It can be bursting with activity alongside Baltimore's small visitors' pontoon

FACILITIES
The summer pontoon is attached to the west face of the south pier. It is run by Diarmuid Minihane, who is Managing Director of Atlantic Boat Services and also the harbour master. **Fresh water** can be obtained on the pontoon. **Diesel** and **gas** are available from Kieran Cotter who has an 'emporium' at the end of the south pier, Tel: 028 20106. Small quantities will be provided in cans; larger amounts may require delivery from the small road tanker. Diarmuid will find a suitable alongside berth for refuelling if necessary.

Two individual **showers** (€3 per person) are situated at the back of Bushe's Bar (adjacent to the harbour). There are also communal **showers** at both sailing clubs, but availability is restricted at times because, in peak season, there are often children using them after their sailing lessons.

Wi-Fi service is available from DigitalForge, Tel: 028 28983 or 086 081 9733 (see page 17 of the introduction).

PROVISIONING
A small but comprehensive Cotters/Gala **mini-market** overlooks the harbour. The staff are very helpful and will look after purchases while the crew go sightseeing or eating. Larger stores can be found in Skibbereen. Limited **postal services** are available from Cotters.

EATING OUT
The pubs play to the maritime theme and some are littered with interesting historical artefacts. Several restaurants, especially the more upmarket ones, do not accept credit cards. Overlooking the harbour are The Captain's Table, Tel: 028 20143, which offers inside dining only, Bushe's Bar, Tel: 028 20596/20125, serving excellent sandwiches, Jolie Brise Restaurant, Tel: 028 20600, named after the first winner of the Fastnet Race in 1925 – highly recommended for reasonably-priced good quality meals with excellent views across the harbour, and Jacob's Bar, Tel: 028 20159. The Lifeboat Café and Wine Bar is newly opened for lunches and teas.

Nearby are Chez Youen, a long established seafood restaurant with a wide reputation, Tel: 028 20136, and Algiers Inn, Tel: 028 20145, which is usually quieter than the bars overlooking the harbour. For finer dining (without credit cards) try The Mews, Tel: 028 20390, or The Customs House, Tel: 028 20200.

A short walk out of the village are Casey's Bar & Restaurant (BIM accredited), Tel: 028 20197, Glebe Gardens, Tel: 028 20232, and Rolf's Country House, Restaurant & Wine Bar, Tel: 028 20289.

ASHORE
The shoreside attractions include the castle, a walk up to Lot's Wife, a 5km hike by road to Lough Hyne or a short bus ride to the local main town of Skibbereen where the Heritage Centre is well worth a visit. Lough Hyne is more fully described in its own section of this chapter on page 179.

The harbour is dominated by *Dún na Séad* Castle

Useful information – Baltimore (continued)

The evening sun warms the outside tables in Baltimore on a Sunday evening in early June

three times a day.
Taxi: West Cork Cabs Tel: 028 22166; Baltimore Taxi Service (Michael's) Tel: 087 131 7313; Dave Long (Coaches & Taxis) Tel: 028 21138; Vintage Car (Pat Connon) Tel: 028 20309; Dolphin Taxis Tel: 028 23323; Waterside Taxis Tel: 086 870 3816.
Ferries: *Cailín Óir – Golden Girl* to Cape Clear Island, Tel: 028 39159/41923, 086 346 5110.
Naomh Ciarán II to Cape Clear Island, Tel: 028 39153, 087 268 0760, 087 282 4008. Sherkin Island Ferry, Tel: 028 20218, 087

244 7828. Ten trips per day. At the time of writing, the Schull and Heir Island ferries have been discontinued.

OTHER INFORMATION
Harbour master: Tel: 087 235 1485 & VHF Ch 09, 16.
Yacht clubs: Baltimore Harbour Sailing Club Tel: 028 20426. Visitors are welcome. It has a bar on the harbour. Glenans Irish Sailing Club, located in the old railway station, Tel: 028 20154.
Police: Tel: 028 20102.
Tourist office: Skibbereen Tourist Office Tel: 028 21766.

('Fort of the Jewels'). The castle was built in 1215 and until 1601, when it became another victim of the Battle of Kinsale, it was the main base for the O'Driscoll clan. It has recently been restored and it is open to the public in the summer.

Anyone entering the harbour from the south will have seen the distinctive conical white beacon, known as Lot's Wife, which was built around the turn of the 19th century as a very early navigational aid. It is about 1½km by road.

Baltimore was notoriously sacked in 1631 by Algerian pirates. Nothing is known of

the destiny of the 100 plus captives, but those left behind sought a more secure location for better safety and founded Skibbereen, 10 miles inland. The Algiers Inn serves as a reminder of the event. Skibbereen is now the largest town in the region. It has a wide selection of shops, a museum and heritage centre, but is mostly known for the Famine Burial Pits at nearby Abbeystrewery Cemetery on the Ballydehob road out of town.

TRANSPORT
Bus services: 251 to Skibbereen two or

Baltimore village. Left to right: Sailing club slipway, *Dún na Séad* Castle, Baltimore Sailing Club and a busy street scene with Cotter's shop in the peach coloured building

Barloge Creek for Lough Hyne
Approach waypoint: 51°29'.00N 09°16'.85W

Barloge Creek is a favourite stopover for lunch and a walk around Lough Hyne, the first ever marine nature reserve to be established in Europe. Protection in the anchorage is good except in south/south-easterlies. The scenery and birdlife are very special. Keep a look-out in particular for choughs.

NAVIGATION
Charts: Use Admiralty SC5623.14, AC/LE2129 or Imray C56.

Tides (approx): MHWS 3.7m, MHWN 3.0m, MLWN 1.4m, MLWS 0.7m. Standard Port Cobh, difference at HW: –00:25min.

Approach: From the west, keep 2½ cables south of Kedge Island and steer 052°T parallel to the mainland coast. From the east, through Stag Sound or from Stags south cardinal mark, make for the approach waypoint, 3½ cables west of Gokane Point.

Pilotage: Proceed north from the approach waypoint to acquire a back bearing of 120°T on Gokane Point; this requires Gokane Point to be in transit with the most south-westerly of the Stags rocks. Enter west of Bullock Island and south of the rocks to the south of it. Note that there appears, falsely, to be a channel between the rocks and Bullock Island through which it can be possible to see moored craft – keep to the west of these rocks, where there is a fading sign saying 'welcome to marine nature reserve'.

The Famine

The Famine had a cataclysmic impact on Ireland. Potatoes, as a crop, were introduced to Ireland as a result of Walter Raleigh's expeditions. It became the main, and in some cases, only food for many poor Irish. When potato blight struck in 1845, nearly one million died of starvation, cholera and other illnesses. The government did too little too late. Those that qualified for the workhouses were five times the capacity. Over a million emigrated, but this was not necessarily an escape as many died en route or in quarantine. Emigrant ships became known as 'coffin ships.' The only organisation to come through the Famine with any degree of credibility were the Quakers, who were 'most giving of relief'.

Entering the anchorage. Bullock Island is to starboard of the yacht. The false entrance between Bullock Island and the rocks off its south-west shore is clearly evident

ANCHORING

Anchor west of Bullock Island in 2 to 3m. Land at the adjacent quay.

LOUGH HYNE

Unusually, Lough Hyne is a seawater lake. The Rapids, which connect the lake to the sea, were narrowed and made resistant to erosion as a Famine Relief project. The lake retains most of its water, but the Rapids cause white water as the level of the sea exceeds or falls below the level of the lake. The ruins of Clohane Castle are on Castle Island in the middle of the lake. It was one of the fortresses in the area built by the O'Driscoll clan. The area is also very popular with walkers as part of the adjoining Knockomagh Wood Nature Trail.

University College Cork (UCC) started research on Lough Hyne in the 1930s and has three laboratories around the lough. As it is essentially a very large seawater rockpool, the water temperature exceeds that of the nearby ocean and distorts the viability of many marine creatures compared to their open

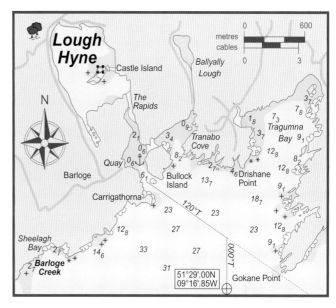

ocean neighbours. It also encourages the continued existence of over 50 species that are not normally found at this latitude in Europe.

Unfortunately, a trip 5km inland to Skibbereen's Heritage Centre, Tel: 028 40900, is necessary to obtain a full briefing on the very special inhabitants of the lough. The exhibition includes an audio-visual presentation and a salt water aquarium housing species from the lough. This trip would be most easily achieved from Baltimore by bus or taxi.

Barloge. The entrance to the anchorage is to the bottom right of the photograph. The boats moored off the quay are in the centre, while Castle Island in Lough Hyne is to the top left

The entrance to Castlehaven

Castlehaven
(Castletownshend)

Approach waypoint: 51°30'.28N 09°10'.26W
(7 cables south by east of Reen Point, in the white sector and due east of Black Rock)

Castletownshend village (Irish: *Baile an Chaisleáin*) is one of the most charismatic places to visit along the coast. This harbour is without doubt near the very top

The Stags through Flea Sound

of the must-do destinations for any cruise. Once inside the haven, protection is excellent, although a strong southerly may bring some swell up the harbour. Do not be deterred by tales of anchors dragging!

NAVIGATION

Charts: Use Admiralty SC5623.14 or AC/LE2129 when arriving from the west. Use SC5623.15 or AC/LE2092 if arriving from the east. Alternatively, use Imray C56.

Tides: MHWS 3.7m, MHWN 3.0m, MLWN 1.4m, MLWS 0.7m. Standard Port Cobh, difference at HW: –00:25min.

Lights & Marks
• The Stags SCM Q (6) + L Fl 15s (also referred to as the 'Kowloon Bridge').
• Reen Point Light Fl WRG 10s.
White sector, 338° to 001°T.
• Also, ruined tower on Horse Island and note use of The Stags through Flea Sound for pilotage.

Approach: From the west, The Stags can be passed to their north through Stag Sound, which has a spring tidal rate of 2kn and 30m depth over a width of 3½ cables, or to their south, which is protected by a south cardinal mark; in both cases, stay at least 2 cables off in a 30m depth during the turn north-east to Castlehaven.

The approach from the east (Galley Head) has no obstructions.

Passage from Glandore (see SC5623.15) is simplest south of High Island. Alternatively from Glandore, the passage through Big Sound is fouled by the uncovering Belly Rock (0.4m) in mid channel south of Rabbit Island: keep the north shore of Low Island in line with the ruined tower on Horse Island (bearing 253°T), breaking away to the north (at the 20m contour) close to Low Island into mid Big Sound and skirting around Low Island's outlyers (Seal Rocks). Continue thereafter towards the ruined tower on Horse Island (approximately 250°T) and turn into Castlehaven when Skiddy Island is due north (at the white-green transition of Reen Point light).

Pilotage: From the approach waypoint, steer 335°T to the middle of the entrance. Clear Colonel's Rock (uncovers – 50m offshore and 2 cables north of Reen Point) by keeping The Stags (3½M south-west) open through Flea Sound as pictured on page 180. Steer 028°T to the anchorage.

ANCHORING

Anchor outside the moorings off the village in 5m, avoiding the well signposted cable which runs across the harbour to the quay on the east shore. Holding is not good and aggravated by the strong currents in midstream. Leave plenty of room to swing and ensure the anchor is absolutely secure before going ashore. Land at the village slip.

Alternatively, anchor north of Cat Island.

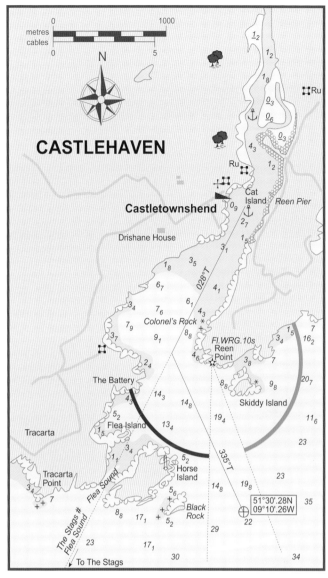

Castletownshend moorings and quays

Useful information – Castlehaven

FACILITIES
Fresh water is available on the town jetty. At high water, alongside access is possible with difficulty.

PROVISIONING
There is a small village **grocery** store with some **postal facilities**. It also sells **petrol**.

EATING OUT
Mary Ann's, Tel: 028 36146, is BIM accredited and highly recommended. This pub and restaurant is enough reason on its own to visit Castletownshend. It is, rightly, very popular and booking ahead will avoid disappointment for those intending to anchor for only a short period.

There are also two bars further up the hill opposite each other, one of which, Lil's Bar, may serve food. The other bar, Collins', was not serving food at the time of writing. Lil's Bar is particularly photogenic and 'a great place to meet the naburs (sic)'.

ASHORE
Castlehaven refers just to the harbour. The village is known as Castletownshend. The harbour area, with its renovated warehouses, hotel and picturesque moorings, is overlooked by St Barrahane's Church – a truly rural idyll. The church has two 'Harry Clarke' stained glass windows (the east window and the window in the south wall of the chancel) and is well known for its classical music festivals which have been held annually since 1980. These usually take place from mid-July to the end of August.

The remainder of the village perches on the hill beyond 'the trees' – Sycamore trees (see photo opposite) obstruct the main street causing vehicles to mount the pavement to pass them. Idiosyncratically, they were deliberately planted in this location to replace trees that had died. The main street climbs steeply and is lined with substantial houses that reflect the historic wealth of the village.

The village was founded by the Townsend family. Richard Townsend fought for Cromwell in England and was eventually despatched

Trees have priority in Castletownshend

to fight in Ireland. After his military career he settled here as a landowner. His descendants still live here and some of their more recent military exploits are commemorated on plaques in the church.

For those who remember the 1985 television series *The Irish RM*, one of the co-authors, Edith Somerville, lived here and drew some of the stories' themes from life here in the 1900s.

OTHER INFORMATION
South Cork Sailing Club: Tel: 028 36383.
Police: Tel: 028 36144.

At anchor off Castletownshend

Glandore/Union Hall

(Glandore – Irish: *Cuan Dor*, meaning Harbour of the Oaks/(Union Hall – Irish: *Bréantrá*)
Approach waypoint: 51°32'.35N 09°05'.10W
(4 cables S of Goat's Head)

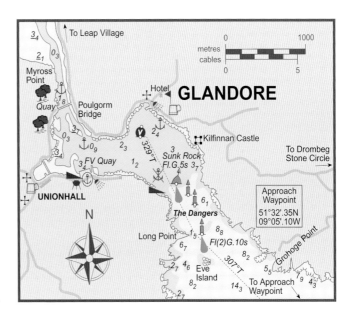

Glandore is a pretty village as found on the cover of any tourist brochure. It is a popular sailing centre with a hotel on the harbour and agreeable pubs overlooking the sheltered moorings in a beautiful setting. Across the harbour is Union Hall, a small but very busy fishing harbour used by over 30 vessels. Union Hall is more workaday and in the tourist shadow of Glandore but does not deserve to be ignored. If Glandore did not exist, it would be a perfectly pleasant and welcome destination in its own right. It can be reached by dinghy or a 3km walk over the single carriageway bridge that unites the two communities.

NAVIGATION
Charts: Use Admiralty SC5623.6E or Imray C56 for detail. Use SC5623.15, AC/LE2092 for the approach. Use only up-to-date charts to ensure the current lights and marks are correctly charted.

Tides (approx): MHWS 3.7m, MHWN 3.0m, MLWN 1.4m, MLWS 0.7m. Standard Port Cobh, difference at HW: –00:25min.

Lights & Marks
• Galley Head Fl (5) 20s.
• Glandore SW Dangers SHM Fl (2) G 10s.
• Glandore Middle Dangers Unlit Perch G Beacon.
• Glandore North Dangers Unlit Perch G Beacon.
• Sunk Rock SHM Fl G 5s.

Approach: Two islands, Adam's and Eve, obstruct the entrance; the trite but clear instructions 'Avoid Adam and hug Eve' are perennially valid. They are quite difficult for strangers to identify as both islands merge

Union Hall – a large group of yachts is moored in the shallow anchorage off the fishing vessel pier (centre). Clockwise from bottom left: single carriageway bridge joining Union Hall to Glandore, Glandore (centre left), Goat's Head (top centre), and Adam's and Eve Islands (top right)

The starboard-hand marks in Glandore Harbour. This view has been taken from inside the harbour to highlight the entrance marks against a clear sky (being green they are much harder to pick out against the verdant background on the way in)

well into the mainland shore. However, it is not difficult to stay well off Goat's Head until Adam's Island becomes obvious and, subsequently, Eve Island soon becomes distinct.

Pilotage: From the approach waypoint, steer 307°T, which leads midway between Goat's Head and Adam's Island to close on the west side of the south-west 'Dangers' lit perch. Leave the perch to starboard and steer 329°T past the middle and north 'Dangers' perches and also Sunk Rock buoy, after which steer due north to the anchorage or stand on for the public visitors' buoys. The channel to the east of the marks is not recommended for strangers.

MOORING

The six yellow public visitors' buoys are moored off the small harbour entrance. Payment (€7) should be made to the yacht club or the Glandore Inn.

ANCHORING

Glandore: There is plenty of space to anchor outside of the moorings. Do not stray too far outside these moorings towards Union Hall as the modern fishing vessels from there need deeper access than their predecessors and are likely to venture to the Glandore shore before turning south-east. To these vessels, at night, a yacht's anchor light will be obscured by the lights ashore in Glandore.

Union Hall: Alternatively, Union Hall anchorages provide good shelter in a south-westerly but are limited in depth. North of the quay, yachts with draughts up to 1.7m should stay afloat at neaps.

Note: Do not anchor where the anchor symbol is shown on chart SC5623.6E.

Glandore Harbour and dinghy pontoon in peak season

There is a splendid view across the harbour from an outside table at the Glandore Inn or the adjacent Hayes' Bar

Landing: At **Glandore**, a very useful floating dinghy pontoon lies immediately within the harbour. At **Union Hall**, above half tide only, there is access to the pontoon at the road bridge in the village itself. At other times, land next to the commercial pier ('Quay' on the chart) either on the beach or in the small dock to the east of the pier, or on the slip to the west of the pier.

If the tide permits, use the pontoon near Union Hall for a visit to the village, which has many more services than Glandore (centre of photograph). Land at the Fishing Vessel Quay (centre right) if the tide dictates or if showers are planned

Useful information – Glandore/Union Hall

FACILITIES/PROVISIONING

There is no ready source of **fuel** in either Glandore or Union Hall. By arrangement with the harbour master, large quantities can be delivered via tanker on the Union Hall pier. The nearest road fuel is at Leap (3km to the north), where additional facilities may also be found.
Glandore: There is no shop but **showers** are available (charged) in Bay View B&B, which is half way up the hill to the Glandore Inn, Tel: 028 33115.
Union Hall: Fresh water, for essential use only, can be obtained on the quay. **Showers** (free) are available via the harbour master. The village has a **post office** and a Centra **mini-market** with a commercial (usage fee) **ATM** and off-licence. It also sells **Kosan** and **Camping Gaz.**

EATING OUT

Glandore: There are three restaurants here: The first two are the Marine Hotel, Tel: 028 33366, on the harbour, and the Glandore Inn, Tel: 028 33468, which is clearly visible from the moorings. The third, the Rectory, Tel: 028 33072, is primarily dedicated to functions and is not for casual dining.

The Glandore Inn is just the place for excellent evening meals and the chance to share experiences with other crews. Nearby, Declan Hayes' Bar, also overlooking the harbour, does light meals in the day and in the evenings offers a convivial, relaxed atmosphere in a very comfortable lounge, Tel: 028 33214. Casey's Bar is up the hill past Hayes'.
Union Hall: This village

Sunk Rock light buoy

has several bars and restaurants, adding more variety to those in Glandore. Casey's majors on seafood and steak, Tel: 028 33590. Try Dinty's Bar, Tel: 028 33373, for a good steak if fresh fish has become too routine. Moloney's Bar and The Boatman's Inn offer further options.

However, if visiting Union Hall briefly, a picnic lunch is possible with the pre-prepared seafood sandwiches (and wine) from the well-patronised The Fish Shop, handily situated near the village pontoon, Tel: 028 33818. Otherwise there is The Coffee Shop next to the Centra store.

ASHORE

Drombeg stone circle (2½km east of Glandore up the hill past the Glandore Inn), is one of the most visited megalithic sites in Ireland. It is an interesting diversion for anyone, especially if the Kenmare River and its archaeology are not on the itinerary.

TRANSPORT

Bus services: Buses regularly serve Leap; Bus 237: Cork-Clonakilty-Leap-Skibbereen.

OTHER INFORMATION

Harbour master (Union Hall): John Minihane has an office on the fishing vessel quay. If advice is needed, he can be contacted on VHF Ch 6 or Tel: 028 34737/086 608 1944.
Yacht club: Has new premises adjacent to the Glandore Inn. Contact Dona Lynch, Tel: 028 33090.

Dinty's is just one of several excellent eating places in Union Hall

Tralong Bay, left, and Mill Cove

Minor harbours in Glandore and Clonakilty Bays

Tralong Bay and Mill Cove are adjacent stopover anchorages east of Glandore. Dirk Bay, South Ring and Dunworly Bay are situated in Clonakilty Bay. All these anchorages are exposed to winds with a southerly component.

Tralong Bay/Mill Cove

Tralong approach waypoint: 51°32'.70N 09°03'.10W
(4 cables SE of Tralong Rock)
Mill Cove approach waypoint: 51°33'.00N 09°02'.40W
(2 cables E of the Black Rocks)

Tralong Bay is more suited to a deep keel yacht than Mill Cove. Neither has any shore facilities.

NAVIGATION
Charts: Use Admiralty SC5623.15, AC/LE2092 or Imray C56.

Tides (approx): MHWS 3.7m, MHWN 3.0m, MLWN 1.4m, MLWS 0.7m. Standard Port Cobh, difference at HW: –00:25min.

Lights & Marks: None.

Pilotage/Anchoring: Tralong Bay: From the approach waypoint, steer 324°T to the cove entrance. Anchor in 3-4m.

Mill Cove: From the approach waypoint, steer 344°T to the cove entrance. Depth decreases rapidly past the first headland to starboard. This harbour is really suited to only shallow draught craft.

Dirk Bay
Approach waypoint: 51°31'.80N 08°56'.33W
(½M due E of Galley Head)

Dirk Bay is a large bay tucked in to the east of Galley Head. The anchorage offers limited protection from westerlies or is suitable as a stopover anchorage if waiting for the tide. The area has mainly eluded the tourist industry and is very secluded. From the anchorage in the west of the bay there is a panoramic walk to Galley Head. In the far north-east of the bay lies a beautiful sandy beach.

NAVIGATION
Charts: Use Admiralty SC5623.15, AC/LE2092 or Imray C56.

Tides (approx): MHWS 3.8m, MHWN 3.0m, MLWN No data, MLWS No data. Standard Port Cobh, difference at HW: Springs –00:33min; Neaps –00:11min.

Lights & Marks
• Galley Head Fl (5) 20s.
Note that Doolic Rock (3.7m) is within the white sector of Galley Head lighthouse, which actually marks The Stags, not these nearby rocks!

Approach: From the west clear Doolic Rock ½M to the south-west of Galley Head.
  From the east and south-east, drying Carrigduff

Dirk Bay: Slipway east of Galley Head

(1.5m), its submerged offlyers, which extend 1 cable south-west, and a submerged wreck (5.2m) obstruct the eastern half of the bay.

From all points, approach the bay from due south on its west side.

Pilotage: From the approach waypoint, steer due north ¾M until abeam a slipway. When entering the bay, keep at least a cable from the shore and anchor in depths of 4-5m. There may be fishing buoys inshore at the anchorage. If going ashore, land at the slipway.

South Ring
Approach waypoint: 51°34'.60N 08°51'.40W
(½M E of Duneen Head)

Shallow draught vessels can reach South Ring Quay, which is within 4km of Clonakilty, a pretty, well-kept and well-established town with attractions such as a Model Village/Train and a full range of services. This is a beautiful but windswept sandy estuary.

NAVIGATION
Charts: Use Admiralty SC5623.18, AC/LE2092 or Imray C56.

Tides (approx): MHWS 3.8m, MHWN 3.0m, MLWN No data, MLWS No data. Standard Port Cobh, difference at HW: Springs –00:33min; Neaps –00:11min.

Lights & Marks
• Wind Rock SHM marks the uncovering rocks west of Ring Head.

Approach: Entrance is ill advised, even dangerous, in a strong southerly as the sea breaks on the bar. Submerged Anchor Rock (2.3m) lies north-east of Duneen Head close to the entrance track.

Pilotage: It would be prudent to assume that the depth is chart datum at the entrance. From the approach waypoint steer 011°T to the west of Ring Head and leave Wind Rock Beacon close to starboard. However, the entrance bar and channel is liable to shift and local knowledge is recommended if entering the harbour.

www.irelandaerialphotography.com

Dirk Bay – a useful temporary anchorage. The Stags are top left, Doolic Rock is off Galley Head, centre left, and Carrigduff is in the eastern half of the bay

South Ring. The shallow winding estuary leading to Clonakilty

BERTHING

There is a drying alongside berth at South Ring Quay, but no facilities are available.

A taxi would be needed to carry purchases from Clonakilty back to the quay.

Dunworly Bay

Approach waypoint: 51°34'.17N 08°46'.00W
(Due W of Dunworly Point; due S of Cow Rock)

Dunworly is a large bay to the west of Seven Heads, which is useful for a stopover or as protection from severe easterly weather. The beach is very popular in peak summer.

NAVIGATION

Charts: Use Admiralty SC5623.18, AC/LE2092 or Imray C56.

Tides (approx): MHWS 3.8m, MHWN 3.0m, MLWN No data, MLWS No data. Standard Port Cobh, difference at HW: Springs –00:33min; Neaps –00:11min.

Lights & Marks
• Galley Head Fl (5) 20s.
• Cow Rock, which dries (2.6m), is in the centre of the bay.

Approach: Approach from the west is direct without any obstruction.

The approach from the east requires the rounding of Dunworly Point and Bird Island 1½ cables south of Dunworly Head.

Pilotage: Keep to the south-east part of the bay because drying Horse Rock (0.4m) fouls the north of the bay. From the approach waypoint, steer 024°T, passing midway between Cow Rock and Dunworly Head. Anchor off the beach in 4m. There are no facilities here.

www.irelandaerialphotography.com

Dunworly Bay

Courtmacsherry
(Irish: *Cúirt Mhic Seafraidh*,
meaning MacSherry's Court)
Approach waypoint: 51°36'.00N 08°38'.00W
(4 cables S of Black Tom SHM)

Courtmacsherry is a very pretty, hospitable, little village and harbour at the mouth of the Argideen River. It is protected from the Atlantic by a high ridge covered in beautiful woodland. To date it has escaped major development, probably because it is neither raw 'West Cork' nor very close or an easy drive to major conurbations. Resting at the end of its 5km cul-de-sac, as it does, no one 'passes through'. Protection is excellent in the harbour but a strong south-easterly breaks on the bar, at which time entry is dangerous. The view away from the unusual single-sided main street of manicured cottages is over their detached gardens to the sandy estuary backed by gently undulating countryside. Those that make it across the bar are well rewarded.

NAVIGATION
Charts: Use Admiralty SC5623.16, AC2081 (Courtmacsherry Bay) or Imray C56 (Inset).

Tides: MHWS 3.7m, MHWN 2.9m, MLWN 1.1m, MLWS 0.3m. Standard Port Cobh, difference at HW: Springs –00:29min; Neaps –00:07min.

The tide in the estuary can be very strong, exceeding 3kn at springs.

Lights & Marks
- Old Head of Kinsale Fl (2) 10s.
- Black Tom SHM, Fl G 5s.
- Barrel Rock SCM (Disestablished decaying ruin).
- Wood Point light Fl (2) WR 5s;
white sector 315° to 332°T (3m white pillar).
- Courtmacsherry SHM, Fl G 3s.
- Three starboard-hand channel markers (spars).

Approach: From the west, Seven Heads (Leganagh Point) is clean, except for drying Cotton Rock (3.6m), which is close in (1½ cables) north-east of the head. There are no obstructions from there to the approach waypoint.

The approach from the east is dominated by the Old Head of Kinsale. In settled weather the head presents no particular difficulty, but a race and overfalls develop in sympathy with the strongest tides (south-west in a west-going stream and south-east in an east-going stream). In these circumstances, plan to stay 1M off. There are no obstructions between the head and the approach waypoint.

Once north of Black Tom, Horse Rock (3.6m) is ½M off Barry's Point (2 cables west of the Wood Point white sector). Note that Barrel Rock no longer has a maintained navigation mark.

Courtmacsherry. The pier with its visitors' pontoon is bottom right. The Old Head of Kinsale can be seen in the far distance

www.irelandaerialphotography.com

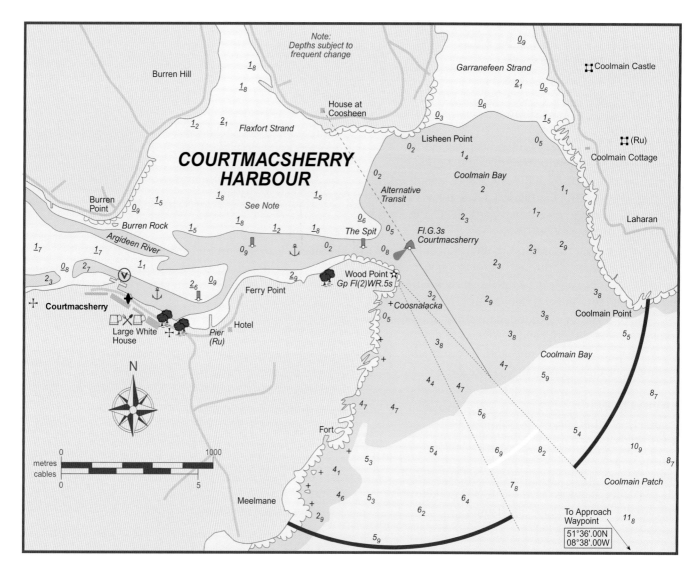

Approaching Courtmacsherry buoy. A possible alternative transit;
Courtmacsherry buoy in line with the white house on the north shore

Pilotage: Courtmacsherry Bar is notorious for shifting unpredictably. Even experienced locals have been known to go aground and the harbour is denied to charterers by some charter companies. Furthermore, the channel marks can be damaged by bad weather and may be missing. For entry, it would be prudent to assume a limiting depth of chart datum in the channel.

From the approach waypoint, steer 319°T towards Wood Point light. Pass Black Tom (2 cables to starboard) and Horse Rock (½M to port). The charted visual transit is Burren Hill, a low hill on the far side of the entrance, over Coosnalacka, which is situated on the shore south of Wood Point, on a course of 313°T. However, this may be of little use to a stranger as neither feature is well defined. An alternative transit, once Courtmacsherry buoy has been acquired, is the buoy in line with a white house on the north shore of the peninsula (approximately 323°T – see photo opposite).

The entrance is marked by Wood Point light to port and Courtmacsherry buoy to starboard. **Notes**:
1. At the time of writing, the entrance buoyage consists of Courtmacsherry buoy and three starboard-hand spar buoys. The first two spars are aligned approximately east-west with Courtmacsherry buoy. The third spar is

Have a spare crew member spotting the third spar buoy. Note the greystone church and the large white house on the shoreline

course for the first spar buoy inside the entrance to cross the bar; at the first spar, adjust course, if necessary, to arrive at the second spar. Have a crew member tasked to identify the third spar buoy; looking between the church and the large (white at the time of writing) house to its west, both of which are partly obscured by trees.

At the second spar, alter the boat's heading to port by at least 40° (more in a strong flood tide) for the third spar buoy.

At the third spar, alter course to starboard for the pier. Keep to the south as far from the sand bar as the moorings permit. The small yacht pontoon is on the upstream side of the pier and, unoccupied, is not visible until the last moment. If turning to berth against the tidal flow, be sure to apply enough power to quickly overcome the tidal stream.

small and is surrounded by moored boats – it is very difficult to pick out! During entry, keep the buoy and the three spars close to starboard.

2. The initial track inside the entrance is due west and therefore may be directly into the setting sun for an evening arrival. This can make acquisition of the first two spar buoys difficult.

3. It is implicit that arrival on a rising tide will mean a significant tidal flow into the river, particularly at spring tides. Helmsmen must be very alert to being set down onto moored boats.

From close south of the Courtmacsherry buoy, alter

BERTHING

The small (around 18m) pontoon is positioned off the main quay. Taken together, there is considerable length of quay for coming alongside. Upon arrival, the very helpful harbour master, John Walsh, will advise on where to berth if the pontoon is unavailable.

ANCHORING

Given the strong tidal flow, extremely robust anchoring is essential. Often the use of two anchors is recommended.

Useful information – Courtmacsherry

FACILITIES
The well-lit pontoon has **electricity**, while **fresh water**, **rubbish disposal** and **diesel** (available during the working day), are on the adjoining quay.

PROVISIONING
A small **store** is at the entrance to the quay.

EATING OUT
Hostelries include Pier House Hotel, Tel: 023 46170, which is at the entrance to the quay and has been in John Young's family for 50 years. Walking east, the Anchor Bar, Tel: 023 46180, is a traditional pub with regular music sessions. It is closely followed by the Lifeboat Inn, Tel: 023 46173, which does excellent evening bar meals and hosts a wide cross section of friendly locals, especially on 'Quiz

Night' – but do not sit in their usual seat at 9.29pm on a Monday night. The quiz starts at 9.30pm! Across the road, the pub also has a delightful garden with a great view of the estuary and the moorings. Further east still is the Courtmacsherry Hotel, Tel: 023 46198.

ASHORE
Courtmacsherry has no exceptional attractions; on the other hand it is a very relaxed, friendly place to come and rest for a while. There is an excellent sandy beach nearby and the walk around the peninsula to Wood Point is a pleasure. A longer walk westwards along the estuary leads to Timoleague, known for its Franciscan friary which was founded by the order in 1240. Timoleague also has a large grocery store.

The ambience may well change in the near future

as there are active plans to develop a 200+ berth marina in the bay close to the third spar buoy and the site of the ruined pier.

The Courtmacsherry harbour festival is held over a weekend near the August Bank Holiday.

TRANSPORT
Bus services: 239 Cork-Bandon-Courtmacsherry. One a day Monday-Friday.
Taxi: Barryroe Hackney, Tel: 087 795 6055/ 210 4964, and James Nicholson, Tel: 023 46444/087 833 0000.

The yacht pontoon is upstream of the pier, but is not normally dominated by the lifeboat!

Kinsale

Kinsale

(Irish: *Cionn tSáile*)
Approach waypoint: 51°40'.00N 08°30'.00W
(2 cables SW of Bulman SCM)

Kinsale is a vibrant, compact and friendly harbour, which also offers a wide range of services. Proximity to such bustle can come as a shock after the remoteness of moorings elsewhere, even in Cork Harbour. There is plenty to see, do and eat and, of course, it is the ideal place to change crews because it is only 20 minutes from Cork airport with its comprehensive list of destinations. Most tourist guides use the word 'gourmet' somewhere in their description of Kinsale. There is no doubt that the restaurateurs work hard to match the acclaim. Bistros, gastropubs and fine dining offer a bewildering choice. There are sheltered beaches in the estuary and the agreeable walk to the Charles Fort ends in a fascinating visit to part of Kinsale's history as a military stronghold. Small coasters frequently berth alongside the town quay to discharge animal feed and well orchestrated lines of lorries appear to transport the cargo to its final destination. Protection is excellent except when strong south-easterlies push into the harbour and raise a chop in the outside berths on the town side of the river.

NAVIGATION

Charts: Use Admiralty SC5623.17 (or SC5622.16), AC2053 or Imray C56 (Inset).

Tides: MHWS 3.9m, MHWN 3.2m, MLWN 1.4m, MLWS 0.6m. The Bar has a least depth of 3m.

Standard Port Cobh, difference at HW: Springs –00:19min; Neaps –00:05min.

The flood tide into the harbour commences 6 hours before HW Cobh and the ebb commences 19 minutes after HW Cobh. The maximum rate on the ebb is 3kn – more after exceptional rainfall inland.

Lights & Marks
• Old Head of Kinsale Fl (2) 10s.
• Bulman SCM Q (6) + L Fl 15s.

Bulman south cardinal mark with Big Sovereign in the background

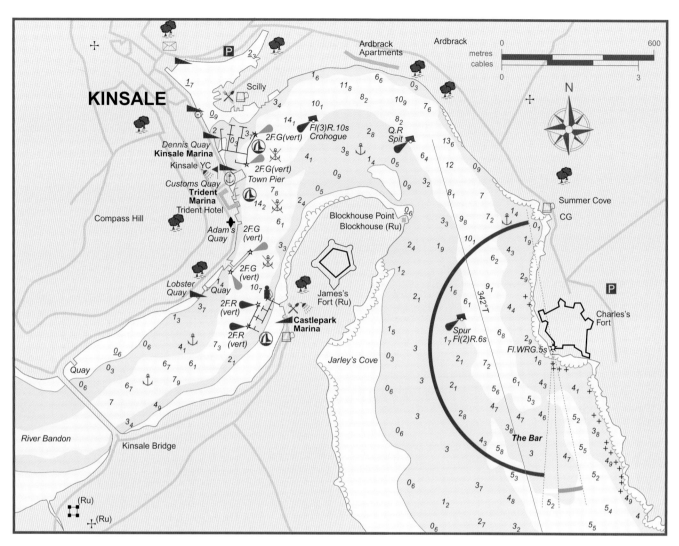

• Charles Fort Fl WRG 5s, white sector 358° to 004°T.
• Harbour PHMs Spur Fl (2) R 6s, Spit QR and Crohogue Fl (3) R 10s.
• YC Marina and Fishing Vessel piers: To starboard, both 2FG.
• Castlepark marina to port, 2FR.

Approach: From the west, the Old Head of Kinsale dominates the approach. In settled weather the head presents no particular difficulty, but a race and overfalls develop in sympathy with the strongest tides (south-west in a west-going stream and south-east in an east-going stream). In these circumstances, plan to stay 1M off.

The approach from the south and points east of Cork is simplest going south of Bulman south cardinal mark.

From Cork, a little distance can be saved by going inside Bulman Rock (0.9m), which lies 2 cables offshore. The transit clearing Bulman Rock keeps the north shore of Big Sovereign and Frower Point in line at 081.5°T.

Charles Fort. The small white light tower is plainly visible against the grey barrack building

After passing the final port-hand mark (Crohogue – centre photo), the Kinsale Yacht Club Marina (right of photo) is ahead. The Trident Marina is a little beyond the commercial quay and Castlepark Marina is to port (upper left of photo)

Pilotage: From the approach waypoint, steer due north towards Charles Fort light (a small white structure backed by a barrack building within the fort). This will track past Easter Point to starboard. Identify Spur and Spit port-hand marks ahead. After they transit, continue north, passing Money Point to port where the depth may touch 5m, until the distant Spit buoy bears 340°T (approximately 1½ cables north-east of Money Point). Alter course (about 342°T) to leave Spit buoy well to port. Cross The Bar (least depth 3m), pass Charles Fort to starboard, Spur buoy to port (keeping an eye on the depth to avoid the shoal to the west) and Summer Cove to starboard. After Spit, follow the buoyed channel to the berth.

ANCHORING

There is a large 'no anchor' zone around the main harbour area. Anchor either south of a line between Crohogue and Spit port-hand marks in 2-3m or south-west of Castlepark Marina in 4-8m. In both places, harbour fees are due and be aware that the ebb tide can reach 3kn.

BERTHING

There is a choice of three marinas in Kinsale. Each is described more fully below, but in all cases, it is best to phone ahead in office hours to discuss berthing arrangements as none have 24-hour staffing.

Kinsale Yacht Club (KYC) Marina

Kinsale Yacht Club Marina is the closest to the town and, with the capacity to accommodate up to 220 yachts, it has the largest number of visitors' berths (50 in total). For berthing availability contact the marina manager, Paul Murphy, on Tel: 021 477 2196/087 678

Kinsale. A freighter unloads animal feed

7377 or on VHF Ch 37, although note that VHF is being used increasingly less in preference to mobile phones. Further information can be had from emailing him on info@kyc.ie or looking at the website: www.kyc.ie/marinainfo.html. Entering the marina at night is possible; in the absence of an allocated berth it is best to tie up along the long outer pontoon.

Berthing fees: Charges (short term rate) vary per metre, depending on the overall length of the boat. Harbour dues are added and these also vary by length but are only charged for the first two nights of seven. Approximately, a one night stay will cost between €3.25 and €3.50 per metre. Rates include electricity.

FACILITIES

Facilities at the marina include fresh water and electricity on the pontoons, showers and toilets in the yacht club building and rubbish disposal and recycling bins in the club compound. WiFi is available in the clubhouse bar via a password provided by the bar staff and is included in the berthing charge for visiting craft. Other services include weather forecasts displayed in the club office window and a slipway adjacent to the marina.

Trident Marina

Trident Marina, adjacent to the Trident Hotel, is now managed by Castlepark Marina and is being redeveloped. The small marina has fresh water and electricity. Wi-Fi is available.

Castlepark Marina

Castlepark Marina is on the shore opposite the town and can accommodate up to 130 craft, including 20 visiting yachts. A night-time entry is possible, but keep well clear of nearby buoys (50m off pontoons). Unless previously advised of a specific berth, tie up on any outside pontoon except the fuel berth. The marina manager, Tadgh Wright, can be contacted in

advance on Tel: 021 477 4959 or 087 750 2737; VHF Ch 06; email: tadgh@castleparkmarina.com; website: www.castleparkmarina.com/. Office hours are 0800 to 1800 seven days per week in season and 0900 to 1700 in winter.

Berthing fees: Rates for a short stay are €5 per metre per night – €20 per metre per week.

FACILITIES

The marina has all the usual facilities, including fresh water and electricity on the pontoons – metered by prepaid card (€3.50 for 10kW-hour), showers and toilets in the marina building, rubbish bins at the marina entrance and diesel available alongside at the fuel berth. The marina office staff are very obliging with weather forecasts but these are also displayed on the marina gate noticeboard. WiFi is free of charge. Access to Kinsale Town is either by dinghy (landing at Trident Marina), taxi or 'Land Train', which operates through Kinsale to Charles Fort.

Useful information – Kinsale

FACILITIES
All services, both marine and town, are available nearby.
Fuel: Diesel can be acquired alongside at the Castlepark Marina. Petrol is sold at the filling station along the Cork Road.
Gas: Mylie Murphy's on Pearse Street holds a wide range of gas, fittings and adapters, Tel: 021 477 2703.
Boatyards: Kingston Brothers, Kinsale Boatyard, Middle Cove, Tel: 021 477 4774; website: www.kinsaleboatyard.com. Facilities include a boat hoist. Kingston Marine, Kilmacsimon Boatyard, Upriver, beyond Kinsale Bridge, Tel: 021 477 5134; email:kby@indigo.ie; website: www.boatsireland.com. Facilities for maintenance and repair.
Chandlers: All chandlers are in Cork City – CH Marine is the nearest to Kinsale at the junction of the Cork Ring Road and the Kinsale Road. Some deliver to Kinsale on a daily basis. Union Chandlery Tel: 021 427 1643; website: www.unionchandlery.com. Matthews Centre Tel: 021 427 7633; website: matthewsofcork.com/index.html.

CH Marine Tel: 021 431 5700; website: www.chmarine.com.
Electronics: For electrical and electronic equipment and parts try Maplin store in Blackpool Retail Park, Cork, Tel: 021 430 9196; www.maplin.co.uk/atoz.aspx.
Sailmaker: Eoghan O'Mahony Tel: 086 326 0018.

PROVISIONING
Two small but well-stocked **supermarkets** are close at hand in the town within 300m of Kinsale Yacht Club Marina. Londis, Tel: 021 470 0467, and SuperValu (will deliver to marina), along with the **post office**, are all on Pearse Street. Alternatively, the **Farmer's Market**, which takes place on a Tuesday on Merchant's Quay, offers a wide variety of produce.
Two **pharmacies** are located in the town: Collins Tel: 021 477 2077 and Moloney's Tel: 021 477 2130.

EATING OUT
Eating ashore in Kinsale should be the easiest of challenges along the coast but the options are so extensive that it can be

difficult to choose. Based on recommendations and experience, lunch would be at the BIM-accredited Fishy Fishy Café, Tel: 021 470 0415 (no reservations), situated between Acton's Hotel and the town park, and dinner at the Spaniard, Scilly, Tel: 021 477 2436. Also worth trying are Toddies at The Glen, Tel: 021 477 7769, which mixes exploratory meals with standard fare, and Jim Edwards (BIM accredited) on Short Quay, Tel: 021 477 2541, which is always busy – a short wait at the

bar usually results in a table coming free.
For a more considered look at the restaurants, take a walk along Main Street and Guardwell Street into Market Place, around the museum to Market Square and on to the junction of The Glen and Pearse Street. Walk back towards the harbour and most of the central restaurants will hove into view. If a decision has still to be made and the weather is pleasant, walk along Long Quay to Scilly. It's only 100m from the Kinsale Yacht Club Marina across

Main Street, Kinsale

Useful information – Kinsale (continued)

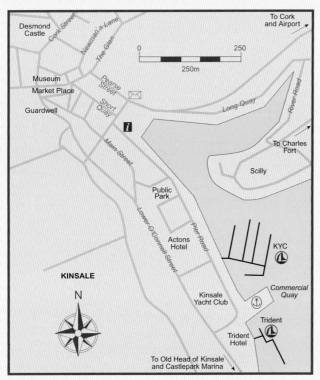

the water, but 1km by road. Here there are three restaurants to tempt and, if they do not, at least stop for a drink in the Spaniard to check out the memorabilia decorating the walls.

ASHORE
Kinsale was first settled in the 13th century and received a royal charter from Edward III in 1334, but only began to have a historical significance in 1601 – the date of the 'Battle of Kinsale', which was the catalyst for the demise of the clan system in Ireland and the flight of the clan chieftains. A Spanish force had taken Kinsale and this threat to the English Crown caused an army to be sent to lay siege to Kinsale. Spain was keen to see English power diminished following the defeat of their Armada in 1588. Hugh O'Neill and his Irish army dashed across Ireland to lay siege to the English laying siege to the Spanish. O'Neill was soundly repulsed by the English while the Spanish failed to support their ally. Thereafter, Kinsale became a Royal Navy stronghold until the size of warships outgrew

the local capabilities.
Kinsale failed to keep out of Irish politics when James II (The Old Pretender) landed with French troops, during the Jacobite Uprising of 1689, en route to an attempt to reclaim the crown from King William III. James was defeated at the Battle of the Boyne in 1690 and escaped through Duncannon in County Wexford.

Through the 17th century, the forts at the entrance to the harbour were built; first James Fort to the west followed by Charles Fort to the east. Kinsale is therefore very much an 'English' town. This is reflected in the architecture, which is notably Georgian in places.

Among the main sights of the town is Desmond Castle (circa 1500), which is actually a Tower House that was built by the wonderfully named Maurice Bacach Fitzgerald for its initial role as a Custom House. During the Spanish occupation it was used as an arms store. It has also housed prisoners of war from the Napoleonic Wars and, later, the American War of Independence. In the 21st century its role is as a Museum of Wine.

The building housing the regional museum dates from 1600. It played a significant role as the inquest venue for the sinking of the RMS *Lusitania* off the Old Head of Kinsale. The exhibits include royal charters and traditional lace.

The best of Kinsale may be seen from a walk from the pier to Charles Fort via Scilly along the east edge of the River Bandon estuary. The route passes the nature reserve in the upper part of the harbour below Scilly and then winds past the restaurants of Scilly to Summer Cove, gaining enough height on the way to have views upriver past Kinsale Bridge, across the town and out to sea as far as the Old Head lighthouse. To answer the inevitable question, Scilly is so called because fishermen from the Scillies used to berth there during fishing voyages. Eventually some stayed and adopted the name of their original home. Looking west, the escarpment is dominated by the façade of the old convent.

Kinsale suffered a massive economic downturn when the British left in 1922. It took until the late 1970s to begin its recovery, at which time it had no restaurants. It has recovered well and Kinsale is not short on ambition for the future. It is now twinned with Antibes-Juan les Pins and Newport, Rhode Island.

TRANSPORT
Bus services: There is a frequent bus service

to Cork from a bus stop near the town park (100m from Kinsale Yacht Club Marina). 249 Cork-Cork Airport-Kinsale.
Taxi: Kinsale Cabs Tel: 021 477 2642; Cab 3000 Tel: 021 477 3000.
Car hire: Is widely available at Cork Airport and includes Avis Tel: 021 432 7460; Budget Tel: 021 431 4000; Hertz Tel: 021 496 5849; Irish Car Rentals Tel: 021 431 8644; National/Alamo Tel: 021 431 8623.
Bicycle hire: The Hire Shop Tel: 021 477 4884 or Murphy's Tel: 021 477 2703.
Rail: Trains depart from Cork for Dublin, Cobh, Mallow, Tralee and Limerick, Tel: 021 450 6766.
Car ferry: Ringaskiddy, Cork for Brittany Ferries to Roscoff, France.
Air: Cork Airport is 20km (20 mins) away.

OTHER INFORMATION
Harbour master: The harbour master, Phil Devitt, has his office above the town quay, Tel: 021 477 2503.
Customs: Forms are available from the Kinsale Yacht Club Marina office.
Police: Tel: 021 477 2302.
Hospital: A&E Cork, Tel: 021 454 6400.
Doctor: Medical Centre Tel: 021 477 2253 or contact a doctor on Tel: 021 477 2717.
Dentist: Tel: 021 477 2788/021 477 4133.
Tourist office: Along the quay from the Kinsale Yacht Club Marina, Tel: 021 477 2234.

Market Quay – Tuesday lunchtime

Crosshaven marinas and the Owenboy River

Chapter eight
East Cork Coast

If voyaging east, welcome to the Irish Riviera! The sunniest and warmest coasts of Ireland lie along the south-east between Cork and Wexford. The countryside is gentle; the remnants of mountainous terrain are largely replaced by rolling hills and cultivated fields supported by market towns and the city of Cork. The one thing that does not change is the power of the Atlantic and its rule over where and when to sail. Expect to encounter more people, see other yachts more than once a day and fewer idiosyncratic anchorages. The 'coast' has become the 'seaside' and its beaches and

harbours are enjoyed by the local town dwellers.

If voyaging west, sail with full provisions, fuel and water tanks and no defects, unless the plan is to stop in Kinsale, beyond which self-reliance moves a long way up the priority list.

Cork is one of the great harbours of the world – reputedly the largest natural harbour in Europe. Since the early 1800s, it has had a hand in the making of the history of many countries. Strategically placed for the European sea lanes and large enough to host the world's greatest liners, it was key to the development

Roche's Point – a very welcome site after a heavy crossing or a long passage! Note the plethora of old signal buildings

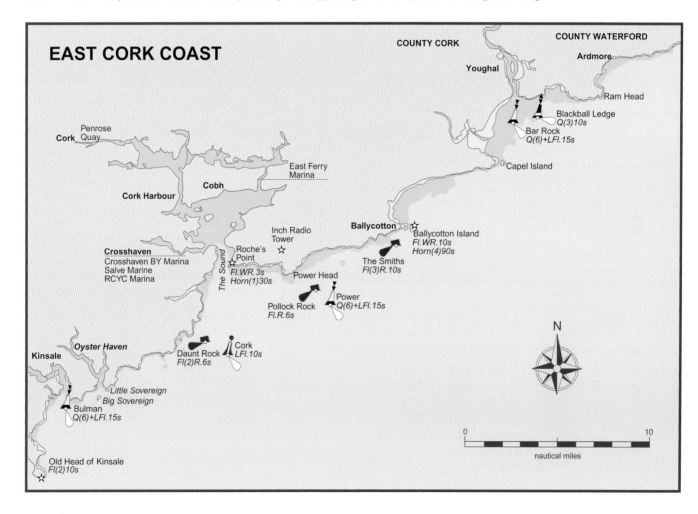

EAST CORK COAST

COUNTY CORK

COUNTY WATERFORD

Ardmore

Youghal

Ram Head

Blackball Ledge
Q(3)10s

Bar Rock
Q(6)+LFl.15s

Penrose
Cork Quay

Capel Island

East Ferry
Marina

Cobh

Cork Harbour

Ballycotton
Ballycotton Island
Fl.WR.10s
Horn(4)90s

Inch Radio
Tower

Crosshaven
Crosshaven BY Marina
Salve Marine
RCYC Marina

Roche's
Point

The Sound

Fl.WR.3s
Horn(1)30s

The Smiths
Fl(3)R.10s

Power Head

Power
Q(6)+LFl.15s

Pollock Rock
Fl.R.6s

N

Oyster Haven

Kinsale

Daunt Rock
Fl(2)R.6s

Cork
LFl.10s

Little Sovereign

Big Sovereign

Bulman
Q(6)+LFl.15s

Old Head of Kinsale
Fl(2)10s

0   10

nautical miles

EAST CORK COAST – PASSAGE WAYPOINTS – WGS84 DATUM		
NAME	DESCRIPTION	LAT/LONG
Old Head of Kinsale	1½M SSE of headland	51°35'.00N 08°31'.00W
Cork Landfall Buoy	1M SE of buoy	51°42'.12N 08°14'.71W
Power Head	½M S of Power Head Rock	51°46'.40N 08°10'.00W
Capel Island	1M SE of island	51°52'.00N 07°50'.36W
Ram Head	8 cables SE of headland	51°55'.75N 07°42'.00W
Mine Head	1½M E of The Rogue, Mine Head	51°59'.50N 07°32'.20W

of North America, trade in the British Empire and Irish emigration. Most famously it was the final port of call of the White Star liner *Titanic* two days before she hit the iceberg. Although many drawings depict her alongside at Cobh's Deepwater Quay, she anchored outside the harbour off Roche's Point. Mail and passengers were ferried out to her.

Oyster Haven, Ballycotton and Youghal are interesting individual destinations and, taken with nearby Kinsale, offer a compact, easy cruising ground based on the extensive facilities in Cork Harbour for those on a quick dash from nearby Europe.

FAVOURABLE TIDES

Off Kinsale for eastward passage – commences 4 hours 20 minutes before HW Cobh. Off Capel Island for westward passage – commences 2 hours 35 minutes after HW Cobh.

WEATHER INFORMATION BROADCASTS

This coast is served by the Valentia Coastguard transmitter at Roche's Point on VHF Ch 26 in the west. An advisory announcement is made initially on Ch 16. In the east it may be possible to hear an identical broadcast from Dublin Coastguard using the Mine Head transmitter on Ch 83.

PASSAGE CHARTS

Admiralty Charts: AC/LE2424 Kenmare River to Cork Harbour, 1:150,000; AC/LE2049 Old Head of Kinsale to Tuskar Rock, 1:150,000; AC1765 Old Head of Kinsale to Power Head, 1:50,000; SC5622.7 Glandore to Ballycotton Bay, 1: 150,000; SC5622.2 Ballycotton Bay to Waterford 1:150,000.
Imray: C57 Tuskar Rock to Old Head of Kinsale 1:170,000. Plans for harbours in this chapter – Cork Lower Harbour, Cork to East Ferry Marina, Crosshaven and Youghal.

SAFETY INFORMATION

This section of the coast is managed by Valentia Coastguard, Tel: 066 947 6109.

ELECTRONIC AIDS TO NAVIGATION

Cork Landfall Buoy	AIS; MMSI 992501100.
Old Head of Kinsale	AIS; MMSI 992501107.
Ballycotton	AIS; planned.

COASTGUARD AIS STATIONS

Cork (Airport)	
51°50'.91N 08°27'.63W	MMSI 002 500360.
Mine Head	
51°59'.60W 07°35'.10W	MMSI 002 500350.

There may be room to anchor at Drake's Pool up the Owenboy River

Oyster Haven

Approach waypoint: 51°40'.94N 08°26'.95W
(Due W of Little Sovereign; due N of east face of
Big Sovereign)

Oyster Haven is a naturally relaxing and quintessential anchorage away from the hubbub of Kinsale and Cork. Good fishing off the boat is to be had in the harbour. The anchorage is well sheltered except in southerlies.

NAVIGATION

Charts: Excellent detailed chart Admiralty SC5622.15 or AC2053.

Tides (approx): MHWS:3.9m, MHWN:3.2m, MLWN:1.4m, MLWS:0.6m. Standard Port Cobh, difference at HW: Springs –00:19min; Neaps –00:05min.

Lights & Marks: None.

Approach: From the west, the simplest approach is south of Bulman south cardinal mark. From Kinsale, a little distance may be saved by going inside Bulman Rock (0.9m), which lies 2 cables offshore. The transit clearing Bulman Rock keeps the north shore of Big Sovereign and Frower Point in line at 081.5°T.

From the east the easiest approach is south of Little Sovereign. However, if approaching using the channel north of Little Sovereign, Sovereign Patch is shallow (2m) and mid channel. It is therefore best passed after half tide in settled weather.

Pilotage: From the approach waypoint, steer due north on the west side of the entrance until 1 cable beyond Ferry Point. This can be achieved by steering a tight back bearing on Big Sovereign east face of 180°T. Before the entrance, do not stray west of the

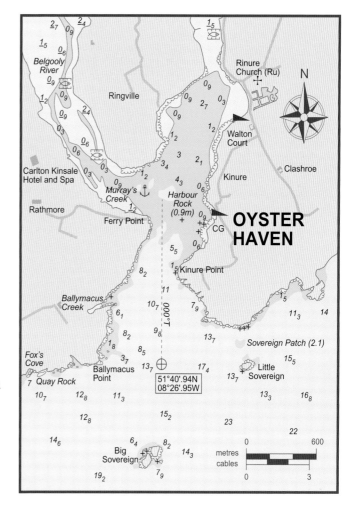

west face of Big Sovereign, to clear shallows cum rocks on Ballymacus Point.

Inside the harbour, clear Harbour Rock (0.9m), which is 1½ cables east of Ferry Point, by staying to the west of Kinure Point at all times.

ANCHORING

Anchor mid-stream in the river mouth to port, which is referred to variously as Murray's Creek or the Belgooly River. It has a heavily wooded south shore. Keep Kinure Point open of Ferry Point for deeper water.

Land on the slip below the large white coastguard building in the south-east corner of the harbour.

Alternative anchorages are possible in mid-harbour or in the northern arm (useful in south-easterly winds).

FACILITIES

There are no facilities nearby, except the four star Carlton Kinsale Hotel and Spa on the hill above the anchorage.

Oyster Haven anchorage. Keep Kinure Point open of Ferry Point

www.irelandaerialphotography.com

Drake's Pool anchorage, Crosshaven and Lower Cork Harbour. The beautiful anchorage is at the bottom of the photograph. Whitegate Oil Terminal heads well into the main harbour, top left. Roche's Point is just out of shot to the top right of the picture

Cork Harbour

Cork Harbour is an ideal place to be for a crew change, should severe weather occur or if spares or repairs are needed. Public transport is good and all major destinations are connected by road or rail. There is a warm greeting for all visitors, but it might be wise to avoid arriving unintentionally in Cork Week (every two years in mid July – even years).

Inside the entrance, the impressive vista is dominated by an island directly ahead. It is accurately named Great Island, on which stands the sizeable town of Cobh, where the spire of St Colman's Cathedral breaks the skyline. Entry to the harbour is uncomplicated but choosing a particular destination is the challenge, because there are so many options for visiting yachtsmen.

SELECTING A DESTINATION

Crosshaven is a cheerful, pleasant holiday village and suburb of Cork that is enlivened further by the large boating community. It is a historic fishing village on the Owenboy River only 2M from Cork Harbour entrance at Roche's Point, reached via a well-marked and lit channel. It offers several berthing possibilities, including mooring buoys, the Town Quay and three

marinas which occur in quick succession near the centre of the village on the south shore of the river. Protection is excellent in most conditions. Good facilities can be found in the boatyards and ashore. Upstream from Crosshaven is the popular anchorage of Drake's Pool. The anchorage has no facilities. The vast majority of cruising visitors choose Crosshaven as a destination and the pilotage notes assume this is the case. A visit to Cork City is easy using the regular bus service but, from here, Cobh is best visited afloat.

Great Island is 7km west to east and 4km south to north. Cobh, the main town, has all the usual urban services – banks, museums, stores etc. Cobh is well worth a visit in its own right. The major attractions include St Colman's Cathedral and the 'Queenstown Experience' exhibition at the Heritage Centre. The centre contains displays which explain the main events in the town's history: convict deportation, the *Titanic*, emigration during the famine and the sinking of the *Lusitania*. As there is no marina or other overnight mooring, a daytime visit may be made from the conveniently situated Quays Bar pontoon. Pilotage notes for Cobh and Cork city commence between Fort Meagher (formerly Fort Camden) and Fort Davis (formerly Fort Carlisle).

Penrose Quay in Central Cork is just downstream of the first river bridge. It is very convenient for access to the centre of Ireland's second city and Union Chandlery, but there is no security and an unattended yacht on this berth is therefore exposed to the risks to be expected in the centre of any large city. There is also a 4m tidal range to cope with if staying for more than a short visit. Working wharfs handling medium-sized merchantmen are the immediate neighbours. Nevertheless, yachtsmen are welcome up the river.

East Ferry is a small full service marina in quiet, wooded, rural surroundings, some would say a backwater, on the east side of Great Island, in scenic East Passage. Although Cobh is not far away, taxi is the only reliable means of transport to and from the town. Further upstream, an isolated anchorage can be found to the south-west of Ahanesk House. Pilotage notes for East Ferry Marina commence between Fort Meagher and Fort Davis.

None of the marinas are staffed on a 24-hour basis; as is usual in Ireland, it is best to phone ahead during business hours to make berthing arrangements.

OTHER HARBOUR ISLANDS (NO LANDING)

Haulbowline Island is just south-west of Cobh and was the hub of the Royal Navy's presence in the harbour. The oldest buildings date from the 1700s; it has a Martello Tower at its highest point. The island has since more than doubled in size because the eastern side is reclaimed land based on slag from an old steelworks. The Irish Naval Service now has its headquarters on the island. It was the founding site of what has become The Royal Cork Yacht Club (RCYC) – see page 207.

Spike Island is positioned centrally in the harbour. It has had a long military history and has only recently been abandoned as a civil prison. The main edifice is a large sunken fort, built as the second line of defence to the two forts at the entrance narrows.

OTHER ANCHORAGES

Just outside the harbour on the western coast are two daytime anchorages – Ringabella Bay and Robert's Cove.

Haulbowline Island headquarters of the Naval Service

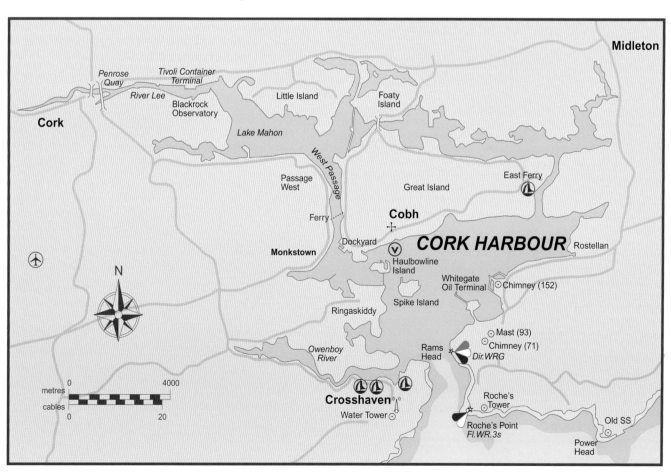

Crosshaven

(Irish: *Bun an Tabhairne*)

Cork harbour approach waypoints:
1) From the west: 51°43'.22N 08°17'.20W
(Midway Daunt Rock PHM and Cork Landfall Buoy)
2) From the east: 51°46'.90N 08°15'.30W
(7 cables S of Roche's Point)
Crosshaven entrance waypoint: 51°48'.80N 08°16'.73W

The entrance to Cork Harbour (The Sound) past Roche's Point is wide and, for leisure craft, deep. For large merchantmen, there are separate leading lights for the west and east 'gates' within The Sound. As the main harbour opens out, Whitegate refinery terminal dominates the view to starboard. Spike Island and Cobh Town are ahead. Forts Meagher and Davis are to port and starboard respectively at the northern limit of The Sound.

Not so obviously, the Owenboy River joins the harbour off to the west. A pair of lateral buoys indicates the start of the well-marked river passage beyond a shallow patch off the Fort Meagher shore (Rams Head Bank). On the north bank of the river is the Currabinny Peninsula, which is an undeveloped rural oasis of calm in the midst of the comings and goings of Ireland's second city.

NAVIGATION

Charts: Admiralty: Cork Harbour Approach; SC5622.9, Cork Entrance (The Sound); SC5622.8 & 10, Crosshaven, Owenboy River; SC5622.10 or AC1765, AC/LE1777 and AC/LE1773, or Imray C57.

Tides: MHWS: 4.1m, MHWN: 3.2m, MLWN: 1.3m, MLWS: 0.4m.

Cobh is the Standard Port for the south coast of Ireland from Wexford Harbour to Fenit in County Kerry. All high water times in this section of the chapter refer to HW Cobh. The flood tide into the harbour commences 5 hours 40 minutes before HW Cobh and the ebb commences 10 minutes after HW Cobh. The tidal rate in The Sound is 1½kn (more over Harbour Rock).

Outside Cork Harbour, the flood (north-east going stream) continues after high water in the harbour, finishing no later than HW+0150 well offshore (HW+0100 at Cork landfall buoy). The ebb ends similarly.

Inside the harbour, the incoming stream generally floods north and west. The stream passes on both sides of all islands, notably around Great Island, where it meets on the north shore.

Lights & Marks (Cork Harbour Approach, The Sound and Owenboy River)

Approach Buoys
- Power SCM Q (6) + L Fl 15s.
- Pollock Rock PHM Fl R 6s.
- Daunt Rock PHM Fl (2) R 6s.
- Cork Landfall buoy L Fl 10s.

Lights
- Roche's Point lighthouse; Fl WR 3s:
– two white sectors; SE Approach 292° to 016°T and The Sound 033° to 159°T.
– three red sectors; Eastern shore/Power Head to 292°T. Daunt Rocks 016°T to 033°T and the Eastern Sound 159°T to shore.
- Fort Davis/Dognose leading lights Dir WRG. FW on 354.5°T (±1°) for the East Gate.
- White Bay leading marks (2 white huts)/lights Oc R 5s (synchronised) on 034.6°T for the West Gate.

Buoys in The Sound
- West Gate laterals: W1 SHM Fl G 10s, W2 PHM Fl R 10s and W4 PHM Fl R 5s.
- East Gate laterals: E1 (Chicago Knoll) SHM Fl G 5s, E2 (Outer Harbour Rock) PHM Fl R 2.5s, E4 NCM Q.
- Upper Sound laterals: No 3 SHM Fl G 2.5s, No 6 PHM Fl R 2.5s, No 5 SHM Fl G 5s.

Owenboy River
All the channel buoys are lit and flash once. The buoys are paired/sequenced as follows: C2A PHM (R 7.5s)/ C1 SHM (G 10s); C2 PHM (R 5s)/ C1A SHM (G 5s); C4 PHM (R 10s); Currabinny Pier Fl G 5s; Crosshaven Boatyard Two Fixed R (vertical) at each end of their marina; C3 SHM (G 10s); Town Pier Two Fixed R (vertical) at each end of the pier.

C3 starboard-hand mark off the Town Pier

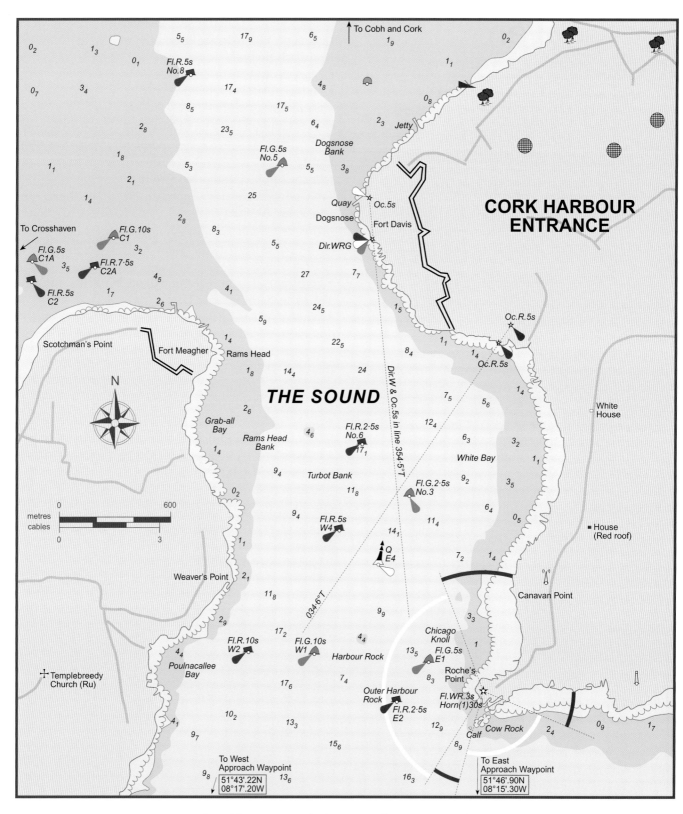

Pilotage (Cork Harbour approach): Head between Roche's Point and Weaver Point and then between the two forts (Meagher and Davis).The south-west red sector of Roche's Point lighthouse protects Daunt Rock and may be ignored once north-east of Daunt Rock port-hand mark. Two deep-water channels (East Gate and West Gate) are marked by buoys and leading beacons/lights, but in mid channel the least depth is 5m and most small vessels will be able to pass freely up The Sound. The entrance is straightforward at any state of the tide, day or night. Be aware of Cow and Calf Rocks 1 cable off Roche's Point, Carrigabrochell Ledge south-west of Weaver Point and Ram's Head Bank north of Weaver Point. Proceed to a point midway between the two forts .

Pilotage (Crosshaven): The Crosshaven fairway is best tackled for the first time in daylight. The Owenboy River opens up to port just beyond Fort Meagher, although it is largely obscured by Currabinny Peninsula. From the entrance waypoint, identify the

The house with the red roof on the tip of the Currabinny peninsula

first pair of channel buoys. In the case of difficulty, the splendid house with a red roof in the sylvan setting (marked on the Admiralty chart) should bear 257°T. Follow the channel markers in the sequence listed above and shown on the chartlet. Once past the Crosshaven

Boatyard Marina and the Town Pier, the Salve Marine visitors' berths are ahead on the south side of the marina cul-de-sac, or, if heading for the Royal Cork Yacht Club (RCYC) Marina or the anchorages, leave the outermost Salve Marine pontoon to port and the moored craft to starboard. The moorings upstream of the RCYC Marina pontoon are 'endless' and eventually lead to the popular Drake's Pool where there may be room to anchor in 2m. Land where the other yachts' tenders are stored.

BERTHING

Besides the Town Pier, there are three marinas with visitors' berths to choose from: The first, to port after Currabinny Pier and before the drying inlet to the south, is Crosshaven Boatyard Marina (where visitors can normally be found a berth). The boatyard is famous for building Sir Francis Chichester's yacht *Gypsy Moth*. After the drying inlet is the Port of Cork Town Pier (suitable for short stays only) with 'C3' buoy close by. Immediately after is Salve Marine, which has alongside fuel and is the closest marina to the village centre. Its one long outside pontoon is followed by the Royal Cork Yacht Club (RCYC) Marina, which has excellent shoreside facilities.

None of the marinas are staffed overnight. As elsewhere it is best to telephone ahead during working hours to make arrangements for arrival. The use of mobile telephones is now commonly accepted and most marinas will call back if left a message or even if

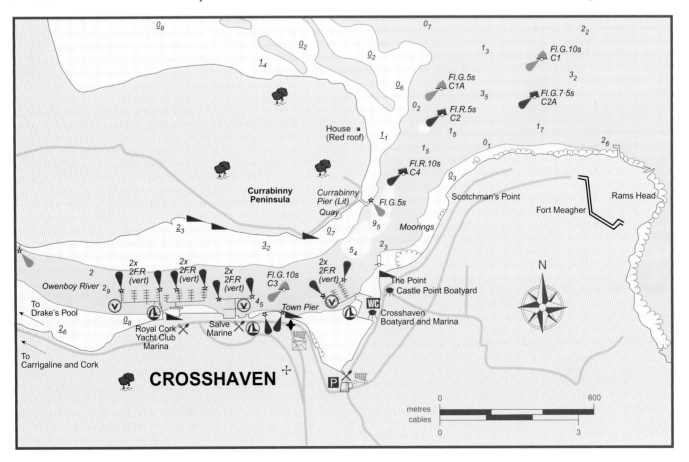

The channel upriver to the marinas is well marked, although strangers may be thrown by the exaggerated track around buoy C3, which lies close to the Port of Cork pier. Salve Marine's long pontoon is to the right of C3 buoy. The visitors' pontoon is far left

they miss an incoming call. (The marinas use Ch M, but use of VHF radio, particularly in the case of Crosshaven, would be problematic because of the surrounding hills).

Tidal flow on both ebb and flood is strong in the narrow fairway past the marinas, the whole river is densely populated with moorings and boat movements are very frequent. Good helming and alertness is essential when manoeuvring. At night, the fairway is well lit for entry but finding a berth may be demanding, especially after a long, tiring passage, in which case consider picking up a RCYC visitors' mooring.

Crosshaven Boatyard Marina

The first marina to port after entering the Owenboy River, Crosshaven Boatyard Marina has no designated visitors' berths but will accommodate visiting yachtsmen if space permits. The marina manager, Matt Foley, can be contacted during working hours (0800-1700) on Tel: 021 483 1161; Ch M; email: cby@eircom.net; website: www.crosshavenboatyard. com. If arriving at night, it is best to phone ahead to make arrangements to be met.
Berthing fees: €2 per metre per night. Electricity is free.

FACILITIES

Water and electricity are installed on the pontoons, while fuel is available alongside at the berth at the bottom of the marina gangway. Showers, toilets and rubbish disposal (all at no charge) can be located at the top of the gangway outside the security gate. Weather forecasts are available from the marina office during working hours. Other facilities include a small chandlery as well as agencies for a large number of manufacturers such as Beneteau, Jeanneau, Dufour and Najad.

Town Pier

This is a Cork Port Authority pier. Alongside berths are possible on the pontoon if space is available and at the harbour master's discretion. Fresh water is on the quay. The charge is €15 (under revision). For more information contact the pier manager, Kieran Coniry, on Tel: 086 310 0095.

Salve Marine

The next marina upstream on the port-hand side is Salve Marine. With 12 designated visitors' berths located in the seaward cul-de-sac adjacent to the shore gangway, the marina can accommodate lengthy vessels with up to a 4.5m draught on the outer pontoon. For berthing availability, contact the marina office on Tel: 021 483 1145; VHF Ch M; email: salvemarine@eircom. net. The office is staffed primarily during boatyard hours – in season 0900 –1800 six days a week and out of season 0915-1700 weekdays; 1000-1200 Saturdays. If entering the marina at night, either contact the marina in advance to make berthing arrangements or tie up on the outermost pontoon.
Berthing fees: Short term rates are €3.30 per metre per night (sixth and seventh nights free). No charge for electricity.

FACILITIES

Facilities include water and electricity on the pontoons as well as on site showers, toilets and rubbish disposal units. Diesel can be taken by hose on the visitors' pontoon as well as the outermost pontoon. Weather forecasts are available from the office during working hours.

Also on site is Fusion restaurant (for more details see page 208). Salve Marine's boatyard capabilities are summarised later on page 208.

Crosshaven berthing: Part of the RCYC Marina is shown at the bottom of the picture. Above that, Salve Marine is followed by the Town Pier, while beyond the inlet to the village centre lies Crosshaven Boatyard Marina

www.irelandaerialphotography.com

Royal Cork Yacht Club Marina

The Royal Cork Yacht Club (RCYC), just upriver of Salve Marine, is reputed to be the oldest yacht club in the world, having its origins as 'The Water Club of the Harbour of Cork' in 1720 on Haulbowline Island. It later moved to Cobh and was headquartered in the fine building on the waterfront now occupied by the Sirius Arts Centre. With the capacity to accommodate 200 yachts, the marina has 20 berths allocated to visitors. For more details, contact the marina manager, Chris Clarke, on Tel: 021 483 1023; VHF Ch M; email: marinamanager@royalcork.com; website: www.rcyc. ie/. A night-time entry is possible.

Berthing fees: Visitors' fees are approximately €2.80 per metre per night for craft up to 13m and €2.50 per metre per night for longer vessels.

FACILITIES

The current premises have excellent facilities, including communal showers that will bring back memories of school days for some. There is also a fine bar and restaurant, not to mention very helpful office staff. Water and electricity are available on the pontoons and fuel can be obtained in small quantities from the marina manager. The mobile phone coverage is good and

Wi-Fi (chargeable) is offered at the marina, but there is no separate internet terminal. Also at the marina is a slipway with scrubbing posts, although this service has to be booked in advance.

RCYC Marina

Useful information – Crosshaven

FACILITIES
For facilities at each marina, see pages 206 to 207 under the marina headings.
Boatyards: There are three boatyards nearby:
Salve Marine, Tel: 021 483 1145, has a marine engineering workshop and specialises in welding and machining stainless steel and aluminium. It undertakes fabrication and repairs and maintenance to hulls/rigging, engines and electrics.
Crosshaven Boatyard, Tel: 021 483 1161. Facilities include a 40-ton boat hoist and a 6.5m dock with 4m draught. Other amenities include shipwrights, GRP repairs, engineering, mechanical, electrical and rigging services, spray painting and osmosis treatments and a small chandlery. Winter storage for all types of craft, both undercover and outdoor, can be provided.
Castlepoint Boatyard, Tel: 021 483 2154, undertakes repairs on GRP, osmosis treatments, painting and winter storage.
Sail repair: Contact UK McWilliam Sailmakers, Tel: 021 483 1505.
Electronics: For those who are self-reliant for electrical and electronic equipment and parts there is now a Maplin store in Cork city at Unit F, Blackpool Retail Park, Blackpool, Tel: 021 430 9196. Its catalogue is online at http://www.maplin.co.uk/atoz.aspx .
Chandlery: If chandlery items cannot be obtained from the local boatyards, there is a small chandlery within O'Connell Paints at Carrigaline, Tel: 021 483 4478. Otherwise the larger chandlers in Cork City comprise: Union Chandlery Tel: 021 427 1643, www.unionchandlery.com; Matthews Centre Tel: 021 427 7633; CH Marine Tel: 021 431 5700, website: www.chmarine.com.

PROVISIONING
The village has a Centra **mini-market** and two grocery stores near the town quay, all within easy walking distance of any of the marinas. Mr Kidney, believe it or not, has a **butchers** shop. There are two **supermarkets** – Lidl and Dunne's – on the Crosshaven Road into Carrigaline. They both have long opening hours. The **post office** and **pharmacy** are situated in the village square.

EATING OUT
There are numerous pubs/restaurants in the village. As this is a holiday village, the restaurants respond to the seasonal ebb and flow of clients. Outside of July and August, it is worth checking which days and times each restaurant opens.
Starting with lunch, the Admiral Drake, opposite the Town Pier, is a good place for a robust, reasonably-priced pub lunch. The walls are decorated with an interesting selection of photos from the harbour's history.
For afternoon refreshment try the Riverside Café on the square (seasonal opening only).
In the evening, and unusually for somewhere that majors on its seafood, the highest recommendation has to go to the China Seas restaurant. The food is superb and the hospitality excellent. The owner is from Hong Kong and his wife is from Beijing. The combination of culinary expertise works brilliantly. Also in the village is Cronin's pub which, BIM accredited, has a reputation for excellent lunches and oysters.
Inside the Salve Marine site is the Fusion restaurant, Tel: 021 483 1000. Run by the boatyard owner's daughters, its menu consists of a little Asian cooking blended with European cuisine. This combination of food, together with the restaurant's outlook across the river, definitely makes it worth a visit.

In season a fish and chip shop-cum-pizza takeaway opens on the village square.
Inevitably, there are many pubs. Most are obvious on a short walk from one end of the village to the other, but do not miss the Anchor, found by going up the hill from the square towards the church.

ASHORE
Fort Meagher, still referred to by some as Fort Camden, remains an impressive structure. On the other side of the entrance is Fort Davis (was Fort Carlisle). A walk up to Fort Meagher reveals a panorama across the inner harbour ranging from the impressive spire of St Colman's Cathedral in Cobh to the refinery at Whitegate. Nearby (3km south) is the beach at Myrtleville, a charming 'bucket and spade' stop.
Carrigaline, the nearest sizeable town, can be easily reached using the frequent bus service that passes the marinas. For those feeling the need to stretch their legs after a long period on board, consider walking the 7km into Carrigaline along the river bank. An old narrow gauge railway line has been converted into a footpath, which is well used by local people. It is a good opportunity to strike up conversations and also appreciate the beautiful surroundings of Drake's Pool. The town, which is now a dormitory suburb of Cork, bustles with life, notably more so than many other towns of equivalent size. It has banks/ATMs, supermarkets, filling stations and a wide range of other shops, including a bookshop and good value restaurants.

TRANSPORT
Bus services: 222. Forty minutes to Cork. Frequent service Monday-Friday. Limited service Sundays.
Taxi: Rahona Cabs Tel: 021 763 1472; Crosshaven Kabs Tel: 021 483 2138; Crosshaven Minibus 086 311 1180.
Car hire: Many visiting yachtsmen head for Crosshaven after a long passage and hiring a car is a favourite activity. There are plenty of companies to choose from at Cork Airport: Avis Tel: 021 432 7460; Budget Tel: 021 431 4000; Hertz Tel: 021 496 5849; Irish Car Rentals Tel: 021 431 8644; National/Alamo Tel: 021 431 8623.

OTHER INFORMATION
Police: Tel: 021 483 1222 (opposite the Royal Cork Yacht Club Marina).
Doctor: A surgery can be found in the village square or, alternatively, in Point Road, Tel: 021 483 1315.
Tourist office: A peak season Information Point is situated adjacent to the Royal Cork Yacht Club Marina.

Crosshaven House

East Ferry Marina

Approach waypoint: 51°50'.20N 08°15'.60W
(Between Whitegate terminal and No 9 SHM)
Entrance waypoint: 51°51'.40N 08°12'.70W
(¾M NNE of EF1 SHM)

East Ferry Marina is remotely situated but offers
modern facilities along with highly regarded bars and
restaurants on both sides of the river. The marina is
accessible at all states of the tide and sheltered from
all but strong south-easterly winds. Cobh, the nearest
town, is 5km away.

NAVIGATION (FROM FORT DAVIS)

Charts: Use Admiralty SC5622.13 or AC/LE1773 and
AC/LE1777 or Imray C57.

Tides: MHWS: 4.1m, MHWN: 3.2m, MLWN: 1.2m,
MLWS: 0.4m. Tidal rates at springs are normally 1kn
to 1½kn in Cork Harbour; but in East Passage they can
reach 3kn.

Lights & Marks
• Main Channel: No 5 SHM Fl G 5s, No 8 PHM Fl R 5s,
No 7 SHM Fl G 2.5s, No 10 PHM Fl R 10s, No 12 PHM
Fl R 5s, Whitegate Terminal Two 2 FG (vertical), No 14
PHM Fl R 2.5s, No 9 SHM Fl G 5s.
• East Channel: EF2 PHM Fl R 10s, Fair Rock Beacon
PHM (unlit), EF1 SHM Fl G 10s.

Approaching East Passage

• East Ferry Marina: Two 2 FR (vertical) on marina
north and south outer pontoon ends.

Pilotage: Proceed as for 'Cork Harbour approach'
described previously on page 204 and continue north
between the forts, following the buoyed channel
(Nos 8, 10, 12, 14 port-hand marks and Nos 5, 7, 9
starboard-hand marks) past Whitegate terminal jetty.
Turn to starboard before No 9 starboard-hand mark
(see approach waypoint above), just north of the jetty
and cross the shallows (approximately 3m) to the
entrance waypoint. The East Passage channel is marked
by EF2 port-hand mark followed by EF1 starboard-
hand mark, with Fair Rock port-hand mark far off to the
north protecting a drying rock (0.2m). After EF1,

East Passage and East Ferry Marina. A quiet corner of Cork Harbour

www.irelandaerialphotography.com

Opposite the East Ferry Marina is the church at Garranekinnefeake

East Ferry Marina pontoons

the church just inside the entrance to East Passage on the east shore becomes visible; stay in at least a 5m depth. From the entrance waypoint, head north into East Passage. East Ferry Marina is to port ½M after entering the passage and opposite the church. If travelling a little way upriver for any reason, the clearance under the electricity wires above Belgrove

House (¼M north of the marina) is 24m. A night-time entry is at the skipper's discretion.

BERTHING

As the marina is quite small (80 places, 10 of which are allocated to visitors), it is best to phone ahead to check for space and to arrange a berth, otherwise tie up on the long pontoon and seek instructions. There are likely to be counter-going eddies off the pontoons. The tide runs very strongly in mid river at springs. The marina owner, George Butler, can be contacted on Tel: 021 481 3390. **Berthing fees:** Rates for visitors are €1.65 per metre per night (sixth and seventh nights free). No charge for electricity.

Useful information – East Ferry Marina

FACILITIES
Water and electricity: Are available on the pontoons.
Fuel: Diesel is available alongside at the end of the central walkway. No petrol.
Showers, toilets and **rubbish disposal:** Are ashore at the sailing school buildings. Note that there is no laundry, Internet access or Wi-Fi connection.

PROVISIONING
The nearest shopping is in Cobh, accessed by taxi.

EATING OUT
The Morlogue Inn is situated on the marina site. Alternatively, on the opposite side of the river (the Midleton side), adjacent

to the disused ferry pier, is Murph's Bar & Restaurant, Tel: 021 465 2676. Both establishments have a good reputation among the locals.

ASHORE
The marina is the primary home of SailCork sailing school; website:www. sailcork.com
There is a small landing beach suitable for dinghies adjacent to the east shore ferry pier, giving access to Murph's Bar. Midleton, with its whiskey distillery, is 7km from Murph's Bar by road. It is either a long, uninteresting hike or a taxi ride away (it may be preferable to visit by bus from Ballycotton's moorings – see pages 215–216).

TRANSPORT
There are no bus services nearby.
Taxi – Cobh side: Contact via the bar staff at the Inn

or Cobh Taxi Association, Tel: 086 815 8631.
Taxi – Midleton side: Maguire's Tel: 086 886 1025.

Murph's Bar and east shore pier

Cobh. The cathedral dominates the town and its waterfront. Kennedy Pier is T-shaped (left of centre)

Cobh

There has been a long debate, locally, concerning the provision of adequate facilities for visiting leisure craft with easy access to the town's many attractions. Fundamental to the debate is the need (and cost) of a substantial breakwater to provide protection for berths overnight. At present, the only simple option is a daytime visit using the pontoon which can just be seen off the bow of the cruise liner in the photo on page 14 of the introduction.

NAVIGATION

Charts: Use Admiralty SC5622.10 & 11 or AC/LE1773 and AC/LE1777 or Imray C57.

Tides: MHWS:4.1m, MHWN:3.2m, MLWN:1.2m, MLWS:0.4m.

Lights & Marks: No 5 SHM Fl G 5s, No 8 PHM Fl R 5s, No 7 SHM Fl G 2.5s, No 10 PHM Fl R 10s, No 12 PHM Fl R 5s, Whitegate Terminal Two 2 FG (vertical), No 14 PHM Fl R 2.5s, No 9 SHM Fl G 5s, No 11 SHM Fl G 10s, No 16 Fl R 2s, Spit Bank Light Iso WR 4s, No 13 SHM Fl G 2.5s, No 18 PHM Fl R 5s, No 20 PHM Fl R 10s.

Pilotage: From Fort Davis, continue north following the buoyed channel (port-hand marks Nos 8, 10, 12, 14, 16, 18 and 20 and starboard-hand marks Nos 5, 7, 9, 11 and 13). At buoy 20, keep to the Cobh shore and identify the Quays Bar pontoon (at approximately 51°50'.93N 08°17'.85W).

BERTHING

Daytime only on the pontoon off the Quays Bar, which is between the Waters Edge Hotel and the Sirius Arts Centre (the old headquarters of Royal Cork Yacht Club), west of the cathedral. Alternatively, for those with a fender board it may be possible to go alongside Kennedy Pier on its south or east faces.

Beware of ferries that repeatedly cross the harbour and cruise-liners that berth immediately west of the Quays Bar pontoon. These massive ships typically arrive between 0700 and 0900 and depart between 1700 and 1900. On average, one liner a week visits Cobh. Also, the waterfront is somewhat exposed to fetch across the harbour from the south and wash from passing vessels. This is especially troublesome to outboard yachts if rafted up.

The Quays Bar pontoon (right), between the Sirius Arts Centre (and Tourist Information Office) and the Waters Edge Hotel

Useful information – Cobh

FACILITIES
There are no marine services at Cobh.

PROVISIONING
Grocery: Full urban services and small stores are on hand. The SuperValu and Aldi supermarkets are a strenuous walk past the 'Top of the Hill' above the cathedral.
Pharmacy: Cobh Pharmacy, 3 East Beach, Tel: 021 481 1341; Wilson, 18 West Beach, Tel: 021 481 1332.
Banks: BoI Tel: 021 481 1088; AIB, 3 West Beach, Tel: 021 481 1408.

EATING OUT
There is an excellent choice of cafés, bars and restaurants to provide refreshment during the day's sightseeing. Because use of its pontoon is free to patrons, The Quays Bar & Restaurant, Tel: 021 481 3539; website: www.thequays.ie, is an obvious candidate for lunch even if it did not also have the benefit of a spectacular view of Cork Harbour from its outside terrace.

ASHORE
Cobh on Great Island is connected to Cork by road and rail and is effectively a commuter suburb of Cork. Cobh has had three names in its history: at the outset it was called Cove (pronounced *Cobh* in Irish), then Queenstown (from 1849 to 1922 it was named after Queen Victoria) and finally Cobh (pronounced *Cove* in English).

From St Colman's Cathedral, there is a panoramic view across the town below and Cork Harbour. The church itself is a neo-Gothic granite epic completed in 1919.

The sinking of the *Lusitania* is commemorated with a peace memorial on Casement Square – an imposing sculpture facing the quay. She was torpedoed by a German submarine U-20 south of Kinsale on 7 May 1915. When she sank in just 18 minutes, 1,198 people died. Many of the *Lusitania*'s victims are buried in Old Church Graveyard.

Conveniently west of the Quays Bar pontoon is to be found the 'Queenstown Story', Tel: 021 481 3591, which explains the main events in the town's history, with exhibits on convict deportation, the *Titanic* and emigration during the famine. Two and a half million of the six million people who left Ireland for the New World departed from Cobh. It is housed in the Heritage Centre, which is part of Cobh railway station, adjacent to the Deepwater Quay (and incorporates a café with a comprehensive menu). On the quay immediately outside stands the much-photographed statue of Annie Moore and her brothers. Annie is distinct in history as the first person to be processed through the, then, newly opened immigration facility on Ellis Island in New York.

Cobh Museum is housed in a former Scots Presbyterian Church, near the Heritage Centre. It has exhibits covering commerce in Cobh in the early 20th century, the Cork Harbour Pilots and a collection of items recovered from the harbour.

Regrettably, the *Titanic* Rooms, housed in the White Star company's old office building on the quay, are not currently in business. The memorial to the loss of the *Titanic* may be found on Pearse Square.

OTHER INFORMATION
Taxi: Cobh Taxi Association, Tel: 086 815 8631.
Police: Tel: 021 490 8530.
Medical Centre: Tel: 021 481 1345.

Annie Moore and her brothers

STATION MASTER'S OFFICE

The Queenstown Experience

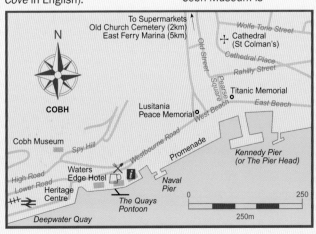

To Supermarkets
Old Church Cemetery (2km)
East Ferry Marina (5km)

N

COBH

Cobh Museum

Spy Hill

High Road
Lower Road
Heritage Centre

Waters Edge Hotel

Deepwater Quay

The Quays Pontoon

Naval Pier

Westbourne Road

Promenade

Lusitania Peace Memorial

West Beach

Pearse Square

Old Street

Wolfe Tone Street

Cathedral (St Colman's)

Cathedral Place

Rahilly Street

Titanic Memorial

East Beach

Kennedy Pier (or The Pier Head)

0   250

250m

Cork, Penrose Quay
(Irish: *Corcaigh*, meaning marshy place)

The 7½M passage from Cobh to Cork City centre begins quite interestingly. To port is Haulbowline Island with its naval vessels, followed by Ringaskiddy Ro-Ro terminals, which are used by the Brittany Ferries car ferry to France. A turn to starboard reveals caissons and piers associated with the dockyard. Thereafter, on the northerly course up the West Passage, to the town of Passage West, there is an absorbing mix of commuter trains, road traffic and a car ferry that holds the record for the minimum time between loading the last car and leaving the ramp! Further on up the river, now the River Lee, the shoreline becomes more industrialised and continues in that vein until Cork. The channel is dredged for quite large ships that frequently pass to and from the many wharfs, docks and harbours along the river. Little concession is given to the leisure sailor – there are no berths between West Passage and Cork City. Unfortunately, the final commercial wharf adjacent to the only possible yacht berth on Penrose Quay is used for bulk grain imports. The associated noise, dust and smell cannot be escaped.

Nevertheless, the trip makes for a fascinating passage through a working dockland, and there is one remarkable edifice along the route – distinctive Blackrock Castle is now open to the public as an observatory, but unfortunately there is no easy access to it from the river.

NAVIGATION
Charts: Use Admiralty SC5622.12A&B or AC/LE1773 and AC/LE1777 or Imray C57.

Tides: MHWS: 4.5m, MHWN: 3.6m, MLWN: 1.6m, MLWS: 0.6m. High water is 10 minutes after HW Cobh.

Spring tidal rates are normally 1 to 1½kn in Cork Harbour; the notable exceptions are:
• Between Haulbowline Island and White Point on Great Island – 2kn.
• At the south end of West Passage particularly in the narrows – 3kn.

Cork. Large freighters still sail up to the centre of the city

www.irelandaerialphotography.com

Lights & Marks: The channel from Cobh to Cork is fully buoyed and all buoys are lit.

Pilotage: From Fort Davis, continue north following the buoyed channel (port-hand marks Nos 8, 10, 12, 14, 16, 18 and 20 and starboard-hand marks Nos 5, 7, 9, 11 and 13) to Cobh. At buoy 20, as a matter of courtesy, it is advisable to inform the *Cork Harbour Radio* on VHF Ch 12 of the intention to make passage north of Cobh. This is a useful way to learn of any ship movements along the river to the centre of the city.

From port-hand mark No 20, identify and steer towards starboard-hand mark No 15 off White Point opposite Haulbowline Island. From here to the narrows of West Passage, the tides are strongest. Give the south-west corner of Great Island a wide berth,

Approaching Penrose Quay (extreme right). Directly ahead are the Port of Cork offices with the *Jeanie Johnston* (Ireland's Sail Training ship – a replica 1847 barque) berthed alongside. A freighter unloading a bulk cargo into hoppers is to port

Penrose Quay is convenient for Union Chandlery

staying in depths of greater than 10m. Ringaskiddy terminal can be seen to port and Monkstown Creek ahead. At starboard-hand mark No 17, start a slow turn to starboard to pass the dockyard and enter the narrows at the south end of West Passage. A rapid and frequent ferry crosses West Passage just north of the narrows. From here, use the buoyed channel north through West Passage to Lough Mahon. Then follow the River Lee buoyed channel port-hand marks – R2 to R24 – and starboard-hand marks – R1 to R21 – to Tivoli Container Terminal. Continue upriver to Penrose Quay, which is on the starboard side of the river. The head of navigation is clearly marked by a very large 'Port of Cork' sign immediately in front of its truly wonderfully restored Victorian offices. Penrose Quay is the last quay to starboard before the road bridge.

BERTHING

Berthing is permitted at Penrose Quay, however, this is a city centre quay with no security and is occasionally used by commercial tourist vessels. The tidal range is approximately 4m at springs, with the attendant problems of first securing at all against the sheer wall and then rigging lines to cope with the tidal range.

The Blarney Stone

High up on the tower of Blarney Castle, Tel: 021 438 5252; email: info@blarneycastle.ie; website: www.blarneycastle.ie, is a visitor attraction that draws tourists in their thousands, despite the need to lie flat on your back and project yourself, with the help of a well-practised gentleman, out and then under the Blarney Stone. Kissing the Blarney Stone, also known as the 'Stone of Eloquence', is supposed to endow the kisser with the gift of the blarney (sometimes called the 'gift of the gab') and it certainly provides the opportunity to take embarrassing photographs!

Visitors are not long in Ireland before realising that eloquence is a national trait and it is reasonable to assume this ability must flow from a source, so why not the Blarney Stone? Even if we go with the sceptics and assume that Blarney is just a tourist trap, it is a five star tourist trap and well worth the trip 8km north-west of Cork City, especially if the weather dictates a day ashore.

Blarney Castle is a substantial building dating from 1446 when it was built by the local chief Dermot MacCarthy. One hundred and fifty years later, Blarney slipped into the language to mean the use of many words to wheedle your way out of your commitments. The then Lord of Blarney, Cormac MacCarthy, was supremely skilled at saying much, offering flattery and delivering little. He regularly exercised this skill on Lord Carew in 1602, to avoid surrendering the castle to Queen Elizabeth I. Carew was an object of derision in London and 'blarney' has been used since then to describe attempts at artful persuasion.

Kissing the Blarney Stone

Useful information – Cork (Penrose Quay)

FACILITIES
Full city services, including Union Chandlery on Penrose Quay itself.

PROVISIONING/ EATING OUT
There is an excellent choice of pubs, restaurants and stores.

ASHORE
First, it is worth emphasising that if a visit to Cork City is on the itinerary the recommended way would be

by using the frequent bus service from Crosshaven. The bus can be boarded at Crosshaven Square or outside the Royal Cork Yacht Club Marina building. Regrettably, Cork is no different to other major cities in the world where leaving an expensive boat and many valuable possessions and instruments on an unsecured berth is inadvisable. Opposite Penrose Quay are the Port of Cork offices and

quays. The site is secured outside of business hours and there is no access to the city.

The simplest way to get an overview of the city is on the Bus Éireann open-top bus tour, viewing the city's famous landmarks with commentary, and then out to Blarney, (kissing the stone is not obligatory – see panel above). The bus normally operates from May to September daily at 1345, returning to Cork at 1745, departing from Parnell

Place Bus Station, Tel: 021 450 8188. Visits on foot may include the English Market and the striking St Fin Barre's Cathedral, with its pillars all having different patterns and no two statues or faces the same.

TRANSPORT
The **rail** and **bus** stations are in the immediate vicinity of Penrose Quay. Buses to the airport depart from the bus station. These are the main transport hubs for domestic and international travel.

Ballycotton. The centre of the village is to the bottom right

Ballycotton

(Irish: *Baile Choitín*)
Approach waypoint: 51°50'.00N 07°59'.12W
(½M due north of Ballycotton lighthouse)

Ballycotton is a traditional fishing village offering visitors friendly hospitality. The moorings are well protected from the west through south, but uncomfortable in northerly and easterly winds. The harbour is distinguished easily by the presence on an offshore island of the somewhat unusual black tower of the lighthouse. It was painted black in 1902 to help distinguish it from the tower on Capel Island to the north-east.

NAVIGATION

Charts: No detailed chart. Use Admiralty SC5622.2, AC/LE2049 or Imray C56.

Tides: MHWS:4.1m, MHWN:3.2m, MLWN:1.2m, MLWS:0.4m. Standard Port Cobh, difference at HW: Springs –00:11min; Neaps –00:01min.

Lights & Marks

• Ballycotton lighthouse Fl WR 10s.
White sector 238° to 000° to 048°T.
• Pollock Rock PHM Fl R 6s.

• Power SCM Q (6) + L Fl 15s.
• The Smiths PHM Fl (3) R 10s.
• Capel Island daymark.

Approach: From the west stay south of The Smiths port-hand mark, in the white sector of Ballycotton lighthouse. Go south about Ballycotton lighthouse at a distance of 2½ cables to the approach waypoint. Ballycotton Sound (between the lighthouse and the mainland) is not recommended to strangers. It has a

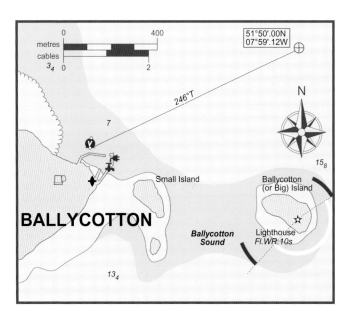

Ballycotton Harbour entrance. A brisk easterly is blowing. The visitors' buoys are off the north arm of the harbour (right)

least depth of 2m, a drying rock and a maximum tidal stream of 2kn.

The approach from the east is directly into the bay and from the north-east stay east of Capel Island (in the white sector of Ballycotton lighthouse).

Capel Island and its tower

Pilotage: From the approach waypoint, steer 246°T to the visitors' buoys.

MOORING
A visit is best served by taking one of six yellow public visitors' buoys, which are immediately north-west of the harbour entrance. Land at the lifeboat station slip or on the adjacent beaches, inside the harbour.

BERTHING
Berthing is possible but the shelving harbour is busy, of limited depth (1.5m), steel pile-sided, not lit and, therefore, is not recommended, especially if entering after dark. If entry is made, tie up outboard of a fishing vessel that is not sailing in the near future.

Useful information – Ballycotton

FACILITIES
Fresh water and **electricity** (no charge for small usage) is available on the seaward end of the south jetty.

PROVISIONING
The **grocery** and **post office**, Tel: 021 464 6832, is about ¾km from the harbour.

EATING OUT
The centre of Ballycotton village, which is about 1km from the harbour, has three bars –McGraths, Tel: 021 464 6085, The Blackbird, Tel: 021 464 6274 and The Schooner, Tel: 021 464 6192, the last of which serves food. Offering some variety is

an Italian restaurant, Nido d'Cigno, Tel: 021 464 6647. Alternatively, why go further than Lynch's Inn by the Harbour, Tel: 021 464 6768, which is a friendly hostelry playing traditional music that can be heard from the moorings when the wind is in the right direction.

ASHORE
There is a panoramic cliff walk for those waiting the return of crew members who took the bus to Midleton, where a visit to a distillery will help distinguish whisky from whiskey.

Midleton is the location of the Irish Distillers Group's

main distillery, making the majority of all Irish whiskey produced. Locals may refer to Ballycotton Island as Big Island.

TRANSPORT
Bus services: 240 Cork-Midleton-Ballycotton. Three buses a day Monday to Friday. Two on Saturdays.

Hospitable Lynch's and the lighthouse

Youghal

(Irish: *Eochaill*, meaning Yew Woods)
Approach waypoint: 51°55'.75N 07°48'.20W
(½M NNE of Blackball Ledge ECM in the East Bar
white sector of Youghal lighthouse)

Youghal is one of Ireland's historic treasures. It has
had a long and varied history – much of which is
well preserved and easy to visit once ashore. If the
right conditions prevail (settled weather with the
wind from the west), a stop here will be very
rewarding. The town caters well for tourists,
particularly those arriving by road. For those coming
from seawards, the offshore approach is hostile in
strong southerlies, anchoring can be unreliable and
a strong river current can tax the stranger. The
provision of an attached or even a detached
mooring pontoon, so common elsewhere, would
make it much easier to recommend Youghal as a
destination, particularly given its valuable cruising
location midway between Kilmore Quay and Cork.
Nevertheless, Youghal is definitely worth a visit.

NAVIGATION

Charts: Excellent detail on Admiralty SC5622.6, AC2071
or the Imray C57 inset.

Tides: MHWS:3.9m, MHWN:3.1m, MLWN:1.2m,
MLWS:0.3m. Standard Port Cobh, difference at HW:
Springs –00:00min; Neaps +00:10min.

The riverbank in town is steep, narrow and long,
causing the river and tidal streams to flow strongly
in the vicinity of the town. Off the town, the ebb
reaches 3kn at springs. After heavy rain inland, river

water will strengthen the stream. Even the neap tides
call for respect.

Lights & Marks
• Bar Rocks SCM Q (6) + L Fl 15s.
• Blackball Ledge ECM Q (3) 10s.
• Youghal lighthouse Fl WR 2.5s.
West Bar white sector 351° to 003°T.
East Bar white sector 295° to 307°T.
Inside harbour white sector 183° to 273°T.
• Also in the northern harbour, west of the Red Bank, a
pontoon has been established by the local sailing school.
It is identified by a special mark with Fl Y 4s. The
charter boat pontoon adjacent the pier is to be marked
by a light (FR).

Approach: To enter Youghal, it is necessary to cross
either East Bar or West Bar in Youghal Bay. In either
case, southerly winds cause a disturbed, heavy sea
in Youghal Bay and the entrance will be particularly
unfriendly on the ebb tide. Also, the tidal streams are
complex and run powerfully over the bar. Entry is best
avoided in strong (>F5) southerlies!

The approach from the east is direct over East Bar
in a least depth of 2.8m, keeping in the white sector of
Youghal lighthouse.

From the west or south, the shortest route is over West
Bar, which has a least depth of 1.7m. However, a passage
plan that uses the East Bar adds little to the distance and
will not be determined by the time and sea state.

If West Bar is used, do not stray east of a southerly
bearing on Bar Rocks south cardinal mark to avoid
Bar Rocks (0.6m).

Youghal is a commercial harbour. Green's Quay at
the north of the town regularly receives coasters.

Youghal. The new private pontoon is visible off the pier. Ferry Point protrudes into the right of the photograph

www.irelandaerialphotography.com

Youghal lighthouse. Maintain a constant bearing on the lighthouse, compensating for any tidal stream in or out of the estuary (right of photo)

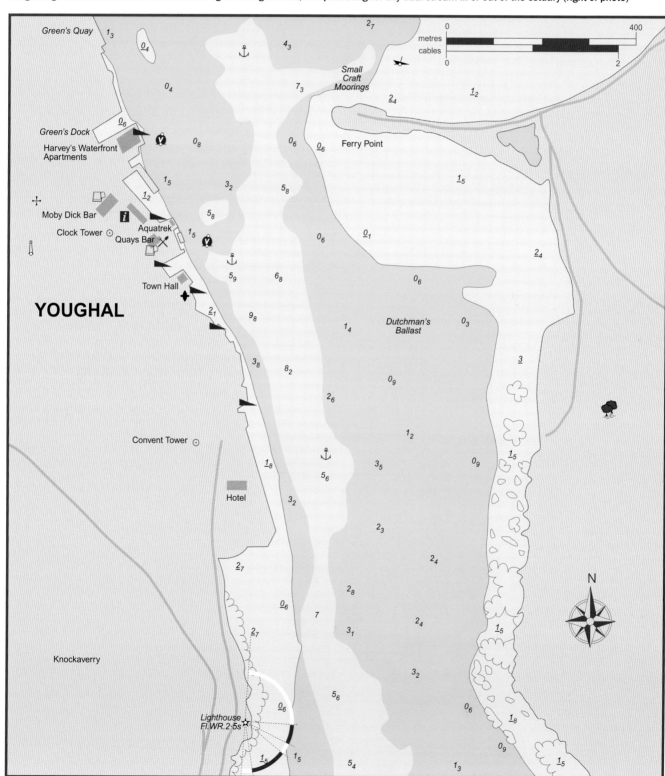

Youghal waterfront. From left to right: Town Hall, Quays Bar, pier and Harvey's apartments. This photo was taken before the installation of the private pontoon at the pier

Pilotage: From the approach waypoint, maintain a bearing of 300°T±5° on the clearly visible lighthouse, compensating for the ebb stream (up to 3kn out of the river). In the entrance narrows, head up the harbour, keeping closer to the town (west) side in 5-7m. Proceed north of the Town Hall to moor. When possible, plan to arrive on the flood and depart on the ebb. Strangers will need to know that the 'Town Hall' from the water looks like a large glass solarium built onto a substantial rendered building a little north of the lifeboat station slipway.

MOORING

Thanks to 'Aquatrek' (www.aquatrek.ie), the local sailing school, two regularly checked mooring buoys may be available free of charge if they are not otherwise occupied. Note that there is no need to contact the school in advance. The first is pink/orange with a brown pick-up float, just off the angling charter boat pontoon. The other, which is yellow, is further north, off 'Harvey's Waterfront' apartment block. In case of difficulty, contact John Innes at Aquatrek on Tel: 086 859 3482.

ANCHORING

Youghal has had a working harbour for 800 years; assume the bottom, between the Town Hall and Harvey's holiday apartment block, is foul. Anchoring is more reliable to the north of Ferry Point (a long spit protruding from the east shore), but if conditions are uncomfortable, proceed past Ferry Point and gain some protection from the spit, anchoring north-east of the moorings. Note that above Ferry Point, Red Bank is repeatedly reported as changing and extending; local advice should be sought if needed. Land at the slip or beach adjacent to the town hall.

BERTHING

All the town quays dry. Going alongside temporarily at high water is feasible on the pier opposite the Quays Bar. A fender board is necessary against the vertical piles. The sailing school is housed in a temporary cabin on this pier and has access to electricity and fresh water for visitors. Call the school on VHF Ch 69 when it is operating (indicated by a blue Aquatrek Flag being flown adjacent to the RYA and ISA training centre flags) or contact John Innes (see above).

A privately-owned connected pontoon was installed in 2008 by an angling charter company. It has a secure gate and CCTV. A notice to seaward identifies its purpose. It should only be used in an emergency.

A private pontoon has been attached to the pier

Ferry Point (far shore – right) is on a spit that narrows the estuary. Alternative anchorages may be found to it's north

Useful information – Youghal

The harbour is controlled by Youghal Town Council, which carries out all maintenance on the docks and quays. The only quay operating commercially is Green's Quay, the most northerly of the quays, which is leased to Youghal Shipping and Storage; it mostly imports steel and fertiliser.

FACILITIES
Until recently Youghal lacked good facilities for recreational or pleasure craft visitors, but the sailing school has been working to develop better services and is always willing to help out in any way it can. Refer to the town website www.youghal.ie for updated information.

Camping Gaz and Kosan are available from Cal Flavin's, 100 Main Street, Tel: 024 92026.

In the event of a critical problem it may be worth calling the very small Ferrypoint Boat Company, Tel: 024 94232, during working hours.

PROVISIONING
Youghal is a large town by the standards of this coast. With a population of 8,000, it supports several supermarkets, including SuperValu, Lidl and Tesco, and a wide selection of stores expected in a town of this size. It would be a good place to stock up if it did not mean a dinghy trip was involved. The post office is situated in Main Street.

EATING OUT
During the day, this busy regional shopping centre offers plenty of cafés, bars and restaurants to satisfy most preferences and appetites. Conveniently situated on the corner of Church Street and North Main Street, midway along the town walking tour, is Treacy's, otherwise identified as 'nookfood', the lunch and afternoon tea section of The Nook Public House, which has been under one family ownership since 1901. Try an open seafood sandwich in these snug surroundings. Live music is played in the evenings on Mondays and Wednesdays.

After business hours, the choice of restaurants close to the quays is limited but interesting. Aherne's, Tel: 024 92424, is a BIM accredited seafood restaurant, The Red Store (Farrell's) has well-priced family dining and The Quays is a modern bar/restaurant which for some reason does not capitalise on the views immediately outside its doors.

Several of the bars serve snacks; of interest may be The Moby Dick Lounge Bar in Market Square. It displays artefacts from the filming in 1954 of the classic *Moby Dick*.

ASHORE
Youghal is a medieval walled town, built by the Fitzgeralds in 1220. Prior to that it was a Viking stronghold. It is situated at the mouth of the River Blackwater, at the eastern border of County Cork. The town walls, which still survive, were constructed in the mid 13th century and extended in the 17th century. Three of the original 13 towers remain. The frequently photographed Clock Gate, which was built in 1777, acted as a gaol until the middle of the 19th century and public hangings took place from its windows! It sits astride the main street. Sir Walter Raleigh was mayor of this town in 1588/9.

The tourist office, Heritage Centre and the start of the Youghal Heritage Walking Tour are all concentrated on the Market Square, adjacent to the waterfront, Tel: 024 20170 – the latter provides an excellent self-guided trail and potted history of Youghal. Some of the more interesting historical sites are:
• The Water Gate, which was built in the 13th century to provide access through the walls to the harbour.
• The Clock Gate.
• The Red House, which was built in 1703 and is a rare example of Dutch domestic architecture.
• The Almshouses: the oldest surviving almshouses in Ireland, these were built in 1610 by the Earl of Cork, who also provided the £5 per year to maintain each resident.
• Tyntes Castle, a 15th century fortified house on the Main Street, was originally occupied by the Walshes, a merchant family of Norman descent. It is thought to have been a secure storehouse with living quarters overhead. The tower passed into the ownership of Sir Robert Tynte in the 17th century.
• St Mary's Collegiate Church was built in 1220. It is one of the few medieval churches in Ireland to have been in continuous use.
• The Town Walls extend along the escarpment behind the town, skirting around St Mary's church. They are in an excellent state of repair and provide extensive views.

Many other attractions ashore include: *Dancing Through the Ages,* which is an Irish dance show performed at The Mall House, Tel: 024 92571, and Fox's Lane Museum which, situated at North Cross Lane, displays vintage domestic gadgets, Tel: 024 91145. There is also a three-screen cinema, Tel: 024 91399.

A trip up the Blackwater by dinghy or on a trip boat passes beautiful scenery and country houses. Depending on draft, it is possible to go as far as Villierstown, 10M upstream past Templemichael Castle, the ruins of Molana Abbey and the handsome stately home, Ballinatray House.

TRANSPORT
Bus services: 040 Cork-Youghal-Waterford; Frequent service. 260 to Ardmore.
Taxi: Youghal Cabs Tel: 024 91818; Worldwide Cabs Tel: 024 91888.

OTHER INFORMATION
Police: Tel: 024 92200.
Hospital: Tel: 024 92106.
Doctor: Dr Declan Matthews, 1 Emmett Place, Tel: 024 93552; Dr Deidre O'Brien, 2 South Abbey, Tel: 024 93411; Dr Declan O'Callaghan, Catherine Street, Tel: 024 92702; Dr Michael Twomey, Grattan Street, Tel: 024 92101.

Public hangings once took place from the windows of the Clock Gate

Hook Head lighthouse

Chapter nine
County Waterford

Ireland's south-east coast is a fine mixture of interesting harbours, a vibrant city and abundant history as well as many navigational challenges and, of course, wildlife. It is also recognised as the sunniest region of Ireland, attracting large numbers of holidaymakers. There is a gradual ruralisation of the features behind the almost continuous low bluff cliffs. Inland 'mountains' thin out until only isolated examples occur, long beaches become more frequent and low, warm sandstone cliffs combine to produce a welcoming ambience. By the longitude of Kilmore Quay the land slopes gently away from the coast.

The County Waterford coastline recedes a long way to the north relative to the direct passage between Cork and St George's Channel, making diversions quite lengthy. Skippers must be aware that the distances between alternative refuges are great and that each has important limitations.

For those sailing west, a good easterly blow invites a fast passage as far west as possible, partly because most of the intervening coastal harbours are uncomfortable in easterlies but also to capitalise on the absence of the prevailing south-westerly. Frequently, however, passage west is dominated by those south-westerlies, which opens the option to shorten the continuous hours motoring into wind by visiting some very individual and delightful harbours described in this chapter.

Sailing eastwards downwind offers the chance of exploring some lesser-visited sheltered locations in preference to sailing quickly past en route to the Irish Sea, Milford Haven and the Bristol Channel.

Without doubt, in all circumstances, good planning, flexibility and working with the weather is required to get the best out of this particular stretch of coast.

At the extreme west of County Waterford lies Ardmore, the birthplace of Christianity in Ireland, with a history preceding the more revered efforts of St Patrick. A little to the east at Helvick, Irish is spoken in one of the most easterly and smallest Gaeltachts, but do not worry, visitors will be welcome and understood in English. Close by, Dungarvan is a major town that warrants the use of the word vibrant. A full range of urban services is available and it provides some very pleasant harbourside restaurants and bars. Finally, Waterford Harbour offers history, a wide range of destinations and interesting river cruising as well as excellent refuge in the worst of weather.

Waterford City is unusual in that its marina is a focal point right in the city centre. New Ross emulates Waterford in a smaller way by having its marina close to the centre of town but uniquely requires the swinging of a railway bridge to gain access, which happens with extraordinary ease.

Although it is well into County Wexford, Kilmore Quay is covered for completeness in this chapter because it is such a useful 'gateway' port-of-call. It is frequently used by cruisers arriving and departing from the south coast. Once in the harbour there is full protection and a good, if small, range of services to refresh a tired crew for the next leg of the passage.

Peregrine and chough are often sighted on the

Gannet in mid flight

more rugged cliffs while kittiwakes can be seen in and around Dunmore East's cliffs. Over the open sea gannets fish with ease and skill.

Many arrivals and departures from this coast will be signalled by the Hook Head lighthouse. This lighthouse was constructed on foundations that date from the original lighthouse, which was built around the turn of the 13th century. The lighthouse has been crucial to navigators for 800 years. It has a few unexpected characteristics, for example, its name, Hook Head. To a stranger, this might imply an imposing structure standing on a substantial cliff. This is not the case. The lighthouse resides at the end of a 10km peninsula that does not rise above 66m. The lighthouse will often appear first apparently 'offshore'. This is perhaps why the coastline to the west is usefully dotted with conspicuous landmarks. The most westerly

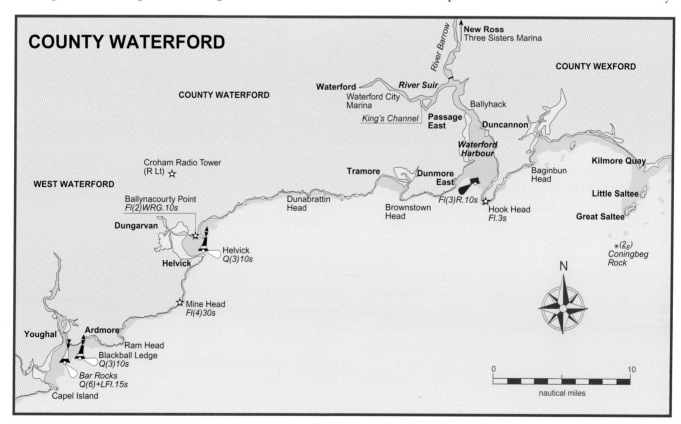

is 'Metal Man', which consists of three towers on a cliff top to the west of Tramore. Surmounting the middle tower at a total height of 20m is a metal figure pointing out of Tramore Bay towards the entrance to Waterford. This warning mark was erected by Lloyds Insurers after the wreck of the *Seahorse*, a troop ship, in 1816.

East of Metal Man is the conspicuous Tramore Church spire and finally, a few miles further east on Brownstown Head, there are two more towers which unambiguously separate Tramore Bay from Waterford Harbour.

The low-lying land on the Hook Peninsula offers little attenuation to the wind. This is also true, but to a lesser extent, for the land on the west shore of Waterford Harbour entrance.

In a good blow, skippers should not expect to have the sea quieten until the River Suir narrows above Ballyhack – 8M inland from Hook Head Light.

FAVOURABLE TIDES
Coastal passage:
Off Ram Head for eastward passage – commences 2 hours 15 minutes before HW Cobh. South of Coningbeg LANBY for westward passage – commences 6 hours after HW Cobh.

Waterford Harbour:
In-going flood – commences 4 hours 25 minutes before HW Cobh. Out-going ebb – commences 45 minutes after HW Cobh.

WEATHER INFORMATION BROADCASTS
The western half of this coast is served by the Dublin Coastguard transmitter at Mine Head on VHF Ch 83, although it may still be possible to hear the Valentia Coastguard from Roche's Point on Ch 26. The eastern half of the coast is served by Dublin Coastguard on Ch 23 from Carnsore Point. In all cases, an advisory announcement is made initially on Ch 16.

PASSAGE CHARTS
Admiralty Charts: AC/LE2049 Old Head of Kinsale to Tuskar Rock, 1:150,000; AC/LE1410 Saint George's Channel, 1:200,000; SC5621.2 Waterford to St David's Head, 1:200,000; SC562.14 Tuskar Rock to Waterford, 1:150,000; SC5622.2 Ballycotton Bay to Waterford, 1:150,000.

Tramore (left) and Brownstown Head

Imray: C57 Tuskar Rock to Old Head of Kinsale 1:170,000. Plans for harbours in this chapter include Dunmore East, Passage East to New Ross/Waterford and Kilmore Quay.

SAFETY INFORMATION
This section of the coast is managed by Dublin Coastguard, Tel: 01 662 0922.

ELECTRONIC AIDS TO NAVIGATION
Coningbeg LANBY   AIS; MMSI 992501074.
Bore Rocks ECM   AIS; MMSI 992501072.
Red Bank WCM   AIS; MMSI 992501076.
Hook Head   AIS; MMSI 992501079.

COASTGUARD AIS STATIONS
Mine Head
51°59'.60W 07°35'.10W   MMSI 002 500350.
Wexford (Forth Mount)
52°18'.93N 06°33'.77W   MMSI 002 500340.

Mine Head

COUNTY WATERFORD – PASSAGE WAYPOINTS – WGS 84 DATUM		
NAME	DESCRIPTION	LAT/LONG
Capel Island	1M SE of island	51°52'.00N 07°50'.36W
Ram Head	8 cables SE of headland	51°55'.75N 07°42'.00W
Mine Head	1½M E of The Rogue	51°59'.50N 07°32'.20W
Helvick Head	3½ cables NE in 15m	52°03'.50N 07°31'.64W
Dunmore East	1¼M SE of harbour	52°08'.00N 06°58'.00W
Hook Head	2M SSW of headland	52°05'.50N 06°56'.50W
Coningbeg	1½M SW of LANBY	52°02'.00N 06°40'.00W

Ardmore
(Irish: *Aird Mhór*, meaning Great Height)
Approach waypoint: 51°57'.00N 07°42'.00W
(3½ cables NE of Ardmore Head)

Ardmore, County Waterford, is a well-kept family resort and small fishing village with beautiful sweeps of beach and unparalleled archaeological sites. On a day with clear visibility and offshore winds (south-west to north), this is a good place to anchor off the village and go ashore. A walk out to the adjacent headlands (Ardmore Head and Ram Head) will be rewarded with excellent views both inland and to the west.

NAVIGATION

Charts: No detailed chart. Use Admiralty SC5622.2, AC/LE2049 or Imray C57.

Lights and Marks: None.

Tides (approx): MHWS: 3.9m, MHWN: 3.1m, MLWN: 1.2m, MLWS: 0.3m. Standard Port Cobh, difference at HW: Springs –00:00min; Neaps +00:10min.

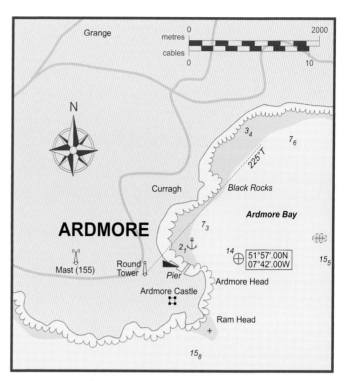

Approaches: The approach from the east is directly into Ardmore Bay. Anyone hugging the coast around from Dungarvan will need to clear The Rogue (3 cables off

Ardmore. The Round Tower and cathedral are bottom centre. The slip and pier have boats moored off. Ram Head is top right

Ardmore panorama approaching from the east

The saints: A short briefing

St Declan (fifth century) was born in Ireland and educated in Wales. He arrived in Ardmore and founded its monastery. This legacy is further distinguished by the adjacent round tower. It was once proposed that, as a native Irishman, he should be the patron saint of Ireland in preference to St Patrick.

St Patrick (390-461AD) was born on the English side of the Irish Sea. When young he was kidnapped by Irish pirates and made to serve as a slave in County Down (North-East Ireland). It took him six years to escape and return home via France. However, something inspired him to study at monasteries in France in preparation for missionary work back amongst his old slave masters. St Patrick and the three leaf shamrock, representing the Holy Trinity, have now become immutably linked with Ireland. As to driving the snakes out of Ireland, that is beyond the scope of a sailing book.

St Bridget (453-524AD) is Ireland's most revered female saint. As she is the saint for animals and crops, it is not really surprising that she ranked highly in a very agricultural community.

St Columba (Irish: *St Columcille*; 521-597AD) was born into a Donegal 'noble' family, the O'Neills. He was very active in the period of conversion to Christianity and founded at least five monasteries. Around 560AD he was exiled and became a missionary in Scotland. He moved to Iona off the west coast of Mull, Scotland, where he founded one of the most famous monastic communities in the British Isles.

Mine Head) and drying Longship Rock (4m), which is 2 cables offshore 1M south-west of Mine Head. In the bay, there is a potentially dangerous wreck on the chart, 1¼M off Ardmore Head, that is readily avoidable.

Approaching from the west, stay 2½ cables off Ram Head and its offlying submerged rock and shallows. Normally, the tall radio mast to the west of the village would aid the approach but Ardmore is blessed with several other unique features to assist navigation! How juxtaposed can they be? One is a 12th century tower and the other a modern public toilet.

Pilotage/Anchoring: From the approach waypoint, steer west-north-west to anchor north-north-west of the pier in 3-5m, but do not stray north of a bearing of 225°T on Round Tower. This avoids Black Rocks to the north of the anchorage. A useful visual mark is the somewhat distinctive and conspicuous building on the promenade looking very much like the bridge of a ship. It happens to house an estate agent and the public toilets. Land on the beach or at the slip. Reference to the rock-strewn gap

between the small pier and the slip as a harbour would be misleading. Locally, it is referred to as a boat cove.

Nevertheless both pier and slip are substantial, lit by street lamps and in good condition, and useful for landing by dinghy. As well as the rocks, there may be loose warps in the water in and around the pier.

Ardmore. The rock strewn boat cove between the slip and the pier

Estate agent, public toilet and useful navigational mark on the Ardmore shore

Useful information – Ardmore

The An Tobar lounge bar on the main street

FACILITIES

Ardmore does not focus on visiting yachts and has few facilities specific to yachtsmen. Tower Garage on the Dungarvan Road, Tel: 086 252 3738, may be able to assist with **mechanical problems** and there is a filling station for road **fuel** also on the Dungarvan Road.

PROVISIONING

Gas, groceries, post office and newspapers are available from Quinn's Deli at the end of Main Street, Tel: 024 94556. Also on Main Street is Mari Mina Pharmacy, Tel: 024 94898.

EATING OUT

Ardmore hosts a small but varied range of pubs and restaurants. Nearest the slip and beach, the Old Forge restaurant offers a simple menu and 'family style dining', where a three course meal will cost about €25, Tel: 024 94750. A little further along Main Street is the White Horses restaurant for a wider range of meals *à la carte*, Tel: 024 94040. Both places change their menus throughout the day and both have good reputations for lunches and teas. For prestigious dining, the Cliff House Hotel (towards Ardmore Head) has a restaurant that is open to non-residents. The set menu is approximately €62. There is no dress code. If fish and chips on the promenade is preferred, try Matt's Takeaway on Main Street.

Scope for a crew pub crawl is very limited as Ardmore has only two pubs, which are situated at either end of Main Street – An Tobar – The Well, Tel: 024 94166, is at the seaward end of the street, with Keavers at the other end.

ASHORE

If researching Ardmore, be sure to identify the correct 'Ardmore', a common place name across Ireland and Scotland. Ardmore's signature landmark is a 12th century Round Tower, which stands over the village and the bay. The purpose of the four storey 30m tower is disputed; some claim it was built as a stronghold for the 'monks' and their religious artefacts and books and that the entrance is 4m off the ground as an added deterrent to incursion.

The alternative theory is that the base had to be raised to maintain the structural integrity of a tall tower without foundations and that the tower's primary purpose was as a bell tower along the lines of a minaret. However, it is certain that it wasn't built to serve the 21st century cruising skipper as a fixing point, as it only just breaks the skyline during the latter stages of the easterly approach. The village's claim to fame is that it is the oldest Christian settlement in Ireland, having been converted by St Declan prior to the more widely acknowledged efforts of St Patrick.

Adjacent to the tower in the still used graveyard is the ruin of St Declan's Cathedral, which has some notable carvings depicting biblical and local scenes. Look out for two pagan Ogham stones, tucked away in small alcoves. There is also a small Oratory dating from the 8th century. St Declan's Well can be found in the vicinity of the footpath which starts east of the pier.

Ardmore Castle is an enigma. The current castle is a watch tower that was built in the 1860s. There is no visible trace of the castle that was laid siege to in 1642 and capitulated within a day or the brutal treatment of the defeated. The siege resulted in 117 men being hanged. It has been deduced from contemporary accounts that the castle stood just below the Oratory outside the cathedral grounds.

Ardmore's winter population is about 350, although there is significant holiday property development in and around Ardmore as well as a large holiday caravan site to the north of the village. This has not yet impacted on the intrinsic attractiveness of the 1½ street central village and promenade where all the facilities are focussed. However, the fast rate of development may delay identification of features from offshore if using old information.

TRANSPORT

Bus services: There are bus services to the east in peak season and to the west all year round: 260 Ardmore-Youghal-Cork. Three buses a day Monday-Saturday. 362 Ardmore-Dungarvan-Waterford. Two buses a day Monday-Saturday (July and August).

OTHER INFORMATION

Tourist office: Ardmore Tourist Office, Tel: 024 94 444, may be open but, if not, the phone call automatically switches to the Dungarvan Tourist Office, where staff will do their best to assist.

Ardmore: St Declan's Cathedral and the Round Tower

Helvick. The harbour is at the tip of the peninsula. At high tide Ballynagaul pier at the bottom of the photo acts as a useful landing alternative

www.irelandaerialphotography.com

Helvick

(Irish: *Heilbhic*)

Approach waypoint: 52°03'.58N 07°32'.19W
(½ cable SE of Helvick ECM – see chart on page 230)

Helvick is a ribbon of cottages on the south shore of Dungarvan Bay. It is a small but very active fishing village. It has some rare qualities that distinguish it from other harbours east of Cork. Most importantly, Helvick Head offers protection from the south-west through to the south, which is extremely useful along a 75M stretch of coast where entry into many harbours or anchorages when there is a significant southerly component of wind or wave is not recommended. The moorings are uncomfortable in westerly to northerly to easterly winds as the bay is wide and exposed in these directions. Entry is unencumbered and straightforward.

NAVIGATION

Charts: Admiralty SC5622.5, AC2017 or Imray C57.

Tides (approx): MHWS: 4.1m, MHWN: 3.3m, MLWN: 1.1m, MLWS: 0.4m. Standard Port Cobh, difference at HW: Springs +00:04min; Neaps +00:12min.

Lights & Marks
• Helvick ECM Q (3) 10s.

• Ballynacourty Point lighthouse (white tower) Fl (2) WRG 10s.
• Helvick Pier Ice Plant – large white building at the east end of the breakwater.

Approaches: From Dungarvan, the safest approach is via the buoyed channel. Then from 2½ cables south of Ballynacourty Point lighthouse, turn for Helvick east cardinal mark. Keep a tight back bearing on Ballynacourty Point lighthouse (153°T) to stay clear of Carrickapane's westerly offlying rocks (1½ cables to

Helvick east cardinal mark and Carrickapane Rocks

Helvick Head, harbour and visitors' buoys in a strong easterly wind

port in the red sector of the light), round the buoy and approach the moorings as from the east.

Approaching from the east, identify Helvick east cardinal mark and track south of it on approximately 245°T, noting that the offshore islands/rocks called the Gainers are only 3½ cables off the shore and 2 cables north of the moorings.

From the south, stay at least 2 cables off Helvick Head (1 cable off its outlying rocks with 15m depth). Turn to port when bearing north of the breakwater and head west to the moorings, keeping well off the breakwater to avoid the shallows to its north.

MOORING
The eight mooring buoys are less than 1 cable off Crow's Point, 2½ cables west-north-west of the breakwater in 3m of water at 52°03'.30N 07°33'.10W. Landing is at the harbour slip. At high water try landing at the old pier at Ballynagaul (6 cables west).

BERTHING
The harbour is protected by the main breakwater aligned east-west and a smaller wall aligned north-east – south-west. Entry is from due west. Shallow keel vessels may berth alongside the inside wall of the fishing pier-cum-breakwater if a berth is unoccupied by fishing vessels, but be prepared to move for a working boat.

If entering the harbour, assume less than 1.5m above chart datum in the entrance. The shore side of the harbour dries. Shelter inside is excellent except in north-westerlies.

Useful information – Helvick

FACILITIES/ PROVISIONING
Helvick is a small remote location with few facilities in the vicinity. Close to the pier are **toilets, fresh water** on a domestic tap and Murray's friendly pub, equipped with outside tables overlooking the mooring buoys. It is a fair step into Ballynagaul, which has a few more facilities, including a **restaurant** and a **grocery**.

ASHORE
Helvick's distinctive feature is that it is the smallest village of three in the *An Rinn* (or 'Ring' in English) *Gaeltacht*, where Irish is the everyday language. *Baile na nGall* (Ballynagaul in English), the main *Gaeltacht* village, is 1km west of Helvick.

Sir John Betjeman, the late English poet laureate, used to visit the 'Yellow House' on Helvick Head. Unfortunately for the area's reputation, his 'local' poem closes each stanza with the line 'Dungarvan in the rain'.

For those on passage to and from the Bristol Channel looking for a daylight crossing to a point as far west as possible, Helvick, with Waterford or Kilmore as backup refuges, has potential as a landfall in the right conditions.

Helvick may not be an undiscovered backwater for long; a government department has identified Helvick as 'having development potential for water-based tourism and leisure'.

TRANSPORT
Bus services: 362 to Dungarvan. One a day on Saturdays and Monday to Friday in July and August.

OTHER INFORMATION
For local advice try Dungarvan Yacht Club Tel: 058 45663.

Helvick Harbour

Dungarvan

(Irish: *Dún Garbháin*, meaning Garbhan's Fort)
Approach waypoint: 52°04'.35N 07°33'.00W
(3½ cables SSE of Ballynacourty Point lighthouse)

Visit Dungarvan now, because in 10 years time the tourist industry will have developed a user-friendly destination for the boating fraternity and everyone will be muttering about how 'you should have seen it 10 years ago…'. This is another way of saying Dungarvan, on the River Colligan, is almost a preferred destination! An excellent start has already been made on redeveloping derelict shops and warehouses along and behind the quayside, which now has a mixture of modern residential space and a commercial centre. Harbour entry is more interesting than challenging and the wildlife en route is fascinating and varied, particularly on Cunnigar (*An Coinigéar*) – a narrow peninsula that projects from the Helvick shore to the pool outside the harbour. No, it is not a must-see destination, but with a few harbour developments and its distance from alternatives, it could easily become a favourite.

The town quay, which is adjacent to the town centre, offers excellent protection, as could be expected from somewhere three miles from the mouth of the bay. This medium-sized town is large enough to enable a full reprovisioning of the boat. Bus and coach services are frequent and excellent, allowing ready access to Dublin, Cork and Waterford on weather bound days. However, and it is a big however, the depths in the harbour (where, with generous hospitality, the Dungarvan Sailing Club welcomes visitors to its pontoon) are insufficient for deep keel vessels. Alongside the club pontoon, keels will sink into soft mud at low water. To stay afloat, these vessels are banished to a deep-water pool immediately outside the harbour where they are exposed to southerly, easterly and to some extent the westerly/north-westerly winds.

NAVIGATION

Charts: Admiralty SC5622.5 or Imray C56.

Tides: MHWS: 4.1m, MHWN: 3.3m, MLWN: 1.1m, MLWS: 0.4m. Standard Port Cobh, difference at HW: Springs +00:04min; Neaps +00:12min.

Least depth in the buoyed channel is best assumed to be chart datum. Entering and leaving on a rising tide is therefore advisable. The flood tide into the harbour commences 5 hours 20 minutes before HW Cobh and

Dungarvan. The entrance, top left, passes Cunnigar, the spit coming from the Helvick shore. The deep keel anchorage is top right. The Sailing Club pontoon is clearly shown, reflecting the sunlight in the harbour

www.irelandaerialphotography.com

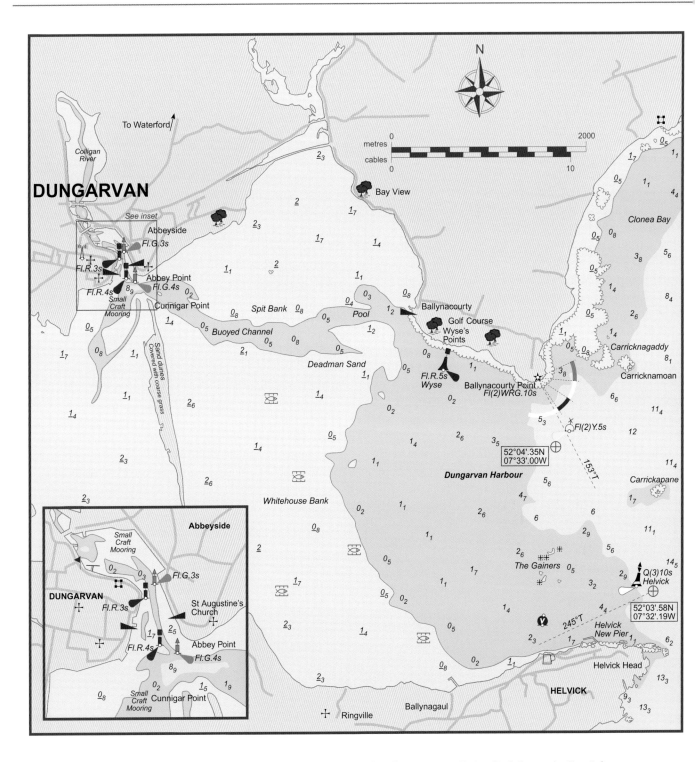

the ebb commences 40 minutes after HW Cobh. The maximum rate in the harbour entrance is 2½kn.

Lights & Marks
- Helvick ECM Q (3) 10s.
- Outfall Buoy (yellow with X top mark) Fl (2) Y 5s.
- Ballynacourty Point lighthouse (white tower) Fl (2) WRG 10s.
- Buoyed channel Wyse's Point to Abbey Point.
- Harbour beacons (south) PHM Fl R 4s, SHM Fl G 4s.
- Harbour beacons (north) PHM Fl R 3s, SHM Fl G 3s.

Approaches: Dungarvan Bay is 1½M wide between Helvick Head and Carricknamoan Islet (½M east

of Ballynacourty Point lighthouse). Carrickapane Islet (known locally as Black Rock) lies midway in the bay between the two. The bay is shallow and totally open to the east, which means entry is not recommended in strong wind and seas from south to east. The bar breaks and can be rough in strong south-easterly winds.

From the east, approach north of Carrickapane, which is in the red sector of Ballynacourty Point lighthouse, steering due west to arrive midway between Carricknamoan, which is in the green sector of Ballynacourty Point lighthouse, and Carrickapane. The northern islet will become distinct only as it clears the background shoreline.

From the south, approach the waypoint from close north-east of Helvick east cardinal mark, staying clear of the shallows west of Carrickapane (in the red sector of Ballynacourty Point lighthouse) and those east of the Gainers.

In both cases pass the yellow outfall buoy (normally with 'X' top mark) to starboard.

Pilotage: Ahead to the west-north-west, identify and approach the first port-hand mark. Off to starboard are the conspicuous greens of the golf course at Wyse's Point. Identify the rest of the buoyed channel; strangers would benefit from having a crew member with binoculars to spot the buoys. Normally there are five port-hand marks and four starboard-hand marks, but some of these may be missing for repair etc. The buoys are moved to reflect changes in the channel.

A typical port-hand mark in Dungarvan's buoyed entrance channel

Follow the channel's winding path for 2M to Abbey Point and Cunnigar Point. The anchorage is close south-west and heavily populated with moorings.

The church and priory ruins at Abbey Point

Alternatively, turn to starboard for the harbour – there are two lateral beacon pairs marking the narrow entrance, after which the harbour opens out.

The tidal flow encountered in the entrance can be strong. The sailing club pontoon and the town quay are immediately to port. Finding adequate space in either location may be problematic at the height of the season. Be prepared to go back to sea while there is sufficient water.

ANCHORING

Deep keel yachts anchor in the pool in about 8m, keeping as far west as possible and not obstructing the fairway. Land at the town slip (1½ cables north-west of the anchorage). Note space is very limited, the tide runs fast and the bottom may be foul with old or disused moorings. It is best to try to borrow a mooring if possible.

Approaching the inner harbour, having rounded Abbey Point

Dungarvan – the west side of the inner harbour. The Sailing Club pontoon is at the far end of the moored boats (centre photo). There are cafés, restaurants and a supermarket in the renovated buildings along the quay

BERTHING

All vessels entering Dungarvan Harbour should be prepared to take the ground at low water. Deep draught yachts can dry out standing alongside the quay wall. Alternatively, go alongside the sailing club pontoon, Tel: 058 45663. Moor port side to as the ebb sets strongly along the quay. Avoid the pick-up/set-down area by using the upstream end; raft if necessary. The club charges €10 for an overnight stay. Payment can be made at the clubhouse along the quay. For more information, refer to the notice to visitors on the pontoon.

As usual in a town centre berth, it is advisable to lock all access hatches when proceeding ashore.

Useful information – Dungarvan

FACILITIES/ PROVISIONING

Dungarvan is the County Town of County Waterford, with a population of approximately 8,000. It therefore has a wide range of shops, **supermarkets** and services. A SuperValu supermarket is situated adjacent to the sailing club pontoon, while Lidl is out on the ring road. The **Internet** can be accessed at the library, located at the quay, or, alternatively, there are several internet cafés in the town.

Showers may be taken in the sailing club's very friendly clubhouse, and road **fuel** is available within walking distance.

Pub sign near to the sailing club

EATING OUT

There are plenty of cafés, restaurants and pubs serving food in the town. Close at hand, The Moorings bar and bistro is one of the elegant establishments that now operate from the renovated harbour buildings. It is well situated for lunchtime refreshment overlooking the harbour. The Tannery restaurant, in one of the restored granaries set back from the harbour, also has a good reputation.

ASHORE

Dungarvan's history can be traced to the third century. Arriving by sea, the most marked features are the tower of the 13th century Augustinian Priory on the east bank of the harbour entrance and King John's Castle, an Anglo-Norman fortification dating from 1185 just north of the harbour narrows on the west bank.

The castle is open to the public while it is being restored. The dominant remains are the corner tower, the gate tower and the 18th century barracks which now house an exhibition and an

King John's Castle

audio visual presentation giving a concise eight minute summary of Dungarvan's history.

The museum on St Augustine Street has a maritime section and is also well worth a visit.

Other attractions in the town include a three screen cinema.

TRANSPORT

Bus services: 040 Express; hourly to Cork and Waterford and local services. 362 Ardmore, 364 Waterford, 366 Waterford, Fermoy & Mallow and 386 Clonmel. There are daily connecting services to Dublin and a nightly service (via the Rosslare/Fishguard ferry) to Bristol and London.
Taxi: Tel: 087 814 4777 or there are usually plenty of taxis available at the taxi rank close to the sailing club pontoon.

OTHER INFORMATION
Police: 058 48600.
Hospital: 058 41125.
Dentist: 058 42961/41155.
Doctor: 058 41106/41063 /42210/41227/42401/ 41262.
Tourist office: The Courthouse, Davitt's Quay, Tel: 058 41741.

Dunmore East

(Irish: *Dun Mor*, meaning Great Fort)
Approach waypoint: 52°08'.00N 06°58'.00W
(1.2M SE of Dunmore East Harbour)

Dunmore East is both a very busy fishing harbour and, at Lower Village 1km north, a well-kept holiday resort with signature thatched cottages, small coves and beautiful red sandstone cliffs populated by a large number of kittiwakes. In calm, clear conditions, the uninterrupted view across to Hook Head, with its reassuring pulse of light, make Dunmore East a very attractive destination. Waterford Harbour Sailing Club (WHSC) is very active in the summer months, holding frequent races and regattas.

Superficially, its location close to and inside the entrance to Waterford Harbour makes it an attractive refuge and overnight stop. However, the heavy fishing vessel traffic, densely-packed moorings and susceptibility to easterly winds must be taken into account. It is therefore difficult to sum up Dunmore East as a destination. It could be anywhere on the spectrum between a very comfortable, unforgettable sojourn and a bumpy stay in the middle of a regatta. Before deliberating on this dilemma, the weather must be considered as a gating factor. Any significant weather from the north-east or east or very heavy weather from the south-east would immediately divert a skipper further up Waterford Harbour, but even a strong south-westerly sea can refract around the headland and cause uncomfortable swell close to the entrance.

NAVIGATION

Charts: Admiralty Leisure Folios SC5621 and SC5622 overlap at Waterford Harbour. Dunmore East Harbour is detailed in SC5622.3B (SC5621.17B) or AC/LE2046.

Immediately outside the harbour in Dunmore Bay use SC5622.3 (SC5621.17), AC/LE2046 or Imray C57.

Tides: MHWS: 4.2m, MHWN: 3.2m, MLWN: 1.4m, MLWS: 0.6m. Standard Port Cobh, difference at HW: Springs +00:08min; Neaps +00:03min.

Lights & Marks
- Hook Head lighthouse Fl 3s.
- Pilot lookout on Black Knob.
- East pierhead light Fl WR 8s:
white sector 225° to 310°T; red sector 310° to 004°T.
- East breakwater extension light Fl R 2s.
- West Wharf light Fl G 2s: green sector 165° to 246°T.

Approaches: From the west, stay south of Falskirt Rock (2M south-west of Dunmore East – *at the*

Dunmore East. The lower village is top left. The harbour is unusually empty of fishing vessels. The yachts in the centre are on private moorings

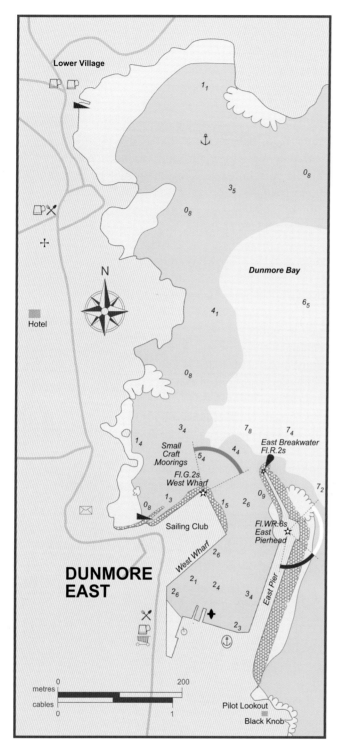

Map of Dunmore East showing Lower Village, Hotel, Dunmore Bay, Small Craft Moorings, West Wharf Fl.G.2s, Sailing Club, East Breakwater Fl.R.2s, Fl.WR.6s East Pierhead, East Pier, Pilot Lookout and Black Knob. Scale in metres (0–200) and cables (0–1).

Dunmore East harbour entrance

2 cables off. At night: steer east until the red sector of East Pier light is sighted before turning to steer north-north-east.

The approach from the east is determined by the weather. In settled conditions the approach from the open sea presents no difficulties – the mouth is 2.2M wide and deep with no obstructions. There is uncluttered passage from Hook Head and the south.

However, tidal streams off Hook Head must be fully considered. Be particularly alert 1½ hours either side of LW Cobh during springs. Spring rates reach 3kn close in, reducing to 1½kn 5M offshore. The conditions are serious enough to have attracted a soubriquet of its own: 'Tower Race'. The combination of a strong Waterford ebb tide with strong south-westerly winds and/or a strong westerly flow offshore give rise to overfalls and hazardous seas up to 2M off Hook Head light.

Pilotage: From the approach waypoint, steer north until East Pier light (a round tower on the harbour wall) bears 310°T (at night – white sector). Alter course towards Dunmore Bay and steer 317°T to the anchorage. The harbour entrance will be obscured because it faces north-north-west and can be reached by turning to port from this course when both the East Breakwater extension and West Wharf marks/lights are visible (the latter is first visible when it bears 246°T).

south-west corner of Chart SC5622.3). **Note**: this can be simply achieved by staying south of an easterly bearing on Hook Head light until the danger is passed. Thereafter by day: follow the coast around at least

BERTHING/MOORING/ANCHORING

There are several possibilities at Dunmore East. The options for visiting craft include talking to the WHSC about the use of one of its moorings or rafting-

Dunmore East – the outer harbour wall

up inside the harbour on the west wharf pontoon. Alternatively, anchor in settled conditions in the bays off the Lower Village.

Anchoring: Even casual observation reveals that the bays off Lower Village between the park and golf course can be uncomfortable in anything but the most settled conditions. If these favourable conditions prevail, anchor in 3-5m – 2½ cables north by north-west of the harbour entrance.

Mooring: WHSC administers three rows of mooring buoys immediately north of the harbour. The outer trot is capable of taking craft of 11m. It is worth checking on availability in advance, Tel: 051 383 230.

There will be a small charge. Outside of the sailing club's moorings are private moorings of dubious reliability, which are less protected from the incoming swell. Check locally to determine which are available and reliable.

Berthing: Visitors may berth in the harbour. Overnight stops are possible rafted up on similar vessels at the south-west end of the West Wharf. The pontoons against the wall are not primarily designed for shore access, which can be a scramble. There is a small berthing charge.

Landing: At a slip either at Lower Village or on the outside (north) side of the West Wharf.

Useful information – Dunmore East

FACILITIES
Fresh water: Is available on West Wharf.
Showers: Can be taken at the Waterford Harbour Sailing Club. The season is nominally St Patrick's Day (17 March) to the end of September.
Fuel: Diesel provision is in a state of flux at the time of writing. Diesel may not be as readily available as it has been in the recent past. Seek local advice from the Waterford Harbour Sailing Club, the fishermen's co-operative (both on the West Wharf) or Brendan Glody, Tel: 087 260 8917.
Gas: Camping Gaz is not currently available locally – check for recent information at the Adventure Centre chandlery, situated in the old fishery hall on West Wharf. Rupert Musgrave at the Adventure Centre carries a small but useful range of chandlery items; Tel: 051 383 783/086 865 8259; website: www.dunmoreadventure.com.
Flogas can be bought from the Dingley's grocery and Kosan from the Londis – both located at the harbour road entrance.
Yacht services: The Synchrolift is not available for leisure craft; however, there is an area in the south-west corner of the harbour where it is possible to dry out between tides.
Lifting facilities are by mobile crane that can be arranged through Shane Statham, Tel: 086 824 5430, who runs a boatyard and can help with anything from engine or electrical repairs to winter storage.

PROVISIONING
The Londis and Centra **mini-markets** along with Dingley's grocery provide a good range of items to top up provisions. Mullaley's **pharmacy** and the **post office** are nearby. Two **ATMs** are available.

EATING OUT
Upper Village: Visiting sailors are welcome in the sailing club's clubhouse where usually it is possible to order food. The club also offers an *à la carte* menu on Friday evenings and a barbecue on Sundays.
The Bay Café, The Lemon Tree and Jenny's Kitchen offer daytime refreshment. The Lemon Tree, which is well spoken of locally, may be found by turning left on leaving the harbour. It is highly recommended, serves seafood sandwiches, savoury pies and is open all year round, Tel: 051 383 164. The Ocean Hotel, Tel: 051 383 136, and The Haven Hotel, Tel: 051 383 150, both do evening bar food. Powers Bar is a long-established traditional pub. More sophisticated Italian dining can be had at the Azzuro, Tel: 051 383 141, before the descent to Lower Village.
Lower Village: It is a 1km walk to Lower Village, which has some excellent pubs and restaurants, some of which capitalise on the fresh fish from the harbour. Prices here tend towards the expensive end of reasonable but not so expensive as to deter large family groups keeping the kitchens busy until 2200. In peak season, it would be advisable to book if a particular restaurant has been selected. There is a slipway directly adjacent to The Strand; dinghy storage is in the car park as the beach is entirely below the high water mark, and immediately ashore is the main road.
The Strand, Tel: 051 383 174, is aptly named and presides over the beach (at low water). Its outside tables are therefore very popular. Inside, the pub is a fine warren of rooms to suit most moods. The separate restaurant, well regarded for its seafood, is BIM accredited.
The Cliff is a newly opened offshoot of The Strand. It is an 'American diner' style pizza restaurant and takeaway, Tel: 051 38 38 39. The Spinnaker, Tel: 051 383 133, recreates a pleasant 'Ye Olde Maritime' feel for its customers. It had the 'Best in Ireland' award for 2007 and has live music at weekends.
A fast food shop is on hand for those that let the peak season queues beat them and opt for a takeaway.

ASHORE
Originally a military stronghold on the west bank of the Waterford Harbour entrance, it was later developed as a cross channel packet harbour for mail, a role that never proved successful, and finally as a large fishing port. Leisure sailors would be a subsidiary interest to the locals if it were not for the Waterford Harbour Sailing Club, which has its headquarters on the North West Quay.

TRANSPORT
Bus services: Suirway provides a regular year-round service between Dunmore East and Waterford.
Taxi: PM Cabs Tel: 087 325 2226; Hogan Tel: 087 279 6959.
Air: Only 10km from Waterford International Airport, it would make a possible place to swap a passage crew for a cruising crew using regular flights from the UK or Netherlands.

OTHER INFORMATION
Harbour master: Captain Hugh Byrne monitors all harbour movements. He administers the area between the harbour entrance and Creadan Head, Tel: 051 383 166.
Yacht club: Waterford Harbour Sailing Club, Tel: 051 383 230; website www.whsc.ie.
Doctor: The Health Centre is in Lower Village.

Waterford Harbour

Encompassing a major city, a large town and rural anchorages, the mostly sheltered waters of Waterford Harbour offer plenty of variety. The passage to Waterford has diverse scenery, ever-changing traffic and is never boring. The passage upriver starts at Duncannon, with its magnificent fort and huge sweep of beach off to the east. The harbour narrows to river proportions within a mile and a half, where a well-used and very frequent car ferry crosses between Passage East on the Waterford shore and Ballyhack on the Wexford side of the River Suir. Ballyhack is a quirky, attractive anchorage if the pub or an urgent shopping trip is the goal. After three further miles the River Barrow diverges and heads north under the railway swing bridge for a further nine navigable miles through delightful rural surroundings to New Ross, which has a small, well-equipped and convenient marina. Here a full-sized reconstruction of a famine ship can be toured. Back towards Waterford and beyond the commercial port, King's Channel separates from Queen's Channel and together they surround Little Island at mile eleven. King's Channel has anchorages, which are excellent for a quiet evening on board away from it all. Finally, at mile fourteen, the rural ideal is replaced by a city centre and Waterford City Marina.

As most visitors' destination will be Waterford and New Ross, the navigation section below addresses this but also provides more detail for each of the minor destinations. Entry to the Waterford Harbour mouth at Hook Head is described under Dunmore East on pages 233–234 and a skipper should be alert to the vagaries of the Tower Race. Once north of the 'Waterford' buoy, tidal streams will quicken and concentrated attention should turn to leading beacons/lights, shoals, commercial shipping and buoyage. In stiff winds with a southerly component, do not expect the seas to totally quieten until north of Ballyhack.

Waterford City
Approach waypoint: 52°08'.95N 06°56'.76W
(1½ cables E of the 'Waterford' buoy)

NAVIGATION
Charts: Use Imray C57, AC/LE2046 or Admiralty Leisure Folio as follows:
'Waterford' Buoy to Ballyhack/Passage East: SC5622.3 (SC5621.17).
Ballyhack/Passage East to Cheek Point to NW Little Island: SC5622.4A (SC5621.18A).
NW Little Island to Waterford: SC5622.4C (SC5621.18C).

Tides: Standard Port Cobh.
'Waterford' Buoy: MHWS: 4.2m, MHWN: 3.2m, MLWN: 1.4m, MLWS: 0.6m. Difference at HW: Springs +00:08min; Neaps +00:03min.
Cheek Point: MHWS: 4.4m, MHWN: 3.4m, MLWN: 1.5m, MLWS: 0.5m. Difference at HW: +00:21.
Waterford City: MHWS: 4.5m, MHWN: 3.5m, MLWN: 1.2m, MLWS: 0.5m. Difference at HW: +00:57.

The flood tide commences 4 hours and 25 minutes before HW Cobh and tends to the western side of the estuary as far as Creadan Head. The ebb tide commences 45 minutes after HW Cobh and flows strongly along the western shore of the Hook Peninsula.

Waterford Harbour entrance. Note the tide offshore has just turned westward off Hook Head (bottom left)

Maximum tidal rate is ¾kn ingoing and 1½kn outgoing in the fairway off Creadan Head but both are stronger in the narrow parts of the river upstream. In the River Suir at Waterford, the tides will reach up to 3½kn.

It is highly advisable, therefore, to plan a visit anywhere in Waterford Harbour assisted by the tide in both directions.

Lights & Marks

a) **Hook Head to Duncannon**:
- Hook Head Fl 3s.
- 'Waterford' PHM buoy, Fl (3) R 10s.

Waterford buoy

- Duncannon Bar laterals, No 1 Fl G 2s, No 2 QR, No 3 Fl G 4s, No 4 Fl R 3s.
- Duncannon Spit SHM (No 5) Fl (2) G 4s (Note No 6 PHM is planned to be added).
- Duncannon leading lights front Oc WR 4s; rear Oc 6s.
- Duncannon Dir light F WRG – white tower on fort. White sector (S) 001.7° to 002.4°T (Al WR to 002.9°T and Al WG to 001.2°T).White sector (NW) 149° to 172°T.
- Drumroe Bank North PHM, QR.

b) **Duncannon to Passage East**:
- Passage Spit, Fl WR 5s (red platform). NW white sector 114° to 127°T; SE white sector 180° to 302°T.
- Passage East Fl (2) 5s.

Passing Passage Spit port-hand mark

c) **Passage East to Cheek Point**:
Upriver from Passage East to Cheek Point, the river is well marked with lit buoys to starboard and beacons on the shore and is therefore navigable with relative ease. New lights & marks at Passage East and upriver were introduced in 2007, for example, Seedes Bank South, Fl (4) G 6s (52°14'.95N 06°59'.32W).

A buoyed channel to Cheek Point (drying) harbour extends to port.

d) **Cheek Point to North-West Little Island**:
The channel between Cheek Point and the commercial quays is marked by special purpose (yellow) buoys to port and beacons on the north shore. Ships manoeuvre in and around the quays frequently. They should be given every consideration. The use of lateral buoys resumes at the commercial quays and continues to the north-west of Little Island.
- Queen's Channel leading line on a back bearing of 098°T heading upstream towards Waterford: Front mark black-white-black beacon (Oc R 6s); back mark white beacon (Q).

The channel also has several lateral buoys.

Queen's Channel leading line sited at the east end of Queen's Channel

e) **North-West Little Island to Waterford City**:
After the north-west corner of Little Island, the river is not buoyed but there are lit beacons on the shore. Keep to the outside of bends.

Pilotage

i) **'Waterford' Buoy to Duncannon**
The first mark encountered in Waterford Harbour is the 'Waterford' port-hand mark buoy, which lies midway between and on an approximate east-west line joining Dunmore East with the large conspicuous building on the Hook Peninsula labelled Loftus Hall on the chart. Take position to the east of the buoy to be closer to the

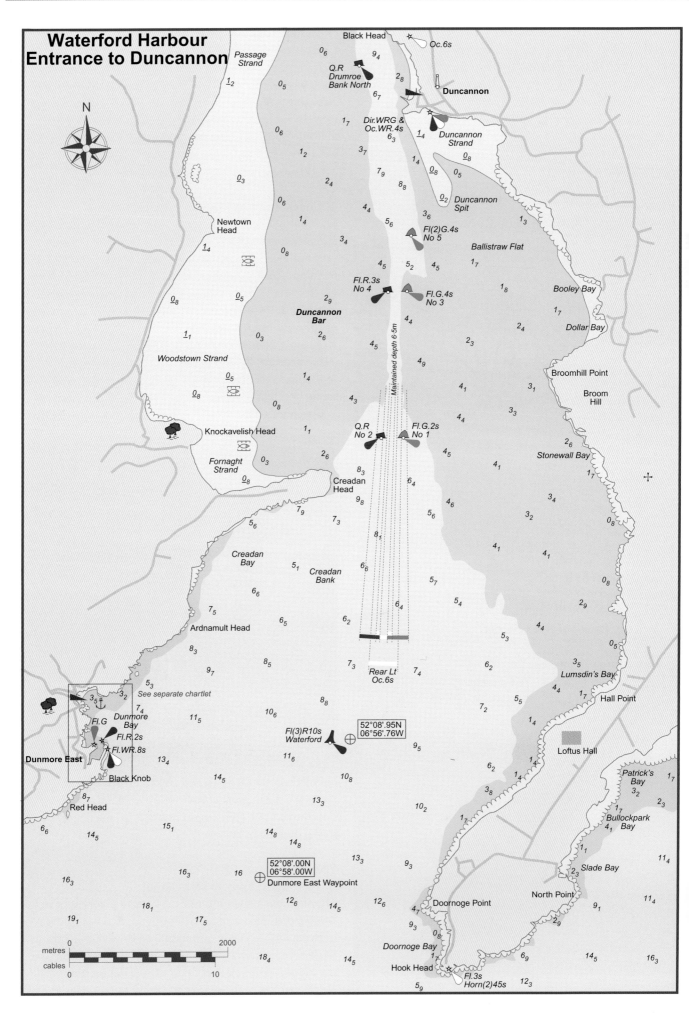

Waterford Harbour
Entrance to Duncannon

Passage
Strand

Black Head

Oc.6s

9₄

0₆

Q.R
Drumroe
Bank North

2₈

Duncannon

1₂

0₅

6₇

1₇

Dir.WRG &
Oc.WR.4s
6₃

1₄

Duncannon
Strand

0₆

1₂

3₇

1₄

0₈

0₅

7₉

8₈

0₈

Newtown
Head

0₃

2₄

4₄

5₆

3₆

0₂

Duncannon
Spit

1₃

1₄

0₈

Fl(2)G.4s
No 5

Ballistraw Flat

0₈

0₅

4₅

5₂

4₅

1₇

1₈

Booley Bay

Woodstown Strand

1₁

0₃

2₉

Fl.R.3s
No 4

Fl.G.4s
No 3

4₄

1₇

Dollar Bay

Duncannon
Bar

2₆

4₅

4₄

2₄

0₅

0₈

1₄

4₃

4₉

2₃

Broomhill Point

Broom
Hill

Knockavelish Head

1₁

Q.R
No 2

Fl.G.2s
No 1

4₁

3₁

3₃

0₈

Fornaght
Strand

0₃

2₆

8₃

6₄

4₅

4₄

4₁

2₆

Stonewall Bay

0₈

Creadan
Head

9₈

4₆

3₄

3₂

1₇

5₆

7₉

7₃

8₁

5₆

2₃

4₁

4₁

0₈

Creadan
Bay

5₁

Creadan
Bank

6₆

5₇

5₄

4₄

2₉

0₅

6₆

6₅

6₂

6₄

5₃

7₅

3₅

Lumsdin's Bay

Ardnamult Head

8₃

8₅

7₃

7₄

Rear Lt
Oc.6s

6₂

5₅

4₄

1₇

Hall Point

9₇

3₂

See separate chartlet

8₈

7₂

1₄

5₃

7₄

Fl.G

Dunmore
Bay

11₅

10₆

52°08'.95N
06°56'.76W

Patrick's
Bay

3₂

2₃

1₇

Fl.R.2s

Fl(3)R10s
Waterford

9₅

6₂

1₄

Loftus Hall

3₅
♁

Fl.WR.8s

13₄

11₆

10₈

1₄

Bullockpark
Bay

4₁

Dunmore East

Black Knob

14₅

13₃

10₂

3₈

1₁

11₄

8₇

Red Head

15₁

14₈

13₃

1₇

2₃

Slade Bay

6₆

14₅

16₃

16

14₈

52°08'.00N
06°58'.00W

4₇

9₁

2₉

11₄

16₃

18₁

17₅

12₆

14₅

12₆

Dunmore East Waypoint

9₃

Doornoge Point

North Point

19₁

18₄

14₅

13₃

0₈

Doornoge Bay

6₉

14₅

16₃

Hook Head

Fl.3s
Horn(2)45s

5₉

12₃

Maintained depth 6·5m

River Suir mouth. Passage Spit platform is at the end of the spit. Creadan Head and Hook Head are in the distance

fort. No 6 port-hand mark may be added in the near future. At the Spit buoy, it is now safe to break from the leading beacon/lights to port to a heading midway between the Fort and Drumroe Bank North port-hand mark. Depths should always exceed 5m.

ii) **Duncannon to Ballyhack/Passage East** Continue past Duncannon and Drumroe Bank North port-hand mark, keeping to the general rule of tracking the outside of river bends for the deeper water.

Identify the somewhat overstated Passage Spit port-hand mark/sector light-cum-cormorant colony to port and, staying in at least a 5m depth, turn gradually to port following the channel. Opposite the beacon is Arthurstown. At this point, the river width has narrowed greatly and the feel is now that of a river as opposed to an estuary.

leading beacon/lights based on Duncannon Fort. A pair of lateral buoys (Nos 1 and 2), which are barely visible from the 'Waterford' buoy, mark the entrance to the channel. They are to the north-east of Creadan Head, the long high headland emerging from the western shore. It is off here that the tidal stream runs strongly as it is concentrated by Creadan Head. The shallows, known as Duncannon Bar, encroach rapidly on the channel immediately after these lateral buoys, but there is nothing to especially trouble the average deep keel yacht.

The readily identified Duncannon Fort is dead ahead to the west of the two shoreline conurbations. The front/lower light is hosted on a white tower which is at the south-west corner of the fort. The rear tower and light is built into the wooded hill north of Duncannon Harbour.

The north end of Duncannon Bar is indicated by another pair of lateral buoys (Nos 3 and 4). A further starboard-hand mark (No 5) protects Duncannon Spit (0.6m), which extends south-south-east from the

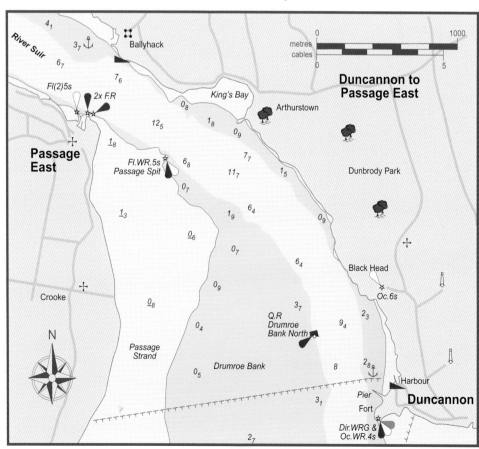

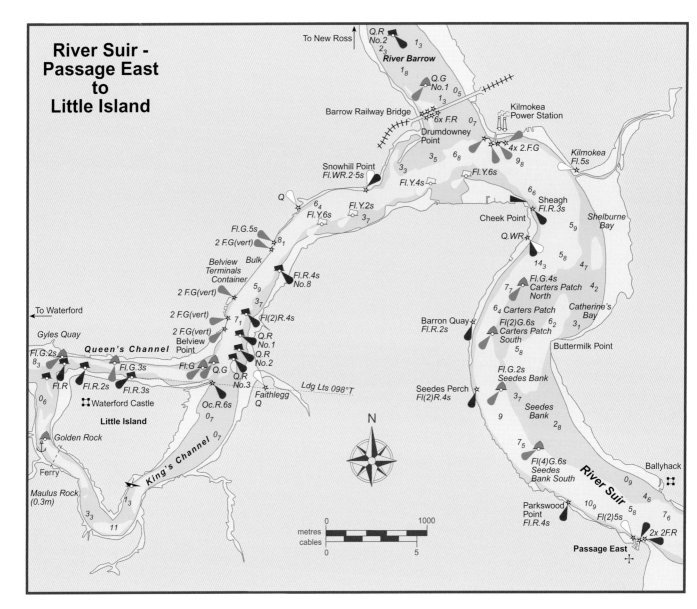

iii) Ballyhack/Passage East to Cheek Point to North-West Little Island via Queen's Channel

From Passage East, follow the buoyed channel, which generally hugs the west shore of the river.

At Cheek Point, Kilmokea Power Station and the railway bridge appear to the north. Here the River

Barrow joins the Suir. The passage through the railway swing bridge to New Ross is described later in this chapter. Ignore the buoyed channel to Cheek Point, which, in the absence of lateral buoys in the main channel, can be confusing.

Between Cheek Point and the commercial quays,

Approaching Cheek Point. The River Suir sweeps left and the River Barrow heads north under the railway bridge to New Ross

After Cheek Point the main channel becomes obvious once the Port of Waterford quays come into view

Yellow buoys mark the channel between Cheek Point and the commercial quays

the yellow buoys should be kept to port.

Once the port and starboard buoys resume, be particularly alert to the imminent hard turn to starboard required to access Queen's Channel, which is marked by the front leading line mark dead ahead and the two starboard buoys in quick succession.

Passage through Queen's Channel is assisted by a leading line on a back bearing of 098°T.

The buoyage further along Queen's Channel remains easy to follow to the westerly confluence of King's and Queen's Channel at the north-west corner of Little Island.

The River Suir has a least depth of 2.5m at its shallowest point, in Queen's Channel.

iv) North-West Little Island to Waterford

This seemingly harmless coming together of the two channels hides two dangers. Firstly, be alert to very strong deflecting currents

as King's Channel merges with Queen's Channel. Also hereabouts on a low or falling tide, stay close to Gyles Quay (on the north bank), as the shallow area at Dirty Tail (off the south bank) is more extensive than the chart suggests. Thereafter, continue to follow the river, staying on the outside of the bends for deeper water.

A departing container ship to port and a moored bulk carrier to starboard. Lateral buoys restart here to mark the channel past Little Island

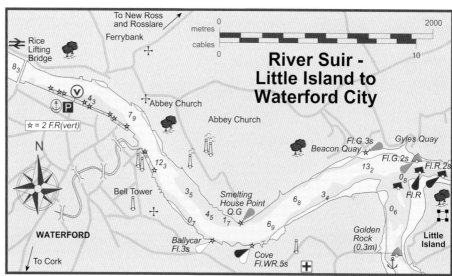

River Suir - Little Island to Waterford City

BERTHING AT WATERFORD CITY MARINA

Waterford City Marina is an excellent initiative. It hosted a Tall Ships gathering in 2005 and will again in 2011. Installed and run by a motivated city council, it is located on the South Quays and could not be closer to the city centre's archaeological relics, restaurants and shopping. The marina is a little west of the Millennium Plaza – a symbol of the city's regeneration. The old commercial wharf opposite the city marina is currently zoned off to be developed into a marina, public park, housing and a shopping centre.

Waterford's Reginald's Tower and Millennium Spire

The first city pontoons are either private or for long-term mooring. They are immediately followed by a visitors' pontoon. The distinctive restored dockside crane just after the Millennium Spire is a good indicator for the first of the visitors' berths. Contact either the marina superintendent on Tel: 087 238 4944 or, if he is not available, the city museum (situated at 'The Granary', further west along the Quay behind the tourist office) on Tel: 051 304 500 during opening hours for berth allocation, the gate keyfob and electricity cards. Although the marina has recently been expanded to accommodate 100 yachts in total, it is worth calling ahead to check on availability of space. **Note**: the tidal flow in the river through Waterford can reach 3½kn, particularly on the ebb after heavy rainfall inland. Approach into the flow is essential.

The marina is accessible 24 hours a day, but if entering at night it is advisable to check ship movements with the Port Authority on Tel: 051 301 400. **Berthing fees**: (short term rate): 7.6 to 10.7m €20 per night, 10.7 to 13.7m €25 per night, >13.7m €30 per night.

www.irelandaerialphotography.com

Waterford. The visitors' berths are on the long pontoon opposite the large silo

Useful information – Waterford City Marina/Waterford City

The marina shower and toilet block – a building listed for preservation

FACILITIES

Water and electricity: Are on the pontoons. Use of electricity requires a prepaid meter card (€2.50 for 10kW-hour), which is available from the marina manager or the museum.

Diesel: Can be delivered in large quantities by road tanker, but this needs to be arranged through the marina superintendent. Road fuel by can is available from the filling station along the road to Dunmore behind the Tower Hotel.

Gas: Some overseas gas bottles can be refilled in Waterford (contact the marina), while Camping Gaz is stocked at Army & Outdoor Stores, New Street, Tel: 051 857 554.

Showers/launderette: The shower block, incorporating a coin-operated launderette, is somewhat idiosyncratic. Located outside the security gate, it is housed in an old corrugated iron dockmaster's hut that has a preservation order on it! It is a rare sailing experience – walking across a public car park with shoppers coming and going when en route to the shower or laundry. Access into the shower block is by key.

Rubbish disposal: Is by bins on the walkway to the quayside.

Communications: Mobile phone coverage in the marina is good, and Internet access is available in the adjacent shopping centre. Note that weather forecasts are not provided by the marina office.

Boat services: Deevy's Marine Accessories, 48 Parnell Street, is a short distance along the Cork Road, Tel: 051 874 477. It has a small but useful stock of items and opens seven days a week in season. A new boatyard company has opened in New Ross, Tel: 087 290 3538. For more information, see New Ross, page 249.

PROVISIONING

The city centre, which is an easy walk from the marina, has an extensive selection of shops and three department stores. There is a large **supermarket** within the Dunne's store in City Square, Tel: 051 853 100, as well as a SuperValu and a Tesco a little further away. Several **pharmacies** are situated in the city centre, including a Boots that is within 200m of the marina. A **post office** can be found at 100, The Quay, while **banks** and **ATMs** are located in the city centre.

EATING OUT

Have lunch in one of the many city pubs or coffee houses (for example, The Gingerman in Arundel Lane, which has friendly service and a wide menu), all of which are within easy walking distance of the pontoons. Much more choice is available during the working day than in the evening, partly because there is not a focal point for the city's restaurants. However, there is a clutch of good restaurants that are well thought of locally close to Reginald's Tower on The Quay: L'Atmosphere (French cuisine), 19 Henrietta Street, Tel: 051 858 426; The Jade Palace (a Chinese restaurant), 4 The Mall, Tel: 051 855 611; The Munster Bar (Traditional Irish bar food); Bailey's, New Street, Tel: 051 874 656; Sabai (Thai & Vietnamese) 19, The Mall, Tel: 051 858 002; Emiliano's (Italian), 21 High Street, Tel: 051 820 333, and Café Goa (Indian), 36, The Quay, Tel: 051 304 970.

Bars and hotel lounges are widespread in the vicinity of the marina and for early drinkers, some bars such as Jordan's on The Quay still have 'Dockers' Licences', meaning they can open at 0900 (it used to be earlier). It is also known as The American Bar because it was once the ticket office for buying emigrant tickets to the USA.

ASHORE

Waterford's closeness to mainland Europe, its highly defensible harbour and the extensive inland reach of the three nearby rivers made it a strategically

Millennium Plaza and long-term pontoon

significant city – Ireland's first, dating back to 856AD when it was founded by the Vikings. Waterford derives its English name from the original Viking name of *Vadre fjord*, meaning a weather-protected haven. They retained Waterford until 1169 when Strongbow (The Norman Earl of Pembroke) eventually broke its defences – it was fortified by a city wall. Six of the towers and sections of city wall still exist – Reginald's Tower on The Quay is the best and oldest example of these relics. It was built circa 1003 by the Vikings. Later, Henry II, the first Plantagenet King of England, made Waterford (along with Dublin) a royal city.

In more recent times, the city gave its name, of course, to the famous hand-cut crystal which has been made for 225 years. A trip to the edge of town is needed to see the Waterford Crystal factory,

gallery & visitor centre. A purchase in the shop might be just the thing as a present for those left at home or as a souvenir.

A simple way to sample Waterford would be to take the one hour 'City Walk', which starts at the Treasures Museum on the quay and visits the principal sights ('two cathedrals, four national monuments, and a gallery of rogues and rascals'), Tel: 051 873 711. Make a visit to the Treasures Museum while there. Inside the old granaries are a collection of artefacts from Waterford's history.

Also in Waterford is an eight-screen cinema situated on Railway Square (Storm Cinemas – Tel: 051 309 110).

TRANSPORT
Bus services: The bus station is just west of the marina gate. There is a comprehensive city, rural and national bus service

from here. Regular express services also run to Dublin and Cork and a nightly service (via the Rosslare/ Fishguard ferry) to Bristol and London.

Taxi: The taxi rank outside Dunne's store is the most used rank; it is more reliable than the rank between the marina and the bus station. Alternatively, contact Rapid Cabs on Tel: 051 858 585.

Car hire: Budget Car Rental, Unit 4 Park Road, Business Park (Near People's Park), Tel: 051 843 747; Tom Murphy, Cork Road, Tel: 051 301 222; Hertz Tel: 053 915 2500.

Rail: The railway station is over the adjacent Rice bridge on the north side of the river. Trains go to Limerick, Dublin and occasionally to Rosslare.

Air: Waterford Airport has direct flights to five countries.

OTHER INFORMATION
Waterford Port Authority: VHF Ch 16 then working

14 – not normally required for daylight passage to Waterford Marina, Tel: 051 301 400.
Customs: Tel: 051 862 212/051 877 011.
Hospital: Tel: 051 848 000.
Doctor: Tel: 051 855 411 (Keogh Practice).
Dentist: Tel: 051 854 110 (Donal Blackwell).
Tourist office: 41 The Quay, Tel: 051 875 788 (Option 1).

Reginald's Tower is the best preserved of Waterford's relics dating from 1003

Duncannon
(Irish: *Dún Canann*, meaning Conan's Fort)

For navigation to Duncannon see page 237. Before opting for long term anchoring at Duncannon, bear in mind that the anchorage is less than 80m from the main shipping channel, which is regularly trafficked by sizeable container and bulk cargo freighters. Also the tidal stream is still strong here. Tidal eddies occur in this area and holding has been reported as poor.

Add to this an underwater cable that extends west of the pier and the lack of protection from winds from the south through west to the north-east, and this combination of factors is hardly a recipe for a relaxed prolonged stay.

ANCHORING
Duncannon Pier aligns east-north-east from the shore; deep keel vessels anchor north of the pier in 3-4m. Landing is at the public boat slip.

Duncannon Harbour's detached pontoon, pier and fort

Duncannon Pier at low water springs

BERTHING

Shallow keel vessels may find space in the small drying harbour to the north-east.

Alternatively, berth alongside the quay over high water (depth may be taken as a little over chart datum towards the end of the pier – see photo opposite). Tying up next to fishing vessels should be negotiated. There is also a privately-owned, detached, three section pontoon that may suit some craft. It is moored off the public slipway in shallow water.

Useful information – Duncannon

FACILITIES/ PROVISIONING
The village has a very small **grocery**, seaside fancy goods store and **post office**. There is an **Internet** café in the fort.

EATING OUT
Sqigl's is a small seafood restaurant (booking essential), Tel: 051 389 700, on Quay Road. It sits adjacent to Roches Bar, which is a more traditional pub with beer garden that serves bar food, Tel: 051 389 188. Opposite Roches is the Strand Tavern, which also offers bar food daily and attracts a large clientele when a Gaelic football game is on television.

ASHORE
As well as being a small fishing port, Duncannon village is a popular tourist destination. The main attractions are the beach and prominent fort that was the foundation of Duncannon.

The splendid beach (The Strand) is over 1½km long, a favourite for kite surfing and the annual sand sculpting festival. The beach was awarded a Blue Flag in 2007, but do not assume that this applies to the water to the north of the fort.

The fort boasts a commanding position over the estuary, which was one of Ireland's most politically significant locations from the third to the 19th centuries, covering Celtic, Norman and ultimately British periods. The fort, which is currently being refurbished, was built in 1588 as a defence against a possible attack by Spain. It is open to visitors from June to September.

TRANSPORT
Bus services: 370 Waterford-New Ross-Duncannon-Wexford.

Duncannon's impressive fort and strand. There is a clear view of the harbour, pontoon and pier (left)

www.irelandaerialphotography.com

www.irelandaerialphotography.com

Ballyhack

Passage East and Ballyhack

For navigation to Passage East and Ballyhack see page 239.

ANCHORING AT PASSAGE EAST/BALLYHACK

The Admiralty chart indicates an anchorage in the middle of the deep-water channel off Passage East. This is probably not going to attract the good humour of the Waterford Port Authority or the frequent freighters heading upriver to Waterford! Given that the harbour dries, a visit to Passage East is best achieved by anchoring in Ballyhack and then crossing via dinghy, if it is capable of countering the tide, or via the ferry. Alternatively, it may be possible to borrow a mooring buoy just north of the ferry slip.

The anchorage is off the Ballyhack shore near the mooring buoys, north-west of the ferry slip in 3-4m, well away from the car ferry which makes frequent crossings. The strong currents at this narrow part of the river can reach up to 3kn. Also, heavy seas in the estuary can carry into the anchorage. The best conditions are therefore in neaps and settled weather.

There are no public mooring buoys; Carrolls Boatyard, Tel: 051 389 164, has only one mooring, which it constantly uses in support of its regular business and it is therefore not normally available to visitors.

Useful information – Passage East/Ballyhack

PROVISIONING
There is a small **general store** in Ballyhack (Byrne's), Tel: 051 389 107, and a **post office** in Passage East, Tel: 051 382 201.

EATING OUT
A small selection of hostelries include:
Passage East: Furlong's New Geneva (Sean Furlong), Dobbyn Street, Tel: 051 383 173; The Farleigh Bar Tel: 051 382 240; Twomey's Snug Bar; Howay Chinese Restaurant Tel: 051 380 749.
Ballyhack: Byrne's Pub.

ASHORE
Passage East is a quaint fishing village built beneath the cliffs as the River Suir narrows. It is based around a large drying quay and two small squares. The car ferry traverses the river frequently (and quickly) to Ballyhack in County Wexford.

When the weather is originating from the south-west, the hill behind Passage East quickly calms the water. There is little evidence now of Passage East's pivotal role in Irish history when it was a fortification on the River Suir. Its main claim to fame is as the landing place for Henry II's liegeman 'Strongbow' and his 1,000 Welsh-Norman troops in the 12th century. They progressed from here to capture Waterford. Henry II landed here one year later.

On the opposite bank, Ballyhack is dominated by its 15th century Tower House, which was built in the last years of the Knights Templar. It is sometimes misleadingly referred to as a 'crusader castle'. It is open to the public in high summer and has a Crusader Knights exhibition.

There is a very busy boatyard in the village. The small fishing fleet is currently not doing well under the combined impact of large fuel price variations and EU fishing limits. Many of these boats are 'resting' in various states of ill repair.

TRANSPORT
Bus services: Suirway Bus and Coach service: Waterford-Passage East. Monday-Saturday. Two buses per day.

King's Channel

The anchorages here are somewhat remote despite their proximity to Waterford and are ideal for a quiet evening on board and some birdwatching. Protection is excellent.

NAVIGATION

Navigation in King's Channel is utterly enigmatic. There can be few places with more inconsistent published pilot data and chart information. Skippers must exercise caution. Also, the sharing of the River Suir's flood and ebb streams between the King's and Queen's Channels causes strong deflecting currents at their confluence. However, taken near the top of the tide, the passage and/or search for an anchorage is a delight and the obstructions easily avoided.

Pilotage: From the north-west of Little Island (preferred):
Enter the western leg of King's Channel using a back bearing (315°T) on Beacon Quay beacon (Fl G 3s) and head for 'Dirty Tail' port-hand mark located at the north-west corner of the island, leaving it close on the port bow (note that this port-hand mark is for those proceeding west along Queen's Channel). Due south of the port-hand mark and midway between the points of land is deeper water (>5m initially), with a least depth of 2.9m half way to the anchorage that is just north-west of the ferry crossing. Keep well off the western extremity of the island shore in depths greater than 5m to avoid Golden Rock by leaving the uncharted (on most charts) starboard-hand mark to port and steering for the mainland ramp of the ferry.

South of the chain ferry: The 'chain' ferry is actually a self-propelled, wire-guided ferry. It was replaced in early 2008. Note that the ferry crossings can be fast and frequent. Turnaround time is minimal.

If following the channel south of the ferry to circumnavigate the island, Maulus Rock (0.3m) lies in wait 40m off the mainland shore (¼ of the channel width), half way between the ferry and the south tip of the island. As of 2008, there is no buoyage south of the ferry.

King's Channel. The private island is bounded to the left of the photograph by Queen's Channel

From the north-east of Little Island: Queen's Channel turns abruptly west as described previously, causing King's Channel to appear directly ahead as a continuation of the main channel. This eastern leg of King's Channel is shallow and should only be explored based on watchful soundings above half tide. The least depth (charted and found in practice) is 0.5m. At the south-east corner of Little Island there is an anchorage in 3-4m.

LITTLE ISLAND

The island was settled by monks in the sixth century and the Vikings in the ninth century. After the Norman invasion, the island passed to the FitzGeralds who held it for nearly 800 years until 1958. The chain ferry was introduced around 1958. The land was then developed into a horticultural glass house complex and, later, a pedigree dairy farm. Finally, in 1988, it started its current role as Waterford Castle – a small luxury hotel and golf course. The peace may be broken if the proposed development of a 250-berth marina comes to fruition.

The one facility nearby is the upmarket restaurant in the hotel on Little Island. Phone for a reservation on Tel: 051 878 203.

King's Channel. Approaching Little Island ferry from the north-west entrance

New Ross, County Wexford

New Ross is like no other destination in this book. It is the furthest inland of all the harbours, the passage requires the opening of a railway swing bridge and a supermarket is situated closer to the marina pontoons than its shower block. Like Waterford, however, New Ross is a very welcome quarter in poor weather.

Even casual observation of the scenery along the river gives clues to its historical significance as one of the main communication and trading arteries of the south of Ireland. With its two sister rivers, the Suir and Nore, it carried much of the commerce locally and to Europe. Extensive earthworks are the legacy of attempts to improve navigation and protect the adjacent farmland from flooding. The River Barrow, at 200km, is second in length only to the River Shannon. The dyke and drainage systems are extensive and it often looks as though the river is higher than the surrounding farmland. There are also ruins of fortifications and limekilns.

NAVIGATION

Charts: Use Admiralty SC5622.4A, B and D (SC5621.18A, B and D) or AC/LE2046 or Imray C57.

Tides: MHWS: 4.4m, MHWN: 3.6m, MLWN: 1.6m, MLWS: 0.8m. Standard Port Cobh, difference at HW; Springs +01:00min; Neaps +00:30min.

Approach: The passage to New Ross diverts from the route to Waterford near Cheek Point (see photo on page 240). New Ross is a commercial port for seagoing vessels. Be prepared to encounter coasters at any

Annagh Castle

point in the river. It is not unusual to see sizeable ships berthed in the town.

Pilotage (From Cheek Point to New Ross): The River Barrow joins the River Suir north-west of Cheek Point under the 15 span Barrow railway swing bridge (closed clearance 7m), to the west of the twin chimneys of Kilmokea power station. The Barrow is well buoyed and navigable, with a least depth of 2.7m to the fuel jetty ½M south of Three Sisters Marina. There is a 2m depth unbuoyed channel to the marina. The river is tidal all the way to New Ross and therefore the benefit of tidal assistance will be noticeable. Where buoys are widely spaced, the usual practice of keeping to the outside bend of rivers is valid.

Opening the railway bridge could not be simpler. Once the decision has been made to go to New Ross, telephone the bridge staff on Tel: 086 816 7826. Inform them of an approximate time of transit. They may request a further call closer to the estimated arrival time (about 15-20 minutes before). Upon arrival, the bridge will be open. The swinging part of the bridge is the third and fourth sections from the west. Pass through, leaving the central pivot column to port in both directions. After clearing the bridge, a quick call of thanks is an appropriate courtesy and also gives the opportunity to inform them of a time and day for the return passage. From the control room high at the top of the balanced section, it is unlikely that bridge staff will be seen!

Immediately upstream of the bridge, the buoyage starts and the river is crossed by four parallel overhead power lines, with a clearance of 40m, emanating from the nearby power station. Upstream, it is a simple matter of following the buoyed channel to just south of the marina.

New Ross and the *Dunbrody* Famine Ship in the evening sun

BERTHING AT THE THREE SISTERS MARINA

Accessible 24 hours a day, the Three Sisters Marina is named after the three rivers (Suir, Barrow and Nore) that converge hereabouts and together they provide access and drainage to a huge part of the south. They can also be used to travel to the far reaches of Ireland, including the Shannon, and to Northern Ireland via the inland waterways. Although the marina, which was opened fully in 2006, is small, there is usually no issue with accommodating visitors who are normally berthed on the hammerheads. (The inside berths are of the narrow, short pontoon variety usually found in French marinas). The fetch caused by a south-westerly exercising itself over the last mile of river is broken by a floating breakwater. Capacity is 66, including visitors' berths, on three main fingers.

As with other small marinas along this coast, the marina is not continuously staffed. It is beneficial to contact the marina manager, John Dimond, during working hours on Tel: 086 388 9652 (email:

New Ross. The *Dunbrody* is central and the marina, to the left, downstream

marina@newrosstc.ie; website: www.newrosstc.ie/marina.htm) to inform him of arrival intentions and particular needs such as electricity cards or gate access fobs.

Berthing fees: Up to 10.5m €10 per night, 10.5 to 12.5m €20 per night. Longer vessels €25 per night.

Useful information – Three Sisters Marina/New Ross

FACILITIES
The marina is equipped with pump-out facilities as well as **fresh water** and **electricity** on the pontoons. Electricity is acquired by a prepaid meter card (€4 per card). Green **diesel** can be obtained in jerry cans from nearby by arrangement with the marina manager, while road fuel and Kosan (Calor) **gas** are available from the filling station opposite the marina gate.

Rubbish disposal and recycling facilities are provided on the marina site, but **showers** and **toilets** are outside the secure area in a nearby public park. Access is by key. For the nearest **launderette**, go to Wash World (9 Michaels Street) in the town centre, Tel: 051 421 505. The mobile phone coverage at the marina is good and an **Internet** café can be found close by on the quay front. **Boat services:** The recently opened New Ross Boat Yard provides storage, winterisation and a dry dock facility. Contact Steven Kehoe on Tel: 087 290 3583. For engine problems try Mick Dunn, Tel: 087 241 8469, and for more general needs, New Ross Outboards (1km along the Waterford Road),

Tel: 051 421 902, may be able to help or advise. It also stocks a few chandlery items. A **slipway** with tidal access is located at the New Ross Boat Club, Tel: 051 421 834.

PROVISIONING
The marina is no more than 100m from a Lidl **supermarket** in one direction and 300m from an Aldi in the other direction. A large SuperValu store can be found half way in to town. The town centre itself is approximately 600m from the marina. New Ross has a wide selection of shops, including **pharmacy, post office** (stamps are also available from the tourist office), **banks** and **ATMs**.

If all else fails, the 24-hour filling station opposite the marina gates has a small grocery and newsagent which sells the basics.

EATING OUT
A good selection of pubs/restaurants lies along the waterfront between the marina and the river bridge.

ASHORE
The town centre is remarkable in that, with the exception of the bookmakers,

there are no chain stores. Unlike the tourist towns in the region, the shops still carry the owner's name over the shopfront in non-pastel colours. Such is the feel of the place that a cow being towed through town on a trailer and mooing loudly in protest does not seem out of place.

The main visitor attraction is the *Dunbrody*. She is a replica 'Emigrant Ship' and illustrates the conditions endured by the many that crossed the oceans to escape the famine in Ireland. A database lists the names of two million emigrants.

TRANSPORT
Bus services: There are excellent express bus services: No 5 Dublin-New Ross-Waterford; No 40 Rosslare-New Ross-Waterford, Cork, Killarney

and Tralee. Other buses operate from the quay adjacent to the river bridge. **Car hire:** Budget Tel: 051 843 747 or South East Car Rentals Tel: 051 421 670. **Taxi:** Paddy Donovan Tel: 051 425 100.

OTHER INFORMATION
Harbour Authority: The New Ross Harbour Authority may be contacted on VHF Ch 14 or Tel: 051 421 303. There is no requirement to contact them in normal circumstances.
Police: Tel: 051 421 204.
Hospital: Waterford Regional Tel: 051 848 000.
Doctor: Walsh practice Tel: 051 421 250.
Dentist: M Quirke Tel: 051 421 453.
Tourist office: At the Dunbrody site (see above under 'Ashore' section), Tel: 051 421 857.

Barrow railway bridge closing!

www.irelandaerialphotography.com

Kilmore Quay approach

Kilmore Quay

(Irish: *Cé na Cille Móire*, meaning
Quay of the Big Church)
Approach waypoint: 52°09'.26N 06°35'.32W
(70m N of SWM on the leading line/lights – the marks
are sited on the beach to the east of the quays)

Kilmore Quay features in this volume because it is a
gateway harbour, the 'Singapore' of South-East Ireland
– with a few perceptible differences! With its marina,
chandlery, boatyards and village services along with
nearby beaches and improved navigational aids,
Kilmore Quay is the obvious, convenient gateway
harbour for a wide combination of North – South and
East – West passages off Western Europe. Customs
facilities are on hand if required. A third of its visitors
come from abroad. Thankfully, it is a harbour of
'necessity' that is also a pleasure to spend time in. If
the weather dictates a longer than expected stay, then
Wexford, with its shops, restaurants and the train, is
only 20km away by bus or taxi. The well-sheltered
marina has only 15 visitors' berths, although all
visitors are usually accommodated. The only time
that predictable pressure on space will occur is when
boats are making their way to/from Cork Week at the
beginning/end of July (even years only). Kilmore Quay
has a few navigational foibles that need to be fully
appreciated for a successful visit.

The harbour has recently undergone a major
upgrade. The west quay is now 250m long with a

3m depth while the east quay is 110m long with a
5m depth. It is constantly active with fishing vessels
coming and going day and night, but noise levels,
mostly caused by continuously running generators
on the large fishing vessels, are not too troublesome.
Conditions inside the harbour are mostly benign in
all weathers.

NAVIGATION

Charts: Use Admiralty SC5621.16 for a detailed view,
but note that this chart is NOT to WGS84. It has an
'undetermined' datum, apparently because it has been
derived from historical 'county' maps and no thorough
maritime survey has been performed in modern times.
All navigation should be based on hard fixing, buoys
and transit marks. Also and regrettably, this is the
one harbour not covered by the duplication across
Admiralty Leisure Folios SC5621 and SC5622! An
alternative would be to use the Imray C57 Inset.

Tides (approx): MHWS: 3.9m, MHWN: 3.1m, MLWN:
1.5m, MLWS: 0.6m. Standard Port Cobh, difference at
HW: +00:03min.

The tidal stream crosses the track into the harbour at
right angles at a maximum rate of 3½kn. The east-going
tide maximises at HW Cobh +1 to +3 hours.

Lights & Marks
• There was considerable change to lights and marks in
this area in 2006/7. Be sure to have the latest published
information! Offshore, this particularly applies to

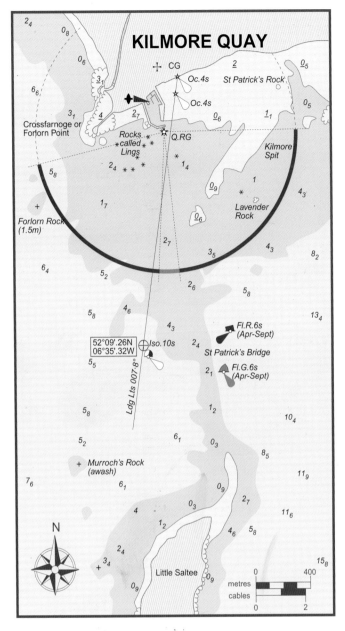

KILMORE QUAY

- Breakwater head: QRG. Green sector, 354°T to 003°T; red sector, 269° to 354°T and 003° to 077°T.
- Leading lights: Oc 4s synchronised on 007.9°T (white pylons with red stripe).

Approaches: A combination of strong currents, shoals and isolated outcrops increases the need for care during the approach. In the summer months, from both east and west, harbour entry pilotage (see below) commences at the seasonal safe water mark. If arriving from the east, make a judgement on whether it is safe to cross St Patrick's Bridge to reach the safe water mark or whether to go south-about the Saltees (see arrival from west – below). The approach across St Patrick's Bridge (least depth 2.4m) is between the seasonal lateral buoys. Do not attempt to cross elsewhere along the reef.

From the west, passage to the safe water mark is clear, with the exception of Murroch's Rock (awash, 6 cables south-south-west), Jackeen Rock (1.5m, 1.2M south-west) and Forlorn Rock (1.5m, 8 cables north-west). The last 1½M of the approach to the safe water mark taken at near due east would be prudent. This also applies to those intending to head to/from the south along the west shore of the Saltees.

Entry in strong southerly/south-easterly winds can be tricky and is best avoided. Look for heavy surf on the beaches.

Least depth on entry near the harbour entrance is 1.9m, increasing to 3m inside the harbour.

Pilotage: From the approach waypoint, steer 008°T and follow the transit marks/leading lights (or, at night, the green sector of the sectored light). Maintain concentration on the leading marks over the 1M run in, as there are shoals on both sides of the channel and cross tides can be very strong. The east-going tide

buoyage south of the Saltees, including new positions and Automatic Identification Systems for Coningbeg, Bore Rocks and Red Bank.
- Direction of buoyage is west to east.
- In daylight, the earliest visual marks are the wind farms to the north-west and east of Kilmore Quay. Closer in, the church end gable is the most prominent feature of the village, standing high above all other features. Once the church has been located it will be easier to identify two 20m floodlights over the harbour entrance and the lens and mast of the retired lightship inside the harbour.
- Note the leading line at 008°T is slightly west of the green sector of the breakwater light.
- Features on Great Saltee that are visible on a westerly approach are not sufficiently distinct for use during the later stages of approach.
- Safe water mark (SWM): Iso 10s (Summer only).
- St Patrick's Bridge laterals: PHM Fl R 6s, SHM Fl G 6s (summer only).

In the final harbour approach, the entrance remains stubbornly hidden to port

It is not unusual to find the harbour entrance narrowed by large fishing vessels alongside the landing berths

maximises one to three hours after HW Cobh, when the danger of being carried onto St Patrick's Bridge is greatest. Just past the breakwater, beware of the shoals immediately ahead. Turn hard port into the harbour entrance, which may be quite congested with berthed fishing vessels as it is classified as a landing berth.

BERTHING

Fifteen visitors' berths on finger pontoons are equipped with water and electricity. Berths cannot be booked but the harbour master is happy to advise on availability a few days prior to arrival.

Useful information – Kilmore Quay

FACILITIES

There is **fresh water** on the pontoons throughout the marina. **Wi-Fi Broadband** in the marina is free of charge once the current 'key' has been obtained from the harbour master, who can also arrange **fuel**; large quantities are delivered by tanker and smaller quantities by jerry can. A **shower** block has been installed in the harbour master's building, which also has coin-in-the-slot washers and dryers. Other facilities on site include CCTV coverage, **bicycle hire** and full **rubbish disposal**.

Within a short walk from the marina is Haven Maritime Boatyard, which provides a 'Mobi-Lift' **boat hoist**, **boat storage** and surveys, Tel: 053 912 9965; email: info@havenmaritime. com. Marine engineering is dealt with by Marindus, Tel: 053 912 9794; email: info@marindus.com. A comprehensive **chandlery**, Hardware & Marine Supplies, also offers 24-hour propeller clearance, Tel: 053 912 9791/9750 or 087 254 4396; VHF Ch 11.

PROVISIONING

Cullen's, the village **general store**, is more than adequate and is open in summer from 0800 to 2200 seven days a week. A **pharmacy** can be found in Kilmore village (5km from the marina/Tel: 053 913 5655), while the **post office** is situated beyond Kehoe's pub.

EATING OUT

Kehoe's pub and parlour houses a host of historical marine memorabilia and provides free Wi-Fi to customers. There is an excellent variety of freshly prepared seafood bar meals and a wide range of 'support acts'. It is extremely popular, particularly at weekends. Last food orders are taken at 2030, Tel: 053 912 9830.

Seafood restaurants within 100m of the marina include The Quarterdeck fish & chip shop (takeaway), which has a tremendous reputation, as does the sophisticated Silver Fox, Tel: 053 912 9888. Le Poisson D'or has a pleasant view to the west; it is recently under new management, Tel: 053 914 8853 or website: www.lepoissondor.ie.

The Hotel Saltees is a BIM accredited restaurant on the fringe of the village along the Wexford Road, Tel: 053 912 9601.

ASHORE

Do not miss the old thatched cottages, a short walk along the road to Wexford, and a visit to the retired 1923 lightship. The Stella Maris Hall is community funded and has showers (€3), Internet access and a café, which is sometimes open for breakfast – not Mondays.

The annual seafood festival is held in mid July.

TRANSPORT

Bus services: 383 Wexford-Kilmore Quay; two a day all year round.

Taxi: Coastal Cabs Tel: 085 846 7277/087 646 5257; T&J Taxis Tel: 087 630 1360.

OTHER INFORMATION

Harbour master (and marina manager): Captain Phil Murphy, KQ Harbour Authority, Tel: 053 912 9955, VHF Ch 9 & 16, Mobile: 087 900 1037, email: hmkilmorequay@eircom.net. **Customs:** Tel: 053 913 3741. **Yacht club:** Kilmore Quay Yacht and Boat club, c/o Ivan Sutton, Commodore, Tel: 087 256 1178. **Doctor:** Tel: 053 913 5296. **Dentist:** Nearest in Wexford. **Tourist office:** In Kilrane near Rosslare, Tel: 053 916 1155 (seasonal).

Kilmore Quay's prominent church

The retired light vessel is now a museum

Pastel painted thatched cottages and palm trees suit the gentle climate of this corner of County Wexford

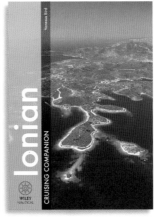

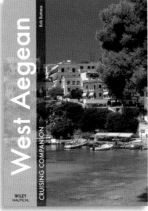
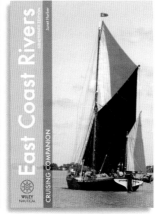

A

Abbey Island	82
Abbey Point	231
Adam's Island	183, 184
Adrigole	108, 123-124
Ahakista	see Kitchen Cove
Alderman Rocks	149
Alderman Sound	149
Amelia Rock	156, 157, 167
Amsterdam Reef	153
Amsterdam Rock	153
Anchor Rock	69, 187
Ardacluggin	102
Ardagh Point	121, 122
Ardgroom	77, 99
Ardmore	16, 222, 224-226
Ardmore Head	224, 225
Ardnakinna Point	109, 112
Argideen River	189
Arthurstown	239

B

Ballinakilla	122
Ballinskelligs	72, 74
Ballybunnion	26
Ballycotton	199, 215-216
Ballycotton Sound	215
Ballycrovane	100-102
Ballydavid (Ballynagall)	46, 47
Ballydehob	166, 168
Ballydehob Bay	166, 168
Ballydivlin Bay	152
Ballydonegan	100, 103
Ballyhack	236, 240, 246
Ballymacus Point	200
Ballymore Point	44
Ballynacourty Point lighthouse	227, 230
Ballynagall (Ballydavid)	46, 47
Baltimore	170, 175-178
Baltimore Harbour	166, 172-173
Banna Strand	39
Bantry	108, 129-133
Bantry Bay	104, 105, 107-110, 125, 139
Bantry Harbour	109
Bantry House	108, 129, 131
Bar Rocks	217
Bardini Reefer	112, 113, 121, 134
Bark Island	126, 127
Barley Cove	149
Barloge Creek	178-179
Barrack Point	172, 173, 174, 175
Barrel Rock	189
Barrow	39
Barrow, River	236, 240, 248, 249
Barrow Castle	39
Barrow Harbour	40
Barry's Point	189
Bat Rock	78, 95
Bay Rock	72
Beal Bar	26

Beal Spit	26
Bear Haven	112-122, 123
Bear Island	107, 111, 112, 121
Beara Peninsula	76, 77, 89, 94, 99, 100, 116
Beenbane Point, Dingle	55
Beginish, Blaskets	50
Beginish Island, Valentia	65
Belgooly River	200
Belly Rock	181
Bere Island	See Bear Island
Big Point	125
Big Sound	181
Big Sovereign	193, 200
Black Ball Harbour	110
Black Ball Head	109
Black Horse Rocks	149, 150
Black Point	55
Black Rock, Ardgroom	99
Black Rock, Bantry	131
Black Rock, Black Ball Hbr	110
Black Rock, Castlehaven	180
Black Rock, Dungarvan	230
Black Rocks, Ardmore	225
Black Rocks, Cahersiveen	67
Black Rocks, Mill Cove	186
Black Tom	189, 190
Blackball Ledge	217
Blackrock Castle	213
Blackwater, River	89
Blananarragaun	160
Blarney Stone	214
Blasket Islands, The	15, 48-50
Blasket Sound	23-25, 48-49, 62
Boar, The	90
Bolus Head	72
Book Rocks	97
Bore Rocks	223, 251
Brandon Bay	15, 44-45
Brandon Creek	45, 47
Brandon Head	25
Brandon Mountain	23, 45, 46, 47
Brandon Point	44
Bray Head	69
Brennel Island	95
Bridaun	101
Brow Head	149, 150
Brownstown Head	223
Bull, The	75, 77, 109
Bull Rock	154, 156, 157
Bull's Forehead, Crow Island	105
Bullig, Ballinskelligs	72
Bullig Reef, Cape Clear Island	150, 157, 162
Bulliga Ledge	123
Bulligmore	152, 153
Bulligmore Rock, Derrynane	80
Bullock Island	178, 179
Bulman Rock	192, 193, 200
Bunavalla Pier	79
Bunaw	96, 97
Burren Hill	190

C

Caha Mountains	76, 94
Caher Bar	66
Caher (Valentia) River	66
Caherdaniel	52
Cahersiveen	52, 66-68
Calf, The	77, 109
Calf Island East	157, 162, 167
Calf Island West	156, 157, 158
Calf Rock	204
Calves Week	145
Cametringane Spit	116, 117
Canduff	49
Canganniv Spit	62, 67
Cape Clear Island	15, 147, 150, 157, 160, 162, 165-167, 170
Capel Island	199, 215, 216
Carbery Island	135-137, 144
Carraig Abhainn Gardens	142, 143
Carravaniheen Island	99
Carrickapane	227, 230
Carricknamoan Islet	230
Carrigabrochell Ledge	204
Carrigaholt	31-32
Carrigaholt Bay	32
Carrigavaddra	112, 123
Carrigbroanty Rock	142
Carrigduff, Garnish Bay	103
Carrigduff, Dirk Bay	186, 187
Carriglea Rock	143
Carrigmore Rocks	157
Carrignakeedu	47
Carrignarone	85, 86
Carrignaronebeg	89
Carrigskye	125
Carrigskye Islet	130
Carrigwee Rock	97
Carthy's Sound	165, 167
Castle Breaker	130
Castle Island	167, 179
Castle Island Channel	156
Castle Island Spit	156
Castle Point	153
Castlehaven	180-182
Castlemaine Harbour	52
Castlepark Marina	194
Castletown Bearhaven	107, 116
Castletownbere	107, 108, 112, 116-119
Castletownshend	16, 170
Cat Island	181
Cathedral Rocks	50
Chapel Island	129, 130, 131
Charles Fort	192, 193, 194
Cheek Point	237, 240, 241, 248
Church Hill	40
Church Island	67
Church Rocks	89
Church Strand Bay	177
Cleanderry	100
Clogher Rock	49
Clohane Castle	179

C (continued)

Clonakilty Bay	186-188
Coastguard Patch	49
Cobh	14, 201, 209, 211-212
Cois Cuain	138, 143
Cold Island	136
Colla Quay	154
Colleen-Oge Rock	55
Colligan, River	229
Collorus	96
Collorus Point	96, 97
Colonel's Rock	181
Colt Rock	112-114
Coney Island	154, 156
Coningbeg LANBY	223, 251
Connor Point	176
Coomagillagh Quay	95
Coon, Ventry	59, 60
Coongar	89
Coosnalacka	190
Copper Point	154, 156-158
Cork Harbour	16, 170, 201-214
Cork Landfall Buoy	199
Cork Week	16, 201, 250
Corlis Point	26, 32
Corrigagannive Point	120
Cotton Rock	189
Cottoner Rock	86
Coulagh Bay	100, 102
Coulagh Rocks	125, 130
Courtmacsherry	189-191
Cow, The	75, 77, 109
Cow Rock	188, 204
Cowdy Point	125
Crab Rock	157
Cracker Rock	131
Creadan Head	239
Croagh Bay	154
Crohogue	194
Crookhaven	15, 145, 149-151, 156, 170
Crosshaven	170, 201, 203-208
Crosshaven Boatyard Marina	205, 206
Crow Head	105, 109
Crow Island	105
Crow Rock	55
Crow's Point	228
Cunnigar Point	229, 231
Curabinny Peninsula	204
Cush Spit	154, 156
Cusleena	167

D

Darrynane	see Derrynane
Daunt Rock	204
Dawros Point	94
Deelick Point	25, 44
Deenish Island	75, 77
Derreen	96, 97
Derreen Gardens	97
Derrynane Bay	83
Derrynane Harbour	15, 75, 77, 79-82
Dingle	23, 52, 54-58
Dingle Bay	15, 24, 51, 52, 61

Dingle Harbour 54, 55
Dinish Island 94, 109, 112, 116, 118
Dirk Bay 186, 187
Dog's Point, Ardgroom 99
Doolic Rock 186, 187
Doonagaun Island 40, 43
Dooneen Pier 138
Doucallia Rock 123
Doulus Bar 67
Doulus Bay 52, 67
Doulus Head 62, 66, 67
Drake's Pool 201
Drowlaun Point 167
Drumroe Bank North 239
DT Marine 146
Dunbeacon Cove 143
Dunbeacon Harbour 141-142
Dunbeacon Point 142
Dunboy Bay 108, 112, 114-115
Dunboy Castle 114, 115
Dunboy House 114
Duncannon 237, 244-245
Duncannon Bar 237, 239
Duncannon Fort 239
Duncannon Spit 237
Duncapple Island 46
Duneen Head 187
Dungarvan 222, 224, 229-232
Dungarvan Bay 227, 230
Dunkerron 89, 94
Dunkerron Island West 90
Dunlough Bay 136
Dunmanus Bay 135-144
Dunmanus Castle 144
Dunmanus Harbour 144
Dunmore Bay 234
Dunmore East 222, 233-235, 236
Dunworly Bay 188
Dunworly Head 188
Durrus 136, 142
Dursey Head 77, 109
Dursey Island 77, 104, 109
Dursey Sound 104-105, 109

E
Eask Tower 54, 55
East Bar, Youghal 217
East Ferry Marina 202, 209
Easter Point 194
Escadawer Point 97
Esheens Rocks 154
Eve Island 183, 184
Eyeries Bay 100
Eyeries Island 101
Eyeries Quay 102

F
Fair Head 112
Falskirt Rock 233
Fastnet Rock 15, 145, 146, 149, 160, 161, 165, 170
Fenit 15, 35-38, 40
Fenit Castle 39, 40
Fenit Island 39, 40

Fenit Without 39
Feohanagh 47
Ferry Point, Youghal 200, 219
Fertha River 66
Flag Rock 105
Flea Sound 180
Foot, The 62
Forlorn Rock 251
Fort Camden 201, 204
Fort Davis 201, 204, 211, 213
Fort Meagher 201
Fort Point 65, 66
Four Heads Point 125
Fox Islands 90
Frower Point 193
Fundy 130, 131
Fungi 54
Furze Island 136

G
Gainers, The 231
Galley Head 183, 186-188
Garinish Island, Glengarriff see Illnacullen
Garinish Island, Sneem 86
Garinish West 107
Garnish Bay 103
Garnish Island 108
Gascanane Rock 157
Gascanane Sound 148, 150, 157
George Rock 112, 121
Gerane Rocks 107, 131
Glandore 15, 169, 181, 183-185
Glandore Bay 186-188
Glanleam Bay 65
Glengarriff 15, 125-128
Glengarriff Bay 108
Glengarriff Harbour 107
Goat Island 154
Goat Island Sound 156
Goat's Head 183, 184
Golden Rock 247
Goleen 152-153
Granny Island 151
Great Blasket 48, 49, 52
Great Foze Rock 50
Great Island 201, 213
Great Saltee 251
Great Skellig (Skellig Michael) 52, 73, 74
Gun Point 126
Gurrig Island, Magharees 40, 41
Gurteenroe Point 130

H
Halftide Rock 99
Hallissy Rock 89
Harbour Rock, Bear Haven 112
Harbour Rock, Knight's Town 64
Harbour Rock, Oyster Haven 200
Hare Island 166, 167, 168
Haulbowline Island 202, 213

Hegarty's Boatyard 146
Heir Island see Hare Island
Helvick 222, 227-228
Helvick Head 227, 228, 230
High Island 181
Hog Island 95
Hog's Head 72
Hook Head 11, 222, 233, 234, 236, 237
Hornet Rock 112, 113
Horse Island, Ballinskelligs 72, 73
Horse Island, Bantry 129
Horse Island, Castlehaven 180, 181
Horse Island, Roaringwater Bay 165, 167
Horse Island Bar 155
Horse Island Channel 156
Horse Rock, Barry's Point 189, 190
Horse Rock, Dunworly 188
Horseshoe Bay 174
Hungry Hill 108
Hussey's Folly 54

I
Ilen, River 146, 168
Illaunanadan 86
Illaunboe 41, 43
Illaunboudane 120
Illaunbrock 157
Illaundonnell, Scraggane 40
Illaundrane 84
Illauneana 167
Illaungowla 90
Illaunimmil 41
Illaunnameanla 100, 101
Illaunnanoon 40
Illaunsillagh 84
Illaunslea 86
Illauntannig 40, 41, 43
Illaunturlogh 40, 41
Ilnacullin 108
Illnacullen 125, 126, 127
Inishfarnard 100, 101
Inishkeelaghmore 85, 86
Inishkeragh 85, 86
Inishnabro (Cathedral Rks) 50
Inishtearaght lighthouse 49
Inishtooskert, Blaskets 41, 50
Inishvickillane 50
Iveragh Peninsula 76

J
Jackeen Rock 251
James Fort 196

K
Kay Rock 66
Kedge Island 173
Kells Bay 52, 61
Kenmare 77, 108
Kenmare Quay 91-93
Kenmare River 75-106

Kenmare Town 91-93
Kerry Head 25
Kilbaha Bay 33-34
Kilcatherine Point 100
Kilcoe Castle 165
Kilcredaun Head 26, 27
Kilcrohane 136, 137
Kilcrohane Pier 138
Killarney 108
Kilmakilloge Harbour 77, 96-98
Kilmokea 240
Kilmore Quay 16, 222, 250-252
Kilravock Gardens 142, 143
Kilrush 14, 23, 26-30
Kilstiffin 26
King's Channel 236, 241, 247
Kinsale 169, 192-196
Kinsale Yacht Club Marina 194
Kinure Point 200
Kitchen Cove 15, 136, 137, 139-140
Knight's Town 62-65
Knockgour Hill 109
Kowloon Bridge 169, 171, 180

L
Lackeen Rocks 89
Lamb Island 67
Lamb's Head 83
Lamb's Island 82, 83
Lamb's Rock 83
Laughaun Point 96
Lauragh 96, 98
Lawrence Cove 15, 108, 112, 113, 120-122
Lea Rock 109
Leaghcarrig 84
Leahern's Point 111
Leahill Quarry 107
Lee, River 213, 214
Leganagh Point 189
Lehid Harbour 95
Limpet Rocks 84
Little Island 236, 237, 240, 241, 247
Little Samphire Island 35, 36, 40
Little Skellig 74
Little Sovereign 200
Lonehort Harbour 111
Long Island, Garnish Bay 103
Long Island Bay 145-168
Long Island Channel 148, 150, 156
Long Island Pier 154
Longship Rock 225
Loo Rock 173-175
Loop Head 23-26, 33
Lord Brandon's Tower 137
Lot's Wife 165, 172, 173
Lough Gill 43
Lough Hyne 172, 178-179
Lough Kay 67
Lough Mahon 214
Lough Tower (Hussey's Folly) 54

Lousy Rocks 166, 173, 176
Low Island, Big Sound 181

M

Macgillycuddy's
 Reeks 51, 76, 94
Magharee Islands 35, 40-42
Magharee Sound 24, 25, 35,
 40-43
Maiden Rock 78, 89
Man of War Sound 156
Mannion's Island 142
Mannion's Rock 142
Maulus Rock 247
Mealbeg 167
Metal Man 223
Mill Cove, Bear Haven 112, 120
Mill Cove, Glandore Bay 186
Minane Island 116, 118
Mine Head 199, 223, 225
Minnaun 41
Minnaun Rock 163
Miskish Mountain 101
Mizen Head 5, 109, 146, 147,
 149, 165, 170
Mizen Peninsula 152
Money Point 27, 194
Mount Eagle 60
Mount Gabriel 143, 147, 156,
 158, 167
Mount Kid 147
Moyarta River 31
Moylaun Island 77, 80
Muckiv Rocks 80
Mucklaghbeg 40, 41
Mucklaghmore Island 35
Mullin Rock 167
Muntervary 135
Murphy Rock 142
Murray's Creek 200
Murroch's Rock 251

N

Natterjack toad 43
New Ross 16, 222, 236, 248-249
Nore, River 248, 249
North Bullig 137
North Harbour,
 Cape Clear Island 162-164

O

Old Head of Kinsale 170, 189,
 192, 193, 199
Oldcourt 166
Oldcourts Boats 146
Ormond's Island 95
Orthon's Island 123
Owen's Island 139
Owenboy River 201, 203, 204
Oyster Haven 199, 200

P

Pallas Harbour 99
Palmer Point 121
Passage East 237, 240, 246

Passage Rock 66, 67
Passage Spit 237
Passage West 213
Penrose Quay, Cork 201,
 213-214
Perch Rock 116, 117
Pig's Rock 72
Piper Sound 109, 110, 112, 117
Pointabulloge 139
Pointanaminnam 25
Pollock Rock 215
Portmagee 52, 69-71, 74
Potato Island 85
Poulgorm Bay 168
Power Head Rock 199
Privateer Rock 112, 118
Puffin Island 53
Pulleen Harbour 110
Puxley Castle 114

Q

Quarry Rock 175
Quay Brack 69
Queen's Channel 236, 237, 240,
 241, 247
Querrin Point 26

R

Rabbit Island 181
Ram Head 199, 224, 225
Ram's Head Bank 204
Rath Strand Bay 83
Red Bank, WCM 223, 251
Red Bank, Youghal 217, 219
Reen Point, Ballycrovane 101
Reen Point, Ballydehob 168
Reen Point, Castlehaven
 180, 181
Reenard Point 52, 62, 65
Reenavaud Quay 99
Reenbeg Point, Bantry 55
Reencaheragh Point 69
Reennafardarrig 41
Reennaveagh 89
Relane Point 131
Rerrin 111, 120
Rineanna Point 26
Ringabella Bay 202
Ringaskiddy 214
Rinneen Island 144
Roancarrigbeg Rocks 123
Roancarrigmore lighthouse 109,
 112, 113, 121, 123
Roaringwater Bay 145-148, 155,
 165-168
Robert's Cove 202
Roche's Point 170, 198, 199,
 201, 203, 204
Rock Island 149, 150, 151
Rogue, The 224
Rose, The 40
Rossbrin Boatyard 146, 155
Rossbrin Castle 156
Rossbrin Cove 155
Rossdohan Island 86, 87

Rough Point 40, 43
Roughty, River 91
Round Tower, Ardmore 225
Royal Cork Yacht Club 202,
 205, 207

S

Saltees, The 251
Salve Marine 206, 208
Samphire Island 35, 36
Scariff Island 53, 75, 77
Scattery Island 27
Schull 145, 150, 153, 156-159
Scilly, Kinsale 195
Scraggane Bay 40, 42-43
Scraggane Pier 42
Scraggane Point 43
Seal Rock, Sneem 85, 86
Seal Rocks, Big Sound 181
Seedes Bank 237
Seven Heads 188, 189
Shannon, River 24, 25, 31,
 248, 249
Sheelane Island 107
Sheelane South 130
Sheep Island 112
Sheep's Head 109, 112, 135,
 137, 139
Sherkin Island 15, 157, 166,
 173, 175
Sherky Island 86
Ship Island 126
Shot Head 123
Skeam Islands 146, 165
Skellig Michael
 (Great Skellig) 15, 52, 73, 74
Skelligs, The 72, 74
Skibbereen 166, 168
Skiddy Island 181
Skughaphort Reef 69
Slea Head 49, 55
Slieve Miskish
 Mountains 100, 102
Smerwick Harbour 46
Smiths, The 215
Sneem 77, 85-88
Sound, The,
 Baltimore 166, 172, 173
Sound, The, Cork 203
Sound Rock 156
South Bullig 137, 139, 140
South Harbour,
 Cape Clear Island 160
South Ring 187, 188
Spanish Island 96, 97, 166
Spanish Point 152
Spike Island 202
St Patrick's Bridge,
 Kilmore Quay 251, 252
Stag Sound 178, 180
Stags, The 169, 173, 178, 180, 187
Streek Head 150
Stromboli Rocks 49
Suir, River 236, 239, 241,
 248, 249

Sunk Rock 183, 184
Sybil Point 24, 25, 49

T

Templenoe 90
Three Castle Head 109, 135-137,
 140, 141, 144
Three Sisters, The 24, 46
Three Sisters Marina 248-249
Timoleague 190
Toorane Rocks 167
Tower Race 234, 236
Trafrask Bay 124
Tralee 35
Tralee Bay 25
Tralong Bay 186
Tramore Bay 223
Travara Quay 102
Travaud Strand 102
Trident Marina 194, 195
Tuosist Parish 77, 94
Turk Island 121
Two Headed Island 77, 80
Two Women's Rock 167, 168

U

Union Hall 183-185
Urhan/Urhin 102

V

Valentia Harbour 52, 64, 69
Valentia Island 62
Valentia (Caher) River 66
Ventry 52
Volage Rock 118

W

Wallis Rock 166, 173, 176
Walter Scott SCM 112, 113,
 117, 118
Washerwoman Rock 74
Waterford City 222, 236, 237,
 242-243
Waterford City Marina 242-243
Waterford Harbour 236-249
Weaver Point 204
West Bar, Youghal 217
West Cove 84
West Passage 213, 214
Wexford 223
Whiddy Island 107, 125, 129, 137
White Ball Head 110
White Strand 50
White Strand Bay 83
White Strand Quay 103
Wild Bank 49
Wilson Rock 173, 174, 175
Wind Rock Beacon 187
Wood Point 189, 190
Wyse's Point 230, 231

Y

Yellow Rock 99
Youghal 16, 199, 217-218
Youngs Island 25, 50